My First Movie

Stephen Lowenstein has worked on television documentaries for Channel 4, ITV and the BBC. He is the writer–director of two critically acclaimed short films and currently has several feature-length projects in development in Britain and America. He lives in London.

My First Movie

edited by Stephen Lowenstein

ff

faber and faber

First published in 2000
by Faber and Faber Limited
3 Queen Square London WC1N 3AU

Typeset by Faber and Faber Limited
Printed in England by Clays Ltd, St Ives plc

A CIP record for this book
is available from the British Library

ISBN 0–571–19669–1

10 9 8 7 6 5 4 3 2

Contents

Introduction

The idea for this anthology came out of a short film that I wrote and directed a few years ago called *The Key*. On the first day of the shoot I awoke at around five-thirty in the morning in a bed-and-breakfast hotel on the Essex coast in a state of blind panic. In a couple of hours' time I would be facing some fifty technicians and actors, all of whom would be expecting me to tell them what to do; to know what I wanted them to do. I must be completely crazy, I thought. Why had I ever wanted to do this? But it was too late for second thoughts: I had gone beyond the point of no return. In fact, my nerves soon evaporated, the shoot proved to be enormously enjoyable and the film went on to be released in London as a support to *The Usual Suspects*.

When my producer suggested I write a newspaper article to coincide with the film's release, I remembered my initial apprehension and decided to write a piece about what it was like to make a film for the first time As a result of the vagaries of the newspaper world, the article was never published. But some time later it struck me that the ordeal I'd been through on that morning must be something that every film-maker, however successful, however high-powered, would recognize: an experience that connected directors of every rank. If it had been worth writing about the experience of making a small film, I realized, it would be worth recording the experiences of those whose debut feature films had made a splash and launched their careers as film-makers on the world stage.

After the release of my second short film, *The Man Who Held His Breath*, I canvassed the opinions of a few movie-going friends, all of whom were enthusiastic, and approached Faber's film editor, Walter Donohue, with the idea of assembling a collection of interviews about the first films of established directors. The aim was threefold: to piece together the inside story of the making of a particular film; to get a sense both of the personality of the director and the subjective experience of making the film in question – in other words to *humanize* the director; and, finally, to glean from the director any insights, technical, practical or otherwise, that would be helpful and interesting to those wanting to make films as well as a wider readership.

Walter was instantly positive about the idea. The next step was therefore to assemble a wish-list of directors. Given the number of times I've been asked who I interviewed for the book and why (usually, it has to be said, by fans of a particular director with a bone to pick), it's worth explaining my rationale. First of all, I wanted to talk to directors whose first films had made an impact on me personally and who had gone on to create a distinctive body of work so that in their early efforts one might discern the seeds of later preoccupations; secondly, I wanted to use the experience of particular directors to shed light on different film-making worlds, including mainstream Hollywood, the American independent scene at different stages in its development, British television of the sixties and seventies, the British theatre, European movies, Asian movies and so on; and finally, I wanted to reflect the extraordinary diversity of film-makers by talking to directors from as wide a range of backgrounds as possible – including those who came from acting, writing, publicity, television, theatre as well as film school. The other element that shaped the list was time. Not wanting to become like a character out of a Sartre novel, limping wearily through the entire modern pantheon of directors, and knowing that the editing of the material I was about to gather would be a task of Herculean proportions, I set myself a limit of six months in which to conduct the initial interviews – a schedule I nearly managed to keep to.

Having drawn up an initial list with Walter, I spent the next few months engaged in the contemporary equivalent of sending messages in bottles. Faxes were sent out explaining the idea of the book and requesting interviews. Anxious weeks passed. Some came back with a positive response, some came back announcing the director was too busy to be interviewed, a small number didn't come back at all. Of those that replied, the response to the idea was unanimously positive. Even the moguls liked it. Steven Spielberg, whose publicity people came back to us saying he was currently too busy to give the extended interview on *Duel* we'd asked for, wanted it put on the record that he thought the idea was 'neat'. The affinity I suspected would exist among film-makers in regard to their début films was alive and kicking.

The same reception greeted me when I began to meet the directors in Europe and America. Everyone seemed to be struck by the simplicity of the idea and saw it as a great way of passing on the baton to film-makers who were trying to make their first movies, as well as speaking to a general audience about their early experiences. Given my desire to scrape away the veneer of PR-puff that usually afflicts interviews with film-makers, I deliberately asked questions about the most humdrum aspects of film-making as well as the most elevated; the most personal and particular as well the most strategic and general. The results were both illuminating and unpredictable. When the American independent film-maker Tom DiCillo read the transcript of his interview for the first time, he sent me a fax with a circle scrawled round a particular question relating to the shoot on his first film, *Johnny Suede*: how were you sleeping? 'No one ever asked me that before', he'd written in the margin. 'Yet it's one of the most important things on any film: as important as how you raise the money; where the story came from and all the rest.'

The personal approach I adopted yielded similarly unpredictable results with many of the directors. Kevin Smith told me that one of the worst things about making *Clerks* was putting on weight due to the fact he was filming in a convenience store where you could snack all day long. Steve Buscemi told me that he locked himself in a toilet and wept when he thought he'd lost the confidence of his crew. 'I asked myself, why did I want to do this?' he said, rehearsing almost verbatim the angst that inaugurated my own short film. Ang Lee recalled in great detail the nightmare of development hell he went through before he made his first feature film, *Pushing Hands*. When I asked him how he spent his time in these years, he replied that when he wasn't writing speculative scripts he was cooking for his wife and child. The kitchen is still my favourite room to shoot in, he added.

A lot of the time I was astonished by the candour of the responses. Even the British directors who were predictably more tight-lipped than their American counterparts opened up to a certain degree. Having described a youthful attack of self-consciousness during the editing of his first film, *Gumshoe*, Stephen Frears announced that the process of being interviewed about his early work was like going through therapy: in the act of talking about an earlier stage of his career he was clarifying certain things that had long puzzled him. 'You've uncorked a vintage bottle, you know,' he beamed.

Whether or not therapy is an appropriate description for what went on in the interviews, many of the directors seemed to take great pleasure in remembering their début films. Although only four days away from principal photography on the fourth in his Baltimore series of films, *Liberty Heights*, Barry Levinson sat calmly in his production office and shooed away his assistants in order to continue talking about the ups and downs of making *Diner*. A one and a half hour slot negotiated with Gary Oldman's management company to talk about *Nil by Mouth* expanded to five hours – and a shared haircut in a Beverly Hills salon – as Gary warmed to his theme: the parlous state of the British film industry and the shock of being turned down for finance in the UK. My conversations with Anthony Minghella included so many lengthy preambles about the nature of film-making in general and the state of the British and American industries in particular, that I didn't switch on the cassette recorder for more than an hour after we met and we were forced to meet no less than three times. Reflecting on this later, my hunch is that the directors enjoyed talking about films that they weren't trying to *sell*.

As the interviews continued, themes emerged that seemed to unite the experiences of many of the disparate group of directors I was meeting: themes that will, I hope, be of interest to those wanting to make films as well as the general reader. For example, it's a cliché that in show business nothing succeeds like success. Yet for film directors, *when* you have success is crucial. Film is such a capricious business that you can be seen as a boy (or girl) wonder then wait for many years for the lightning to strike a second time. P. J. Hogan and James Mangold were both star graduates of distinguished film schools at the age of twenty, who, apart from the odd burst of film-making, spent the next few years languishing in the stable of wannabe film-makers, unsure how to cross from the purgatory of unemployed talent to the heaven of the greenlit project. Ang Lee, too, was a star pupil of New York University Film School who, on the basis of his graduation film was wined and dined by talent agencies promising the earth, but then discovered the hard way that although everyone is paid to compliment you, no one is paid to help you make a living. Only you can do that.

What you have your first success with is also crucial. Ang Lee was convinced that if he had been successful with the Chinese-language fight pictures he was trying to write to bring in some money when he was in the depths of his development hell, he would never have had the chance to join the world of serious independent movies. Likewise Bertrand Tavernier made a brace of short films in the early sixties, which he now describes as imitative and unimaginative; he was subsequently advised by his then wife, Colo Tavernier, to 'live more' before attempting to make his first feature film. It was, he says, the best advice anyone could have given him.

When Tavernier finally made his first film, *The Watchmaker of Saint-Paul*, in his early thirties, he discovered another elemental rule about film-making: no one wants to say yes. Producers who had willingly hired him as a publicist on their films shut the door in his face when confronted with a script he wanted to direct; or, worse, said the script *weighed* too much to be any good. Their behaviour was disgraceful, he says now. Disgraceful maybe, but in the film industry, all too predictable. In many cases, the brick wall of indifference that confronted directors in their early years was another theme of the interviews. As was its effect: the sheer frustration of *not* making your first film. Directors as different as Tom DiCillo and Oliver Stone provided eloquent testimony to the sense of time running out; of the mortality of the artist, growing older with the sense that nothing of significance was happening in their lives. Despite this sense of doom, however, *they went on*. And, prior to the break that launched their careers, that's what all the directors I met had done. They went on because they could conceive of no alternative. P. J. Hogan said the alternative to directing was the dole. Ang Lee said there were only ever two things he could do in life. Cook and direct. Directing was better paid than cooking so he directed. Even if this is faintly disingenuous, it raises a serious point. What separates those who do it from those who talk about doing it isn't just talent or luck. It is the inability to do or even conceive of doing anything else and the willingness to continue along your chosen path until you find a chink in the wall; until someone finally gives you a chance.

Since those who have the power to give directors a chance – studios, distributors, TV channels, financiers of different kinds – often want to satisfy themselves of a director's practical abilities before they take the leap, those who want to become directors are frequently caught in the Catch-22 of not being allowed to direct until they have *already* directed. Technical know-how was therefore something I wanted to ask about. I was surprised to discover how little some of the directors I met knew about the technical aspects of film-making when they made their first films. The Coens freely admitted that when they arrived in Texas to work on *Blood Simple*, it was the first time they had been on a professional set. They were saved by the fact that, ignorant though they were, no one else knew anything either. Likewise Neil Jordan admitted that his technical knowledge was almost non-existent when he made his first film, *Angel*, with the result that he relied almost exclusively upon his DP, Chris Menges. Allison Anders, meanwhile, went as far as to say that she is so untalented a photographer that even now, when she goes into a photo bureau to pick up some snaps, the assistants will try to give her lessons on how to light her pictures. Unsurprisingly, she keeps quiet about her profession.

The fact that many of the directors I spoke to were by their own admission technically ill-equipped when they made their first films was interesting in itself for it showed that first films are not about flashy technical proficiency; they are about individuality, about making your mark, getting noticed in what is a fiercely competitive marketplace. According to Ang Lee, first films are all about saying, Look at me! Here I am! It is only when you have made a few films, he says, that you can try and be more subtle and let the audience do more work. There is an interesting paradox here, for although it is hardest to persuade people to back you when you haven't made a film before, you are also, in a sense, at your freest. As Stephen Frears put it, you can't help but be original when you make your first film: 'There's no one to say, don't be an idiot because, after all, *you* are the director.'

The freedom that first-time directors enjoy is something that all directors covet. For once established, the pressure of living up to your reputation, of working with larger budgets, with bigger stars, means it's easy to be risk-averse, to settle into an established *modus operandi*; yet part of being a successful director is the obligation constantly to re-invent yourself. Directors must never coast on earlier successes for therein lies artistic death. As Neil Jordan put it, every film requires a new pair of eyes. In other words, to live up to your reputation you have to forget you have one.

In this spirit, several of the directors I spoke to said they treated every film as a first film. Having explained how uninterested he was in technical matters on his first film, *Pepi, Luci, Bom . . .* , Pedro Almodóvar said that he is now burdened by an almost unbearable number of possibilities every time he has to decide where to place the camera, what lens to use. Despite the almost iconic use of his name in his films, he added that he fantasized about changing his name, starting again so that he could be free now in the way he was free on his first films. I think that if there were a patron saint of first films, he or she would urge all film-makers to remember that despite the difficulties of making their first film they may never again have as much artistic freedom. They should accordingly make as much use of it as they can.

Finally, a word about the interviews. Spread over a half year, they took place in offices, restaurants, apartments, hotels, dubbing theatres and, in one case, a garden. I would be the first to admit that they are more conversations than hard, journalistic inquiries. I wasn't trying to give anyone a hard time about their work, simply trying to understand what inspired it and how they went about making it happen. It is a shame that a book with surround-sound has not yet been invented for so much of my memory of these meetings is bound up with the voices of the directors I was talking to. If such a device had been invented, readers would have been able to hear the gentle, understated tones of P. J. Hogan whose laconic, self-deprecating humour punctuated our conversation about *Muriel's Wedding*; the gales of mirthful and mischievous laughter that accompanied the ping-pong conversation of the Coen brothers; the instantly recognizable Long Island drawl of Steve Buscemi – so easily identifiable, in fact, that the friends in whose New York apartment I spoke to him kept for posterity the answerphone tape on which he left a message before he arrived by yellow cab; Ang Lee's soft New York-Chinese haiku, dampened even more by his trip into London on the red eye from New York; the strange hybrid of working-class south-east London and translatlantic drawl that characterizes Gary Oldman; Bertrand Tavernier's wonderful, dawdling French-English; the fast and furious east coast banter of Barry Levinson. And so on. I can only hope that something of the voice of each director will have carried through on to the printed page.

Acknowledgements

On a project like this thanks are due to many, many people. If I omit any names I can only apologize and offer to buy them a drink at some future date. First of all I'd like to thank my agent Jane Turnbull for her tireless enthusiasm for a project that has grown much larger and taken much longer than I think either of us ever anticipated. For their sterling work typing up transcripts of the interviews, I want to thank Emily Briggs and Tam Ly; for her speedy translation of the Pedro Almodóvar interview, I want to thank Susan Mushin; for support, moral, practical and other, I want to thank Marjorie Ann and Harold Lowenstein, Sean Rainbird, Neil Heathcote, Justyna Brewczynska, Sara Boas, Toby Poynder, Nick O'Hagan, Mark Carlisle, Jake Arnott, Chris Dickens, Gill Polonsky, Rich Hardcastle, Simon Harsent, Adam Hunt, Felicity Campbell, David Birn, Robin Campbell, Freddie and Jacqui Freiman, Fred and Sarah Jackson, Natalie Carroll, Ian Denning, Bryony Gammon; for the use of their production stills, thanks are due to Sooni Taraporevala, Sophie Baker, Dan Hassid, Patricia Sullivan and Jack English; for their forbearance and level-headedness when assailed by numerous phone calls, e-mails and faxes from the editor, the assistants, colleagues and agents of the various directors interviewed are owed a deep debt of gratitude: they include, in no particular order, Alan Schoolcraft, David Lee, Liza Moore, Rachel Blackney, Amy Solon, Donna Hunt, Karen Siplin, Nelly Reifler, Kim Loughran, Alexis Brandow, Michel Ruben, Neda Armian, Rob Wilson, Lance Stockton, Tim Bricknell, Cassius Matthias, Sarah Jordan, Cian MacDonald, Shana Eddy, Louisa Garnier, Pam Marshall, Alex Reed, Deborah Reede, Audrey Brasseur, Richard Miller, Kate Lenahan, Tim Curley and Doug Urbanski.

Finally I'd like to say a particular word of thanks to my editor at Faber, Walter Donohue. When I took the idea for this book to Walter, I had a track record in television documentaries, two short films to my credit and a burning desire to make films, but no form at all as an editor of anthologies. Walter not only gave me the chance to edit the book but generously opened his crammed address book to help me with the initial contacts. This is unusual. As I said in the introduction, people who say yes to first-timers are far rarer than those who say no. In a spirit of gratitude, therefore, I'd like to dedicate this book to all those who have somehow managed to resist the forces of inertia and given first-timers in whatever field their first chance.

Joel and Ethan Coen: *Blood Simple*

Were you always passionate about movies? Did you see lots of movies when you were kids?

JC: We always went to a lot of movies. But when we were kids it was watching movies on TV. I guess our earliest film education came from a guy called Mel Jazz who had a movie programme on during the days. He was an eclectic programmer. So we were exposed to a lot of strange things – through the eclectic programming genius of Mel Jazz. Ethan once kidded that he had just about the whole of the Joe Levine catalogue because he'd have *8½* one day, you know, Fellini, *The Nights of Cabiria* or something. And the next day he'd have *Sons of Hercules*. So it was a mixture of European art films and badly dubbed Italian muscle movies, essentially. I mean it was very strong in that area. He also liked a lot of the golden age of late fifties, early sixties studio comedy product. Doris Day, Rock Hudson movies. *I'll Take Sweden*, you know. Bob Hope stuff.

EC: Later, *bad* Bob Hope.

JC: A little later on there was a film society at the University of Minnesota that showed the kind of stuff that you wouldn't normally be exposed to: Godard, and the Marx brothers – who were both kind of hip at the time.

EC: I guess that doesn't exist any more. But for a period people would show black and white 16 mm prints on some crappy projector in a basement in the university building somewhere. I guess video ended that.

When you saw movies did you think, 'I want to do that'? I mean, you started making films when you were kids, didn't you?

EC: Yeah. Super-8 things. But it didn't rise to the level of serious ambition. It was another way of goofing off. I don't know when it got sort of serious for me. Certainly later than Joel, since he went to film school and I didn't. For me it was more an opportunity that presented itself through Joel's work than any long-harboured ambition I'd had.

JC: But these things are sometimes just pursuing what might be a casual interest in the path of least resistance. Even the decision to go to film school. Something that strikes you at that moment as being a bit more interesting than something else. It's not as if you really know what you're going to do with it. Or if you're going to do anything with it.

EC: Yeah. There are other people you read about like Scorsese for whom it seemed like a religion from an early age. It certainly wasn't that with either of us.

Could you have imagined going off in a completely different direction?
EC: I never seriously thought about any career so I couldn't honestly say. But, yeah, I suppose it could have happened.

Can you say a little about your experience of NYU film school?
JC: I think film schools are quite different now from when I went. First of all, a lot of people on the undergraduate programme weren't really that interested in movies. A lot of kids who had to go to college thought, this might be fun. I'll go to film school. You know, taking the path of least resistance. And it started that way for me. But it ended up being a fairly interesting place to be. If you took advantage of the school's resources, which were extremely limited but were at least something, you could go out and make little movies and sort of screw around with it without essentially having to pay for it beyond the tuition. I also met people there who we ended up working with later.

What kind of films did you make there?
JC: It was just an extension of what we were doing with Super-8 cameras when we were little kids. Just kind of screwing around. It was all pretty crude. But even that stuff is kind of an interesting thing to have done. When you think about people who are making a first movie, it's a little bit different having had to look through the camera and frame a shot or imagine how it's going to get cut together, than it is if you're coming to it from a completely different discipline like a writer, who's never even made a Super-8 movie and is having to figure it out intellectually. So I think it does have some value even if what you're doing is a very crude exercise.

What happened once you got out of NYU?
JC: I started working as an assistant editor on low-budget splatter movies. Ethan and I were both living in New York at that point and we started writing together. We would get these writing jobs from producers who had these low-budget movies and sometimes wanted stuff written or rewritten. We got some writing jobs together that way at that point and that led to us writing something to do ourselves – which was *Blood Simple*.

How did the idea of writing Blood Simple *come about?*
JC: We wrote a little thing for Frank LaLoggia, one of the directors I was working for as an assistant editor; we wrote a screenplay with Sam Raimi. So we just sat down and thought what kind of movie could we make that was sort of producible on a really small budget like these horror movies, but that isn't necessarily a horror film.

EC: The inspiration was these movies that Joel had been working on which had been done mostly by young people like us who didn't have any credentials or credibility in the mainstream movie industry. But they'd gone out and raised money underground for their little exploitation movies, got the movies made and subsequently wandered into the place where Joel was working to have them cut. It was that evidence that it could be done that led us to try it ourselves: notably Sam's movie, *The Evil Dead*, because Sam was the most forthcoming in sharing all his experience with us.

You said you chose the particular kind of story because it was manageable at a certain budget. Was it also because you loved noir *movies?*
JC: On the one hand, we were both interested in and had read a lot of pulp fiction like Cain and Hammett – and Cain especially when you think about movies that involve murder triangles. On the other hand, as Ethan said, the sort of financial model for the film was also, to a certain extent, a creative influence on it. So it was kind of a mix of those two things.

EC: Also, there were a couple of notorious Texas domestic murder stories that had just happened in the early eighties. I'm sure that figured.

Did you write from beginning to end, or did you write particular scenes down as they came to you?
JC: We start at the beginning and work through to the end. On *Blood Simple* that was definitely the case. It was just a scene by scene accretion, wasn't it?

EC: Right. We don't outline and we don't really know where we're going. We might have some vague feeling that we're going to arrive at some point in the future but it's the vaguest sort of feeling till we actually write ourselves to that point.

But Blood Simple's *plot is so intricate, so exquisitely crafted. Is it really just an organic process by which you arrive at such a complex structure?*
JC: Yeah. Sometimes writing yourself into a corner means that there is no way out and you just have to bag the whole thing. But sometimes writing yourself into a corner means that you have to think of a way out of the corner. If you read the whole thing, you might think 'Oh this is very intricately plotted out.' But just because, by putting yourself into a box you figured a way out of the box, doesn't mean it was all premeditated. *Blood Simple* started something else that we've done pretty much on every subsequent movie, which was that we've always written parts for specific actors. And as we've made more and more movies and got to know more and more actors, they're frequently people we know personally from one place or another or that we've worked with in the past. In *Blood Simple*, we wrote the part that Emmet Walsh played for Emmet just because we knew his work. The other parts were written without knowing who would play them.

What's the starting point for a story like Blood Simple? *Is it a situation, a kind of equation: a man wants his wife killed and gets killed himself? Or a character: a slip-*

pery private eye like the character played by M Emmet Walsh? Or is the dichotomy between plot and character a false one?

JC: It is, inasmuch as who does what to whom has to be consistent to some sort of idea of who the characters are, even if they're rather crude. But in this one the balance probably tips more towards the story than the characters. I guess this one was conceived more as a thriller. I remember that it was an early idea in *Blood Simple* that someone would fake the murder, and then do another murder that made more sense. That was there as an equation, as you say, at some point fairly early in the writing – earlier than the point that we got to that scene. Our initial thinking about it was probably more about plot than about the people in it. But maybe it's just something you just assume after the facts, since the characters in it now seem pretty crude.

What were you doing while you were writing Blood Simple *to make a living? And how long did it take to write?*

EC: I was working as a temporary clerical typist. It took a long time because it was an evening and weekend type proposition. Months.

What did you do once you had a screenplay? You were still not 'the Coen Brothers' as you are today.

JC: Cro-Magnon Coen brothers dragging our knuckles across the floor! (*Laughs.*) We followed the example of Sam Raimi. Sam had done this trailer, almost like a full-length version of *The Evil Dead*, but on Super-8. He raised sixty or ninety thousand dollars that way, essentially by taking it around to people's homes to find investors. He financed the movie using a common thing that people making exploitation movies had used, which was a limited partnership. This was a business model taken from Broadway shows where the general partners were the people who were producing or making the movie and the limited partners were just individual investors who were putting in a certain amount of money and buying equity in the product. So, Sam also told us how to set that up and we did that in conjunction with a lawyer here and then went out and shot a two-minute trailer in 35 mm.

Can you describe the trailer?

EC: Well, it was rather abstract, as it had to be. We didn't have the actors: we didn't know who the actors would be, of course. Actually, what we also borrowed from Sam and the other models was that it was presented more as an action-exploitation type movie than it ended up being, and in fact than we knew it would be. It was pretty much of its time. In the early eighties there was a real vogue for these low-budget horror movies, some of which did really well commercially and made their investors lots of money. So we were passing ourselves off as one of those – which to a certain extent we were, of course; but to a certain extent we were not. And we just ignored the respects in which we were different.

JC: The trailer emphasized the action, the blood and guts in the movie. It was very short. We had a very effective soundtrack, which is very cheap to do. And we schlepped that around for about a year to people's homes and projected it in their living rooms and then got them to give us money to make the movie.

EC: The thing is when you're trying to attract someone who might invest, you have this legal prospectus which is really dry. It's worse than dry – it's a document that's basically warning them off the investment, presenting all the risks. You have to be able to show them something that's a little more intriguing than the legal document that they're eventually going to have to sign. Which was Sam's rationale for doing his little featurette.

JC: There were two or three people that we knew or who were connected to our family somehow. But beyond that, they were all people we'd never met before in our lives. If you call people up and you say, 'Can you give me ten minutes so I can present an opportunity to invest in a movie?', they're going to say, 'No, I don't need this', and hang up the phone. But it's slightly different if you call up and say, 'Can I come over and take ten minutes and show you a piece of film?' All of a sudden that intrigues them and gets your foot in the door. That's something Sam made us wise to which was invaluable in terms of being able to raise the kind of money we were trying to raise, which was essentially much more money than Sam had. He'd raised about ninety grand initially and we were trying to raise a threshold of five hundred and fifty and up to seven hundred and fifty.

How much did you raise?
EC: Seven hundred and fifty ultimately. We started actually working on the movie once we'd raised the five hundred and fifty.

This was all going on in New York?
JC: New York, Minneapolis and Texas.

Because you were going to shoot in Texas?
JC: Right. And because we knew some people. I think there ended up being about sixty five investors in the movie, most of them in five- or ten-thousand dollar increments. I think sixty to seventy per cent of them were from Minneapolis.

EC: The good thing about Minneapolis is those horrible phone calls you have to make to people you don't know – you've just got their names from whoever. They're too polite to hang up.

JC: That's absolutely true. In New York, they'd just go, 'Yeah, yeah', and hang up; because the dangerous thing with any salesman is to keep talking to them. (*Laughs.*)

EC: But people actually put up with us! We'd walk into their living room with our projector and before they'd even offered us to sit down we'd be like finding the outlet, sticking the cord in, setting the projector up and opening up the screen. (*Laughs.*) There was one investor we went to and we hit his car, parking. And we had this big debate out on the driveway whether we should tell him we hit his car before the sales pitch or after the sales pitch. We decided that we wouldn't tell him until we showed him the movie and made the sales pitch.

JC: Obviously he didn't end up investing in the movie!

What kind of people did end up investing in the movie?
JC: Not professional people, by and large. They weren't doctors and lawyers and dentists and that sort of thing. They were small business people, entrepreneurs who had started a small business themselves twenty years earlier with very little money and had made a lot of money doing it and related to the entrepreneurial aspect of it. They liked the show business thing but that was actually secondary. It was more that they related to the enterprise of just going out and trying to start a business that way. And that's where most of the money came from. These people owned little businesses. You know – I've got a business that supplies hair driers to beauty salons or I've got a scrap-metal yard or I've got fifteen bowling alleys or something like that. It's those kind of people.

EC: *Fargo* was based around our fascination with the Minneapolis business community.

JC: Right. It was raising money for *Blood Simple* that we met all these business guys who could wear the suits, get bundled up in the park and slog out in the snow and meet us in these, like, coffee shops. We came back to that whole thing in *Fargo*, the car salesman, the guy who owns the bowling alley, you know, whatever. That was very much part of it.

And your family helped you out?
EC: They put in fifteen. I don't know why. I don't know why anyone did at the end of the day.

Did the investors make their money back?
JC: Oh yeah. It took a while though.

EC: In fact it took so long that they might have done almost as well putting the same amount of money in the bank and collecting bank interest. But you know, they certainly did fine. And most of them were quite pleased because it is an interesting thing to follow if you're not in the movie business.

Did you try to raise money from any distribution companies?
JC: We went to certain people after we'd raised a certain amount of money hoping to bring in a partner who could basically end the agony of having to go out and find all that money – because it just took for ever. Each time they either wanted too much or it seemed they'd be interfering and controlling and at the end of the day it would

be better to struggle on and control it all ourselves than it would be to relinquish any control to these groups. They all wanted to talk about the script. I'm sure they would have taken us to the cleaners. Not that that was such an issue at that point.

EC: It would have been complicated since we already had investors who'd signed up under terms which forbade us being taken to the cleaners.

How long did it take between finishing the script and raising the money?
JC: It must have been at least a year and half.

Did you ever think you weren't going to make it?
JC: Oh yeah. Until we had raised the threshold amount that we needed to start the production, neither of us thought that it was anything but a long shot, that we'd actually succeed in doing it. I think we thought there was a good chance it wouldn't work out.

Do you think first-time film-makers have to have a kind of crazy faith in what they're doing because if they looked rationally at the odds they'd never try?
JC: That's definitely true. All the things we didn't know are what enabled us to do it and be successful. If we knew what we know now or even what we knew when we finished the process we probably wouldn't have attempted to do it or at least attempted it that way. The odds of succeeding at it are very slim and the process is very difficult. That's why it's kind of hard to recommend it to people.

EC: Right. There is something a little unhealthy about the monomaniacal frame of mind you have to put yourself in. Right after we got it done we kidded that the reason we got it done was because we got ourselves so deeply in debt that the only way to pay back the money was to make the movie.

JC: We ended up getting dangerously in debt just to live and to keep the operation going. There was absolutely no way we could have made good on that money without actually making the movie and have the movie make money and pay off. So it's all a little crazy. It's all something that's a lot easier for people who were in our position than it is for people who are a little bit older or have financial responsibilities. We didn't have kids. We were just kids. We didn't have any commitments so we could gamble that way. People who are making a lot of money doing commercials or videos or that sort of thing, a year or a year and a half into the process that we went through, they're factoring in all the income they've lost, thinking 'Jesus!' We weren't doing that.

EC: It's an irony that even back then some of our peers were actually making serious money at serious movie industry jobs. They wouldn't have done what we did because they did have something to lose. They would have to relinquish something in order to embark on something like that.

Once you'd raised the money, how did you begin to prepare for the filming?

JC: The first thing we did was hire Mark Silverman who we'd gone to school with and I'd been to NYU with.

EC: Mark actually did have a little experience. He'd done a couple of really low-budget horror movies.

What was his role?
JC: He was the line-producer. And he was really the one who put the movie together from a nuts and bolts point of view, who really helped us organize it at a professional level.

How long was your shooting schedule?
EC: It was October to November. Eight weeks, I guess.

That sounds quite long for an independent movie. How did you manage that?
JC: We didn't pay anybody anything. Well, we paid them the minimum. That's the one thing I always say when people ask about this type of thing: it makes more sense to find people who don't necessarily have the experience doing what you want to do, but who you think are ready to do it and shoot for longer, than it does trying to find some four thousand dollars a week DP who you think is going to save you time and allow you to shoot for a week less. It doesn't work like that. That was something Mark helped us achieve and appreciate. That was the philosophy that he brought into the movie and it was really helpful for us. The other thing we did, which I think in retrospect was really smart, was we gave ourselves a very long pre-production, too. Because we were dealing with very limited resources we gave ourselves a really exhaustive pre-production and that ended up paying off.

EC: Yeah, we storyboarded extensively, pretty much everything.

Did you work on that together?
JC: On *Blood Simple* we did it together and then we worked with some storyboard artists down in Texas.

How did you end up working with Barry Sonnenfeld?
EC: We met him through a mutual friend. He was in fact the person who introduced us to Mark Silverman.

What had he done at this time?
EC: Odd things here and there. You know, 16 mm industrial type things. But he hadn't shot a feature before. In fact I think he hadn't shot anything on 35 mm before.

JC: There was almost nobody on *Blood Simple*, ourselves included obviously, who had ever done a feature film before. Certainly not in the jobs that we had hired them to do.

How did you work with Barry in terms of the look of the film? I thought some of the scenes looked almost colour-coded. Blue when Marty is sitting out on the back step looking at the incinerator or when the private eye is breaking into John's house; red for Marty's bar and back office.

JC: Some of these things were conscious. But you may be reading more calculation into it than actually happened. As most of these things are, it was half by calculation and design and half just because that's what there is. There was a conscious effort to make it crisp. Use hard sources and make it cold.

EC: The thing you mention, looking at it again, I actually think we went too far. We wouldn't have gone quite that far if we were doing it now. But that probably came from talking to Barry about single light sources. There's a blue bug zapper in that scene. There's a lot of neon in the bar.

How did you go about finding your key locations?

JC: Some of the actual locations in the movie were places that we were aware of when we were writing the movie. Beyond that, I think we did it just the way we normally do it. We hired a location manager who started looking for places and showed us different options when we went down there. I don't think it was any different in that respect from the other things we've done subsequently.

EC: It's funny you ask about that. Looking for locations is always weird. It's always surprising how specific you can get in your descriptions of what you want and how you realize when you get shown things, how much you've left out: what you really need. Everything superficially matches what you're asking for but it's all basically kind of wrong. It's funny. That never changes.

JC: So at the end of the day, you have to find these places yourself or go out with whoever's looking.

EC: We would frequently choose things out of ignorance. The house that we shot in, for instance, was so ridiculously small that when the AD came down –

JC: – she told us we were crazy, that we'd never be able to get the crew in, the lights and blah blah blah. It ended up actually working out okay but she was right.

EC: We really made life difficult for ourselves out of ignorance.

I understand you had to vacate the bar at the weekend?

EC: That's right. It was empty during the week, then the swingers came in at the weekend. They said, we got to keep it going at the weekend. So we had to get out of there.

Let's talk about the casting. What made you think of M Emmet Walsh for the part of the private eye? Did you know of him already?

JC: We hadn't met him. He was a Los Angeles guy. We knew him only from his work, notably from a movie he did called *Straight Time* in which he was really good. It's an interesting movie in which Dustin Hoffman is a parolee and M

Emmet is his parole officer. M Emmet's character was sort of sleazy. Actually it was a more interesting character than what we came up with in *Blood Simple* inasmuch as it was more ambiguous. So, yeah, that was the notable thing that we'd seen him in. We had our casting director send him a script not in the expectation but in the hope that he'd be interested in it and he was. It was a pleasant surprise that he was interested in doing it.

Where did you actually meet him for the first time?
EC: In Texas. We met him only when we were ready to shoot. He was the one person we offered a part without an audition. All I remember is we didn't know what the hell to call him! I mean, what the hell do you call him when you meet him? 'M'?

Was he like the character he played?
JC: Emmet? No. He was a bit of a curmudgeon, certainly, but he didn't have the sleaze that his character in the movie has.

EC: His sort of curmudgeonliness is not a cloud on the set. As a matter of fact it's the opposite.

JC: Emmet's kind of crusty.

EC: He's kind of a coot.

JC: He's basically any noun or adjective that starts with a 'C'!

Did he ever give you a hard time?
EC: Yes, but in a half-kidding but only half-kidding kind of way. He never tried to intimidate or make us feel insecure because of our lack of experience although he had by far the most experience of anyone on the set.

What about the rest of the casting? How did that go?
EC: It was just the usual process of meeting actors. In our case, it was here in New York, for the four main parts excluding Emmet. Actually, we met Dan Hedaya, John Getz and Sam Mart fairly early on but hadn't met anyone we were happy with for Fran's part until we met Fran. We met Holly Hunter and liked her but that quickly became academic. She wasn't available because she was doing a play in New York.

JC: But she and Fran were room-mates at the time, in the Bronx. Holly went back and told Fran, I can't do this movie but you should go and get an audition.

EC: She said, there are a couple of geeks you should meet!

JC: So Fran got an audition, came in and we went okay, let's go with that one. Right after we met Fran we went to Texas. Within a day or two.

Can you remember the first day on location?

JC: I remember Ethan and I driving to the set the first day and both being very impressed by the number of trucks.

EC: It's probably the first thing anyone would notice on their first day working on a movie. It's the most striking thing – the number of trucks.

You hadn't been on a film set before?
JC: The first day of shooting on *Blood Simple* was the first time I'd ever been on a feature movie set in any capacity, even as a visitor.

EC: Everyone was the same. You know, Barry hadn't done anything before.

JC: Right. Barry'd look at the dailies then he'd go up the parking lot and throw up, he was that nervous. Everyone was in the same boat. The gaffer had never gaffered a feature. The sound guy, the mixer on the set, had never mixed a feature. Everyone was doing their job for the first time. Jane had designed a lot of stuff for the theatre and a couple of short things, like after-school specials, little short things. But she'd never designed a feature.

EC: Yeah. The one person who had just loads of feature experience was the key grip who lived in Austin.

JC: He was a survivalist. He was in his sixties and he believed the world was coming to an end and had decided to move to Austin and buy a lot of guns and stuff and get out of the film business. We went down there and found him. I think he'd been sitting there waiting for the world to end for about six or nine months and was really bored. He was willing to work on our movie cheap because the world hadn't ended so he might as well take the movie!

So how did you feel being on the set of your own film?
JC: It is a little freaky to have that many people waiting for you to make decisions. But again the nature of the set and the nature of the kinds of people we were hiring and what we were asking them to do conspired to make it as low-pressure and as comfortable as you can get, doing it for the first time.

How did you feel about about directing actors given you hadn't done it before?
JC: Well, it helps if the actors have also never done a feature. If you walk out on the set for your first movie and you're dealing with Gene Hackman, it's going to be really intimidating and a pain in the ass. On the first day of the shoot, the first shot was in the strip bar. I remember standing there and seeing Fran who's off-camera about to go on. It was the first time Fran had ever been on a movie set or ever acted in front of a camera. I was watching her before she went on and I saw how nervous she was. And that was the thing that made me think she's just as nervous as I am: I'm not the only one here who doesn't know what they're doing. So, what the hell, you know. It was also interesting how she managed to go on and not betray any of that nervousness. It was very impressive.

EC: John Getz had done a lot of TV. He'd been in front of a camera. And Emmet, of course. Emmet was the only one who gave us some shit – but in a way that was quite refreshing and put you at your ease!

Given this was your first professional movie, did you feel confident about what you were doing?
JC: We had to be taught the nuts and bolts of how a professional set works by the people who had some limited experience doing it, like Mark Silverman and Debbie Reinisch. But the actual process, what we actually needed to make the scene work, we had enough experience of our own, either making our little movies or preconceiving this one in terms of doing the storyboards, or working as an editor, to see what kind of raw footage you need to make a scene work – which you can also learn if you're watching movies closely enough. So I don't think either of us felt intimidated about what the process had to be or what we needed to get from an intellectual point of view. That wasn't such a big deal.

How did you work in terms of the basic elements of directing: staging the action and deciding where to place the camera?
EC: It's funny. It was more a question of accommodating Barry than accommodating the actors.

JC: Barry lit the movie with very hard sources and used a very fast stock and very low light levels. We were really shooting wide open, which means that we had a very limited depth of field. Everything had to be laid out very rigidly in terms of the actors' marks.

EC: Barry doesn't light by areas. He lights everything very specifically then has to flag that specific light off with everything else. There's a thicket of fixtures and flags behind the camera, advancing to within an inch of encroaching on the frame.

JC: It's actually more the way black and white would be lit than how most colour cinematographers would light. They don't use hard sources in such quantities. But we were learning from Barry, and then accommodating him. We would come in with a basic idea of how we wanted the scene to be blocked, and then, shot by shot, Barry would force us to become more specific about it.

EC: Through whining, in a sense. Like, 'You want me to pan? 'Cause if I got to pan, I got to have flags over here!' (*Laughs.*)

JC: Barry was the personality on the set: the high-maintenance person. But when we say 'high-maintenance', you have to realize maintaining Barry is not something that feels like an obligation or a chore. It's an amusing pastime.

EC: And his incessant whining is always about wanting to improve his work.

JC: Right. People often characterize actors as being needy and like children but they've obviously never met Barry.

JC: It was only when we started working with Roger Deakins that we realized that there's actually a way to light such that you can decide to pan at the last minute.

But you did work with Barry again?
JC: Oh yeah. We shot three movies with him. (*Laughs.*) The other big asset we had on the movie, was Debbie Reinisch, who was the AD. She really was quite brilliant showing us how everything had to be scheduled and keeping us on track with all that.

EC: We got through a lot of set-ups every day. In the teens, definitely.

Did you stick closely to the storyboards?
JC: It's been the same in everything that we've done, including *Blood Simple*. The storyboards are something that you do and then might not even refer to when you're shooting the scene. You have them somewhere in the back of your head, and then start to accommodate whatever it was that you were thinking about with the storyboards to the reality of the shooting: the spaces or how it ends up feeling when it's actually blocked or what the lighting requirements are. So fairly closely, but not religiously.

What was the most difficult thing about the shoot?
JC: No matter how much time you have, you're always shocked at the uncompromising nature of the day: having to get the shot and move on and that being your chance to get this little piece that you've been imagining for so long; and then it is what it is. This may be lacking, that may be lacking but you've done it and you've got to move on. And there's always very little opportunity to re-shoot or go back. Although we did once or twice, actually.

EC: That's true. That's what you're confronted with. That actually never changes. It's just the uniform pressure of having to make the day.

JC: And when you're doing that for the first time, you're often psychologically unprepared for what it really means. That's why you see a lot of directors on their first features looking really shell-shocked. I think I was that way and Ethan was that way and probably Barry, too. And it's something you can recognize in other people.

Did you find the shoot physically punishing?
JC: Right. It's exhausting. You get very little sleep. You have this constant, inexorable pressure in terms of time. And you haven't really been psychologically prepared for what that really is going to be – I think on a first film you feel that more.

EC: But we went into it to a certain extent with our eyes open, even though we had never done it before and scheduled a reasonable amount of time. We were never in that horrible position of having to throw out set-ups just to make the day. Deciding what to sacrifice. We were never really confronted with that, the production nightmare.

How do you think you coped?
JC: I remember it being tiring and being relentless. I've made movies subsequently where I've actually felt like I can go home at the end of the day and, it sounds funny, you can actually leave it behind to a certain extent. But it didn't happen on *Blood Simple*.

EC: There was a lot of pressure on that movie. It was so new to all of us – again, it was mostly the three of us, me, Joel and Barry – that even though we were shooting six-day weeks, on our day off we were so keyed up that we just wanted to keep shooting. Every movie since then I've loved having the one or two days off.

JC: Whereas then we didn't know what to do with ourselves on the day off. I think the keyed-up nature of it came from the fact just that we were actually finally doing it. It was all so new and relentless that a different kind of monomania takes over from when we were raising the money. The monomania of actually doing it and being unable to think about anything else or know what to do with yourself in any other context. But I don't think we were so concerned about how it finally ended up. I think we were probably more fatalistic about that.

EC: We didn't have this weird artsy attitude that it has to be perfect or whatever.

JC: It is what it is.

Do you remember your reaction to the dailies?
JC: I remember Barry being very upset with us that we didn't constantly tell him how great they were! (*big laugh*) We didn't know whether it was working or not!

EC: The first day's dailies, I remember being really shocked because they were printed too bright and Barry said it looked like a porno movie. That was a printing problem that just worked itself out.

But were you pleased with what you were getting?
EC: I don't think we knew enough to be pleased or displeased.

JC: Our reaction was much more focused on the details of whether certain little things worked or didn't work, as opposed to any sense of knowing whether or not things were working and going to cut and come together in the right way. You know, did the newspaper hit the window at the right moment? It was much more detail-oriented, almost exclusively that way in my recollection.

Once you'd finished shooting you brought the film back to New York and began editing. That took quite a long time, didn't it?
EC: Yeah. We took a lot of naps. Since we'd raised the money ourselves there was no outside deadline. It was Joel primarily, but the two of us with a friend of ours, Don Wiegmann. (*laughter*) How did it take so long?!

JC: We were just really slow. We weren't really pushing ourselves. We were doing bankers' hours. There was something we liked about the process of editing that meant there was no reason to make it go any faster if it didn't have to. And then in addition to that there were about forty set-ups in the completed film that were shot after we started cutting or had done a rough cut: stuff that was shot here in this apartment.

Such as?
JC: Apart from the one shot, all the stuff with Emmet in the darkroom was shot here. The door that goes into that room over there is the door that the bullet goes through, that kills Emmet at the end of the movie. There's a lot of stuff shot out here that was in the scene in the back office at the back of the bar. A lot of fish stuff, insert table top stuff. We shot a lot of exterior stuff out in Barry's backyard in the East Hamptons.

Did you plan it like that?
EC: A couple of them we knew we could afford to put off so we did – as in the darkroom scene. We knew all we really needed was Emmet's coverage, and we'd get everything else later; some of it in the course of cutting.

JC: We realized we could solve problems in the cutting with very simple shots. Because it was just the three of us essentially: Barry, Ethan, and me. So we shot stuff over the course of the nine months or so that we were cutting the movie – the stuff in the car, the rainstorm – and we plugged it in. Actually, the plate shots at the very beginning of the movie that Ethan and Barry shot in Texas – they were done later.

And the opening scene in the car with the wipes for the credits?
JC: That was done in principal photography.

EC: It's just a car on a stage with lights being run at the car.

So the way you financed the movie gave you a lot of freedom when it came to your post-production schedule?
JC: Yeah. We could bring the movie out whenever we wanted. We could cut however we wanted. We could do it on any timetable we wanted. There was nobody who was calling us up and saying, 'What's going on? When's the movie coming out?' All we had was sixty-five people, the investors.

Had your financial situation improved at all?
EC: When we were cutting we actually started paying ourselves. We hadn't on the movie, but as editors we paid ourselves two hundred dollars a week so we could live. The immediate worry was allayed.

JC: That was another reason not to speed the editing up! That was the only moment in the whole process we got a pay-cheque. We didn't pay ourselves anything for directing the movie or producing it or writing it.

So what were you living on?
JC: From the point that we got the money pretty much through pre-production, well certainly when we moved down to Texas, the production was paying for the place we were living and we were getting fifteen dollars a day which we were living on. But we were making no money.

Let's go back to the editing. Did you have to cut much out? Did you find the film worked differently as a film rather than as a screenplay?
EC: A couple of scenes. Nothing radical.

JC: We did a cut of the movie during which we lost certain things that were in the script. And the movie was maybe six or seven minutes longer than the length at which it was released. We actually did a print, went out and sold it, then decided to go back and shorten the movie. After we'd lived with it for a certain period of time we realized there were certain cuts we should make that would make it play better.

EC: Yeah. Once we'd raised seven hundred and fifty thousand, we realized we wanted to shorten the movie a little but we also needed finishing money for some music rights and some outstanding lab stuff. We got an advance from this foreign sales company of seventy-five thousand which allowed us to pay everything off and shorten the movie a little bit.

JC: We went through this process of cutting it, finishing the movie and trying to find a distributor.

Where did you take it?
JC: We took it to Los Angeles and showed it to the major studios.

EC: We showed it to everybody.

JC: It wasn't like now, where there's seven hundred movies in various stages of completion trying to get into Sundance. If you went out to LA and said, 'I got a finished movie', anybody would look at it. So we showed it to all the major studios, starting with Warner Brothers, I think, where we knew the brother of a friend. They all said no with the exception of Orion. They said they would distribute the movie but they wouldn't give us anything up front.

EC: They actually offered two hundred and fifty thousand as an advance on a deal so onerous that it was clear that would be it. Our investors wouldn't get anything.

JC: We were in so much trouble we made this deal with the foreign sales agent to start to sell the movie. It was a way of getting an advance to do a little bit of work we needed to do. It was a risky move, not that we realized it at the time. But separating it out like that – selling the foreign rights without having a domestic distributor – was risky. But we did it anyway.

EC: It diminishes the interest of domestic distributors because they don't have the foreign rights as well.

Who else did you show it to?
JC: We took it to Crown International Pictures and the guy would say, if you have some nudity you can put in there maybe we can distribute it. We saw everybody from the studios to the lowliest sleaze-bucket distributors in LA. And they all said no.

How did this make you feel?
JC: It was frustrating. It's not like we went out there expecting to start a bidding war. But at a certain point when people like Crown International said 'Go screw yourself' we were getting a little bit worried. I mean, it wasn't just the majors who were saying no. It was these people who distribute crap.

EC: Trouble was, it was a little too arty for the sleaze studios and a little too sleazy for the majors.

JC: But the whole business was really different then in terms of independent film. I remember while we were out in LA, we were trying to get an agent so we could get a job writing a script or something. We were recommended to this one agent and she said to us, 'Give me samples of your writing.' 'We can do better than that,' we said. 'We can show you our movie.' And she actually wasn't interested in seeing the movie. She just wanted writing samples – which we thought was crazy! Not only had we written a script but we could show her how it had turned out on celluloid. And it wasn't the celluloid she was interested in. It was really curious! I don't think that would ever happen now.

How did the film end up getting a distributor?
EC: Two things sort of happened at once. It got accepted into the New York Film Festival and it got shown in Toronto.

JC: We started putting it into festivals and it started getting good reviews and then it got accepted for New York which is unusual for a first film in that they have a first film section, but it's unusual for a first film to be in the main festival. At the same time it was shown in Toronto where it got very good reviews. All of a sudden, everything changed because of that. What happened was that Ben Barenholtz saw it in Toronto.

EC: Ben was the principal one of three partners in a company called Circle Films.

JC: The funny thing is we knew Ben because we'd gone to him when we were trying to raise money for the movie. He had a company called Libra. And he was interested but at that point we'd raised three hundred thousand dollars and we realized it was a little bit crazy to give anything away when we'd done so much work on our own. So we said thanks and we went away. And then in the meantime while we were off making the movie, he had started this business with these guys in Washington, Circle Films. And seeing the movie, he was one of the first people to make us an offer and I think it was a combination of the fact that we knew Ben and liked him personally that made it happen.

EC: Also he was partners with Ted and Jim Pedas who were in the movie business as exhibitors but were actually a little outside the mainstream. They were happy to work out a deal that the Hollywood majors and sleazy companies we'd been talking to wouldn't have been comfortable with.

JC: They said, look, none of us know what the film's going to do. But we'll structure a deal such that if it makes money we'll all make money. It'll be very transparent how it's set up. And you guys can see what we're about and we can see what you're about. It was personal and small. And that just seemed right.

What happened once Circle had picked it up?
JC: It was released in New York on a very limited platform, a kind of art-house release where it did very well. And then they experimented in trying to release it wider.

EC: As an exploitation movie, but it failed abysmally. Its only success was as an art-house picture.

JC: It certainly was a financial success in relation to its budget. It did very well. But it didn't become like *Halloween* or something. I think when they saw the admission numbers in the art-house market, Circle's hope was that it would go out and make a ton of money like *Halloween* or something.

EC: I don't even know if it was a hope. I think Ben was realistic about it. His attitude was – it's worth trying, see what happens.

JC: And at the same time, the critical reaction to it was very positive. It was being written about in all these national magazines, you know, *Newsweek*, *The New York Times*, big articles.

I guess your investors must have been very proud of the movie?
JC: The interesting thing that we learned in retrospect is that with this kind of high-risk speculative investment it's fine if you never make a dime because everybody who goes into it is quite savvy from a risk-reward point of view.

EC: They go, it's a failure. I lost everything, oh well.

JC: It's fine if it makes a ton of money because that's the other end of the risk-reward equation. But if it makes a little money you're in trouble because then they think they're being screwed, especially if they know nothing about the business. And none of these people knew anything about the movie business and how it works.

EC: That's where the Minneapolis base became a liability. They figured rightly,

I'm from Minneapolis, I don't know what's going on. Somebody somewhere in Hollywood is screwing me with this movie that's gotten all this attention but it doesn't seem to be making a huge amount of money.

JC: Right, I can't open a newspaper or magazine without seeing stuff about this movie and yet I've only made my investment and fifty per cent back, that doesn't make sense. I'm being screwed somewhere. So the answer is that there was a small group of investors in the movie who weren't at all happy. Even though they'd already come out fine, they were positive they were being screwed. That was a sticky situation for a while until we were able to demonstrate that they weren't being.

Once it had got its platform release, your fate was sealed – you could raise money for more movies?
JC: Right. It was because of the fuss the press made of it that it was considered successful. You actually look at the numbers, they're fairly small. But even at the time, Warner Brothers, who were the original company that had passed on it, went to Circle after two weeks in New York and tried to buy the movie back. They were reading the reviews and the numbers and they thought, all right we made a mistake. Let's go see if we can buy the movie back.

Was this the same with all the people who'd up until this point been saying no? Did everything suddenly change?
JC: It only changed in the respect that as I said before we realized that we wouldn't have to finance our next movie the same way. In fact we did a deal with Circle to do three movies with them up to a certain budget which they agreed to finance for us. So from that point we didn't have the same traumas in terms of financing and distribution.

Just a small problem with the original investors.
JC: Right. One of the things the investors objected to was that we had made a deal to make several movies with this distribution company. And they felt that that was a conflict of interest, because we had a fiduciary responsibility to them as the general partners, which was clouded by the fact that this company which we had another kind of relationship with just involved us. It didn't involve the investors.

How do you feel about the movie now?
EC: It's crude, there's no getting around it.

JC: On the other hand it's all confused with the actual process of making the movie and finishing the movie which, by and large, was a positive experience. You never get entirely divorced from it that way. So, I don't know. It's a movie that I have a certain affection for. But I think it's pretty damn bad! (*big laughs*)

Tom DiCillo: *Johnny Suede*

Have movies always been a big part of your life and, if so, when did your obsession begin?
My father was a colonel in the Marine Corp., a rather strict person. He was very adamant about encouraging my brother, sister and I into activities he hoped would develop our minds. One of the things he did was to refuse to allow a television in the house. So in the late sixties and early seventies, a time when network television was one of the biggest social influences in America, we never watched TV. We would go to school and all the kids would be asking each other, did you see *Laugh-In* last night? *Star Trek*? *The Man From U.N.C.L.E.*? We'd always get the strangest looks when we said we hadn't seen them. Ironically, my father would then go away for thirteen months at a time, stationed somewhere by himself. And the first thing my mom would do when he was gone was rent a television and we'd go through these sessions of sometimes forty-eight hours of watching television, like it was a drug. I think part of my fascination for film, for the sexiness of moving images, came from being denied it for so long.

When did you make the transition from secret TV viewing to movie going?
It wasn't until I was in college that I saw a film that made me think of movies as more than just 'go there and eat popcorn'. My cinematic experiences up until that time were mainly limited to that: go there, sit there, lose your brain. I had seen *Rebel Without a Cause* when I was eleven years old and it was a very disturbing film to me. But beyond that, I'd just go to movies on Saturday afternoon and zone out. When I was in college I was majoring in creative writing and someone said, we're having a film class. Why don't you come by? And the first film they showed was Fellini's *La Strada*. Watching that film gave me the actual physical sensation of having my brain ignited in my head. The quality of the story; what he chose to tell a story about; the complexity of the characters. It was a story about human beings involved in human activity dramatized in a way that I'd never seen before. It was an absolutely mind-blowing experience. And it was at that point that I said I'd like to try and do this.

Did you start making films at this point?
I was really into black and white photography at the same time as I was writing. But no. Nothing with film. You have to remember this was 1976. The whole idea of the American independent scene, you know, anyone can pick up a camera and do it, had not even begun. It wasn't even a concept. Most of the people I knew still

thought of film as something that only rich people in Hollywood could do. The idea of somehow getting a camera and making a film seemed completely impossible to me financially. So I decided to go to film school. I began investigating film schools and then had to make a decision between schools in LA and New York. I got accepted by NYU in the masters programme and decided to stay on the east coast.

Can you tell me about your experience at NYU?
My degree at NYU was in writing and directing. I wrote and directed six short films there. They were little slices of life. Some were autobiographical, some were made up. In one, a guy was lying in bed thinking about a woman that he was really in love with but who had rejected him. I took thirty seconds of time and made a five-minute film about it. It was the most successful thing I'd done at school. It was just a guy lying in bed. I was working on his emotional state, how to cut into the flashbacks to give the information about his being with this woman and then the break-up. I was very pleased with it as an exercise and it was well received. But I was very angry there most of the time. In terms of what I learned there, I learned nothing. In fact, apart from meeting Jim Jarmusch, it was one of the most destructive experiences of my life. There were several people there who were expelled because their films did not meet a certain aesthetic requirement of the faculty, who said, 'This is a film; this is not a film.' To me, that was the most absurd thinking that I'd ever heard – especially in a school. Let's say you attempted to make a little film, something that you thought was interesting and it didn't quite work. Well, what is the most beneficial thing for the film-maker at that point? To be made to feel like you tried something and you failed miserably? Or to say, hey, what did you learn from that? So you stumbled? Get up! You cannot be fearful about being decapitated every time you stumble. If you are, you'll never try anything. In fact the reality of film-making is much more about stumbling than anything else.

How did you end up working with Jim Jarmusch?
Jim and I were in a seminar once at school where they showed Godard's *Vivre sa Vie*. We were the only two in the entire group of students that responded favourably to the film. Everyone else was going, I don't get it. It's not about anything! That initially drew us together. Then by complete accident we were assigned to work together on a class project. The teacher said, Jim, you write a two-minute sketch. Tom, you shoot it. That's how it happened. I knew something about composition from my photography but that's about it. I'd never studied cinematography. There was something about my sensibility that suited Jim: the fact that I was not overly concerned by a pretty light here and the exposure matching there. Essentially we worked together on a visual idea level to bring out the emotions of the film. Most DPs don't work that way. They work the opposite way, which is, I can't shoot that. I have to wait another four hours for the light to be right. It was

that class exercise that led me to shoot Jim's first feature, *Permanent Vacation*. Although Jim had a very strong sense of what he wanted to do, he gave me almost complete freedom to visualize the scenes. This person should walk in here on this line and do this and the camera should make this little adjustment. It was good practice for me. *Permanent Vacation* won several awards in Europe which helped put Jim on the map. Meanwhile I was studying acting and writing and painting apartments to make money. Jim then asked me to shoot *Stranger Than Paradise*, which led to a lot of offers to shoot no- and low-budget movies. But shooting was never something I really intended to do. I sort of stumbled into it. I then began to see that the only way out of it was a complete cut because, especially after *Stranger Than Paradise*, everyone identified me as Jim Jarmusch's cameraman. So I quit shooting. I shot my last film for Jim in 1984. And just to let you know how pervasive that association was, ten years later I was in Barcelona for the opening of *Living in Oblivion*. I'd already made *Johnny Suede* which had opened in Spain. There I was in 1995, at the press conference for *Living in Oblivion* and someone asked me, so, Tom, will you be shooting for Jim Jarmusch again? I said no. The next day in the paper, the headline in the arts section was DiCillo will not work with Jarmusch again! With a big exclamation mark!

When did the idea for Johnny Suede *start to take root?*
That idea hit me roughly about the time that I began taking acting classes. At this time something very exciting was happening in the music scene in New York: one of the very few rare moments of truth in American music – the punk movement. I know it started in England but for a brief moment when it came here it was incredibly exciting. You'd walk down the lower east side and see these extraordinary characters. One element of punk led a group of musicians back into a pseudo-fifties sub-genre, like early Elvis Costello, The Stray Cats and The Clash. And that's when the idea of a character enmeshed in the fifties came to me. So in my acting class I began to play around with the idea of a guy who's a bit slow but looks like an idol. I said, is there a way the guy can look like a hero on the surface but underneath he's as foolish and as a fearful and as vulnerable as everybody else? That enabled me to treat him as an innocent but have him do some pretty horrific things. I began writing monologues about certain experiences I'd had in New York – drawing on myself, pouring myself into this character.

Can you describe the process by which you turned your monologues into the screenplay for Johnny Suede?
You have to take a look at my state of mind at that time for a moment. It was about 1985. I'd graduated from film school over six years earlier in 1979. I'd shot some independent films; I was studying acting, painting apartments, working occasionally as a waiter for a catering service. But at the back of my mind was this daily reminder pounding on my head. You went to film school. You have a Master's Degree in Directing. When are you going to make a film? Finally I realized I could

use these monologues in a one-man show. So in 1985 I put it together. I knew someone who had a theatre. I even remember making the call, going, listen, I've written something I'd like to put on at your theatre in a one-man show. Getting up and acting, putting up the money myself to produce it – that was an enormous challenge for me. But I had to do it. So mounting the show, taking out an ad in the *Village Voice*, that was the next big milestone. And the fact that the theatre read the piece, liked it and was extremely supportive gave me the confidence that the idea had value. The next big incentive to go further with the piece was the response from women in the audience. They seemed to really appreciate being able to see this particular slant on the male psyche. It was this response that gave me the first real vision of the piece as a film. Getting the first draft down on paper was both exhilarating and horrifying. My major problem was that in the monologue, which was a stage vehicle, all the information was expressed in words. It was in the Mark Twain storytelling genre: 'I was walking down the street and this girl said, "Wow, where'd you get those shoes?"' I was really just telling the story with words. The first draft of the screenplay reflected this dependency and I had to start all over again and try to tell the story visually. I had to keep reminding myself, 'You've got a camera here. Let the camera relay information.' I wrote four drafts before I felt I had made the transition. But ultimately I still think that the original dependency on words was a problem that made its way into the finished film.

How long did you take to write it?
It took about eight months to get to the fourth draft. You have to remember that prior to this, the longest thing I'd written was a full-length play (about one and a half hours) and the *Johnny Suede* monologue (about an hour). This was only the third time I had wrestled with longer form structures. It was tough, therefore, to think in terms of telling a story over almost two hours; two hours seemed enormous and overwhelming. But once I had the first two pieces done, the longer form concept of *Johnny Suede* as a film seemed far more achievable to me.

How do you work when you're writing?
I need total concentration when I write. I shut myself in a small room and literally enter the world of the film. There is something exhilarating about isolating myself for six to seven hours a day and just creating the film as I see it. My acting experience helped me enormously in terms of writing scenes and dialogue for *Johnny Suede*. I would pour myself into every character. I would be rocking around the living room acting out all the scenes: me being Darlette; me being Johnny; me being Yvonne. And just saying the lines, working on the lines over and over and over until it felt right. It was tremendously exciting to bring the characters besides Johnny to life. Previously they'd only been spoken about or referred to and dramatizing them really helped me specify his world. The first person to read my scripts is always my wife, Jane. She's an amazingly gifted and astute observer of the most critical thing that needs to be happening at any point.

She can immediately tell when the script veers away from believability or strays into digression. I also talk to friends and show the script to people. But mainly it's just me alone.

A lot of people watching the film might have asked themselves what exactly was it about suede that inspired you?
There's a section of the film in which Johnny has a fantasy of himself in front of a group of women and starts trying to say what he loves about suede: 'Suede is rough but smooth. It's strong but quiet.' You don't notice it right away. It doesn't stand out in a crowd full of leather and vinyl but once you do see it, you can't take your eyes off it and you wonder why you ever overlooked it in the first place. About a year before, I'd found those pointed black suede shoes. I was walking by a pile of garbage and I noticed a small suitcase. My curiosity struck me and I said, I wonder what's in that suitcase? I opened it up and there were those shoes. I tried them and they fitted me perfectly. And they were those black suede shoes. And something about that seemed almost magical to me. And I wore those and everyone'd look at me and they'd go, my god, where did you get those shoes? No one in the entire city had a pair of shoes like this. It made me start thinking about suede. More than anything, Johnny feels that the world is overlooking him. He's not flashy in a sense. He's not leather and vinyl. He's got something he feels is a bit more subtle, that takes a little more effort to see the real value of. Ironically, he's right. He doesn't really know how right he is because he's still very much into his surface. But his 'suedeness', so to speak, is revealed at the end of the film. I was trying to say that, particularly in the art world, now even more in the film world, it's what grabs your attention immediately that usually gets talked about. There's even another speech in the film that's associated with this – when Deke comments on one of Johnny's songs and says it's old-fashioned. It's not 'now'. We want something 'now'! Whenever I think what 'now' is, it's absurd. All you've got to do is look and see what people looked like in 1972 and the concept of 'now' becomes meaningless. If you didn't wear the bell-bottom pants, you weren't cool. I can remember going to school and having people ostracize me because I didn't do what they thought was the essence of cool or 'now'. To me it's still very bizarre. I wanted to have Johnny state my feeling about that: my belief that sometimes you have to look a little closer at things to see what their real value is. That's why I chose suede.

Where did the idea for Johnny's enormous pompadour come from?
Some people said to me after I made the film and the posters were coming out, it's too bad about his hair. I said, what are you talking about? They said, well, he looks so stupid. I said, that's the point. Whatever he was trying to do to himself had to be so exaggerated that it made him look stupid even though he didn't know it. I got the idea when I was in Japan and I saw these groups of kids that would dance every Sunday afternoon in Yoyogi park and they had these pom-

padours that were like thirty feet tall. They took the whole idea of the American fifties and exaggerated it almost to the point of monstrosity. I said, that's what I want. To me it was the most critical thing I could have done to show that I wasn't try to make *Johnny Suede* as an exercise in cool. I wanted him to look like a fool from the moment you see him. Even then I was aware that there was a danger that people would look at the film and think that the film itself was trying to be cool. I was really trying to do the exact opposite which was to show the futility, the pointlessness of anybody trying to be cool.

Was the story in any way autobiographical?
A lot of it was autobiographical. For example, I had been in a relationship with a woman like Darlette who encouraged me to see her as a troubled, beautiful princess who loved me and needed me to protect her from some abusive outsider. But it was all exaggerated in the film. I even gave her boyfriend, Flip, a gun to accentuate the sense of danger! Johnny's image of himself was as a protector of women and once that fell away he was shattered. After a while, women get bored of being protected but Johnny had very little to fall back on. Which is why he initially has so much trouble when he starts a relationship with a woman as self-confident as Yvonne.

Yvonne is such a contrast to Johnny. What does she see in him? Apart from the pretty face?
I think she sees that there is the potential for something real in him; that he is struggling to be honest with her. I think that most men have a very difficult time being honest with women, revealing themselves to them. And this happens even in the simplest ways like being able to talk without feeling threatened or needing to exert control. So in this way Johnny is at least several steps ahead of a lot of men. If you look at their relationship, you can see that he's absolutely honest with her even if he doesn't know it. The scene in bed where he reveals he doesn't even know how to give her an orgasm is potentially very humiliating for him. If it had been another guy, it might have been, fuck you! But look what he does. He stays there. He allows her to instruct him. And he doesn't give her any attitude about it. I believe that's one of the reasons Yvonne would feel maybe there's something to this guy.

What did you do once you had a screenplay?
I had absolutely no idea what to do with it. It was like being dropped in the Atlantic Ocean and trying to swim for land. You have to remember this was 1987. The whole concept of the 'profitable' independent film scene was barely an idea. There was no *Millimeter*, no *Premiere*, no *Independent Film* magazine. There were very few places in the country that were financing independent films. That didn't really begin until a few years earlier with *Stranger Than Paradise*. It was the first independent film to première at the New York Film Festival. This was a huge achievement. The idea of someone taking the smallest possible amount of

money, making a movie and having it playing next to Hollywood movies, in the same venues and having critics see it, that had never happened before. So one of the first things I did was show the screenplay to Jim Jarmusch. He was very positive and gave me some helpful advice. He was getting all his money at the time from European financing. German television, ZDF, had given him money for *Stranger Than Paradise*. So I approached them and they gave me eighty thousand dollars right off. I was stunned. I said, wow! I didn't even have a producer. I was doing all of this myself. Making the calls, sending out the scripts. Jim actually gave me a pamphlet on how to apply for grants so I went down to the library and I started filling out forms for grants. I got a grant from the National Endowment for the Arts for twenty-five thousand dollars. At that moment someone read the script and said, why don't you take it to the Sundance Lab? I said, after my experience at NYU? Fuck that! I don't even want to see another teacher. That was how I felt. But they said, maybe you should consider it. In the end I said all right. So I sent it into Sundance and it ended up being tremendously helpful to me. It definitely helped with the script. For the first time it enabled me to shoot a scene, look at it and go, oh, now I see what to do. What a tremendous relief to feel that you could try it once, come back in and try it again and not feel that you had one shot at it. In low-budget film-making, unfortunately, that's one of the worse pressures and the most persistent. Most of the time you only have one shot. Sundance helped me in many ways, not least of which was that they gave me a Panavision package; they gave me an entire camera which is worth about thirty thousand dollars.

What happened next in terms of raising the finance for the film?
By now it was 1988 to 1989. The last film I'd shot as a cinematographer had been accepted into the Directors' Fortnight at Cannes. The director was kind enough to pay my way over there. I was proud of my work on the film so I went over there to support it. Ironically, the moment I got off the plane I ran into someone who had heard about the screenplay which then led to someone else. Before I knew it, within two days, I had a deal. It was totally out of the blue. I was utterly jetlagged. All I wanted to do was go to sleep. But I was having to make all these phone calls and go to all these meetings. And there's a guy saying, 'Yes, I'd like you to sign an option.' So I ended up signing a deal in a hotel room, the Hotel Majestic, for three hundred thousand, giving this guy worldwide rights to the film. He was from South Africa. It was not an absolutely fair contract for me but for a first-time film-maker it was great to hear someone say, here's the money: you can make the film. But in a sense he was going to hire me to work on my own film, with the right to fire me if he felt so compelled. A shaky thing but still I felt it was worth the risk so I decided to go ahead with it. We went into pre-production, started casting, hired a casting director, began the search for Johnny which was enormously difficult.

I heard you had to go to LA for casting because actors in New York didn't understand the character of Johnny Suede?

Yes. They all tended to play him like this character called the Fonz out of this stupid American TV series *Happy Days*. It was absurd. 'What are you doing?!' I'd say, 'just be yourself.' So we ended up staying in this sleazy motel in LA. Again we're talking about a budget of three hundred thousand, so just to fly myself and the casting director out there was a considerable expense. At the end of our search, the second to the last guy we saw out of maybe five hundred guys, walked in. On his résumé, he had two things: one, a Canadian TV series I'd never heard of; two, a film called *Thelma and Louise* that no one had seen. This was Brad Pitt. I knew immediately he was the guy for my film. Then as I looked at him I realized that in American film at this point, there wasn't anyone like him. There was Tom Cruise. But Tom Cruise was a bit of a jock, a sports guy. There was no one who could do the James Dean wounded-hero kind of thing. And, as you can see, Brad slipped right into that. Anyway, my financier said, 'No, you can't cast him.' I said, 'You're crazy!' He said, 'I want you to meet Timothy Hutton. He's interested in the film. He wants to do it.' I said, 'Oh, come on, man!' Finally, I insisted. I said, 'It's got to be Brad.' And he let me cast Brad. Then we were in pre-production and the entire deal fell apart. I'd begun to mistrust this guy. I didn't like what he was doing. I didn't like the fact that he had complete ownership of the film, that he could fire me, that he wouldn't give me final cut. We'd been location hunting, we'd done everything. But I just really, really began to mistrust him, especially when he put this piece of paper in front of me and asked me to sign it. Ironically, at Cannes I'd met Ruth Waldburger, a Swiss producer who knew one of the producers of *Stranger Than Paradise*. She'd already expressed some interest in the project through the South African producer who was now insisting on a controlling personal involvement himself. Unbeknownst to me, he had misinformed her about some of the more crucial elements of the film, so she'd walked away. And feeling I had no other options, I'd signed a deal with the South African. Jump forward again. I'm in this deal with this South African. I'm all cast, I'm ready to go and I start getting this uneasy feeling that I don't really trust him. At this point I had a very supportive producer working with me, Yoram Mandel, who strongly agreed that in order to save the film we needed to get out of the deal. The day the South African's option expired, therefore, Yoram and I called Ruth Waldburger and explained how we had originally wanted to make the film with her. She was elated. I was out of one deal on a Friday and in another one on a Sunday. She gave me final cut without question; complete choice over the actors and a much better deal in terms of what I was being paid.

Was there any fall-out from the South African producer?

Yes. He sued us over the money that he'd spent. And, of course, he inflated all the figures. It was really ugly. He hadn't spent anything. As I told you, I hadn't even got paid a dime. That's why I will always be indebted to Ruth Waldburger. She just assumed the debt. She just picked it up and paid the guy off. And that was that.

When was this happening?
By now we're now talking 1989.

Five years since you came up with the idea of Johnny Suede?
Yes. It's hard to look back on it now and have any clear perception of what the hell I was thinking. Because if I apply what I know now about what goes into making a movie, I would say, Tom, you were insane! It was as if I was looking at the ocean and saying I can walk across it. Well, Tom, how are you going to do it? You can't walk on water. I know. But I'm going to do it. It's almost about mind over matter. Convincing yourself that you can actually do the impossible. It is a kind of insanity. It forces you into these absolutely schizophrenic states of mind. Each little victory is elation. The most money I'd seen in my life was five thousand dollars. And I was looking at a total budget of four hundred thousand!

What were you living on at this point?
Painting apartments. Sometimes I'd take a loan from Jane. It put a real strain on our relationship. But she was amazingly supportive. I was really just putting my head down and not even looking at what was around me; saying I will not stop until I make this movie. A lot of things were driving me at this point. I'd been to film school but I hadn't made a movie. I felt I had a lot of potential but I just wasn't realizing it. That was probably one of the main motivations in my life: Tom, what are you doing? If you're going to do it, do it! After a certain amount of time, there isn't going to be any more time. So if you have these hopes and these dreams, fuck it, you're going to have to do it! My naivety protected me from the disappointments, the complete impossibility of things. I essentially worked for free for four years. It was like blind faith.

Had you been paid anything from the budget at this point?
No. But the thing is I never even considered it. Even then I knew that in order for me to make this film I was going to have to make it my way. That if I couldn't get the money to make it on 35 mm, I'd make it on 16 mm. And if I couldn't make it 16 mm I'd make it on Super-8. I never even considered taking the script and showing it to anyone in Hollywood. People keep asking me, did Jim influence you at all? On an ideas level, the answer is no. But on a reality level, absolutely. The fact that he was the first one who took a personal idea and made a public cinematic event out of it was very inspiring. It wasn't until I worked with Jim that I realized I wasn't alone. So I respect him enormously. I still do because he's continued to work that way. He hasn't sold out.

Did you ever think, 'I can't go on'?
Not in the money raising, no. I was so excited that I'd even made that step. I can't tell you how many millions of people are in this grey area of 'I want to be a film-maker'. And even after going to film school, I was in the grey area too! I remem-

ber going to meetings and events and people saying, what are you doing, Tom? And I was saying, 'Oh well, I got an idea for a screenplay.' That's where I was at. Still at the ideas stage. So to have moved from the ideas stage to the action stage was unbelievably exhilarating.

With Ruth on board as producer, how did you begin to prepare for the shoot?
I knew I wanted to give the film a particular visual style: something that wasn't ostentatious, that wasn't just tacked on. But at the same time I knew it should be a little twisted, a little off. I began by looking at pictures of things that gave me that feeling – for example there was something I liked about the quality of light in an Edward Hopper painting. I showed it to my cinematographer. I said, look at that light. It's the inside, outside. The quality of the way the light is hitting the body in this picture: it's Johnny in his apartment. The first big surprise came when I realized that the East Village where I was going the set the story had completely changed. It was no longer the East Village as I remembered it – wide empty streets with nobody on them. It had completely changed. It had turned into the Gap, Banana Republic. We ended up going out to Brooklyn and finding this whole area of Williamsburg that was completely deserted and had this very strange atmosphere. I said, wow! I like this better. I can get a shot of him walking down a deserted street. And in his ridiculous outfit, it's going to have some significance.

Given your reputation as Jim Jarmusch's cinematographer, was it difficult finding a DP?
This is a nightmare story. After an exhaustive search I ended up hiring a guy who seemed to me to have some creative ideas which had nothing to do with just technical things. We were down by the river, shooting the scene with Johnny and Deke and we had to send a grip to the truck to get a light. We're all standing around waiting for half an hour. No big deal. The sun starts to go down a little bit. Across the river, Manhattan was rising up, half in shadow. Out of the shadow, up along the river, came this old Chinese freighter. It was incredibly beautiful. Something about the rust on the ship made it feel like it could be part of the world I was filming. It wasn't a pretty shot but it was really powerful and the light was incredible. We're all looking at it, a little astonished, and I turned to the DP and I said, 'Just spin the camera round, don't even look, just get me a shot of that boat.' A moment later I looked round and the guy hadn't even moved. He was still standing by the camera. I said, all right, maybe he didn't hear me. So I said, 'Just turn the camera around over here and get a shot of the boat.' And he does it. I thought, that's really strange: what the hell is going on with this guy? But I didn't get a chance to think of it again because there were millions of things happening. The next day we went to dailies. About thirty of us were sitting there and the shot comes up on the screen for a split second. Because of the incredible beauty of the shot the entire room goes wow! Then the camera started jerking all over the place. It never stabilized. The shot was completely unusable. I looked at the DP afterwards and said, 'Why d'you

do that?' 'I don't know,' he said. This continued. I'd ask him to do a shot and the shot would be executed. Then I'd see it in dailies and it would be unusable. After two weeks, I fired him. Jump ahead three months. I was in the editing room. I needed a cutaway: something to help me put two things together. I said, let's go back to the shot of the boat. Maybe there's four seconds we can use. We drag it out of the dusty bin, put it up on the Movieola and look at it. There's not even four seconds of material I could use. I was so furious that I called the DP. I got on the phone and said, 'Listen, man, I got to ask you something. You shot almost a third of this film. If you want your name in the credits, you better answer me this question. What the hell were you doing?' He broke down in tears over the phone. He said, 'You're absolutely right, Tom. I was so jealous of you directing your first film that I was intentionally sabotaging your film.' I couldn't even conceive of somebody being that destructive. So Joe DeSalvo ended up shooting the film. He came in in a difficult situation – we were already two weeks into shooting. I had no prep time with him. It was literally a phone call: can you come in tomorrow and start? So considering that, he did very well.

How did your collaboration with Joe DeSalvo work in terms of your decisions about how to cover a scene?
It depends every time on where the strongest visual focus of a scene is. There's usually something in a scene, somewhere you step and suddenly realize this is where the camera wants to be. The exteriors were usually chosen for a very specific visual reason: for the wide empty streets; for the decrepit buildings; or to emphasize the absurdity and isolation of Johnny's character in this odd wasteland. Most of the interiors had to be carefully worked out in terms of the shots. Basically you're in a room so you have to plan it all out. Sometimes I would get to a location and just looking at it, discover the shots right while we were there. We had a very careful shot list. There was never an instance where I was able to stop and say let's do it again. We were grinding out the shots. We shot the film in four six-day weeks doing about twenty set-ups a day. It was brutal.

How did you sleep during the shoot?
Not at all. That was when I first started having anxiety dreams. Even though I'd have a horrific day on the set and knew that the most important thing for me to do was to sleep, I'd go to bed and be shooting the same scene over and over. It never ended even into the editing. I would be editing and then having these dreams that I was still on the set. Sometimes I'd wake up and yell at myself, 'Tom, you've finished shooting! Stop it!'

It sounds strangely reminiscent of Living in Oblivion?
Absolutely. *Living in Oblivion* was my revenge on *Johnny Suede*. The DP that I fired was the absolute basis for Wolf's character in *Living in Oblivion*. But, as you can see, I was too kind on him. Wolf comes off as a lovable guy. *Living in Oblivion* could very easily have been like Bergman's *Hour of the Wolf*. It could have

been a horror movie. The twisted personalities that are in this business are amazing. Most people are involved in the film-making business for all the wrong reasons. I talked at length with my production designer about how I wanted Johnny's apartment to look. We looked at four or five books with very specific pictures of distressed, run-down-looking rooms. I walked into Johnny's apartment on the first day of shooting and everything was immaculate. It's all painted, it's beautiful. It looked better than my apartment! I said, 'What the fuck are you doing? We are supposed to be shooting in here in twenty minutes!' I literally picked up a hammer and started pounding at the walls. Sometimes there are just personalities and people who are not going to listen no matter what you say. That's one of the aspects of this business that's very tough to deal with and I had an abnormal amount of it on *Johnny Suede*.

How did you feel before you began the shoot?

The night before I didn't sleep at all. I drank half a bottle of vodka and I still couldn't sleep. Then I woke up in the morning, drunk. My experience on some of my own student films had been so horrific that I knew that if that little ball of luck rolled the wrong way it could be brutal. So I was very apprehensive. It wasn't that I didn't know what I was going to do. My eight years of working with actors made me feel very confident that I could deal with that side of it. I knew that if I could get the dramatics of the scene to work, it didn't matter where I put the camera. I was very excited. It wasn't all a nightmare. I looked at myself at times and I thought I can't believe I'm here. Three years ago I was sitting in a room looking at the collected notes of my monologue, going, Tom, are you ever going to do this? And here I was the day before shooting my first film. I was proud of myself. I said, no matter what, you have accomplished something just by getting here.

Was your excitement at getting Brad Pitt for the part of Johnny borne out by his performance?

What had happened was that the Hollywood machine had already started rolling. The buzz had already started about him even though *Thelma and Louise* hadn't been released yet. His agents were at the point where they were saying, maybe you shouldn't do *Johnny Suede*? When *Thelma and Louise* comes out you're going to be so big! So I would say this about Brad: once he committed to the film, he committed a hundred per cent. He did things I would never have expected in terms of his commitment. And I still consider it one of the bravest roles that he's ever done, the most revealing. He didn't manifest any of that egotistical shit that most stars have. Our first day we shot a lot of the exteriors of Johnny walking alone and everything went perfectly. The light was incredible. We got all the shots. Brad was great. The sense of exhilaration was beyond belief. Day two: (*sound of massive explosion*) it was literally as if my entire world had collapsed. It was the first scene with Johnny doing dialogue and it was awful. I suddenly realized that Brad had this whole concept of the character that was wrong. I'd told him, one of the things about Johnny is that he thinks and behaves like a child. What I meant was that if you look at a child, their attention is focused here and then if they lose their focus, after two seconds, they're still focused over there just as intensely. I said to Brad, it takes a tremendous amount of energy to be a poseur because you're constantly thinking, how am I doing? Can people see through me? And Johnny knows that he's faking it! I saw Brad get excited about this and I said, okay, I've said enough. But Brad had taken the note the wrong way. He thought I meant Johnny was infantile, slow, like a baby. All the way through the shoot I was thinking, why is he talking this way when he should just be using his own voice? Ultimately as the director of the film I take responsibility. I realize now in retrospect that I probably could have been clearer to him, spent more time explaining what I was thinking about to help him. Again, I didn't find this out until the end of the film. And it's a lesson that I keep learning: you have to be ruthless as a director. You have to be! But I had so many distractions, so many things fucking up! The set for his apartment began falling apart. The walls were literally falling away from the floor to the point that the fire department closed down the building and said you can't come back in here. We had to find another apartment to shoot in and match it. All these distractions prevented me from focusing on the main thing, which was: Brad, you've got to speed it up! Don't take it personally; but you've got to speed it up! I never ever expected Johnny to come off as a dimwit but he does. To me, that's a critical oversight.

Did you get all the material you wanted?
I lost so much. For many reasons. As simple as the film was, it was extremely ambitious for four hundred thousand dollars. And we were moving at such a frantic pace that I didn't have the ability to see the most basic problem: that Brad was a little off. Quite honestly, I missed the wildness of the character I had created. Why's Johnny doing this? How much energy does he put into being this guy? I missed that. But I got some things, too. I think on a scene by scene basis I found some things that enabled the actors to take some real risks. And visually the film is unique.

Apart from your dissatisfaction about Brad's performance, were you happy with the way the shoot went?
For some reason in hindsight you only tend to remember the nightmares but there were moments. In particular, all the scenes with Brad and Catherine Keener were very exciting. They had a great chemistry about them and we all instantly agreed on what the scenes were about. I really enjoyed working with Calvin Levels who played Deke and I had a great time with Nick Cave. Even so, the entire experience seems racked with frustration. Each day I was forced to remind myself before coming on to the set, this is a new day. Forget the catastrophes that happened yesterday. Be positive. There was a particular day when this reached an almost Kafkaesque absurdity. I'd wanted Johnny to look like a prince out of time

but the costume designer had had some problems in realizing the style I had in mind. So the night before shooting Brad and I went into my closet and put together all of his costumes. Fortunately my clothes fitted him. Every single bit of clothing that I'd bought in thrift stores and vintage clothing stores over the past fifteen years became his costume. Anyway, two weeks into the shoot, I come back from lunch. It had been a pretty gruelling morning and I was giving myself my usual pep talk in an attempt to rekindle my 'positive energy' for the rest of the afternoon. Think positive, I was telling myself. The moment I walked on to the set, a wardrobe assistant came up to me and said, 'Tom, I hate to tell you this but during lunch the wardrobe van was left unattended.' I said, 'Yeah?' 'And some of the clothing got stolen,' this woman went on. Still, I'm thinking it's probably just a raincoat or some shoes or something. 'All of Johnny's wardrobe got stolen,' the woman went on. 'All of it.' As I said, we were two weeks into the shoot. All of Johnny's wardrobe had been established in the film. I was so furious I kicked the wall and nearly broke my foot. We were in Brooklyn which was the most crime-ridden area I'd ever seen and someone left the wardrobe van unlocked? How could anybody be so stupid? Well, they *were* that stupid. And all the clothing got stolen. We had to shut down for a day and do other shots while they went and made replicas of all the clothes. They ended up looking fine on film but afterwards we just threw them out because they looked so fake. I mean, they were fake. Anyway, having my personal stuff stolen as a result of someone else's stupidity did a number on me. I know that other directors have sacrificed much more for the films. I mean, Francis Ford Coppola had to sell his house to make *Apocalypse Now*. But for some reason, this particular catastrophe hit me hard. I think it had something to do with the fact that the clothes had been so personal to me, so much part of my identity.

After the craziness of the shoot, how did you feel about the first cut of the movie?
It was devastating. In my mind I was still seeing the movie that I hoped was going to launch my career and show me it was worth the ten-year wait. And the first cut of the film was just dreadful. It was two and a half hours long. An hour had to be cut out of it. That's a lot of film! I had to be ruthless about it. I said, Tom, you can't use that scene. The pacing of the film there is so slow you can't cut within that scene, so you've got to cut the whole scene out. It was really painful. I realized that some of the nuances of Johnny's character that I liked, the little undercurrent of violence in him, I had to take out. That first screening – when you're sitting there and expecting the magic to come and suddenly you see that it's slow, some things weren't realized – it was very tough. I think that's one of the most difficult things for any film-maker: when you finally take it off the editing table and you screen it for the first time and part of you is expecting it to spring to life. Sometimes it does but this time it didn't.

How long did you go on working on it?

About another month and a half. I cut another hour out of the film. Some people still say the film is slow. It is. But it has a deliberate pace to it. The crazy thing is if you'd seen the original monologue, the guy was bouncing all over the place. I thought it would be more of an exciting film. I said, what did I do wrong? Ultimately I realized the thrust of the film, the tension, was unfocused. It's something I have to be constantly aware of: keeping that ball of tension rolling.

What happened once you had a completed film?
I said, we're going to apply to Cannes, which is something every film-maker in the world says. So we submitted the film. Every day we were waiting for the answer. And finally Ruth Waldburger came walking down the hall to the editing room. She looked at me and said, they rejected it. I was devastated. They had seen the film in rough cut form and said, no, definitely not. Two months later we finished the film and got accepted into the Locarno film festival. We had no US distribution but having gone through the experience with Jim and some other film-makers, I wasn't too worried. What they did was make the film first and then get a distributor. Jim made *Stranger Than Paradise* before he got a distributor. To me, it didn't seem that risky. Obviously Ruth Waldburger didn't think so either. I think by this point she'd sold the film to France and Switzerland but we had no US distribution. So we went to Locarno. I was basically thinking this is my first film festival with one of my own films. I'm just going to enjoy it. And I did. I had no expectations. Nothing. I said if we get some good press out of this, that would be great. The next thing that I know, I began perceiving this almost physical buzz. Everywhere I went I heard people saying, that's the guy that did *Johnny Suede*! *Johnny Suede*! *Johnny Suede*! All of a sudden, it came down to the awards night. They said, Tom, you are up for one of the awards. I said, I don't believe it. They said, you are, you are. An hour before the award ceremony, Ruth Waldburger comes up to me and says, you won the Golden Leopard for Best Film. Next thing I knew I was standing up in front of seven thousand people. It was in this huge outdoor piazza in Locarno. I felt completely disembodied looking out on this sea of people, all the lights. It was the first time I'd ever really won anything in my life: anything that I thought was significant. I felt really bizarre. I couldn't quite believe it. Then what followed was a night of complete celebration travelling around to restaurants holding this ridiculous Leopard. I wanted to leave it in the car, but Ruth said, no, bring it in. Everywhere we went we were carrying this Leopard and people would start applauding. Tom! Tom! It was my first taste of the addiction, of the pure buzz of acclaim. How dangerous it is, because it's like a fix: as soon as it's gone, you want it again. Meanwhile, *Thelma and Louise* was about to open and the buzz about Brad Pitt had started. The name, Brad Pitt, was now on everyone's lips. So Miramax bought the film. Harvey Weinstein bought *Johnny Suede* without even seeing it. We came back from Locarno and we went to the Toronto film festival. And I remember it screening there with Harvey Weinstein right in front of me. This was the first time I'd ever met him. I remember

someone tapping him on the shoulder and saying, 'Hey, Harvey, hope you like it.' Then began what I call my 'trial by fire`, my coming out of the state of childhood into adulthood. Harvey Weinstein picked up the movie. He had a screening. The press in Toronto liked it. He had a good response to it. He came back to New York. He said, I'm going to have a test screening. I'd like you to come down. I said fine. I'd never been to one. We went down. We had the test screening. The audience was laughing throughout the film and responding. At the end, though, as they began to ask the basic questions, one, did you like the film? and, two, would you recommend it to your friends? the responses weren't very good. He called me into an emergency meeting the next day and said I had to cut ten minutes out of the film. I was really naive. I was thinking, what are you talking about? No, no, no. I mean, this was the film that had won the best film at Locarno. I was proud of my resistance because a lot of people just cave in to him immediately. He looked at me and he said, 'Well, if you're not going to cut it, I guess we know what that means.' I jumped up and said, 'What does it mean?' And he looked over at his head of distribution and said, 'Well, we don't know how many prints we're going to strike.' I said, 'Are you threatening me? You're going to dump my film?' We ended up with a compromise which was that in the American version I wrote a narration in which Buck Henry tries to clarify certain things that some audiences seemed to have problems with.

What was the public reaction to the film?
The film very clearly affected some people and didn't affect others. Some reactions were very confusing to me. There was a British review that said if MTV had a contest for a first-time superficial film, this is it. I was astounded. I said, did they look at the movie? Did they see that underneath all of his fancy clothing Johnny Suede walks around wearing the rattiest underwear? That he can't even play the guitar? That he doesn't know the first thing about sex? That he ends up punching a woman in the stomach? I mean, did they watch the fucking movie?! In America, the critics were pretty much evenly split. There were those who denounced the film as being about absolutely nothing. Then there were other critics who said there's something going on here. This is an interesting film. Nonetheless Miramax's release of the film, based on what they thought was going to happen to the film, ended up in a run of three weeks in New York. And that was the most depressing, the blackest period of my life. I felt utterly betrayed. After all the work I'd put into the film, all the effort to try to drag it into existence. But there was nothing I could do about it. It then went on to other openings. It did very well in the UK. But it didn't in any way put me on the map. Most people think that *Living in Oblivion* was my first film.

Maybe you wouldn't have had the material for Living in Oblivion *if you hadn't had the experience of* Johnny Suede?
Much as I value *Living in Oblivion*, I hate to think I have to go through that kind

of catastrophe every time I make a film. It's a little exhausting. *Johnny Suede* was definitely a film made in the spirit of let me try something, let me put an idea out there. It was not a film made to put me on the cover of *Premiere* magazine. I still feel, based upon the kinds of movies that were coming out at the time, that *Johnny Suede* is an absolutely original film. It's no better or worse than any of those films that were getting so much attention at the time. But it didn't happen. It made it incredibly difficult to finance my next film.

So no calls from LA?
Ironically, there were. After Miramax bought the film and it won at Locarno, I came back from Switzerland and listened to my messages. I should have saved the tape. In one day, there were messages from Spielberg's company, from Coppola's company and some others. I immediately returned the calls but no one at any of the places had any recollection of anyone calling me. It was tough. I tried to make a film, a subtle film and what I was really trying to say was a little too subtle. People either wanted Johnny Suede to be a hero or they wanted him to be a complete fuck-up. To suggest that he could be both was unacceptable.

What were the main things you learned from the experience?
One has to be ruthless in terms of the way you interrogate the people you hire. I didn't make a single call to anybody about anyone who worked for me. If I had, I would have found out some things about them. I can guarantee you, anyone who calls me now to ask me about the cinematographer that I fired, you know what I would say about him. Low-budget film-making is too precarious to have even one member of your team against you. You have to be ruthless in terms of weeding the destructive elements out and making sure that your creative crew is there for you a hundred per cent. I didn't know that. Now I do. I learned that no matter what's happening, it is critical that you somehow find a way to enjoy what's happening on set. If you don't, no one else will. It doesn't mean that you sit around blowing bubbles. For example *Living in Oblivion* was in a way a much more difficult shoot because we shot the film in twenty days, but I was having a blast the whole time I was making it even in the midst of enormous difficulty. *Johnny Suede* was like I said, a ton of bricks falling on me. It was tough to find a moment of enjoyment on it. I learned more than anything that the element of tension is incredibly crucial in a film. It has to be there. I look at *Johnny Suede* and to me at times it's like watching paint dry. At the same time, I'm very proud of it. I feel that I put on film some things that I had never seen before.

With the light of hindsight, what advice would you give the younger self that made Johnny Suede?
It's this, Tom, listen man. Slow down. You're doing this because you love it. Put a little a bit more attention, a little bit more energy into the enjoyment of it as opposed to the agony. It doesn't mean the agony's going to disappear but it's like

what happens in *Living in Oblivion* when Steve Buscemi says, 'You just got to roll with it, man.' You just got to roll with it; because if you don't roll with it, it will crush you. That's something I at least know now. Whether I can keep putting it into use is another question.

Allison Anders: *Gas Food Lodging*

When did you first discover movies?
The first movie I remember seeing was at a drive-in when I was about three. I was sitting in a car with my parents, and on the screen was this man with a turban on his head; and I had no idea what the movie was, but because I was hearing this big, booming voice, I thought this man was talking to us from the sky. I didn't realize there was a screen there, that this was being projected. So I actually thought this must be the voice of God. I had no idea why everyone was being so casual. I mean, this was not like an everyday occurrence. This was really weird! There was a man in the sky with this big, booming stereophonic voice. So I guess movies were God, right from the beginning!

Can you remember what kinds of movies you saw as a child?
I remember it was a big year when I was five, because I saw *King Solomon's Mines* and *El Cid*. Ironically, another movie that I saw on TV that year was *Citizen Kane* but I didn't know that was the name of it and in fact I kept looking for it my whole life. Where was this movie? What was it? I remembered very distinctly the whole thing of him tearing up the room and I remember crying. But the most significant movie I saw that year was *A Stolen Life*, which is one of the great melodramas, and the first film that Bette Davis produced for herself. She cast Glenn Ford who was an unknown then and hired the director, Curtis Bernhardt. She played twin sisters, one who's really tarty and another who's very introspective, artful, lonely. This sister meets a lighthouse keeper, played by Ford, and they talk about loneliness. But then the tarty sister can't help herself, and Ford falls in love with her because her cake is better frosted than her sister's! By the middle of the film both sisters are out on a boat and there's an accident and the tarty sister drowns. The lonely sister tries to haul her back on to the boat, but all she ends up with is her sister's wedding ring, which she's wearing when she wakes up. So everyone thinks she's the sister who's married to the man that this woman has always loved. So she decides to feign this whole thing; to pretend she's her dead sister – only to find out that their marriage is a disaster, and he's miserable with this woman and they're getting a divorce. So it's just a nightmare. But it set up my idea of romantic love, of soulmates, for life. In fact the original ending for *Gas Food Lodging* was the next to last image of that film.

What was that image?
Bette Davis standing, hands behind her back, with the wedding ring in her hand

and Glenn Ford walking out of the mist towards her. As I remembered it, they looked at each other and it was clear that they were going to be together. Later after seeing the film again, I realized that they came together and kissed and that's the last image. But for *Gas Food Lodging* I basically duplicated what I thought was the ending. Instead of the ring, it was the rock that Trudi had behind her hand. I didn't even realize that I had stolen it until the film came on TV and I was like, oh my God. There it is!

You saw this movie when you were five? You must have an amazing memory.
I had to commit so many things to memory when I was little because we didn't have VCRs; we didn't have the luxury of seeing things over and over again. When a film came out you would go and see it many, many times because you weren't going to be able to see it again for least three years, until it came out on TV. So you committed more things to memory. I didn't see *A Stolen Life* again until I was fourteen years old, smoking pot in my bedroom with the TV on late. I was stoned and I'm like, oh God, it's that movie!

One of the enduring images in Gas Food Lodging *is Shade going to the cinema to watch the films of the fictional Mexican film star, Elvia Rivero. Were movies already a passion for you when you were Shade's age?*
When I was her age I think that movies were mainly about getting stoned then going to a movie like *2001*. There was a movie theatre right across the street from my house in Coco Beach, Florida. I watched the movie theatre being built and I went to every movie that played there. But I think pop music was even more important to me than movies, because I could own records and play them to death. The Beatles were a really big deal. Paul McCartney songs in particular were really important to how I ended up writing. Basically I learnt how to write female characters from Paul, from 'Eleanor Rigby' and 'Yesterday'. He just painted these vivid pictures of women which, God knows, nobody else was doing or has done since. I mean, when Mick Jagger painted a portrait of a woman it certainly wasn't any woman that I ever met. Paul really wrote narrative stories about these females which was really interesting. He continues to do so actually.

Did you have a moment when you thought film was something you wanted to do? Or did movies still seem a long way off?
For a long time I don't think I even knew that movies were made by anybody. Probably Stanley Kubrick was the first director I ever heard of, because people would talk about 'Stanley Kubrick's *2001*'. And then I remembered his name from *Lolita* because the weekend that movie came out, they wouldn't let me in the theatre because I was too little, and I wept the whole weekend. But even if I had known what a director was, I would have assumed that I couldn't do it because I was a girl. But I do remember that when I was in third grade, eight years old, they went around the room and asked people what they wanted to be. Everyone else was very content to be in small-town jobs. But I was like, 'I don't know. A writer, a singer,

someone famous!' I just had this basic idea that I was artistic. But saying I wanted to be a director would have been completely out of the question.

What other movies did you see in your teens?
When I was seventeen one of my friends out here in California who considered himself a film buff started taking me to movies. I then saw Godard movies. I saw Truffaut movies. The usual things: *Jules et Jim*, *Breathless*.

By then you were starting to seek things out?
Yeah. But I was writing poetry by then, and movies weren't something I ever thought I could venture into. It was still like directors were guys. I think I was probably nineteen years old when I realized that there were some female directors like Ida Lupino. When I fell madly in love with *The Trouble With Angels*, I had no idea that Ida had directed it. So I think it took a while before I realized that this was what I wanted to do. What I liked about film, what I started to see about movies was that you could tell a story, which you can't necessarily do in poetry. Poetry seemed to be where I was headed, although I also tried music. I'd been all over the place but had absolutely no artistic ability in terms of fine arts. But I felt with movies you could work with actors, you could tell stories, you could have music, you could have cool clothes. It just seemed like, God, that's so much freedom to be able to do all of that! And I still feel that way.

You went to live in London for a while before deciding to go to film school. How did that come about?
I followed a boy I met on a Greyhound bus, went to England and conceived a child. I worked as a barmaid at the Hope and Anchor pub on Upper Street in Islington. It was right before punk rock. It was really quite a scene. The boys had more make-up on than their girlfriends! It was like something out of *Velvet Goldmine*.

Did your interest in movies continue in London?
The man I lived with introduced me to movies that had not come to America yet; for example *Solaris* and a lot of Russian films. German films were also starting to make an impression on me: Wim Wenders and Fassbinder had just begun to make movies. And when I came back to the States, the new art-houses had begun to show these kinds of films. I also went to see old movies, John Ford movies, stuff that I hadn't been aware of over here before.

When you came back to Los Angeles you went to UCLA film school. What material did you submit to get in?
Poetry. Actually they don't allow you to submit films; you have to submit a written piece of critical theory on a film. Then you have to write a personal essay on why you want to go there and then you submit some kind of creative written work. My producer and co-writer Kurt Voss and I had actually already met at junior college and we both applied to UCLA at the same time. We were dating at the same time and then we both got in, which was amazing because it was still difficult to get

into that school. I think your chances were one in nine or something like that.

Spielberg didn't make it!
Exactly!

What were you living on when you applied to UCLA?
Welfare and student grants. I had two kids by this time. I was a single mom, a welfare mom. Any time I saw any information about a grant, I applied. I still have that mentality!

Can you tell me about your time at UCLA?
It's funny because both Kurt and I had both been very good students at junior college and then we came to UCLA and it was a whole different world. We found out that, 'Oh shit, we don't know how to write. We don't know how to do what they want at all.' So it was interesting through the first quarter because we were split up for a while. I saw him walking down the hall and he holds up a paper he'd written and goes, 'All right. Another D.' And I'd just gotten a D too! We finally started to get it and he goes, 'You know what? I've figured out the thing. We write this Feminist–Marxist shit and they love it.' And I was like, 'Fuck that! I'm not kissing anyone's ass. I'm not writing what they want.' So I started writing very personal stuff.

About you or about movies?
I'd write about what a film meant to me personally. If I saw a movie in class I would write my personal musings about the films while Kurt would write the Feminist–Marxist stuff. And we both started getting As! By this time we were living together and he was so pissed off he was like, 'How do you get As when you write all this personal stuff and use all these personal pronouns? That's not academic. You can't use 'I' and 'me', you know.' So he stops our teacher in the hall one day and goes, 'How can you give her an A for that? Look at all these personal pronouns!' And the teacher was like, 'Allison's work is so subjective that it's radical', and she walks off. And I'm like, 'Yes!! I've found the key!' And he was like, 'Yeah, well, I'll see you at home. You can make dinner.' And I said, 'Yeah, the Marxist–Feminist!'

Did you make any films at UCLA?
Yes. I made a film in the second quarter. Once I got the hang of the critical studies thing I decided to make a movie. My first little film at UCLA was called *Nobody Home*. It was in black and white and was shot by Dean Lent who later shot *Gas Food Lodging*. The whole first quarter I was really dismayed by one of my teachers, Janet Bergstrom, who was a very big film theorist. I think she was quite irritated by the students; she acted like she thought we were very stupid. One of the things she was constantly talking about was 'off-screen space'. I didn't know what the hell she was talking about. But one day we were talking about *Stagecoach* and one of the students said, 'I don't understand. What happened to the colonel?'

The answer he wanted was that he shot himself. But instead Janet gave this long exasperated sigh and said, 'The colonel was taken care of by off-screen space.' So I used to walk through the hallway saying, 'The colonel was taken care of by off-screen space.' In fact, Janet ended up becoming a great friend: I did a lot of my important film classes with her and took my most significant projects to her for feedback. When I made my first film I realized how much I'd learned about film language from her and how truly brilliant she was at telling us this stuff. This is why I don't subscribe to the Robert Rodriguez school of 'Just get a camera and shoot'. Film is not just about pointing a camera at anything. You've got to learn how to create meaning. When D. W. Griffiths moved the comera, it wasn't just to go, 'Whee! I can move the camera!' Chances are, anything you point a camera at and shoot was shot a hundred years ago at the beginning of cinema, and you're not doing anything new at all. Maybe you can cut it quicker. But even there, you have to know why you're making that cut.

Did you make any films at UCLA?
Yes. Once I got the hang of the critical studies thing I decided to make a movie in the second quarter. My first little film at UCLA was called *Nobody Home*. It was in black and white and was shot by Dean Lent who later shot *Gas Food Lodging*.

Did you make use of off-screen space in Nobody Home?
It's basically about a day in the life of this one guy, and most of the action took place off-screen. But you heard things going on in the house of this guy's daily life, and a lot of it was told through the incoming calls on an answer machine and through photographs.

Didn't you win a few prizes for your writing while you were at UCLA?
I did. For a script called *Lost Highway* – not to be confused with David Lynch's film. It was the first feature I wrote and it won the Samuel Goldwyn Award and also the Nicholl Scholarship. By this time we were already starting to write *Border Radio*, which we made while we were at UCLA.

What was Border Radio *about?*
It's about a rock musician hiding out in the desert in Mexico. His wife is trying to find out if he stole some money and who he fucked over, and if he's fucked her over. So she goes through the LA punk rock scene of the time, trying to piece it all together. Kurt, Dean and I decided to do this feature on two thousand dollars. Our big motivator and inspiration was Billy Woodberry who'd made this beautiful movie, *Bless Their Little Hearts*, which we'd all seen and loved. Billy worked at the check office at UCLA. Charles Burnett had actually written the script and shot the movie for him. After he saw our second film at UCLA he said, 'You know what? You guys need to make a feature.' Our movies were very different from the films that anyone at UCLA was making at the time. There was this weird excitement about them, because they weren't trying to be Hollywood movies and they

weren't experimental movies. But they were personal, and very reminiscent of German cinema at the time. They were all shot in black and white and I think that really appealed to people. Dean shot all three of them. The second movie was also called *Lost Highway* and I expanded it in a different way as the script that I ended up writing. This was basically the beginning of American independent film. We later realized that what happened with *Border Radio* was happening all over but we didn't realize that's what was going on for a while.

About this time you met Wim Wenders. How did this come about?
I started writing letters to Wim before I went to film school. He actually read the script for my very first film: sweet. It was amazing to me that I had this contact with this hero of mine. At the end of the first year at UCLA, he called me up and said, 'Hello, Allison. This is Wim. I'm coming to Los Angeles and was wondering whether you can find time to show me your movie?' I nearly died! I was like, 'No, I don't think so.' I got so excited I screamed throughout the house. So he came and saw my movie; and Dean and Kurt's movie. And meanwhile I finagled a grant to go and work for him on *Paris, Texas*. I lied to the grant people and told them that he had invited me. But I hadn't even asked him yet. I told him I won this grant and he was like, 'Oh, congratulations'. I told him, 'Well, it's to come and work and study under you.' He then gave me this faraway look and goes, 'Well, I guess you have to come then.' And then I told him that as two of my other friends had applied for the same grant all three of us had to come! So I went to work on *Paris, Texas* and was a big pain in the ass. I didn't drive so I was a horrible PA in that way. I was constantly resentful of having to take orders from anybody and I was constantly judgemental of everything he was shooting. I was just awful. In fact I kept a detailed journal from which I would give him weekly instalments. One entry would be like 'Well, today I learnt how Wim manipulated all the women on the crew', that kind of thing. I thought he's never going to read this stuff. These journals are sixty pages long and he's too busy. So one day I'm walking past him and he goes, 'You! Come here!' I was like, oh shit, I'm totally busted now. And he goes, 'Ha, she thinks she's so smart; she thinks she knows me so well. Just remember the production always reflects what the film is about.' And, of course, being a smart-ass, I was like, 'Ha, I think this production reflects what your *last* movie was about' – which was *The State of Things*, where the production got shut down – which nearly happened on *Paris, Texas*. But in fact, what he said comes back to me all the time. He's absolutely right. The production will always reflect what the film is about. It's very weird but very, very true.

Did you find that on Gas Food Lodging?
Yes, I definitely did. It was about these women trying to come to terms with men. Which I don't think I did necessarily. But I'd say the production was pretty optimistic and I think the film's pretty optimistic.

Gas Food Lodging *was based on the novel by Richard Peck,* Don't Look And It

Won't Hurt. *What appealed to you most about the story when you read it?*
I thought, God, I can't believe that I didn't write this because I was a single mom myself. I'd been raised by a single mother, and the story really got that poverty down well. It showed the kind of tensions that happen when you're poor. I mean, I had middle-class friends and I never knew what was going on in their parents' lives or in each other's lives and I always thought, God, why is that? And finally I realized that poor people always know what's happening with each other because it's so goddam crowded! Middle-class people can go for years without knowing anything about each other because they get their own rooms and everyone's blocked off, whereas when you're poor everybody's on top of each other. Richard Peck had put the family in a duplex but I wanted an intensely confining space so I moved them into a trailer. My mother and my stepfather and me lived in a trailer, with a corrugated roof there on the side. So there was a lot that I drew from that particular period, from living in that trailer park.

You've made no secret of the fact that you were raped as a child. Was the scene where Trudi talks about being raped in the book?
No. This was the first time I really put my own experience into something. Basically I had acted out when I was a teenager after I was raped when I was twelve. In the book the character I renamed Trudi was a very promiscuous girl who was also very popular. I felt like: you can't be both. You're either one or the other. You can't be the slut and the most popular girl in class. The slutty girl is popular for a night. So, this isn't to take anything away from Richard Peck's wonderful book, but I decided that Trudi is a girl who's been sexually abused in some way. Because that's why you act out like that. I named my rapists in the script and my producer was like, 'Please can we change the names?' Because in movies you go through all this stuff of checking the names of people who might possibly sue. But I was like, what? Are these rapists going to come forward and say how dare she? I'm going to sue her! I said, boy, I would love that. I would love it if it drew them out of the woodwork. In the end he just stuck behind me.

What was it like for you to see this scene taking shape when you were preparing to shoot the film?
Some very good actresses came in to read, and that was the scene where they would always fall to pieces. The way they chose to play it was to cry and be hysterical. But it wasn't written that way. In the script it said she always sounds like she's talking about something that happened to someone else. That's because there's an odd detachment with most survivors of rape and sexual abuse. You have to be detached, otherwise you'll be in a state of hysteria all the time and you won't survive. So I wanted a very detached reading. Ione read the script, saw that and did it just beautifully. She gave Trudi this numbed-out quality which was just right. Afterwards, I always hugged every one of those girls who came in. Because even if they'd never experienced this themselves, they really had to go into a very

dark fucking place to do that. And I'd always make sure that they were okay when they left. This was my first time in a casting session, and people were so amazed that I would do things like that. I just thought, well, Jesus Christ, don't you know that that's what you're supposed to do? But of course most people don't. They just let people walk out the door like the scene had no effect on them at all, like they were just doing a part.

How did you feel when you were shooting the scene?
I felt very privileged, actually. Before we started, I was sitting there thinking, God, here I am on this beautiful set, with this beautiful lighting and this beautiful girl. And we're talking about the worst thing that ever happened to me in my life. And it's really wild! I'm a director! I get to do this! It's my job, in a way, to put this stuff out there. The strange thing is that people think that when you put personal stuff into your work that it's cathartic. It's not really – or not entirely. I think it definitely helps along the way. But it's not like now I'm done. This is why writing doesn't help me any longer because I've written through just about everything in my life.

Did it have an effect on Ione?
I comforted her a lot during the scene. And I think she was just very pleased to have gone through it. We did have this triumphant feeling about the sex scene in the cave. A feeling of, yeah, we did it! I think we left poor Rob Knepper who played Dank out of our mutual triumph. In fact one of the lessons I learned from this was that I spent so much time making sure my actresses were OK that I was ignoring the guys, and they were already feeling a little lost in this movie anyway because they weren't taking the action. Each one felt there was a scene that was missing where they could take that action. I kept thinking, why do they all come to me saying there's a scene missing? You know, where I go in there and I tell her, I love you. I finally realized, oh that's right!

Why is Shade such a big fan of these Mexican movies?
In the first draft of the script she went to big-budget movies, but they were like fantasies of forties movies, where everybody's happy and middle class and sitting down like at Thanksgiving dinner. I was like, you wouldn't get those kinds of movies in a small town. And what are those movies anyway? I don't even know what genre that is. So I figured maybe we could have this Mexican movie theatre; and I thought, what if we invent a really beautiful Mexican film star, who represents a lot of female archetypes in one woman, someone Shade really looked up to? So Elvia Rivero plays a wife, a daughter, a lovesick elegant woman, a nun. I basically went through all these different archetypes. Not only could it be fun but we can also see where she gets her ideas about female archetypes. 'Elvia Rivero' was actually the name of my landlady who let me stay in my apartment for ten months, rent-free, because I was so broke. And when I got *Gas Food Lodging* and another writing job I paid it all off and honoured her with this character. Originally Yasmin Le Bon was supposed to be Elvia Rivero and something that no one

ever notices, thank God, is that the Elvia Rivero posters for the set dressing are actually of Yasmin Le Bon! But Yasmin pulled out of the project at the last minute so I had a matter of days to find someone who looked like Yasmin, could speak Spanish and could act. And, thank God, I found her!

So both the sisters were very close to you?
Yes, I thought so. In fact, my mother was always very confused because she thought Brooke Adams was her. So she was confused about Trudi being me and Shade being my little sister. I was like, 'Mom, that's not how it works. They're actually all me, you know – even the men!' The one thing about the mother in the book that's the same in the script is that she was always miserably tired and had no sex life. I thought, well, if she's got to be tired all the time – which I've been when I was waitressing, it's horrible, very, very tiring – at least she's got to have some kind of sex life. So I gave her a sex life with Hamlet and also with Chris Mulkey, the guy she was having an affair with. James Brolin was the father, which my dad was very pleased about. He said, 'I'm glad you got somebody good looking enough to play me!'

Gas Food Lodging sums up the movie's twin themes of mobility and immobility so well. Where did the title come from?
You see these signs all over America: Gas Food Lodging. Someone called it an inverted road movie. Because instead of dealing with people who are on the road, it's about people who are locked into a lifestyle off the main road, who have pulled into the truck stop and stayed there.

Why did you want to set it in New Mexico?
Cineville kept telling me, 'You could shoot this in New Mexico.' Finally I came in and asked them, 'I'm just curious; why are we constantly talking about New Mexico?' And they go, 'Because we want to go there!' So I say, 'Okay, sounds good.' I went scouting with Bill Urich and found the town of Demming, which was perfect because it was not quaint and not Sante Fe-ish and not arty. It was just an almost charmless town and the landscape was not immediately intoxicating. It wasn't some beautiful desert like Tucson or something like that. It was just bleak and empty. And we shot pretty much everything there, except for a couple of things in El Paso.

Did you have a script you were happy with by this point? Or were you writing while you were looking for locations?
I think I went back to do another rewrite after we found the place.

How do you work when you write? Do you write from the beginning to the end? Or do you write scenes as they come to you?
I write from the beginning to the end. I think that's kind of what I always do: personal journeys. *Mi Vida Loca* (*My Crazy Life*) was like that. So basically you have to start from a place: where is the character when we meet them and where do we want them to end up?

Can you give me an example from Gas Food Lodging?

I think with Shade it would be that she wants to find a father figure. She wants to find her dad, basically. And she does, but first she sets her mom up with a man her mom's been trying to get rid of. And then she finds her dad's not exactly what she thought he was going to be. In the process meanwhile she's trying to find love herself, goes after the wrong boy for her, and then finds the most unlikely right boy.

The film has a wonderful non-linear quality. Do you think your characters always take priority over the plot?

I start with characters because I really don't have any plots and I'm always amazed at the end of it going, 'Wow, I can't believe that it works!' Plot is not one of my things. Probably a lot of it comes from Wim, because I'm not terribly interested in resolving the plot. I'm more interested in my characters resolving. Wim was always like, yeah, the story just seemed like some bothersome thing that I had to hang everything on. I think that's how I feel too. It's like a clothes line, and you've got the colourful textures, which I'm really interested in. I'm interested in what's on the clothes line, not the clothes line itself. This is pretty anti-Hollywood. For the most part, Hollywood is all about the clothes line, and they think they can just hang anything up there. Like, maybe we'll put Bruce Willis here. Maybe Arnold Schwarzenegger there . . .

Kevin Smith's producer, Scott Mosier, told me that Hollywood executives aren't interested in reading scripts; they like short ideas that don't take long to pitch.

Yeah. I think anything you can pitch like that is probably a piece of shit. I'm phenomenally bad at pitching as you can imagine because stories don't pitch, they go all over the place.

Did you have to pitch Gas Food Lodging?

Yeah, I pitched it to Larry Estes, who was the guy financing low-budget independent films of the time. Larry often had to green-light low-grade genre films, some of which were very bad. But that left him free to do films he cared about too, and out of that came some of the early gems of the American indie movement: *sex, lies and videotape, My New Gun, One False Move*. Anyway, Cineville had development money, so we sent the script in, but they didn't have enough to finance it. There was coverage on the script which was not great. The girl kept saying that *Welcome Home, Roxy Carmichael* was a better movie. Larry was at RCA Columbia at the time. What they would do is a video pre-buy and finance the movie that way. So I had to go in to Larry's office, never having met him before, and say why Larry should do this movie never having met him before.

And how did the meeting go?

Larry says, 'You know, you set us up for all these things in the script like Shade finding her father, bringing the family together and none of that happens.' I was like, umm ... So I just started to make up shit. I said, 'Well, that's true but you see that's the way a woman's life works. A man sets a goal and what he does next in his life is very determined by that goal, whether he fails or succeeds. Women go off on all kinds of directions, we're not linear like men are.' I was just babbling by this point. I didn't know what else to do. My producers were practically bent over ready to get their asses kicked out the door. But then I see that Larry is looking at his little female assistant, who's nodding her head going, 'Yes'. And I'm going, 'Stay with me, sister, stay with me.' Finally I go, 'I'm babbling here, aren't I?' And Larry goes, 'No, no, no, that's fine. I don't know anything about women.' Then he says, 'Get me a budget', and I'm like, oh my God, we've just got the money for the movie! Somehow he bought it and I laugh about it to this day with him. It was just this kind of attitude like: well, this must be some new Female Cinema thing I know nothing about. Then he says, 'Now, I've got to ask you about sex.' And I thought, oh, my God, do I have to blow him to get this? No problem. I'll do it! So I said, 'What do you mean?' He goes, 'Well, you've got sex in the movie.' I said, 'Yeah.' And he goes, 'Are you going to shoot it?' I said, 'Well, that's why I wrote it.' And he says, 'I've got to tell you, these guys come in here with all this macho bravado. They write these sex scenes to please me and when it comes down to it they don't shoot it.' I said, 'No, no. I didn't put it in there gratuitously. I put it in because it was necessary. I plan to shoot it.' He was happy about that. In the end, he was very happy with the sex scene in the caves so that was fine. I actually had a sex scene of Brooke with Hamlet too but in the end I cut it because it was better just to do the post-coital scene.

So Larry agreed to put up the money. What was the budget?
One million, two hundred thousand dollars.

How easy was it to cast?
Casting was actually really hard. Originally I wrote Trudi for Christina Applegate but it didn't work out, which was a real nightmare because a lot was predicated on her committing. Then I wanted Ione Skye. I asked the casting office to bring her in, and someone said, 'Well, you'd have to "read" her. And besides, she has a tendency to get a little chunky.' I was so outraged! Not only by the look-ism of that remark, but also Ione is a beautiful, talented girl, and at the end of the day, I was asking to see her and they should have brought her in right away. She came in and that was that. But with Shade I had a problem as well. This casting director kept bringing me women who were twenty-four years old, and just didn't look like they could be experiencing a first kiss: they couldn't access that. Drew Barrymore was brought to me many times, but unfortunately she'd just done *Poison Ivy* or was about to do it, and she was just too lusty. By now the head of Cineville, Carl Jan Calpaert, was getting frustrated too. He was down in the casting office one day and saw Fairuza Balk's picture thrown in a pile. He said, 'What about this girl? She was in *Valmont*.' And the people in the casting office were like

saying, 'She's only sixteen.' And I said, 'Well, that's what I want, you idiots.' This was my first experience with a casting director.

I suppose you get a better sense of who's out there if you do it yourself?
Yes and no. You may know people the casting directors don't know, and you may have ideas that come from the rock world or young actors just starting that you've seen somewhere, or a great face you encounter somewhere. But the great thing about having a casting director is that they can introduce you to some great character actors. Brooke Adams I knew already. She was a friend. So I brought Brooke to the picture. James Brolin was actually Larry Estes's idea. That was very funny because my producers were so cautious when they told me, 'Larry just wants you to meet James Brolin . . .', in other words implying 'but you don't have to cast him'. You have to understand, we were looking at people like Sam Shepard and Scott Glenn who really had that weathered Marlboro Man vibe. And James Brolin's image was so far removed from this, his fame was from TV shows like *Marcus Welby* and *Hotel*, he was not someone who would ever come to mind when casting a down-and-out small town boozer. But I said, 'Are you kidding?! I love James Brolin!' They were so shocked! I was in New Mexico and I flew back to meet with him and he was such a sweetheart. He's such a fabulous actor. When I see the movie again and I look at all of the stuff that he does when he's trying to tell her that he's sorry, that he thinks about her every day, it's just the way it is with fathers like that.

Did you have any problems casting the English character, Dank?
Originally I cast an actor who had only done a couple of movies called Hugh Grant! He was all happy to do it and then at the very last minute he backed out of it. It was pretty traumatic because I had fought so hard for him. Nobody wanted him, they didn't know who he was. Not my main producers but there was one producer on the film that I've never worked with again who was very aggressive about casting and he was really hassling me to cast this one actor who was a very good actor. I liked him a lot but he was wrong for the part. The day that I found out that Hugh wasn't going to do it I just bolted downstairs into the basement of the building we were in and just burst into tears with all of my three Cineville producers. So I ended up having to recast at literally the last minute, the day before we went to New Mexico. That was the first time I was dissed by Hugh Grant.

It happened again?
It's Hugh's favourite thing to do. He likes to back out of movies. I mean, the second time he did it to me, I was green-lit and people had quit jobs to come and work. It fell apart. I haven't gotten it back together yet and it's the project that's most dear to my heart.

Once you had a cast, did you do a lot of rehearsals?
I only had about three days for rehearsals. I worked with Jacob and Fairuza. I

worked with Fairuza and Donovan and I worked with Ione and Fairuza. I don't think I worked with Brooke at all.

Maybe because you knew her best?
Yeah, exactly.

What about visualizing the movie? Did you commit anything to paper prior to the shoot? Did you have a shot list?
Yes, I had a shot list and I did a little bit of storyboarding. Not much but a little and I never looked at that stuff again.

When you were looking at locations, did you have a sense of how the scene would play; where you would put the camera?
We would definitely always have a sense of that but of course it would sometimes change once the actors were in the room. And of course the scenes in the trailer were really shot in a trailer so we were pretty limited, which I liked. I mean I believe very strongly in using the real location. I hate building.

What about your technical knowledge? Did you delegate quite a lot to Dean or did you say I want a 35 mm or I want a 8 mm?
I still don't know anything about the camera, nothing. You know those disposable cameras? That's what I take pictures with. And they turn out like shit. I'm such a bad photographer. In fact, I'm so bad that when I went to pick up some pictures of my son and his puppy, the woman behind the counter gives me the pictures and goes, 'You know it's better if your subject is in the light.' I'm not even going to tell this woman what I do for a living!

So you would rely quite heavily on your DP?
Very heavily.

It sounds like performance is more important to you than flashy visuals?
Exactly. In *Gas Food Lodging* I didn't want to move the camera unless it was for an emotional reason. I use it when Dank looks over and sees Trudi crying in the coffee shop. I come in on him and his look and then go over to her. We carry a lot of moments of recognition in one take. Also in the scene where she's talking about her rape, there's a slow dolly in on her. There's a steadicam on Elvia Rivero coming down the staircase. But I only used it either for drama or for emotional reasons. I was just so tired of all the tedious, dizzying camera movements and the constant cutting. I was like, I want to go back to doing something really simple. And I still feel that way. I mean we had a lot of close-ups in *Gas Food Lodging* but wherever I can I get things in one.

Approaching the shoot, were you nervous?
I kept thinking that I was going to get nervous and I never did. Not once. I was nervous every single day on *Border Radio*. I felt, 'I can't do it. Don't make me say "Action".' I was ill. And on *Gas Food Lodging*, I thought, well, it's the first day and

I'm going to be really nervous. And it never once happened. In fact, the guy from the bond company left after a few days. He was like, you're doing great, honey. I've got some films that are really in trouble so I'm leaving you now. I mean, the shoot itself was absolute bliss. The actors would go back to LA and agents would be like, God, what are you doing to our actors? They're all coming back going it was the greatest experience I've ever had! So it was really a fantastic shoot. Great people, a lot of on-set romances, shit like that.

So it was a completely positive experience?
Well, there were a couple of things that bothered me. Some girl who was a stand-in was getting laid a lot by a bunch of the crew. At one point they had made a little drawing of the *Gas Food Lodging* symbols that have these little stick figures. And usually the bed was for the lodging and they had her lying in the bed with five guys standing around. I got really furious. I was like, you guys, this is bullshit. This is a feminist movie. But you get that on almost every film. I've a great affection for the grip and electric department, I'm always deeply impressed by how hard they work. And needless to say, they're usually very good-looking. On *Gas Food Lodging* I spent the pre-production hiring people, but it was so crazy that I didn't remember anything. So when I got on the plane to Mexico my first reaction was, oh my God, who hired all these cute boys? Then I realized that it was me! I liked one of the electricians a lot. He actually worked again for me on *Grace of My Heart*. I was sort of flirting with him on the way to New Mexico and he's flirting back. Then Monday came and he was all buttoned up. This persisted throughout the remainder of the film. So at the end of the shoot I go, 'What happened?' And he goes, 'On the plane I thought you were the wardrobe chick. I didn't know you were the director. Then the guys told me, "The redhead who was yakking it up with us? She's the director, man."' Unfortunately this kind of tedious respect has continued with my crews ever since. It's a hard thing for women directors: you don't get laid as much!

How did the shoot compare to Border Radio?
I actually found out that my job was in some ways much easier because on *Border Radio* we did everything. On this movie it was like, now what do I do? The actors are in make-up and the DP and I have already talked so what do I do with myself for the next hour and a half? Well, I guess I'll just hang out. I'm not a stresser at all. I'm actually calmest when I'm on the set. I'm a lot more crazed when I'm in pre-production, worried about making sure that everything is going to be there: the clothes, the locations.

Was this the case on Gas Food Lodging?
Yes, that was one thing that I was thoroughly unprepared for: just how much had to be done. My friend Chris Connelly, who was the editor of *Premiere* for many years, asked me, 'What do you do in pre-production?' And I said, 'Well, basically I have meetings all day long with people who come in and ask me questions that

only I can answer and they go off and do things based on those answers.' And he says, 'Ron Howard says that you can just make up anything really.' And I said, 'Well, on his budgets he probably can. But I can't.' Also, I'm trying to create intimate environments so if we're making up some family history which, for example, we did for the trailer, I'd sit with the production designer, Jane Stewart, and Jane was like, okay, how long have they lived in this trailer? Of course you're making it up because there is no reality in any of this. But it's going to be very different if I say they've lived here a year as opposed to seven years. Seven years is a long time for children. And then there are other questions. Would the father ever have lived here? Maybe there was an argument? Maybe something was thrown against the wall and that stain is still there? Maybe there's still some silly little thing that Shade made when she was ten years old that's hanging in the kitchen? How long has the carpet been there? You can't arbitrarily make this shit up. It has to be genuine. The same thing with the clothes: you have to know what kind of thing some woman was in two years ago; that maybe they still have that sweater they wear with a different skirt. That's the type of thing that I spend a lot of time on.

Did you find it easy to come up with the answers to people's questions?
Yes, because I knew the characters.

What was the hardest thing about the pre-production?
I would say learning what everybody did! Or learning how to work with the script supervisor.

Hadn't you done that before on Border Radio?
No. I was the script girl; a very bad script girl!

A lot of the story took place in the confined space of the trailer. Was the action rehearsed beforehand or blocked on the day?
It would definitely happen on the day. We just really didn't have any time so it was whatever happened at the time.

Was there anything that you disliked about the experience? Do you think the director, male or female, is always slightly isolated from the rest of the people on the set?
Yes, a little bit. On *Gas Food Lodging*, the crew would go party in the bar next door every night after the shoot and I would watch my dailies and go to bed, that was it. But I kind of like being isolated that way. I don't tend to get involved socially with my crew or my cast. I don't think there was any real downside that I can remember about *Gas Food Lodging*. The only thing was that producer who was disrespectful of everything. But that was okay. I've never worked with him again.

How did you feel when you first saw the rough cut? Were you happy?
Yes, I don't find assemblies too horrifying. I find them horrifying later because I think, oh God, why did I think that was good? And I showed it to people. But I like the idea that it was Wim-esque, if you get my meaning. It contained long

languid pieces. One thing I knew about Wim's stuff was this sense that if you cut it shorter it doesn't do what it's supposed to do. For example, a lot of times when I was watching *Kings of the Road*, I'd be like, Jesus, this is so long! Do we really need all these shots of telephone wires and things? But later I'd realize that these things build a mood. So I was very well aware how important it is that you shoot things like that: how you place people in a landscape. Some of my favourite shots in *Gas Food Lodging* are extremely simple: Shade showing up to the door of her father's house, shot through that screen; or Ernesto's mother, the deaf woman sitting out against the wall of the adobe house. And it's just long and kind of quiet and still and I like things like that a lot. So there's things like that which I think are all integral pieces. Editing doesn't do anything for those.

Where did you first show it?
We had a screening at the DGA, a cast and crew type thing and that went really well. And then we screened it at Sundance.

How did your backers respond to it?
Larry really liked the movie, which astounded him, because I think he was just assuming the worst. I remember when he first came to see it, he said, 'Come on then. Let's let this dog out of the gate.' Then he looks at me and says, 'I'm sorry, Allison. I mean, let's let this puppy out of the gate.' He was so used to these films being dogs, but he always hoped for a gem, and I guess *Gas Food Lodging* really was a puppy, not a dog.

How were you feeling when you showed him the movie?
I was pretty nervous. But at the same time I really liked the movie. I had the same reaction when I screened my very first movie at UCLA, *Nobody Home*. When I screened that I thought, well, fuck it, I really like it so I don't give a shit what anybody says! At UCLA you had to go up in front of two hundred people and defend yourself. There was this one guy who was a real prick that tore slightly experimental stuff apart, hated women and he said, 'God help me but I really like this movie.' So with Larry I felt a similar kind of thing. Even so, the producer I didn't like was still pressuring me about cutting certain things and filling Larry with all this crap. The one thing that Larry wanted me to change, and this happened on the second screening too, was the deaf mother dancing. He wanted me to take it out and by the second screening I came to him with like some ammunition. I said, 'Look, I cut so much out of this movie now that I'm not personally attached to anything in it. There's no individual scene that I'm personally attached to. But this consistently comes back as everyone's favourite scene. I think it would be stupid to take it out.'

Did he explain why he wanted to take it out?
From the very beginning they thought it would come off really bad somehow. That it could be misread by people; that people would think it was too crazy, too

weird, too much. And he said, 'Can you just change the music for me?' So I got a piece of music written that worked for him. That was it. That was the only interference from Larry Estes. You can't really call that interference because I've experienced interference now and that's not interference!

What reception did you get at Sundance?
It was pretty exciting. I've never done press before. I was excited by the turnout to the screenings. I was kind of astounded that I could get up in front of all these people and talk about the movie and not be nervous. So I was pretty happy at Sundance. I mean, we didn't win any prize. I was a little hurt. But my producers were so non-competitive. They were like, oh well, we didn't win. So we all went out to dinner afterwards. Later I was on the jury at Sundance myself and these young film-makers were in tears. I took this one girl aside and said, 'Look, I didn't win anything either but when I first met you, you said I'd inspired you. Well, how the fuck did you see my movie? You saw it anyway.' Sundance has become so competitive, which is really unfortunate for the film-makers. I keep wishing there was a way I could have a pow-wow with them ahead of time and say don't freak out over the prize.

Did you already have a distributor at this point?
Yes, IRS. But they didn't really have the chops for distributing movies. And I had no control over the poster or any of that stuff. I was like, what is this? They're not wearing these clothes in the movie. But recently this guy who'd been in the army told me that the most rented video in the army was *Gas Food Lodging* because it had these pretty girls on the cover, which I thought was so hilarious. These army guys watching *Gas Food Lodging* and being sorely disappointed. But then I thought, well, maybe they *did* know what they were doing with that poster!

What was the reaction once the movie got into the cinema?
I probably got consistently better reviews for *Gas Food Lodging* in the States. But the biggest thing for me was that this very serious feminist film critic actually didn't like *Gas Food Lodging* because she said that the women were all looking for men. And that really perplexed me and hurt me. Now I know they just don't like my work, which is fine. It's not all feminist. There's a group of feminists that feel that way. They wouldn't mind it if they were lesbian characters looking for relationships but they don't like women looking for penises.

Salvation in men?
Yes. I just think it's hilarious because if I put my life against any feminist, I'm sorry, but I win hands down! If we arm-wrestle, I win! You can't come up with a more feminist life than mine.

What were the main lessons you drew from Gas Food Lodging?
With women it is very shocking. I mean there are a lot of women directors but there's only a handful that get to keep making personal work. Of course, there are

the mainstream big-budget women directors with bodies of work, and some write their own material such as Nora Ephron, and some are directors for hire. Some women directors who work with the studios and bigger budgets don't necessarily write their own work but certainly are auteurists such as Martha Coolidge or Randa Haines. You know one of their films when you see it. But for those of us who work outside the studio system, women making dark, personal work, the number is reduced dramatically. I mean it is pretty horrifying when you think that there are really only a few of us American Indie chicks with bodies of work: me, Nancy Savoca, Mira Nair, and Maggie Greenwald. Recently a few indie women directors have made second films: Mary Harron, Lisa Krueger, Gurinder Chadha. But this is rather shocking when you figure how many male indie directors have made a third or fourth film in the meanwhile, male directors who started at the same time as these women did. Internationally the stats are no better: Jane Campion, Gillian Armstrong, Claire Denis, Agneiska Holland, Sally Potter. Alison Maclean has only now made her next feature. It is enormously unjust. Women directors have to restart their careers each time they make a movie, and that's just wrong. And it needs to change.

What do you think that says about movies?
I think once they've heard a woman's voice they're like, okay. Thank you. I've heard it now. Especially women of colour. Forget it. They never make a second film. Take Darnell Martin who made *I Like it Like That*. Our films came out at the same time. She got better reviews than I did. But only now is she making her second feature. That really troubles me, it offends me. I mean, she directed episodes of *ER*. But once they've heard a black woman's voice their attitude is like, oh, I've heard that already. I think you mustn't depend on them. You have to go from scratch every time. You make the first film going, fuck it! I'm just going to do it. And you've got to have that attitude each time because I think unless you're going to go into Hollywood film-making and be a director for hire you're not going to get to make a second movie as a woman. Why would they do it?

Did this happen to you? Was it a struggle to make your next film?
Yes and no, actually. The fact was that I had a script already and that's the thing: to be prepared with your next script and not wait for them to hand you scripts. You've got to say this is what I want to do next. You've got to be willing to want to do it under the same circumstances next time. You can't sit around thinking that you're going to get what the boys get. It's not going to happen. I mean, they've yet to call a woman film-maker a genius. There's always a boy wonder. There's always a Todd Solondz, someone they'd be just apeshit over. But they've yet to do that with a girl. And, you know, I blame the critics in large part too because I think the critics are often harder on women directors.

Really?
In America, absolutely. Not in Europe. I love the critics in England. I read any-

thing that they write because even if they slam me it's just so bright and all-encompassing. But here I think they're a lot harder on women directors. I've seen it not only with myself, but up in Sundance they'll just trash a woman's film mercilessly, much worse than they would a boy director because they think, well, they're nobody; they're not here to stay. Even a successful women director like Kathryn Bigelow has projects she's desperate to make that she can't fund, because she's got a big vision and she needs big money for her vision. I was talking to Kathryn about how women directors never get their asses kissed and I said, 'You know, I've seen some editor kissing some young boy's ass who's made one film.' This editor's edited hundreds of movies and he's kissing this young boy's ass. And I said, 'God, I'm sure glad that's never happened to us.' And Kathryn says, 'They don't think we're here to stay.' Which I think is very much the case.

So it's still very much an uphill struggle?
Always. I don't think it's going to disappear in my lifetime.

Kevin Smith: *Clerks*

Were movies something you were interested in as a kid?
Yeah, I grew up with movies. I wasn't athletic, I didn't play sports, but I liked to play around. And a lot of the stuff I played was based on flicks I had seen, like *Star Wars*. My father was always taking me to movies. On Wednesdays we had a half-day at school and he'd pick me up and take me to the multiplex. So I was always seeing a more disparate array of flicks than most of my contemporaries. I remember seeing *The World According to Garp* and then trying to explain it to a bunch of thirteen-year-old friends. They were going, 'So Mork's in it? Is it set in space?' And I was like, 'No, it's a weird character thing, and it's based on a book.' But I never once thought that I could put any of this to good use, and do movies to make a living. I always assumed that I would either wind up owning a deli, or working in someone else's deli, for the rest of my life.

So when did you realize you wanted to get involved in film?
After I graduated from high school I was studying writing at the New School for Social Research in New York. But I used to cut class and walk down to the Rockefeller Centre where they tape *Saturday Night Live*. And I'd just sit in the lobby, hoping to be discovered. Not that I was doing anything amusing; I was just hoping someone would come and say, 'You look like an introspective lad who could write a funny little cut-and-slash sketch.' It never really panned out. And meanwhile I had that typical late teenage angst of thinking 'my life is going nowhere' but I wasn't doing anything constructive about it. So I dropped out of school and went to a local community college back in New Jersey. I had already worked at a string of convenience stores, and then I saw a listing in the paper for a video store clerk. And I thought, 'God, that I would love to do! What a great job sitting there, controlling the ebb and flow of movies in this region, making sure the right people get the right movies.' So I went in for the job and the video store owner, Mr Thaper, owned the convenience store too. He said, 'You'll have to work both stores.' I said, 'Well, I have plenty of experience.' So I started there, and I met this kid Vincent who came in at night to mop up the floors. He was younger than me but had a real passion for films, and he so wanted to be a film-maker. Vincent knew stuff that I didn't. He would tell me, 'You should get into laser discs. Most of the films are in the correct aspect ratio.' And I was like, what aspect? I don't know what you are talking about! A lot of my early education came from Vincent.

Was there a particular epiphany for you?

Vincent and I started taking these trips into Manhattan, to Film Forum and the Angelica, to check out these weird flicks that we'd read about in the *Village Voice*. And that's how I saw Richard Linklater's film, *Slacker*. It was the night of my twenty-first birthday, and we went in to catch a midnight show. And that was 'the moment' you know? The audience were just loving it. And I thought it was really clever and whatnot. But part of me was thinking, well, it's good but it's not that funny. If these people think this is funny, I think I can give them something really funny. It was a moment I've often referred to as a moment of awe and arrogance. I was awed by *Slacker*, that it existed. And Richard's story was kind of compelling too. This guy from Austin, Texas – not from Hollywood, not from New York – had made a film that's playing here in New York and look at all these people here to see it! And he'd made it for such a low amount of money. But by the end of the film I was thinking, I could definitely do this! And oddly enough it was the reaction that *Clerks* would have a few years later. Film students told me, 'Your movie made me want to be a film-maker. Because I knew that if you can do it, I can do it.' Anyway we're driving back to New Jersey and I say, 'You know, Vincent, I think that's what I want to do. I think I want to make a film.'

And this hadn't really been in your head prior to this?

Never, never. The best case scenario, beyond wanting to write sketches for *Saturday Night Live*, was thinking, 'Maybe I can write scripts.' I knew I could write. I knew I was good with a turn of phrase: decent at dialogue. I'd written sketches for these high school talent shows I'd been in. So I knew I could handle that much. I just never applied it to a feature script or a full script. So, I started thinking about it a lot more seriously and started reading up and watching the people that had done it along the lines of Richard's film. I watched Hal Hartley's films on video, *The Unbelievable Truth* and *Trust*. And I just fell in love. I looked at Jim Jarmusch's work and I realized that they're revolutionary in terms of shooting. I mean, he set the camera up and let things happen in front of it. And it really broke the process down for you, made the camera seem less intimidating. Suddenly, it's like, well, I can set a camera up and orchestrate action in front of it. So then I started sniffing around for film schools because I knew that I needed the skills to actually pull it off. So I saw an ad, again in the *Village Voice*, for the Vancouver Film School. It had a 0800 number so it was worth a call – and they told me it was an eight-month programme and nine thousand dollars. They said, 'What we do is teach you hands-on; you get your hands on the equipment, you make films. We skip all the bullshit theory of most film schools.' That sounded good to me. I wanted to learn how to operate a camera and a Nagra, how to record sounds, lights. I remember the day I told my best friends, Walter and Brian about it, I said, 'I'm going to go to film school out in Canada and when I come back we will make a movie.' And they looked at me like I had just offered them oral sex or something; like I was insane. They said, 'People in Hollywood make movies. You don't know anybody. How are you going to make a movie?' And I said, 'That's the point. I want to get an education, come back and do it. In less than a year we can be up and running.' They wished me well but they were still very sceptical. So I pulled together some student loans and went off to Vancouver. But it wasn't all it was cracked up to be. The best thing that happened there was that I met my producer, Scott Mosier, and my DP, David Klein. In Scott, I basically found the enabler, the guy that would get me out there and able to do it. He understood what I wanted to do, and he wanted to do it too.

Did you make any films while you were at this school?
We did these High-8 documentary projects. There were about twenty-six of us in the class and everybody had to come up with a proposal. Then they picked four proposals and everyone would crew up on those four documentaries. Scott and I pitched this little ten-minute documentary about a transvestite guy we had met. I don't know what his name was, but his name was going to be 'May'. He was taking hormones for his breasts but he hadn't been to the chopping board yet, so to speak. Now we were known in class for being somewhat the jokers who sat at the back of the class and laughed and passed notes to each other like we were still in high school. Then we had to get up and present something very serious and show how we were going to handle this topic very sensitively. And we did. It was the greatest performance of our lives. So we were one of the four projects, and three other people crewed up with us. We had a week to shoot it, and two days in, May dropped out: he wouldn't do it. Our crew was blaming us. They went to the school and said, 'Look, we don't want to fail just because these guys fucked it up.' And the school was like, 'Well, you guys, there's nothing we can do, you're going to fail.' So Scott and I said to the school, 'Look, can we do a documentary about how our documentary fell apart. We've got five days. We've got the camera. At least give us a shot.' And they were like, 'Well, if anyone doesn't object.' The crew were into it so we played the director characters, going, 'Gee, we don't know what happened.' And we encouraged the crew to give their true testimony on the whole event, and they duly told us what terrible, terrible directors we were. And then we talked to our instructors at the school, who lambasted us for how this thing fell apart. Then we put it together and it was great. And out of the four, it was definitely the best documentary the class had done. They still use it to this day as part of the curriculum.

Was that the only film experience you had in Vancouver?
Yeah. I was approaching the four-month mark at film school, where you either stay in or bow out; but if you bow out you get half your tuition back. So I thought, this is just pointless. I might as well keep my cash, go home and put it into my own flick. So I bowed out of film school and talked to Scott and David. I was just like, 'Look, I'm going home, right? When you're done, whatever happens, we'll help each other, like I'll come up and help you shoot in Canada, you

come here and help me.' Now one thing I'd done in Vancouver, on a day off, was that I'd written the scene in *Clerks* where Randal is sitting on the counter at the video store and the woman is asking which movies are good. 'I don't appreciate your ruse, Ma'am.' My example was Robert Rodriguez. In an interview he'd said, 'Take stock of what you have and work with that. I had a bus and I had a turtle, so I worked them both into the script!' I thought, I can get my hands on a convenience store . . . So I went home, and got my job back at the convenience store, fully intending to shoot a flick there. And I started writing like mad. I guess the first draft of it was about 164 pages, pretty long, so I handed it over to my friend Vincent. I was like, 'What do you think?' And he was like, 'It's really good. I think you should do it.' I sent it up to Scott, and he dug it, so we agreed that he'd come down here and we'd do it.

Did you get any kind of career guidance at Vancouver?
They were urging us to work our way up the Canadian film ladder after film school. You know, start as a PA and so on. At least in Canada you can appeal to the government and get all sorts of grants. There are enough studios up there and you can get government funding for films. But we don't have that in the States. And I didn't want to spend my life as PA and then an intern and maybe moving up to a third AD. That's not what I wanted to do. And we told them in film school when Scott and I were expressing our desire to go out and do a guerrilla film, they looked at us like we were stoned. They were like, 'Oh why? Why risk all that money? Why would you want to do that? You don't know how to make a movie.' And I'm like, 'Well, that's what we are here for, we are here to learn how to make a movie.'

What did you do about raising money?
You read up on everyone that has gone before you and figure out how they got their money. Robert Rodriguez had spent some time in medical experimentation. Sam Raimi had gone from dentist to dentist and local physicians to raise money for *The Evil Dead*. I didn't have enough confidence to do either. I certainly didn't want to take my 164-page script to potential investors and say, 'Do you have any cash?' I mean, 164 pages of dick jokes at a convenience store? It's a sure bet! But over the previous three or four years, a friend of mine, Brian, and myself had this running competition to try to get as many credit cards as possible; it's one of those things you do when you're bored and unsatisfied with your job! I would always put on my application that I was the manager of RST Video and I made fifty thousand dollars a year and invariably they'd call the video store to check me out. I would answer the phone: 'Yeah?' 'We're checking out a credit loan for Kevin Smith, the manager.' 'Oh. He makes fifty thousand dollars a year.' They'd say, 'Excellent!' and hang up. And sure enough, within a week I'd get a credit card! So I had about ten to twelve credit cards out of which I'd maybe used one. But it was a point of pride for me and Brian, just to have all these cards in our wallets. But

suddenly I'm looking at these cards going, 'Well, Robert Townsend put his movie *Hollywood Shuffle* on a bunch of credit cards. So I decided this was it: let's do it this way. We had a rough guide to a budget because of this article we'd read in *Filmmaker* magazine, by Peter Broderick, about *The Living End*, *El Mariachi* and *Laws of Gravity* where they broke down their budgets and talked about how much everything cost and whatnot. So I figured, 'Look, we can make this movie for twenty-five thousand dollars and I have enough room on my credit cards to do that. So let's just shoot and start cutting it, and when we hit twenty-five thousand we start worrying.' So Scott came and we started.

It sounds like a big gamble?
It was. But you don't think that way at the time because what are your options? The option was to continue working at the convenience store for the rest of my life, until I got fired. And if not that convenience store, some other convenience store. And I was just no good at labour. I was just a very, very lazy person, and still am to a large degree. But when it came to this, I never felt lazy because it didn't feel like work. It's my passion; it's what I want to do. So I guess it was a gamble and when I told my parents I wanted to make this movie, I think they figured, this'll get it out of his system. Now he'll settle down and get a good job like his brothers. But they were very supportive.

Given you were doing everything yourselves, where did you begin? Casting actors? Finding camera equipment?
Scott was making calls from Vancouver to New York to set up the equipment. I had this little film Yellow Pages book that he was working off of. I went to this local theatre and held casting calls: you know, put an ad in the local papers in Atlantic Highlands where I was living. Some local actors came in and most people didn't quite understand it but kind of went with it anyway. We pulled together a cast. I had written the role of Randal for myself but as we got closer it was just like, I can't memorize dialogue and direct and work in a store. So I started looking for a new Randal. Nobody we had seen in the audition was really any good but there was a friend of mine who I had known from high school who was coming into the video store a lot around that time and saw me writing. I was working on my big clunky word processor which was bigger than Scott's computer. He was like, 'What are you doing?' And I was like, 'I'm just writing this flick.' And we started talking about it and he just said, 'Yeah, I'll come down to the auditions. I think that would be fun to do.' He read for the part of Jay, which of course I had written for Jason Mewes, but at that time I didn't know if Jason was going to do it or not because he was kind of scared of being himself on camera. He committed in the end. So then I sat down with this guy again after the audition because I was like, I think he may be good for Randal. And I read the entire script from beginning to end with him and at the end of it I was like, 'You're it.' And that was Jeff Anderson, the guy who wound up playing Randal.

I'd written the role of Silent Bob for a friend of mine at high school, a big quiet guy. But once I was not going to be Randal any more, I thought, you know what? This could be the only movie we make and if it's going to be a mistake and I'm going to pay for it my whole life, I at least want to be able to see myself in it. So I took the part of Silent Bob. And I didn't have to memorize any lines! So we were all set to go.

When did you start shooting?

We were going to shoot in January '93 but in December we had a huge storm which rocked the Eastern seaboard and the home where I still lived with my parents was decimated. I had a couple of old, beat-up Volkswagens. Me and Jason Mewes were sharing one and we were fixing up the cell on the other. And they were flooded, too; they were lost in the flood. So after the flood calmed down, FEMA, the Federal Emergency Management Agency, came round and started reimbursing people for shit they had lost. And I submitted for my cars and we got some cash that I split with Jason. So it gave me a little money towards the budget. I also had some money left over from my tuition, having dropped out of school. And I had a comic collection that I traded in to the local comic store for two thousand dollars in store credit, which I then sold to my friend Walter. So he would buy books on my credit, give me eighty bucks and that helped to pay the minimum payments on the credit card. The one thing we hadn't counted on came up at the place where we rented our film equipment, Spiracorp up in New York. They had this old clunky Arriflex SR camera, so loud we had to throw a leather jacket on it to barney it, to keep it quiet. But when we went there, they wouldn't take credit cards, only cash. So I told my parents, 'We need three thousand now, otherwise we can't get the equipment.' And they helped me out.

Could they afford that?

My father worked in the post office, he was the guy who basically cancels your stamp. He had done that for many years and was kind of checking out of that job over health reasons because he was really diabetic and he had a stroke at one point. My mother was a homemaker. We were basically living off of the half-pension he got when he retired early. So we were not well off at all. In fact I would say we were borderline poverty. But my parents still somehow managed to put together some cash they had saved. And I said, 'I will pay you back most assuredly.' Now, since my house was flooded, Scott and David couldn't stay with me so I put them up at a town called Segar. I had to rent some rooms at fifty dollars a week. And I had been rehearsing the whole previous month with the cast every night after work. Every night we shut down the convenience store and Brian and Jeff and Lisa, Lisa Spoonauer and Marilyn Ghigliotti, would come down to the store and we would all rehearse. Over the course of the rehearsal, Jeff, who'd had a girlfriend, fell in love with Lisa and they hooked up, which was nice. Love bloomed in the convenience store!

Had you worked with actors before?
No. But when I was at community college at Brookdale, I had taken this acting class. I picked up a little there. And one day – it's so weird that I just remember this now – our class was done and two girls came in, they were rehearsing a scene for another class. They asked my opinion, and I was like, well, if you really want to know . . . And it was kind of harsh, I guess. But they said, 'Well what would you do?' And I told them. They said, 'What do you know about acting?' And I started bullshitting, saying I'd directed theatre in New York, and then I started basically directing the scene. And it really improved tremendously. Telling people how something should be done – that essentially is directing. But then I was always one of those people who knows how everything should be or sound or look. Very opinionated, I guess, but not obnoxiously so. I had written the script, so I had heard it in my head all the time. I knew how the script should sound. I think that's what made it easy to direct the actors in rehearsal.

What about staging the action? Did this come naturally?
It was figuring it out as we went along. There wasn't much space to manoeuvre. The whole movie kind of takes place behind the counter, so it works like a theatrical piece. I worked in that convenience store. I lived and breathed it so I kind of knew how to move around in it. I was just like, imagine filming me throughout the day. So it didn't seem like an insurmountable task. Plus, having seen Jarmusch's work I was primed to set the camera up and let the stuff happen in front of it. As long as the performances were on – that's what I cared about. There's only one or two times when the camera is really active and that's once when the boys are going to the funeral parlour and the back of the car's swinging from side to side. And the other time is when we are hand-held and Lisa, the Caitlin character, comes out of the back having fucked the dead guy. I said I wanted to have this weird feel to it and Dave said, 'Well hand-hold it.' I never had a waning in confidence where it was like, I don't know what I'm doing. I'm bullshitting here.' It seemed like, well, I wrote it so I should know exactly how it should sound and look. And to this day, that is why I won't direct someone else's script. You get a lot of offers, and exorbitant monies thrown at you just for directing, and I wish I could do it because, God, I could collect fat pay-cheques. But I just could not interpret somebody else's script.

Did you storyboard it? Don't you have an interest in comics?
Yeah. But I can't draw for shit. Otherwise I probably would still be in comics. I mean, me and Scott sat down and talked it through and Scott's good at drawing so he drew storyboards and there is one sequence that we actually stuck somewhat close to the storyboard. The rest of the sequences – never. Last year Sundance wanted early material from film-makers that had been there. So they asked us if we had any storyboards for *Clerks* and we were going to send them one piece of paper with a frame and Dante behind the counter and go like, 'This is the storyboard!'

Did you write a shot list or did you literally just turn up and turn the camera on when you were ready?
We did a basic shot list. I sat down with Dave one day and talked to him about what I wanted to do. I think Dave wanted to do a little more, he wanted to get crazy with it – because he still had that film school stuff in his blood. And I think most people's first instinct is 'more is more' when it comes to shooting. That's why in most student films, they try out moves. But I was like, let's keep it simple, basic and that had a lot to do with laziness and lack of confidence. But it also just made sense to me. Just set the camera up and things will happen. There is very little coverage in the movie. I don't think there is a single over-the-shoulder. Basically we are always looking in one direction.

Did your time at Vancouver give you any technical knowledge?
Nothing. I didn't get a damn thing. Thankfully, Scott and David had stayed so David knew how to operate that camera and Scott knew how to operate the Nagra. It's amazing we got such great clean sound. We had such crappy equipment in such terrible conditions. That was Scott actually just mixing and figuring it out as we were going along. There was no boom operator. Just occasionally, whoever was not in the scene would hold the boom and try to keep it out of frame.

But the camera was David's responsibility?
Exactly. Periodically he would set up the frame and he'd be like, 'What do you think of this?' And I'd look through the lens and go, 'It looks wonderful.' It's the only movie I've ever done without a video tap. It was just a real exercise in faith and trust; we wouldn't know what we were getting because we didn't have dailies, we had 'weeklies' or 'bi-weeklies'! We watched most of our footage two weeks into the shoot and the rest of the footage long after we were done shooting. So it was kind of frightening. I remember there was one reel that was burnt, when we were covering Scott. Scott played the guy who's snowballing with a bushy beard and we had a burn right through that reel so we had to re-shoot that footage. Thankfully that was in the first batch that we watched within the first two weeks, so we were hoping that when we watched the rest of the stuff that it was all there, because we didn't have the money or the time to get the people back for the stuff we didn't shoot.

Was the decision to shoot in black and white driven by budget?
At first, my attitude was, let's shoot in black and white – it's arty. Then, as we got closer to production, I said, 'We should shoot colour, because nobody is going to want to watch a black and white movie.' But Scott said, 'If we shoot colour we are going to have to rent an entire light package because we can't use the store's fluorescent lights unless we get gels and proper lights.' And I said, 'So if we shoot black and white, we can just use the store lighting and some keys? Fuck it – shoot in black and white!' And it wound up being cheaper to develop, too. DuArt, which processes most of the film on the East Coast, did black and white on a very

regular schedule and it was pricey. So Scott found this lab in the Yellow Pages, which has long since closed. We called them up and were like, 'How much do you charge?' I think it was twenty cents a foot. We asked them, 'Is there a student discount?' and they said, 'Sure'. So we went in, went up this creaky elevator. There was a slot in the door, big enough to put a can of film through. Some guy who didn't speak English took our film and Scott was like, 'Do you need to see ID?' He goes, 'No.' And that was that. He took our film and we were just like, are we ever going to see it back? What are they doing back there?!

Another leap of faith?
Yeah. I guess we didn't know any better. We were all like, maybe this is how it is done! At that point too, before we had started production, we were trying to find ways to nip and tuck the budget left and right. Kodak had a programme for film school students where you get fifteen per cent off your stock. So we went in there, we had Vancouver film school IDs but Kodak only accepted people from the city. So we went in and ordered up the complete film stock package and I had my credit card ready to go and they were just like, 'Right, now I am going to have to see your film school ID.' And I was like, 'Oh. I don't have mine. Scott, do you have your school ID?' And Scott's like, 'Well, I think I left it downstairs in the car.' So the guy took the film back. He could tell we were bullshitting. But I was like, 'We're not beat.' We went down to the New School for Social Research and looked through their catalogue for a one-day course we could join. We found this course called 'Roasting Suckling Pig' and the fee was fifty bucks. I signed up for the course, put it on the credit card, got ourselves a school ID, went back up town, gave him the ID and the guy had to give us the film stock at fifteen per cent off. It was still warm from the laminating machine! Then we went back down town and I took my name off the course. So I didn't have to pay the fifty bucks because fifty bucks was a lot of money.

So you had your stock, you had your equipment and you had your cast. How long were you in pre-production? I guess this might be a very formal title for what was going on!
It was really a very informal pre-production. It was a good month. Because I was rehearsing for the first two weeks while Scott was still out on the West Coast making calls back to the East Coast about renting equipment. And when Scott came out we still had two more weeks of pre-production and Dave was there for some of the rehearsals to see the blocking. And we had to go pick up the equipment and check it out. So it was a good month before we started shooting.

Were you working at the same time?
I'd been working in the convenience store and the video store all that time. I would work the six till eleven a.m. shift, then the boss would come in from eleven a.m. and he'd work from eleven till about five or six. From eleven to five we were either sleeping or preparing for the next night's shooting, bringing stuff into the

city, to get developed, stuff like that. From five or six till ten-thirty at night I was working again. Then from ten-thirty till six in the morning we were shooting the movie. And then the day would begin again. Sometimes we would end a little earlier than six a.m. and we would go crash in the video store. We had pillows and some blankets and went and slept on the floor in the video store and hung a sign on the convenience store shutter gates that was just like: 'The store isn't open. Knock on the video store window'. Sooner or later somebody would be knocking on the thing, I'd stumble out there, hair all messed up, half awake, and open up the store. I'd try to jockey the register and stay awake at the same time. Then occasionally I would switch with Scott and he would go run the convenience store while I was catching some zzzs in the video store before the boss got in.

There wasn't any problem with getting the use of the store from your boss?
No. When I came back to work after I'd come back from film school, they were in a bad way. I guess they needed my help. And they were like, 'Are you going to come back?' I was like, 'I will come back but I want to use the store as a location.' And at first they didn't think it was a big deal. You know, we were a couple of kids and there were a couple more kids and we were running around with film equipment, had to set up lights and move shit around. You know, there were cables everywhere. But I remember one day we shot the sequence where they have the food fight; where Dante and Randal kind of beat each other up and all that candy and doughnuts is splayed on the ground. It was about four-thirty or five in the morning and Jeff kind of hit a bump and was trying to get dialogue out so we wound up going another hour and we actually shot up until six. That was the morning that Mrs Thaper, the boss's wife, came at six o'clock. She walked into the store, saw the floor the way it was, saw everything, all this broken merchandise, saw all the equipment, turned around and just walked out. She sat in her car and we cleaned everything up and then I went to get her about a quarter after six and I was like, 'We're done' and she was like, 'Did you pay for all that food?' And I was like, 'Yeah. I marked it on my sheet in the tally book.' That was about the only time they kind of got a glimpse at it; saw how the process worked.

How did you feel the day you started shooting? I mean, you had a lot riding on this movie. For a start, twenty-five thousand dollars.
We were hoping it'd be less. But at that point I never thought about the money because I was like, it's credit cards. As long as I can make the minimum payments every month, that's fine. If it takes me twenty-five years to pay off the bills so be it. At least I won't be in gaol or something! So I never worried about the financial aspect too much. I remember that day I worked and people started showing up about nine o'clock in the evening. The video store closed at nine o'clock so we started putting everyone over there. I remember the first sequence that we shot was Dante and Caitlin crying and hollering and Lisa Spoonauer when she comes and they have this seven-minute exchange in the video store. She comes in and

then they walk next door to the video store essentially. That was the first thing we shot and I remember there was the basic crew, which was me, Scott, David and our friend Ed Hapstack who basically worked as a gaffer, doing all the hook-ups and whatnot. And that night, the first night, there were a few more people. My friends Brian and Walter were there; Vincent was there; the store owner's son, Ajive, was there hanging out watching. There were a few other people; we had a good ten people crewing up on this thing. And there was all this excitement of making a movie; it was so bizarre! We laid out everything as it would be for the next twenty-one days: where our movies were on the shelves and whatnot and posters here and there. And then shot that first sequence which is a seven-minute scene. We had rehearsed that scene to death so when we got up in front of the cameras Brian and Lisa did it flawlessly in one take, no mess-ups: we ran the camera, we ran the film, and, boom, the scene was over and I was like, 'That's it! We don't have to do it again.' And everyone was like, 'Wow, it's going to be like this every time, isn't it? Just one take! We'll always nail it in one take!' Of course, that wasn't the case. There were a lot of shots, a lot of set-ups, that wound up going way more than one take but that one was the key because it was the longest sequence in the film without cutting. So we shot that, and we shot Veronica coming back into the video store where Randal's saying, 'That's it. So he doesn't love you any more.' And if you look at that scene Randal's make-up is much heavier than it is in the rest of the movie. It was the first night that she made him up, and this girl, Lesley, who was doing the make-up, she'd been to some make-up school round the way and really just put on some heavy duty make-up and made him look like a racoon! I didn't know shit about make-up or how it shows up on film but I was just like, 'I think that is too heavy. I don't know what it's going to look like on camera.' So she brought it down a bit, but still in the finished film you can see it is heavier than it is in the rest of the movie. So that was the first day. By the end of the first week I'd say we were down to four people and that was it. Like all those people who are like 'wow, they are making a movie' just go away because you get on a set and unless you have one of the key jobs it's boring. It's just boring and repetitive! Plus, we are doing it all late at night so nobody wants to devote all their nights to this thing.

What was the hardest thing about the shoot for you?
The hardest thing was finding people to fill the roles, the side roles, because these people would drop out like flies. You know, 'We are shooting tonight. We need you at two a.m.' 'Oh, I'm not going.' So if you watch the movie that reached theatres, my friend Walter plays four roles; in the first cut he played five! We just kept changing his appearance. He plays the guidance counsellor, the guy who's spinning the egg; he plays the guy in the beginning with this wig on and a little hat and army jacket where Dante's getting the cigarettes thrown at him; he's the guy that's like, 'Ughhh . . . packet of cigarettes?' He played the guy who was like, 'Cute cat. What's its name?' And Randal says, 'Annoying customer.' He goes, 'Fucking

dickhead.' And he played another role too. He just kept on popping up in the movie because he was around. Walter didn't go to sleep until early in the morning, about four or five or something so he would come and hang out. And every time somebody didn't show up for one of the roles, we were like, 'Walter, throw this jacket on. Put this thing on.' And basically we would kind of change his appearance a little bit. But people wouldn't show up and that was kind of tough: that was about the toughest thing. The other tough thing – and probably tougher, way tougher than finding people for these side roles, was just finding sleep. Finding a place to sleep, finding time to sleep. But at that point you are cruising on your volition, on your passion for it. 'We're making a movie. This is phenomenal.' So your adrenalin is pumping and you don't really need sleep that much, but God, it would get to five o'clock in the morning and it would be time to fall asleep. Then most people could go home and there were other people who had jobs too, but they didn't have to go to their jobs till nine or ten. Some days I had to like turn around and jockey the register ten minutes after we'd done shooting. That was tough!

Did it ever get the better of you?
There was one night I fell asleep. We were shooting the fight sequence with the boys. Dave knew what I wanted to do. I was like, 'We need to do this, this, this and this.' And so they are shooting Dante getting hit in the face with bread, and Dave keeps wanting to do another one because it's not quite right in terms of lost focus on one. And in one, Dante goes out of frame and in one, you could see Jeff was wearing a watch which he shouldn't have been – we didn't have a continuity person on the movie so there's continuity glitches where we caught a few things. And then there were a lot of insert shots in this scene and candy going this way and that. And I am sitting on the coolers and I just laid down while they were setting up again and I just fell asleep. I just fell asleep for ten minutes – just flat out – I went out and I came to and Scott was just like, 'We finished it. We just shot the other inserts.' And I was like, 'Excellent!'

Time to go back to sleep!
Time to go back to sleep! But yeah, you tend to miss out on some hours while you are making a flick. And I thought we missed out on a lot of hours but I found that over the course of production, you never get as much sleep as you need because you are always so psychologically awake. You are so awake in your head and you are always anticipating and thinking about what is going to be needed and how. And, 'Oh God, that scene wasn't very good in rehearsals. Can it be better here on film?' Or whatever issues there are; time, for example. People love saying, 'We are running out of time.' Or, 'You are burning too much film.' So your head is always going. And at a certain point, even if your body wants to go to sleep, you can't. Your mind is just racing. So you lie awake for hours and finally fall asleep and suddenly the phone rings and it's time to get up. So yeah. I think, you can never

be prepared. The best thing to do before making a feature is get as much sleep as possible.

Is that still the case? Do you get a nice big rest before you actually go on to a set?
Definitely. I once read that Spielberg works out before he makes a feature. You know, he drops a bunch of weight. I thought that was kind of cool because the first thing that happens while you are making the movie is that you start gaining weight like mad. Most times when you are directing, you are standing around or sitting around and people are always going, 'Do you want some snacks?' Or you are cruising over to the table with that snack tray and you are just always noshing! Always eating and noshing! I put on thirty pounds when we made *Clerks*!

I guess you were in a convenience store!
Yeah, that was the great thing: we never had to cater that movie. We were just grabbing. People would be eating Fig Newtons and Yoo-hoos and whatnot. But you just wind up gaining weight.

Were there any major bits of good luck or bad luck? Any technical disasters or things that went so well that you couldn't have foreseen them?
My friend, Ed, had built a dolly for the movie and it was kind of like an overgrown skateboard dolly. And we put it on PBC piping for rails but it just didn't work: it didn't flow very smoothly. We did nine takes. It was the scene where Dante is counting milk and Randal comes in and he says, 'Let me borrow your car. I want to rent a movie.' And we follow them up the aisle. And Dante exits frame saying, 'You work at the convenience store, you work at a video store.' And Randal goes, 'I know I work at a video store but I want to go to a good video store so I can rent a good movie.' So it's not a long move – a couple of yards I guess – but we did it eight times with this dolly. At the end of it I was just, 'You know what? Let's just do one hand-held, just to be safe.' And sure enough, when we watched those dailies later on, every dolly one was just like (*waving hands all over the place*), kakakakakaka! So we wound up using the hand-held one. Thank God it was good. One night we had a cat that's in the movie and we lost that cat. We spent two hours looking for it. It was my friend Vincent's cat that we lost and the production shut down while we went to look for the damn cat! Because we needed the cat and the night we needed the cat to shit on cue we brought him to the video store and kept him there all day and any time he looked like he was going to crouch or any time he went towards the litter box we just picked him up and started holding him and whatnot. So this cat was waiting to shit all day. We basically kept him busy all day and so we figured we'd put the box up on the counter and, boom, it would just happen! So we put the box on the counter, we rolled and he jumps over the counter and we were like 'no, no, no'. The second time we got the cat up, the cat went into the box and started scraping around and then sure enough, just delivered on cue! A wonderful historic moment in the show because it went right. But we were worried that this cat was going to

wind up dead from some sort of digestive failure from us not permitting him to take a shit!

'No cruelty was involved in the making of this motion picture.'
Exactly. I'm not sure it was cruel but it was definitely not too favourable for the cat!

How were you faring in terms of your budget at this point?
We'd never known how to take cash advances off credit cards. We knew how to charge services like you charge for anything else. But we never knew you could just walk into the bank, give them your credit card and get money off of it! The day we figured out how to do that was just a banner day on the production. Because suddenly we had liquid cash to deal with.

I assume no one was being paid?
Nobody. Most people just did it for fun. Until the day he saw the movie, Jeff Anderson just assumed it was like some sort of thing that would be for family or friends. It never felt like a movie to him. Most people didn't get it. I remember the first reaction many people, friends and family had when they saw it was, 'Wow, it looks like a real movie!' I was like, 'Well what do you think we were doing – jerking off?'

Can you tell me about cutting your movie?
We brought a Steenbeck into the video store so the schedule of the movie proceeded into the post-production period. Everyone else was gone; it was just me and Scott. Scott would be editing during the day and I would be in the convenience store and then periodically through the day I'd switch off and watch what he'd cut and then do some cutting while he was running the convenience store. And then when the store shut down at ten-thirty we'd both go and edit for a while and then we'd go to sleep at around three or four, wake up at six, open the store again and try and grab some zzzs somewhere during the day, then come back and start again. So Scott and I saw the movie all the way through as we were cutting it.

Where did the idea for the titles that intersect the film come from?
You can almost take any number of scenes out of *Clerks* and play them out of context and it works as a short film. So the idea was to string them together with intertitles that read 'The first circle of Hell' because his name is Dante and it is kind of like a modern-day film of Dante's 'Inferno'. So basically the day would begin with the first circle of hell, the second circle of hell, the third circle of hell. And then I thought that was a little too pretentious, and a little too 'on the nose', particularly because the main character's name is Dante. So we were heading into the city one day, to the title house. They were going to do our opening credits and our closing credits. And we needed things to bridge the scenes sometimes because you couldn't cut from one to the other. So as we were going in I took a dictionary with me. There were some words that I loved. And then I started looking up words and reading the meanings and going, 'This describes a scene. I like

this.' So what I decided to do was throw a bunch of so-called fifty cents words on the screen so that we are at least guaranteed to play to a college audience.

What do you mean 'fifty cents words'?
There are nickel words like 'fuck' and 'butt' and fifty cents words like 'vilification'. So just by putting up some impressive vocabulary words we figured that college kids will watch the movie because it will make them feel smart for some reason. That was our backwards logic, but it worked out nicely.

Was it exciting to see your film take shape?
It was great. You just want to show everybody. The first thing you want to do is bring your friends in and your family and go, 'You've got to see this. It's pretty funny!' So you are proud. You know, it's just like having a kid! You just want to show it off!

That's interesting. A lot of people seem to hate the first cut of their movie.
Really? See, I didn't. I loved the first cut of the movie. And I loved every subsequent cut. The first time we put it together and it was mixed and we had a crappy little video copy of it, but with mixed sound, we all went over to my friend Ed's house and kicked back and watched it on his TV. Just really revelled in it! Like, wow! We made a flick! That's kind of cool! The next time I watched it, we wanted to screen at the IFFM. That's what we were working towards the whole time. The Independent Feature Film Market which is held at the Angelica. That's where Richard Linklater had taken *Slackers* as a work in progress. You pay five hundred dollars and you get a screening slot and you try to pack it with as many potential distributors or print media or just potential investors or whatever as you can. I had gone there the year before and found out what it was like so that was what we were gunning for. So we finished the film, we submitted it and we got in and we were like, this must mean something. But at that time the IFFM took every film that came in. You wrote them a cheque and you got in! So they gave us this screening slot on a Sunday morning at about eleven a.m. and it was the last day of the market, so when we got the schedule, the slot, I was just like, this is great. They gave us the whole week to build the hype – they must really believe in the movie! Then we found out that Sunday morning is the graveyard slot because nobody gets up that early on a Sunday when they don't have to. We didn't spend every day of the week at the IFFM; we watched a few other people's movies; we hung posters, hand-made kind of Xerox posters, ads for the film, saying what theatre and what time. We got there on Sunday morning and there were like ten people in the theatre and most of them were the cast and crew! And there we were in an empty fucking theatre. We had gone to other people's movies during the week and they were packed and there we were sitting in an empty theatre and at first it was like, wow, I can't believe how big it is. Here it is projected on the screen. This is amazing and it sucks that nobody is here. But God, this looks cool. But then they started talking and I'm sitting there going, oh my God. I can't

believe I spent twenty-seven grand – because at this point the final budget was about twenty-seven thousand, five hundred and seventy-five dollars – and nobody is here and nothing is going to happen to the movie and our dreams are crushed and why do they keep cursing in the movie. Everybody keeps saying 'fuck' and oh, the language! What will my mother say? I was just like, this is horrible. And then about twenty minutes after that I calmed down. I was like, you know what? This is my first effort and most people pay more than twenty grand to go to film school so this is kind of my film school and it's only money and I can pay it off and we did it at least and just kind of 'kick back and enjoy it and don't worry'. So I did just sit back and enjoy it. At the end of the movie there were four people there that had nothing to do with the movie. They had come in late, I guess. There were a couple from Canada who said some nice things about it. There was a woman who was asking, she said to me, 'Yeah, it's a funny film. But it is sad. And very angry.' I was like, 'Really?' And she was like, 'Yeah, I mean the people in the movie are so full of hate. You know people like that?' And here I am standing amongst my friends and I'm just like, um, yeah, one or two. And she was like, 'Yeah. I've got this theory that all the Nazis got reincarnated and are living in New Jersey.' I was just like, '. . . interesting!' And then she was just like, 'I guess I'll give you my headshot.' And she gave me her head shot and her résumé and I was like, 'Thanks!' Meanwhile Scott was talking to this guy by the name of Bob Hawk who was saying he really enjoyed the movie and he thought it was funny and had something to say and it was very original and we should submit it to Sundance. The trick of the IFFM is that you are always looking at everybody's badge to see if they are anybody important or if they are working for anyone important. Bob Hawk's badge said ICI which is his company, Independent Consultation for Independents. And that was it. This guy said we should go to Sundance and he was going to tell his friends about the movie and that was it. Our screening was done. It was over and we all just kind of went our separate ways.

How far in debt were you at this point?
We were probably close to the twenty-five grand mark. You also have to account for the incidentals that you pay while you are making the movie which have nothing to do with the hard cost of the movie. The little things that didn't get thrown into the budget like putting up Scott and David in the house and buying food and gas and tolls into the city: they boosted it up to around forty grand. And we had run out of credit card space and my parents were strapped for cash. I borrowed three grand from them at the beginning of the film. So we needed another three grand to make the print. And Scott's parents ponyed up and we made a very official deal with Scott's father who loaned the money on an interest rate and we had to pay it back in payments. But at that point, the cards were stacked up and the bills were starting to roll in and I was paying the minimum on every card, two hundred dollars every month; less than that, I don't think it was as high as two hundred. Sometimes it was just like fifty or sixty dollars. So it was stuff I kind of

struggled through and made the payments. But when we got close to the twenty-five mark we did start getting worried because we didn't know how much more it was going to take. And if we had gone the Robert Rodriguez route, the film would have cost us ten grand. Because Robert processed his film and popped it on video; he never printed it all out. Robert didn't do a sound mix. He didn't edit. He edited it on his VCRs. So if we had gone that route, it wouldn't have cost us that much. I think to get to the same place Robert did with a video tape, it would have cost us about ten grand.

So, how did you feel after the screening?
Very deflated. I was dating Scott's sister at the time and we lived up in Mount Clare in New Jersey. We all sat around that night going, 'Well. This is it.' Scott had got it into his head that he was going to walk the earth; he was going to go hiking. He was like, 'I'm young, even if I took seven years off to go walk the world I could still come back and make a movie by the time I'm thirty. You know, I don't know why I'm rushing.' We were all kind of making excuses for ourselves. It was just very depressing. Then the next morning I had a phone call at the apartment from Amy Taubin of the *Village Voice*. I knew her name because she had written this article about Richard Linklater when *Slacker* was at the IFFM. She says, 'I've heard some wonderful things about your movie, *Clerks*. I was wondering if I could get a video copy of it?' And I was like, 'Yeah, right. Who is this really?' And we played this game for ten minutes. I was saying 'Fuck you! Who is this?' like I thought it was one of my friends. And she was like, 'It's real. It's me. I called the number that was in the book and it was your parents and they gave me this number and a friend of mine told me I should watch the movie. He said it was the undiscovered gem of the marketplace.' I said, 'That piece on Richard Linklater at the IFFM? I have that piece framed, it's hanging above my desk.' And she was really flattered and we chatted for a little while and so I said, 'Yeah. I'll bring a tape up. By all means.' Then a while later I get a phone call from Larry Kardish who programmes for New Directors New Film Festivals, at the Museum of Modern Art, which is kind of the companion piece to the New York Film Festival. It was like, 'Yes, I've heard it is very good and I want to see a tape.' I was like, 'Nobody was there! Who told you?' And he was like, 'A friend of mine, a man whose opinion I trust a great deal.'

This was Bob Hawk?
Right. We were never told who it was though. So I was like, 'Yeah, I will certainly send a tape in.' A while later we got another phone call from Peter Broderick who wrote that influential article for *Filmmaker* magazine about *Laws of Gravity* and *El Mariachi* and *Living End* and he was like, 'Yeah, I've heard about the film, I wondered if I could see it?' I was just like, 'Who are you people talking to?' And he was like, 'Well, he is a friend. His name is Bob Hawk. He has been around for years and if he says something is good they kind of pipe up and listen.' So all these

people wanted to watch the movie, gave great feedback on it and Amy Taubin made it the focus of her piece about the IFFM that year and called it the 'undiscovered gem of the marketplace'. And wrote about our dialogue on the phone. Like when I was 'Who is this really?' She said how wonderful it was. She wrote: 'His style is that he has no style.' That was really great. It was our first piece of press on the movie and it was major press. It was the *Village Voice*. It just meant loads to me. I finally spoke to Bob Hawk and Bob was just like, 'Yeah, I was a real big fan. I told you I was going to tell people. I think you guys should submit to Sundance. I advise them from time to time, so I could put in a good word for you guys.' Now for us Sundance had films like *sex, lies and videotape*, a colour film, 35 mm, with stars. We didn't think *Clerks* was really in that league but he was telling us to submit it and then he said, 'The other thing I want to do is put you in contact with John Pierson who is a producer's rep. He sold *She's Gotta Have It, Roger and Me* and *Amongst Friends*, amongst other things', and listed all these films. 'You should talk to him. He should see the movie.' So I spoke to John Pierson and he was like, 'Yeah, send the tape up.' People had made John out to be very iconic and huge but he called me one night, a Friday night at about ten o'clock, and I couldn't believe this power player was calling me at ten o'clock at night! So I sent him the film and he got back to me a week later. I'd spoken to his wife in the interim, Janet, who works very closely with John and she was like, 'I watched the movie and I thought it was wonderful. He hasn't watched it yet. He has been away but he is coming back and I'll make him watch it.' And John had told me later that he didn't want to rep films any more. But when he got home, Janet handed him the tape and she was just like, if you want to get out of film repping, don't watch this. So John watched it. He called me up and said, 'I watched the movie. I laughed and had a really good time but I don't think the market for this film exists so if you are ever in the city I'd be happy to buy you dinner.' I was like, 'Gee, thanks. All right. Bye.' A week later, John Pierson calls up and he goes, 'I watched the film three more times and I think there is something we can do here. I think we can do something.'

Did you put it into any festivals?
Yeah. By that point we had submitted to Sundance. We got accepted, which was another big day. They called the convenience store. Bob was out in Los Angeles where he lived at the time. He called me at one point and he was saying they had programmed twelve or fourteen movies, I forget what it was at the time, and we were one of the finalists. He was saying, 'It is not written in stone but you are hanging in there for the dramatic competition.' And I was like, 'God! Really?' And he was like, 'But you are not in yet. You could get booted out but isn't it nice to know that out of six hundred movies, you got this far?' And I was like, 'Yeah, it is very cool.' He called me back a half hour later and he was like, 'You're in!' And I was like, 'My God! We are in the competition. We are in Sundance! This little movie is in Sundance!' Scott had gone back to Vancouver where he lived and I

called him up and I remember I had this long preface where I was just like, 'I don't know, dude. We are kind of screwed! My mother accidentally threw out two of the reels so our film is incomplete and my father spilt soda on the other reel.' I just went off on this long bizarre story and Mosier was like, 'My God! You're kidding me.' And I was talking about the negative and he was just like, 'Well, we are absolutely fucked!' I was like, 'Nah. I'm just kidding, we got into Sundance!' He was like, 'Wow!' So Scott came back and John Pierson had come on board officially to rep the film. And John had taken the film to every distributor – to Miramax, to October, to Sony Pictures Classics, to Fineline, everywhere before we had even gone to Sundance, and in every company there was a person who loved the movie. Unfortunately that person was never in a position of power. So our distribution chances were shot before we went to Sundance. Nobody wanted the movie.

Given the reaction of Bob Hawk et al, why do you think this was? The humour? The way it was put together?
After the Miramax screening Harvey Weinstein said, 'It looks like hell and everyone's talking and nothing happens in the first five minutes.' Also in the first five minutes there's that whole cigarette diatribe and Harvey is a huge smoker. And he was just like, 'I don't need to hear this.' He'd just got off a plane from New York and he was tired and he walked out of the screening. They were like, 'Well, we will see how it plays at Sundance but it is really not for us.' Right before we went to Sundance, John says, 'There is one thing you have to do with the movie: you have to cut that ending off.' And I knew that a few people who loved the movie, including Bob Hawk, John Pierson and Amy Taubin, hated the ending. The original ending is that some guy comes into the convenience store and shoots Dante dead and takes all the money. And Pierson was like, 'Look, man, you can't grow to love this character overnight and then kill him because you didn't know how to end the movie.' To me it was like, that's the ultimate joke. He is not even supposed to be there and he gets killed. But John was like, I really think you should cut the ending and if I am wrong you can put it back later on. You can talk to the distributor and ask if you can put it back. So we cut it right before we went to Sundance: cut that clip where Dante gets shot so in Sundance it ended with this POV where the camera comes into the store – that was the killer's POV – and it's on Dante and Dante goes, 'Can I help you? Oh, I'm sorry we are closed.' And then cut to credits. For a theatrical release we cut it back even further, to Randal throwing in the sign and saying, 'You are closed.' And Dante walks out of frame and the movie ends – which made a little more sense.

How did it go at Sundance?
We had four screenings. The first three were well attended. It was the first time we saw the movie with a full audience and just to hear the cacophonous laughter, the roaring, it was like watching the *Slackers* screening at the Angelica years before, but to the nth degree. I felt right about myself. It was like, 'I knew I could give 'em

something to really laugh about.' It was a really satisfying feeling. Still no distributors were interested. The last screening we had was at the Egyptian theatre at Sundance on a Friday and we were playing right before the Friday night première, *Reality Bites*. So we screen. It goes like *Gangbusters*. Mark Tusk, who worked at Miramax and who was a big fan of the movie – he had come from New Jersey originally himself – was lobbying for us the whole time. Harvey had passed on it and Mark made Harvey go to that Friday screening at the Egyptian. He'd promised he would deliver Harvey and he did. So Harvey was watching the movie and Mark says he feels Harvey start to stir at the same point that he stirred while watching it at Tribeca, and he said to him, 'Just stay and keep thinking thirty-seven.'

What do you mean, 'keep thinking thirty-seven'?
The movie kicks off for a lot of people when Dante accuses his girlfriend of sucking thirty-seven dicks. Harvey has a very distinct guttural laugh, you could hear him louder than anyone else and he loved it. We did this big Q&A afterwards, great reception. Then after that, we were just sitting there talking to people, and Guin Turner, who was there at the festival with *Go Fish*, came up to me and Scott, and said, 'John wants you across the street. He is sitting down with Harvey now.' So Scott and me ran across the street to The Eating Park, and sat down with Harvey, Jon Gordon who is now our production exec at Miramax, David Lindy who was the lawyer at Miramax at the time, and John Pierson. Harvey is smoking like a fiend, eating these greasy potato skins. And he says, 'You made a fucking funny movie. I'll take it and put it on a bunch of fucking screens, show it to the right fucking people, put a fucking soundtrack in there . . .' And me and Scott were like, 'Yeah!' He was our kind of people: very blunt and very frank. So he put an offer out there. Now John had dealt with Harvey before because he had sold him *Working Girls* and *The Thin Blue Line*; and he was like, 'Well, Harve, the movie has had four screenings. It's proven it is not a pig in a poke. So you might want to boost up your offer.' And so he made another offer. And every figure he threw out was golden to Scott and me. We were like, all right! But then we went to the Saint John and John pulled us to the side and said, 'Now, here is the deal. No other distributor has offered to buy this movie. Miramax is the only bidder. For some reason they think they are competing with other people but they are not.' The sum they offered us was very low. It was two hundred and twenty-seven grand. Twenty-seven grand paid for the hard cost of the movie, not even the interest on the credit cards. A hundred grand had to go toward blowing the movie up to 35 mm. And then we were left with a hundred grand to split between us and pay more bills and all the people on the cast. But I'd never seen a hundred grand in my life; never thought I would! So we didn't care about the money. And John was like, 'We could really push for more cash but is this how you want to enter into a relationship with these people? This way we go in low. If the movie breaks out they will love you for the rest of your lives.' For us it was about distribution. It was about getting the movie with somebody who got the movie and

would get it to the right audience. So we went back to the table and I was like, 'Yes. Let's do it.' And David Lindy had a yellow legal pad right there and was writing up the terms of the deal. And John was making all these demands: 'It has to play at this many cities, it has to play on this many screens.' Harvey at one point excused himself, he had to take off, we would see him in the future, blah, blah, blah. So there it was. We sold our flick and we were dumbfounded. I don't think Miramax would ever buy an under one hundred thousand dollar movie again, unless it was pure genius, because Miramax isn't in the ultra-small movie business. They will make movies for under a million and buy movies that were made for under a million, but under a hundred, they haven't done it since us and we're always theorizing about the reason they did it. I think Harvey did genuinely like the movie. But it was also a very shrewd move to buy the movie because Miramax had just acquired Disney.

You mean the other way round!
Sorry! Disney had just acquired Miramax a few months prior to that. And there was some bemoaning in the press that they were going to lose their art-house image, blah-blah. So buying this scrappy black and white American independent film shot on the ultra-cheap was a great PR move for them. And then the movie did really well for them. It never played more than fifty screens, but they made three million theatrically and overseas made another four to five, I believe.

On their two hundred and twenty-seven thousand dollar investment? They must have loved you!
Plus the video did really well. Of course there is no TV sale because the movie is what it is. It made it on to a few airlines though. I remember people saying, 'I watched that movie in first class, on the little pop-up screen.' So Miramax did well by it. It was a smart buy for them and our loyalty will always be with Miramax. I mean, they really took a chance on us. And while it was a shrewd move for them as well, they didn't have to. They really could have just flat out passed and said, 'No, your movie is too small for us.'

How do you think you came out of the overall experience of Clerks?
Smart. Knowledgeable, worldly. A lot of wisdom came out of it. We spent a year on the festival circuit with the movie before it came out. Theatrically it came out in the States in October, so we spent a year going to all these festivals, and as you travel, you learn about the business aspect. We went through every step of the marketing with them, figuring out what the campaign for the movie would be. The cutting of the trailer. The numbers. Where that money comes from. How all this money to send us to these festivals somehow gets applied back to the movie.

What do you mean, 'applied back to the movie'?
Well, we went to Cannes, and Miramax was also taking *Fresh*, *Pulp Fiction*, and one other. What Miramax does is they take all the money they spend in going to

Cannes, divide it by four and apply them to each movie. Now they had a yacht and threw a huge *Pulp Fiction* party. Also they put up Bruce Willis, Quentin, Sam Jackson and the entire cast of *Pulp Fiction* in the Hotel du Cap which is a very expensive fucking hotel. Meanwhile, me and Scott are sharing the hotel room the festival gave us. Basically if they spent an inch on us, they spent three yards on *Pulp Fiction*. Yet, somehow, we split the bill four ways. It's like going to a restaurant with a party of fifty, getting a glass of water and being handed a bill for your share!

Where does the money that pays the bills actually come from?
It comes out of your grosses at the end of the picture. So you find out all these things as you go along. You go, 'Who's paying for all this?' And they go, 'Well, actually, you guys are.' The back end of the movie is paying for it. So we never saw a back end on *Clerks*, whatsoever.

Did you learn much from the response to the movie?
Storywise, what is incredibly helpful is reading the reviews. Uniformly, across the board we got really good reviews, good to wonderful. But even in the great reviews they say, 'Well, the camera movement leaves much to be desired . . .' And that kind of stuff sticks with you. You are like, maybe I should start thinking about moving the camera. And getting a little ballsier. I don't care what a filmmaker says. Every review does something to you, bad or good. The good reviews, of course, are great, and make you feel a sense of relief. The bad reviews are the ones that stick with you because those are the people you are always trying to win over. You are always trying to prove yourself to that one guy. I was talking to Chris Rock, who is in *Dogma*. And Chris talked about doing his comedy act on stage for a thousand people. But you are never playing to a thousand people. You are playing to the one guy in the fifth row who just keeps looking at you and hasn't laughed yet! And it's true. I think one grows in terms of craft by thinking about the people that nay-say you.

Surely you learn by actually doing it?
Yeah. There is something about it too where the second time round you are like, 'I think I can do this a little better.' But for me it has a lot to do with the reviews. And I read them all, too. I always think it's important to hear what somebody has to say. As long as you take it with a grain of salt!

Do you think you're progressing as a director?
I think so. Particularly in terms of performance. I used to be very rigorous with the performers in terms of giving line readings, especially on *Clerks*. If they weren't saying it right I would tell them, 'Say it like this', and tell them exactly how to say it and basically they would then mimic me saying the line. Then when I started working with professional actors, I realized they hate that. They hate it! So then you have to find new and interesting ways to lead the horse to water, so to speak, without telling them exactly how to say it. I think visually I have gotten

better too. I have learnt more about the camera. I've learnt the difference between a 100mm and a 50mm lens.

What did your parents make of Clerks? *Had they seen the script before they saw the film?*
My mother watched the movie and when she was done she said, 'You spent twenty-seven thousand dollars on that piece of garbage?' And I was like, 'Thanks, Mom!' I was never mad at her. I was like, it is not her kind of movie. As soon as the movie got acknowledged, her tune didn't change. She was just like, 'Obviously there is something to it I am not seeing.' And yet she wept when she saw *Chasing Amy* and thought it was wonderful. I asked her, 'Why this movie?' And she was just like, 'I identify with this movie in ways you will never understand.' And I was like, 'What? The lesbian movie you identify with? You are my *mother*.'

Should they have recognized the world Clerks *was about? Was it autobiographical?*
All the films thus far have kind of been little snapshots of my life at the time. But my life is never that interesting. It's definitely not compelling enough to put up on the screen. So what you do is take a seed of truth and build incredibly on it. There was nothing in the movie that happened in real life. But I was very much the Dante character, and Dante's two girlfriends, Veronica and Caitlin, were both based on my girlfriend at the time, Kim, who runs the office here. So that was in there. As was the subtext of not knowing what to do with one's life. And complaining about it or feeling lost and realizing, finally coming to the realization that you just have to do something, just take it in hand. All the whining in the world isn't going to produce results. So I was my own Randal. Dante was the guy I was and Randal was that inner voice, the guy that you want to be. The guy that always wants to have the witty rejoinder, at the right time, the guy that wants to spit a mouthful of water at the occasional jackass who passes by the front of the counter. It was also a way of reaching out and seeing if people laughed at the same things as you did. Like, I always figured me and my friends would really laugh at this movie, because it is our kind of sense of humour. And there was always this worry: is it regional? Will it play outside of New Jersey? And if it plays outside of New Jersey, will it play outside of the States? And it did. No matter where we went with the film, people laughed at the exact same things. No matter what the translation. So either we were getting guys who were translating the film who were writing a way funnier film than I was, or people universally laughed at the same things. It was also a little bizarre to have them laugh at the things you didn't think were that funny!

Do you think you were helped by your time at film school?
In as much as I like hearing people react to my writing – that was positive. But nobody taught me anything about the craft or anything like that. I think, more or less, it is in you or it is not. And I think you either have something to say or you don't, much like with directing. I think with directing, a lot of times it comes

down to you can or can't. For me I know, and with a lot of directors, it is about visually telling a story but that has never been my strong suit. My strong suit is telling a story verbally and creating interesting, believable characters and whatnot. I think to direct, all you have to know is how to communicate. That's it. And if you can convey a thought to an actor, they can convey a thought to the audience. And so if I can communicate with my DP and give him a general idea of what I want to see, if not a very specific idea, then the audience is seeing what I am hoping that they will see. It is all about that communication skill.

Do you think film students understand how hard it is to break through?
There are more students in film school now than in law school, I think. But I've never met anyone that used their film school degree to segue right into their production gig. I mean you don't walk into a studio with a film school degree and go like, 'OK. I am certified. I can make a movie.'

Do you think you've been lucky?
I make no bones about the fact that *Clerks* tapped into the zeitgeist at the right moment. And it is not so much about talent as it was about timing. If we'd made that movie a year earlier or a year later I wouldn't be talking to you like this. But thank God, Bob Hawk went with me. It wouldn't have happened otherwise. Many of these film-makers you read about in the press really think they reinvented the ashtray. They really feel that they are God's gift to the craft and they don't credit all the other people that helped them get where they are. The problem with the average young film-maker today is they make their movie, and if, God willing, it's picked up, the first thing you see across the screen is 'A film by Blah-blah-blah'. And that always irritates me, because this is a collaborative medium, and then one jackass says, 'A film by . . .' There are very few people who can get away with it. Obviously, it's 'A film by Martin Scorsese' or with Spike Lee, it's a 'Spike Lee Joint'. I give those guys credit. But these first-timers who get out there and feel they have to announce their brand name of themselves to the world are just so irritating. There is no way in hell that I could have made *Clerks* or anything beyond it without Scott. And it is about that team effort, at the risk of sounding cornball-ish. I write and direct and that is the credit I deserve. Scott puts together every physical aspect of the production whether it is crew or if it is just the simple fact that he is there, which makes you feel comfortable enough to go like, 'All right I think I can do this, with a little support.' Whoever is shooting, whether it be Dave or Bob Yeoman, they are responsible for the look of the film, and I will tell them what I want to see, but at a certain point you have got to let them do their job and bring their craftsmanship to it.

So in reality you're at the mercy of the machine you assemble?
Absolutely. That is so true.

And that for a director's talents to shine, you need a good producer?

For me this is how it is. I mean, maybe other cats know different, but without Mosier, I don't think I could have done it or would have ever taken the first step. I would have dropped out of film school and gone back to the convenience store, maybe written a script that would sit on the shelf. It is about finding that other person who gets you completely and knows where you are going, and knows how to make that happen with you and for you, and is on your side as you are on his. And every flick we have ever done is as much his as it is mine.

Will you ever go to LA?
No. It's a nasty little business out there. They ask us to go out to LA the whole time. They say, 'How come you're still here in New Jersey?' And I'm like, 'I didn't make my movies in LA. We made our first one here. It's not about LA.' I'd much rather stay in the suburbs, and be a big fish in a small pond. A lot of people want to go to the parties, they want to attend the screenings. I don't. I have zero interest in it. They send us screening invites and premières. I'd rather watch a movie in a theatre with a real audience.

You still live here in New Jersey?
Yeah, I live down the street.

Stephen Frears: *Gumshoe*

When did you start going to the movies?
I started going to the cinema in 1944 when I was three. There were forty cinemas in Leicester, and there wasn't anything else to do so I would just be taken along by my mother, or whoever was looking after me that afternoon. Then in some barbaric way I went away to school when I was eight, and at school they would show you a film every Saturday, and repeat it on Sunday. So in fact, this was making me a rather informed scholar without my even being aware of it.

Are there any of those films that are still with you today?
Oh, lots. Most of the films I saw were British war films like *The Way to the Stars*. Ealing comedies. I can remember being terrified by a Will Hay film about a headless horseman called *Ask a Policeman*. David Lean's Dickens films. And much more mundane things: Launder and Gilliat. Solid, ordinary British films. American films really weren't around a lot. I think they were probably thought to be rather vulgar; not that my family was particularly genteel, we were just ordinary and conventional. I can remember one terrible occasion when my mother wanted to see *Red River* and I was much more interested in seeing some British rubbish. There was some historical reason to do with the war why there weren't American films being shown in Britain around that time. Also, Britain slightly found its subject during the war.

At this stage, was film-making something you dreamed of becoming involved in?
No, I was just a punter. I haven't changed, really. At least I hope not.

Did you have any idea of what you wanted to do when you left school?
I wanted to work in the theatre. It was the only thing within my imaginative range. My dad was the doctor at the local theatre. Therefore I had an entrée, and I used to go there a lot and was rather seduced by the place – because it wasn't like home, really. It seemed free and liberal and full of sex and things like that. There was an actress in Nottingham called Anne Bell, and I'd never seen anyone so beautiful – walking down the street in black stockings and a beehive hairdo. So as a child I was really completely seduced by this life that seemed bohemian to me. I'm sure it was an illusion, but at the time I was ready for one. Then I met Lindsay Anderson on holiday somewhere and was astonished to meet someone so intelligent and provocative.

What period was this?

1958. There was a boy at school whose mother was a rather distinguished woman called Daphne Rye who was the casting director at Tennants. I used to go on holiday at his mother's house in Majorca, and actors would go and stay with her, too. I was always taken there as a sort of chaperone for her son. And so I met these rather glamorous people and became completely seduced by the glamour. It was my fatal flaw – my Achilles Heel.

What did you do about it practically?
At Cambridge I started directing plays. Theatre played a very large part in university life, and I was an absolute sucker for it – a groupie. Plus, there were very clever people there, such as Trevor Nunn, John Cleese.

Did your passion for the theatre at Cambridge leave much time for movies?
I went a lot. It was a wonderful time. What was happening was that European cinema was being opened up to the world. There would be a masterpiece playing in Cambridge every week. And there were at least three really top-class cinemas. I can remember seeing Truffaut's films, Antonioni, Fellini, Bergman, Russian films. And American films started to get rather good around this time.

So at this stage, you were still a punter, albeit an informed one?
Yes. I was a sort of intellectual punter, by then.

What happened when you left Cambridge?
My eighteenth birthday sort of coincided with the transformation in English society, around the time of the 1959 election. When I left Cambridge I went to work in a theatre in Farnham in Hampshire, then I ended up at the Royal Court, which was where I really wanted to go. It was a rather austere organization in those days, and it had a sort of sideline making films. I was drawn to that kind of material and that way of treating material. But at this point I still didn't think I was going to work in the cinema. I mean, a lot of my life has been spent being prised open to imaginative possibilities that I wasn't brought up to think about. Film directors just didn't exist in my world. They just came from outer space.

What did you do at the Royal Court?
I was an assistant to Anthony Page, which involved a lot of getting him scrambled eggs and parking his car. But also witnessing *Inadmissable Evidence* being born, and being apprenticed to some extraordinary, brilliant people – Anthony, George Devine, Samuel Beckett, Bill Gaskill. Terrifying people. It was like being an apprentice at the Borgias. I was like a boy with straw in his hair. But then, in the end, if you sit at the feet of the Borgias, you eventually learn an enormous amount.

Were you learning much about directing during this period?
No. I was learning about life – how it could be lived on this sort of emotional level, and with this much intensity. I'm rather old-fashioned in that I believe that art is a way of learning to live. And these people were teaching me.

How did you end up working in film?

Karel Reisz came to the Royal Court to do a play. And Lindsay Anderson said, 'Oh, get Stephen to be your assistant.' Then Karel couldn't cast the play, but he said, 'Come and work on my film.' So I became his assistant on *Morgan, a Suitable Case for Treatment*. Nowadays you watch a film and there'll be a credit for 'Assistant to the Hairdresser'. Ridiculous. I wasn't anything like that. I was just a presumably bright kid whom Karel, out of the goodness of his heart, thought would be good to have involved in this film. He said the other day that I was a very good assistant. I don't know what he means. I mean, I would ask an idiot's questions, which was quite useful, I suppose.

Do you regret that the role of assistant director in the sense of an apprentice no longer exists?

If you look at Renoir, his assistants included Visconti and Becker. But it isn't like that now. Now it's just people arranging appointments. The first assistant director is an important role but it's quite different from what used to be the assistant director. It's a kind of sergeant-major.

How do you think working as an assistant for Lindsay and Karel helped you as a director in your own right?

What I've discovered is that I am in some sort of humanist tradition. And it's quite reassuring to discover a tradition that you're part of. Lindsay was very good because he'd always say 'Make things matter!'

How did you progress from working as an assistant director to directing your own short film, The Burning?

After working with Karel, I went off to work with Albert Finney on *Charlie Bubbles*. I was like a sort of parcel being passed around. I was very naive and unformed, all over the place, really dependent on these parental figures to shape me. Then one day I found this short story which was rather good, so I filmed it. It was rather a Chekhovian story, set in South Africa on the day the revolution breaks out, and it concerned a white family with tumultuous events going on around them. Being startled to discover fires and dead bodies. It was really about the decline of empire. The film did rather well. It played at the Curzon with *The Bride Wore Black* and got noticed. It was well acted. It had the qualities that I imagine my work has continued to have.

What happened next in your career as a director?

Everything was so tied up with trying to find out who I was, trying to earn a living, trying to pull myself together. Some of my contemporaries had got into television companies and sorted themselves out. By then, Mike Apted and Mike Newell were doing *Coronation Street* and *World in Action*, so they were earning proper money. I was much more at sea, writhing around. I'd been turned down for all the proper training schemes. But after I made *The Burning* I got an agent called Clive Goodwin, and he started to get me work on the strength of the film. He got me a job in children's TV, working for a loony called Tony Essex. He had made *The Great War* series, he'd been an editor and a sort of impresario before he became the head of documentaries at Yorkshire Television, which had just started operating out of a raincoat factory in Leeds. And he loved film, so he'd bring in proper directors to do these children's stories properly. And somehow it was an inappropriately good opportunity to shoot a lot, and learn that way.

Wasn't it one of the episodes you did for him which led to the idea for Gumshoe?
That's right! It was about two kids who pinch a car, and it was written by Troy Kennedy Martin's brother Ian who invented *The Sweeney*. The kids would drive down the Great North Road acting out scenes from films. The scenes had been written but I'd just give them the clip from the film and say, do this, and they were absolutely wonderful. They'd do imitations of Rod Steiger and Marlon Brando! And then I met Neville Smith. He'd been an actor. Then he'd become involved with Ken Loach and Tony Garnett. He wrote something rather good about Everton FC called *The Golden Vision* which Ken did and which mixed real people and fiction. Then he wrote another wonderful script that Ken did, called *There's a Kind of Hush or the Pope and Alan Ball* about the death of a trades unionist. We were both out of work so I said why don't you write a thriller, a cop show? And he said, okay, and he wrote the first bit of *Gumshoe*. It was a wonderful piece of writing. I wasn't bright enough or on the ball enough to realize just how good it was. What Neville could write was the sensibility; he was great at writing jokes and creating an imaginative world. But we were both hopeless at creating a plot. Then a friend called Maurice Hatton made us go and write the plot properly. He was much more aware of what we were doing. Anyway, the script got written.

What do you think of it now? To my mind, it didn't seem to be able to make up its mind whether it wanted to be comedic or serious, Philip Marlowe or Billy Liar.
I think it's caught between the two things. But I think it's an absolutely wonderful piece of writing. It was absolutely what our world was like in those days. It was more a description of my generation than anybody realized. That split probably existed in all English people of my generation. So the film is split in many ways and I'm inclined to blame myself for that. But it was the first film that anyone had made about people who went to the pictures in England. I mean, it was exactly the same time that Woody Allen was making *Play it Again, Sam*.

Once you had the screenplay, what happened?
Albert Finney had made a lot of money out of *Tom Jones* and he set up a film company with the producer, Michael Medwin. It was called Memorial Enterprises, after the Albert Memorial, and they invested in plays and films. For example, they contributed to *The Burning*; and to Mike Leigh's first film. And they made *Charlie Bubbles*. So I took the script to Albert, because I guessed he would

like it. And he did. And that was sort of the end of it. Raising the money was a doddle. Because Albert was a world star at the time, even though *Charlie Bubbles* had been a catastrophe.

Was there any resistance to you directing Gumshoe?
No. But I was always expecting there to be. And I was curious to find out what price I would sell out for. I don't know if there were conversations about my directing it or not. Not in my presence, anyway.

So it had a fairly painless birth?
On the contrary, it was full of pain. It just wasn't painful where you'd expect it to be.

Where did the pain come?
Columbia Pictures, who bought the film, thought Albert Finney was playing a private detective. You'd say, 'Well, no, it's actually a film about a bingo caller who thinks he wants to be a private detective.' So it was as though all they could see was a bloke in a trench-coat, but actually what was on offer was a rather more complicated film about a bloke who wanted to be a man who wore a trench-coat. I mean, wearing a trench-coat is easy; but being Humphrey Bogart is presumably harder. So the film was always caught in that gap.

What, concretely, was the problem?
You had very modern people and very traditional people banging into each other. The people closest to me – Neville, and my cameraman, Chris Menges – were very modern, albeit inexperienced. But the people who were making the film with us were very experienced but very traditional. Chris was absolutely firmly on this side of the line, which didn't please the people on that side of the line. For instance, Chris is a great realistic cameraman, so all his work was geared toward the reality of the film. For Chris, I'm sure the film was clearly about someone who had read too much Raymond Chandler. So he knew what the pastiche was within it. But this other set of people just wanted a conventional action thriller, and they didn't know why we were putting the emphasis on certain things. And I was in the middle, trying to resolve certain intellectual things in my head, things which you know if you can pull the contradictions together will make it interesting.

But you didn't manage to reconcile the two things?
Listen, I was very young. I didn't even know this was the problem. It's easy for me to speak about it now with hindsight. But at the time I just sort of blundered on by instinct. It's in the nature of being new to the job. As you get more experienced you're able to explain to people, to carry them with you. But when you're the newcomer, people sense your anxiety and they step forward to offer advice – which might not necessarily be the best thing to do. I mean, nobody was malicious. People were well-meaning and tried to be helpful. But what you really had

was a completely contradictory set of attitudes, and it causes you a lot of pain because you're being pulled in several different directions. Every time you do a shot you're split in two.

Did having Albert as your star mean it was easy to cast?
Well, I used a lot of actors out of the Royal Court: Billie Whitelaw, Frank Finlay. So that wasn't difficult. Janice Rule I remembered seeing in a film called *The Chase* in which she was terribly good, terribly sexy. I'd never come across anyone like her before. Her character's name was taken from an Olympic runner, Fanny Blankers-Koen, a woman who ran in the Wembley Olympics in 1948. You see how everything in the film comes out of some *Beano*-reading view of England!

What about the fat man who started the film off by giving Eddie a package containing money and a gun?
I was in Liverpool on a recce with Chris, and we saw this man crossing a road and Chris said, 'Oh you want people like him in it. Go on, go and ask him. It's Sidney Greenstreet.' I said, 'I can't!' Maybe the car stopped at a traffic light. He kept saying, 'Go on, ask him!' So eventually I went up to him. It turned out he was Cecil Bernstein's brother-in-law. And all my friends knew him, because he ran the Wimpy in Oxford. He was an extraordinary man, a rather touching man and he ran a theatre in Liverpool called The Everyman which was why he was there. I said to him, have you got an Equity ticket? He said, is it good if I have one or don't have one? And he arranged it all. That's what I mean by these contradictions in the film. In order to emulate somebody who appeared in a thriller in Hollywood we'd found a man crossing the street!

Given that some of the cast hadn't acted before, did you spend much time rehearsing?
I don't remember rehearsing at all. There wasn't really anything to rehearse. I mean, Albert knew how to do all that stuff. Albert was the first person I came across who used to imitate Bogart. I've seen Belmondo do it since but Albert used to do it, too.

What was it like working with a big star?
If you think about it, Albert was exactly the same as we were. He was a bloke from Salford. English to his fingertips. Riddled with Englishness. Hopelessly, provincially English. But, of course, he'd also become a big star. And the big star was also the boss of the company making the film. Which sometimes got us into difficult situations. For example, Chris was always wanting to shoot towards windows, which means you have to balance the light. If the light drops outside you have to drop the light inside so they're always in relation to each other. Well, that's quite a delicate thing to do, particularly in November when we were shooting. Albert would say, why don't you just get me up against the wall and shoot me?

Looking at his watch?
Well, slightly. He couldn't understand why we were interested in things other

than just photographing him. Because that's what happened in Hollywood. But it's one of his great performances.

What was it like for you to direct a major star, as someone who at that point had made one short film?
I guess if he did something that didn't make sense to me, I would ask him why. But it just seemed to me that what he was doing was good. If people are being good, what is there to talk about? What was complicated was that Albert had really been taught by Karel and Lindsay too. So of course it was rather complicated when I turned up, somehow connected to them. He was always rather suspicious of educated people. I think he thought I was too clever. I probably drove him mad. But he was great. The good side of it was that I was working with my friends, with Neville and Chris. I was beginning to find myself. Albert was really from an earlier period, from my life as an apprentice, as it were. With Neville and Chris I started to emerge as who I really was.

How did you come to work with Chris Menges?
Well, in this generation that I belonged to, the really interesting work was being done at the BBC by people like Ken and Tony. Chris came out of that. Among my contemporaries, he was regarded as a sort of genius. He was a very considerable presence. In fact, there was a terrible row about him. I asked Chris to shoot the film and he agreed. Then Ken asked him to shoot *Family Life* and of course Chris got into a terrible state because he didn't know what to do. Anyway, eventually I held him firm to the agreement. Chris taught me an enormous amount. He was years ahead of me in terms of what he was doing and I was always out of my depth with him. Except that I could clearly offer him opportunities that were interesting. Perhaps because I was interested in doing work that wasn't entirely realistic. I did five films with Chris which were always very difficult, very complicated struggles between the two of us. He was very, very dominant, slightly bullying and always pushing you to do better work.

How did you work with him during the preparation for the film? For example, did you prepare shot lists or storyboards together?
No. Chris was more confident in his own sensibility, he was very clear about his values. Whereas I was always a late developer, much more tentative.

How would you describe your technical knowledge at this point?
Non-existent. Didn't have any. So I relied on Chris entirely, and I was happy to. I still do rely on the cameraman, though of course I know far more than I did then. But with Chris I wasn't able to question what he was doing.

What about when you arrived at a location? Would you have had a clear idea of where to put the camera or was that also a source of diffidence?
Diffidence and fear. But it was also ignorance. I didn't even realize the camera position mattered. But I would have also had some quickness of wit: people like

me live on our wits. Also, an awful lot of photography is done out of necessity. If you're in a car there are a limited number of places you can put it.

Did you have much input in terms of the look of the film?
We had a very skilful designer. But I was so out of my depth. People would come up to me with four watches on their wrist and say, 'Which one do you want him to wear?' At the time I thought, Christ, I didn't know my job description included being able to tell you things like this! And I don't give a fuck, because in one sense it doesn't matter. Now I've learnt to say, you decide and I'll tell you if you've made the wrong decision.

It sounds like you were fairly happy to delegate?
Well, nothing's changed. And you delegate to talented people. I remember that when I made *Dangerous Liaisons*, a big step in my life, when I went back into the *Gumshoe* ring, as it were, big stars, big budgets, I worked with very, very clever people. It was about the eighteenth century and I thought, I know fuck all about the eighteenth century. One day the costume designer, who had quite a wicked sense of humour, said to me, 'Do you want this set in 1762 or 1760?' And I thought, you bugger! In the end I thought, I am not actually going to conduct this conversation. I will question you on what you're doing but I will just concentrate on the bits I can do. Actually, it often seems to me that the director is the most redundant person on a set. The technical people are very clever and they often don't need me. Likewise the actors will generally give good performances without the director. There's something going on that's much harder to grasp – which is what I try to do. I try to think about the bits that no one else is going to think about. And of course those bits aren't technical. It's really to do with the content, the overall thought, the sensibility of the film. That's quite exhausting enough so you end up just doing that.

Let's talk about the shoot. Was it easy to find locations, easy to make decisions?
There was all that business about the expense of shooting on location; they always want you to do as little as possible that involves people staying in hotels. So then you set about trying to find bits of London that look like Liverpool.

Can you remember how you felt when you were just about to start? Were you apprehensive?
No, it was all going too fast for me. I remember we started shooting in the working man's club, which was half full of real Liverpudlians. I dropped the highly sophisticated Albert who'd just been working with Audrey Hepburn, into the middle of this working man's club. Years later I made a film with Ian McKellen, *Walter*, where he played a disabled man. I cast a lot of eccentric actors to play disabled men. But after the first day I said, it's ridiculous, so I released the actors and left Ian in the middle of these disabled men. And, of course, it was monstrous of me but it was probably extremely good for him. It meant that he had to deal with

the whole thing on a highly realistic level. The same with Albert: I surrounded him with locals. Billy Dean, I remember. These were all guys that Ken Loach had found in working men's clubs and I was rather dazzled by what Ken was doing at the time. Billy's great in the film. He's very funny and he's absolutely truthful. But of course he hadn't been trained at RADA. So again there was a clash of two cultures which was very difficult.

Albert must have been amazed to find himself acting with these northern comedians, except that, of course, a part of him came from the same world. After he was in that, Billy Dean was in a film with Elizabeth Taylor. He was always very impressed to have been in scenes with Elizabeth Taylor.

Did you feel confident of your abilities?
No. All I had was originality. *Gumshoe* was a very, very original film. But I didn't see how original it was, because to me it was just what had been going on in my head for the last year since Neville had brought it to life. But, in fact, it's your originality that is really interesting. In a first film you can't help but be original. I suppose because I've turned out to be a film director I must have had some tenacity or obstinacy or cleverness so that the originality didn't get knocked out of me.

Do you think in this respect it was lucky that you hadn't done a BBC or Granada training course?
Yes and no. I think if I'd made the film at the BBC, Neville would have probably played the lead and it would have been made without those contradictions. The irony is that such an original project was made within such a conventional system. With *Gumshoe*, I was being original in a completely unsuitable place. In hindsight, we might have been better off making it within a less conventional system.

Did your newness to the process cause problems?
In those days the film industry in Britain was like a closed masonic world. You had to go into that world to make a film but actually all your ideas were opposed to it. It's like going into a feudal system to make an anti-feudal film. I imagine the crew saw me as very difficult, because I didn't know how to say 'this is what I want to do' and lay it all out for them. It's not a crime not to be experienced. But they were used to working with skilful, experienced people, that's all. I probably conducted myself in a rather sulky way, because I could feel the originality of what I was doing but I couldn't articulate it.

What were the implications of your inexperience in terms of how you worked i.e., coverage, set-ups etc?
Some scenes were done in one shot, with very little depth of focus, which rather shocked people. Also it puts a strain on the actor, because you need to do a lot of takes; whereas if you just stand an actor up against a wall, they do it and it's all about the performance. But we hadn't told anybody we were going to shoot in this elaborate way. It just sort of bubbled out of us because we didn't know any better.

And Chris was very influenced by people like Raoul Coutard in France. But of course, Coutard was shooting a different kind of film, and he wasn't shooting with big stars. So all this got into a terrible muddle. Albert kept saying, 'Why am I doing twenty takes?' The answer was that it was going out of focus at some point. But all the focus-puller knew was that if it was out of focus, he'd get sacked. Also, the scenes between Albert and Billie Whitelaw had very complicated camera move-ments where you wouldn't expect them. The production people expected the scene to be shot in a certain way and take a certain amount of time. But we would quite innocently drift into making a very complicated shot. Now I've learnt to deal with all of this. You say to your actors, 'Look, this is a very difficult shot. You'll need some patience with this.' Now I've learnt to allocate time: how much time you need to do certain things. If you want to do something complicated you'd better do something simple to make space.

How did you work with Chris on the shoot itself?
You'd work out a scene and Chris would say, it's rather good from over here and then we could come round here and then you'd start and before you know where you are you're building up this very, very complicated, rather interesting shot.

Based on a piece of action you've already arrived at with the actors?
Yes, in the normal way. However there was no one who could say 'don't be an idiot, shoot it like this' because, after all, I *was* the director. So we would take much longer to shoot things than had been allowed. As I said, no one could say to me, you've got to do it in a simple way because I didn't quite know I wasn't doing that anyway. I was just doing what Chris said. Well, this must have driven people bananas as we started to move the camera around and put chalk marks on the floor. They'd just think, this is going to take for ever, this shot, this simple scene.

Did this lead to any frayed tempers?
Yes. Because even though what you're shooting is of course rather interesting, you start spending more money than you should. So, yes, that caused trouble. Now I think about it, that was the main problem. Because I got behind. I started to go over budget. I started to go over schedule. Then people start asking, 'Why?' To make films, you have to be on top of the schedule, and I never really got on top of it. It wasn't *Heaven's Gate* or anything idiotic like that. It's just we took longer than we said we would and people were going to have to work longer hours than they'd expected to. So all those pressures started, and I wasn't clever enough to stop them.

What did Albert and Michael make of this?
I imagine it drove them bananas. It wasn't as if we were idiots. It was just that if you want to make an unconventional film then you do it over there. You don't make it in the middle of a conventional film. Nowadays the cameraman will say

to you, look, if we shoot what you're asking me to shoot, it will take five hours. Are you sure that's the decision you want to make? And I've learnt how to deal with all of that. But that's what I didn't know how to deal with on *Gumshoe*. All I knew was that, however inarticulate he was, what Chris was doing was more interesting than if we'd been trying to do it in the conventional way.

What was it like working in Liverpool?
There was a wonderful moment where the whole of the film industry was supposed to go on strike, and there was a meeting about whether the film crew should go on strike. And I, of course, supported the strike because politically I would – because that was what you did in those days. But if you were a director you weren't somehow supposed to get involved. You weren't supposed to have a political thought in your head. I think the film company must have brought pressure to bear and there was then a second meeting and the vote was changed.

Would you describe it as a fairly easy shoot in terms of the physical demands it imposed on you?
Well, we didn't have to go to the South Pole or climb Everest. As I've said, the main problem was my ignorance and inexperience. It wasn't much fun. I had no idea it was like this. It was just painful. Intellectual confusion is always painful. Confusion in your thinking leads to confusion in your actions and that has consequences. And these consequences were painful for me. I remember trying to sort out these private feelings while the film was galloping along like a racehorse. Nowadays I can enjoy the contradictions, let the film float, go with it, and be confident that it will resolve itself in the end. At that point, people wanted me to be clear. And I hadn't learnt to say, I'm not clear but it doesn't matter that I'm not clear. Let's still make the film!

Did the muddle in your head continue into post-production?
I started off cutting it with a young editor, Charles Rees, who was very clever, terribly nice and very bright and we just got into a sort of mess. In fact, we dubbed the film and finished it and then Karel Reisz saw the film and said this simply doesn't make sense. It's about somebody who lives in a sort of Walter Mitty-ish world. That means that you have to see a moment when he reacts to something, thinks, then enters his imaginative world. You have to see him *live* that moment. Well, we'd simply left that out. So intellectually it was ridiculous. Then a very experienced editor was brought in who cut it. I can remember him watching it and saying, there's a perfectly good film inside here.

So the new editor came along and sorted it out?
He just went bang, bang, bang and put in the right bits, and brought out the film that's there now. But it was as though the central idea of the film had been buried in the way we had edited it. We had somehow contradicted what we were trying to say. In other words, we'd failed to express the central idea. And in the end all

you really have is the central idea. And since the central idea is a rather wonderful idea I could never understand why people couldn't see the magic of the idea. Of course, we'd edited it in order to conceal it. I had edited the film to conceal what it was I was trying to say.

Why?
Whatever it was I was trying to express, I didn't want to be caught expressing it. The idea of self-expression was too frightening. Still is. I've learnt to live with it – I think. But I come from a middle-class professional family, I wasn't brought up in an atmosphere of self-expression. The woman I live with now is a painter, and she was brought up among paintings. Expressing herself is what she's done all her life. Well, nobody told me about expressing myself. When I eventually came to express myself, I felt embarrassed and as if I had no clothes on. So, of course, I put some clothes on. And this turned out to be a very elaborate exercise in deception. But I notice it with my students at the National Film School. They conceal things for all sorts of complicated, neurotic reasons. They'll shoot something and then they'll edit it in a completely different way. You ask them, 'Why?' Then they show you the rushes, and there's the whole scene laid out: exactly what they intended. But they completely suppressed it because they've got embarrassed.

Can you remember when Gumshoe *was first shown in public?*
It got absolutely wonderful reviews. I mean, reviews you'd shoot yourself for!

How old were you when you made it?
Twenty-nine – which in those days meant you were a prodigy. Now you'd be an old man.

Did you feel there was a lot at stake?
Not really. I was still too self-obsessed, too muddled to be ambitious. I was like a teenager dealing with acne or something. What really impresses me about some younger directors is that you can be young and clear-headed at the same time. That's what I notice: emotional clarity at an early age. That seems to me fantastic. It's what interests me in looking at people's work, really. 'Was the person making this clear-headed?'

What was Gumshoe's *impact on you in terms of future work?*
I don't think I was doing anything when it finished. I remember being asked if I'd make a film of *Steptoe and Son*. And then it opened in December a week after my mother died. Alan Bennett, who was a great friend of my wife, had written his first television film, which had been drifting around at the BBC. Eventually it found a producer. I went to see him on the Monday after the Sunday it had had these incredible reviews. By the time I arrived, they thought Orson Welles was arriving, somebody very substantial and impressive instead of this person full of uncertainties. By the time I arrived they would have given me anything. So I went to the BBC and began the process of pulling myself together.

You didn't have any sense that moving from cinema to television was a step backwards?
Getting into the BBC was by far the best thing I could have done, by far the most constructive. It added stability and continuity to my life. I was with people I was comfortable with. And I was allowed to develop at a much more realistic pace. These were golden days in a way. Success was less important. And I was ideally suited to it. So my feet started to settle on the ground and I started to learn my trade rather than dealing with these glamorous gods of the cinema.

What would you say were the main lessons you drew from the experience of Gumshoe?
You just take one foot down the road for the rest of your life, really. You just start. Of course it was painful. Look at any teenager and you can see what pain they're in. So it's just growing up. But what's good about the film – I mean, I still think Neville's script is wonderful – is that there's some spark, some originality there. Mercifully, it didn't get squashed, and I was alert to that in some untutored way.

Ken Loach: *Poor Cow*

When you were growing up, did you see a lot of movies?
Not particularly. I was more interested in the theatre. And in the early days, the fortunes of Nuneaton Borough football club. And then I got into theatre. I used to cycle to Stratford and sell programmes for the local repertory company which used to visit the Co-op hall in Nuneaton three days out of every three weeks.

How far back can you trace your interest in the theatre?
I suppose it was going to the grammar school. I was always first to put my name down for school plays. I guess I was stage-struck, like a lot of kids.

Was there any interest in the theatre in your family?
No. The radio was the big entertainment – or the wireless, as it was known. My father used to work seven days a week, Saturday mornings and Sunday mornings. When he got home he was pretty much knackered, so it was the radio and early to bed. But when we went on holiday, which, when I was young, was to Black-pool, we'd go to five or six shows in the week. My parents loved the variety shows with comics and singers and acts and all the rest – which I think barely exist now.

Did you have a moment of 'that's what I want to do' when you went to the theatre?
You didn't think like that, really. You just thought that belonged to some other world. It wasn't something kids from Nuneaton ever did.

What did kids from Nuneaton do?
Towns in those days were very self-sufficient places, unlike now. There was the usual round of solicitors and teachers and dentists and doctors and accountants. If you were lucky and went to the grammar school, then you might be one of those people, rather than a factory worker or a miner. It was still a mining area in those days.

So you acted when you were at school?
Yes. Though school plays are a very coarse form of acting.

But you got your hands dirty?
Oh yes. I thought of nothing else.

And when you got into Oxford, you continued this?
Yes. And through national service as well, which was two years, nearly as long as university. When I was in the RAF I was based in Nottingham and I lived out in Ely. I'd get a five-thirty bus back to the airbase having been in amateur shows. We

did one as a company in a huge aircraft carrier in Hereford. It's a bizarre thing to think about now.

Were you interested in politics yet?
Not at all. The *Daily Express* was the paper that would come into our house. That had Beaverbrook's politics, so if I absorbed any it would be those. And very little at Oxford, which I regret because there were some very sharp people there. Obviously you couldn't fail to absorb some politics, but I didn't really take an active part in it. There were such huge opportunities to see plays and to be in plays that that just absorbed all my energies. It was a very single-minded enthusiasm, which in a way was quite immature. I think we probably took a longer time to mature in those days.

Can you remember any particular theatrical triumphs at Oxford?
No, they were all various grades of disaster, I would think. It's something I would hate to revisit. But, you know, we tackled all the classics, with the effrontery of youth. In the second term I was in a production of *King Lear*, playing Kent. I don't know if it was any good but it was great to be in it. We did reviews, musicals, modern plays, everything.

Cinema wasn't on the agenda at this point?
There's always been a good cinema in Oxford in Walton Street, where I saw some films.

Nothing that made you think, 'I want to be a film-maker'?
Not at all.

What about the law? Was this gradually slipping away as a serious career option?
Yes. Again, Oxford could be very bad for people like me because productions got a lot of attention from the national press so you were flattered into thinking that you were better than you were. People had gone from university into the profession and I guess I had hopes of that. But I still ate dinners at Gray's Inn – that's what you did to be a law student. And then I didn't work hard enough at the law degree to know if I could have done it or not and in the end got a not very good degree and left and tried to do something in the theatre.

What happened after graduation?
My friend Bill Hays and I tried to form a theatre company in Bedford. I mean, a ludicrous venture, total lunacy! Then I got a job as an understudy in the West End, which made me feel ten feet tall.

That was in a Peter Cook revue?
Yes. Fortunately I didn't have to do anything much. Then I got a job as an assistant director in a rep company, which was very good because it meant putting on a show every two weeks. I did all the odd jobs and directed three plays, very badly. But nevertheless I was working with seasoned pros. That was very instructive, because it demystified the whole process. It made you a professional. In a way

you remained inexperienced at it but nevertheless after that I felt I was a pro rather than somebody who was messing round on the edge.

What were the main things it taught you?
How to be with people, really. What you could ask actors to do and what you couldn't. I found that out the hard way by asking them to do things that were totally inappropriate. So you'd get your knuckles rapped but in the nicest way.

Can you give me an example?
I remember I directed a farce, which I was totally ill-equipped to do because it's about arranging bits of business all the time. And I had it in my head that you had to have run-throughs so that the actors got a sense of the overall shape of the piece. This was before we'd worked out what the business should be that would get the laughs. And of course it ground to a halt. And finally the main actor said, 'We cannot do this. You're working the wrong way round.' And I was. I mean, they just taught me lessons. The same kind of lessons the *Z-Cars* actors taught me.

You then went on in 1963 to an assistant director traineeship at the BBC. How did that come about?
I was out of work for a time. I applied for everything. I applied for the BBC and got in. They were taking a lot of people from the theatre, which I still think is the best route – perhaps because I did it. But I feel it's a much better training ground than film school.

Why?
Because directors are responsible for what goes in front of the camera. You've got a cameraman who can teach you about shooting and you've got an editor who can teach about editing – and anyway in terms of editing, all you've got to do is watch films and see where they make the cuts. I mean, that's something you can do in your spare time. No one will teach you how to move actors around in a space and how they function. And that's actually what directors do. At seven o'clock in the morning the camera assistant will unload the camera, the sound recordist will get a mike out. You have to know what to say to the actors and if you don't know what to say, go home. And the theatre is where actors function. That's their space. When they come to a film set, all too often they're peripheral and all too often directors are afraid of them so they talk about something they feel comfortable with which is what's the light? What lens should we use? Or is it a wide shot or a close shot? Which is an escape really.

What were your first impressions of the BBC?
I was just glad of the wage-slip, after four years existing on biscuits. I hadn't had a decent wage-slip apart from the few months in the West End and I knew that was only temporary. I think I had a six-month contract at about a hundred pounds a week which in those days was a lot of money – when pies were three-pence. Quite soon afterwards I managed to get a mortgage on a small place.

What was the training like there?

You were given a general description of how the BBC functions. It was nothing to do with film-making; it was television-making. One morning, a television director, John Jacobs, came and addressed us on the subject of 'what to do with your cameras'. That was the sum total of technical training. I mean, in the studio you had three cameras. You'd have one doing wider shots and two doing closer shots. That's it. It's not difficult.

You first did a drama called Catherine, *which was how you met your future producer, Tony Garnett. What was that about?*

All I remember is that we did it in Manchester and I got through it somehow. It was a script by Roger Smith who was someone I knew at university and who's been a friend since then. We still work together.

You said that you learnt a lot from the actors on Z-Cars. *Can you elaborate?*

The good actors in *Z-Cars* understood how really good acting for the camera is about working at a conversational level and about behaving and responding. So from working in the theatre, where it's all about projection and pitch, pace and power and picking up the cues and all the rest, I suddenly saw a whole different way of working, a whole different way for actors to be. Again, I'm sure my work on it was crap. But the main actors, almost all of them, were very congenial, very helpful. I mean, one or two of them got a bit intolerant of young lads coming in who didn't really understand what they were doing, so they could be a bit intolerant and that was all right, that was probably no more than I deserved.

Were you starting to take an interest in the cinema by this stage?

No, that came in the mid-sixties when I started working with John McGrath and Troy Kennedy Martin. I'd done some television and I started to think how pictures go together. And it was the time of the French new wave where the styles of editing changed completely in an non-naturalistic way and the things that the French new wave were interested in was a talking point among the people interested in cinema. Troy wrote a piece in *Encore* about all that and then he and John McGrath wrote a six-part series, *Diary of a Young Man*, which incorporated some of their ideas. Again, I was lucky enough to direct three of those. That forced you to consider different ways of presenting a story, some of which were very modish, but the underlying ideas were always important, were always challenging, were always something you had to consider.

Can you remember any?

Only showing the audience what you want to show them. Don't get bound up with people getting in and out of cars and going in and out of rooms. It's tedious. Just show the audience what you want to show them. That was when there was a vogue for cutting things to music, using stills to tell a story. Some of that was really useful when we were doing things like *Up the Junction* and *Cathy Come*

Home. And then it became very much the preserve of commercials and they did it to death so you had to find a way of doing something else.

Let's talk about the Wednesday Play *period. They were very significant in terms of the subjects they covered. How did they differ from what had come before in terms of the way they were put together?*

I think that when people talk about it, they often miss the point. The point was not the style. The point was the substance. Why it was done. Everything was driven by the subjects they wanted to tackle, and by making drama out of the stuff of everyday life. It was about relating the struggles that people were experiencing and taking away from that sense of either high art or what was becoming the soap operas – basically actors walking about in sets talking about who was falling out with whom. So it was trying to take it away from that and to throw it out into the public arena: trying to say 'Look, this is going on; that is going on.' And to really capture the taste of people's experience and not just to do it as an impression but to draw political conclusions from it. The subtext was always, 'There's something wrong in the state.'

Do you think of it as a particularly formative period for you in terms of style and substance?

I think it was formative for everybody who was involved really because we were at that age to be formed. We were late twenties. And whatever you do at that age forms you. We were just lucky enough to have the opportunity, the equipment, the space and the air-time to try things out and, if we were lucky, have them communicated to half the population – which was extraordinary. It obviously wouldn't happen now because with the multiplicity of channels the audience is divided up. We were lucky to be there when there was a door to push open and fortunate enough to push it open.

You've talked elsewhere about your modus operandi as a film-maker, not using wide-angle lenses because of the distortions they impose on your characters, keeping the camera at a respectful distance from your characters, etc. Were these ideas already taking shape in what you were doing?

No. It's an old cliché but you only ever learn from your own mistakes. In *Diary of a Young Man*, for example, I remember we found ourselves in a situation and it seemed the only way out was to put on a very wide-angle lens. I remember being really horrified by the results and thinking well, I never want to do that again. I suppose I admired the Czech films of the time, which I much prefer to the French new wave, because they seemed to have an interest and a space for people, which in Godard just got silly and insulting in the end. In the best of the Czech films you came out with a warmth for people, which I like. Then you think, now technically how did they do that? And they're very simple films to take apart. This is why film schools are so overblown. You take one or two of those films and just sit through them and think, okay, where did they put the camera? What sort of lens is that?

Is the camera moving or is it allowing the people to move? And how does it affect me? How do I look at the people differently if the camera allows the people to do it rather than if the camera insists on whizzing around all the time? And what's a trick and what's a genuine attempt to elucidate something? I mean, it's very simple. You can see the answers as plain as a pikestaff. It's a simple business complicated by people with a living to make, really.

So you think film schools make too much of a virtue of technique rather than what the technique is there to serve?
Yes. They have a course to fill so you can't reduce it to its simplicity and then all go home. Which is what I think people should do. So the whole thing has to be elaborated: books have to be written, films have to be disinterred and argued over, people have to be criticized before they've done anything. And I think that's absolutely not the way to learn. Just go out and do whatever work you can and you'll find a way and make up your own principles because in the end that's what you have to do.

Do you think directing is something that can be learned? Or are great directors born rather than made?
The bones of it you can learn as a craft, like you can learn to be a carpenter or a plumber or fix the telephones. Film-making is like thinking laterally, really. It's just shaking the kaleidoscope up so that the patterns fall differently.

But that doesn't mean you'll make great films?
No, because there needs to be a degree of originality in every film. I mean, there needs to be, but there isn't, obviously.

You're very much identified with naturalism or 'critical realism` as it's been called. Is this something you've always identified with?
I used to go along to Stratford-upon-Avon and see John Gielgud and Olivier and fall under their theatrical spell. But I think film is a different medium. You can see behind what an actor's doing. You can see right to the back wall, as it were: the actor's mind. When I started doing television, that dawned on me within a year or two. So after that, you're very aware that what you're filming, as far as what's in front of the camera, should be true, should be authentic. But that you can put it together in a way that is quite unrealistic or surreal, or juxtaposes images that you want the audience to see as a conscious juxtaposition. I think this again is where there is a lot of confusion when people talk about naturalism or realism. They don't differentiate between what you photograph and how you assemble it. You can photograph something that is real or looks real, has the sense or taste of being true or real and you can assemble it in a way that's quite unnaturalistic and unrealistic and that's one thing. But people talk about realism in a way where under the excuse of wanting something to be stylized, they just get people to overact. That's not stylized acting, that's overacting.

Does your identification with naturalism extend to your tastes as a viewer? Are you very catholic in your tastes as a viewer?

I'm not very catholic as regards films, no. I am in other things but not in films. I've never been a cineaste, really. If you're pursuing your own way of doing things you have to keep refining it and defining it, holding it up and scrutinizing it, rejecting some things and trying to move on. If you're doing that, it's difficult to have a wide taste at the same time because the two things are in conflict. You're thinking all the time, I don't want to do that, I want to do that.

Let's talk about Poor Cow. *How did the idea of turning Nell Dunn's book into a film come about?*

Its birth was rather unfortunate in a way. I'd worked with Nell on *Up the Junction* and then I'd worked with her husband, Jeremy Sandford, on *Cathy Come Home*. And I'd worked with the producer Tony Garnett on both *Up the Junction* and *Cathy Come Home*. We were very much a partnership and I relied on Tony a great deal. I then got an offer from Joe Janni to do two films and at the same time Nell's agent was contacted by Joe for her new book. Joe had a great eye for the contemporary mood so because the television films had been quite successful and a scandal and all the rest, he thought this was something he wanted to get involved in. Obviously I liked the idea of making a feature film and also wanted to work with Nell again. I tried to include Tony in the process but failed. Joe initially talked a great deal about working with Tony then when it came to it, as was his way, put all sorts of obstacles in his way and made it impossible for him to be involved. By which time I was committed. But I've always felt that I should have pulled out. It's something I've always regretted.

Because of your loyalty to Tony?

Yes, and not only that. We could have done it together and it would have been a better film. The other key element in setting it up was Carol White who'd been in *Up the Junction* and *Cathy* and who was someone who was just emerging, very talented; people responded to her.

How did you first find her?

I auditioned her for *Up the Junction*. She was a Hammersmith girl. Or Fulham. Very ordinary girl, nice girl.

Did Joe Janni put all the money together?

Yes. That was something I never knew about really. He'd done a whole series of successful films without understanding any of them, I think. As I got to know him it became plain that he didn't understand a word of it, as far as I could see. Others would speak differently. But I found him a very difficult man to deal with because he was one of those people who didn't actually listen to what you said. He had an idea in his head and he would pursue it.

You're credited on the film as co-screenwriter along with Nell. How did that work?

From what I remember the book is very cinematic, as is all Nell's work. It was written in that particular style she's got which I liked a lot, which is fragments and moments put together. So really I just took the book and tried to make the screenplay match the rhythms of what I thought a film should be rather than the rhythms of what I thought a book should be.

It felt very real. Did the characters in it, Tom, Dave, Joy, have real life counterparts?
No. I think they were fictional creations. But obviously Nell had people in mind for two or three people.

You had a very interesting mix of professional and non-professional actors in the film, including Carol White, John Bindon and Terence Stamp. How did you go about casting?
Obviously, Carol was part of the thing at the beginning. Nell and I imagined her in it from the start. At the same time I was very much trying to find authentic people to be in it. I'd just go round looking, meet people, just make contacts. John Bindon was very much part of that. There was a lad who I had in mind for the part of Dave. But Joe wanted a bigger name and I lost out on that. I think we met Albert Finney for the part of Dave. Joe didn't appreciate that Albert Finney is from Salford and this was set in London. He wouldn't notice things like that. So we went with Terry Stamp who was always very pleasant and worked very hard. But I think it gave it the aura of a film rather than something I had in my mind which was something grainier. Terry Stamp was well known and his face was known, so inevitably that meant it became a feature film.

What was John Bindon's background?
I think he was involved in various kinds of villainy. He's dead now. As is Carol, sadly.

What happened to her?
I think she got into very dodgy company. People exploited her. She was a very pretty girl and I think people just ripped her off. She was married to Mike King who was a very nice guy and that didn't last and I think all this wealth and apparent glamour was just too much. She did some parts that she was unsuitable for. What she had was very special, and very particular to her. She could be very touching, very sharp and very bright, very funny, excellent. But she was very vulnerable to people flattering her and telling her she was going to be the next big star.

Like the character she plays, Joy?
Yes. She was quite close to Joy. But the sad thing was that she'd lost it a bit by then. I think *Up the Junction* and *Cathy Come Home* were her best work. And when she was doing *Poor Cow* she'd had a lot of notice obviously with the other two. And she was getting offers for films. Stupidly, I agreed that she could do another film that overlapped with ours, *I'll Never Forget What's 'is Name*, which

she was desperate to do because she wanted to look pretty on the screen. The sad thing that people don't understand is that if they look pretty they'll look pretty whatever they do to their hair. But she did it and they were sending a big car for her and I was saying go home on the Tube. They were treating her with all that stupid flattery and nonsense that destroys people. So in the process of making the film you could see her start to go.

How did you work with your DP, Brian Probyn?
Brian had shot a film I'd done called *The End of Arthur's Marriage*. And we talked about how to get various effects, how to make it not look like a film. And he did all kinds of things in trying that, we tried to desaturate the colour, he would sprinkle talcum powder into the air to try to thicken the atmosphere, this was even before smoke guns. So he tried all kinds of things. He was very nice but the production company put him under a huge amount of pressure. They gave him a crew, which apart from Chris Menges was mainly old feature people, and they, by and large, didn't understand what he was trying to do and he got very impatient with them, so there was a kind of split in the crew. It was very valuable for me to meet Chris, and Brian and Chris worked well. There was that and then there was like a shadow crew and they didn't understand what was going on. The lights weren't big enough for them. It was this old-fashioned macho film crew business. Again, you learn from your mistakes. I vowed that I would never have that again and I never have.

This was also a result of having Joe Janni as your producer?
Yes. Half the crew or a third of the crew I'd brought from television and the others were from old-fashioned feature films.

What was the difference?
A whole different attitude, a whole different way of working. Brian was a documentarist, Chris was a documentarist. You went into a place to learn from it. The standard feature-film crew goes into a place to remove all traces of it, to obliterate it. So the idea of observing something was something they didn't actually understand. I got on with everybody personally, but that was the training they came in with. Also there was a production manager who was put in by Joe to make sure that no one ripped the film off. So this immediate them-and-us attitude sprang up. He'd be sniffing around like a robber's dog, trying to find out who's doing what? what's going on? Not trying to understand or contribute to what the film was about but seeing it as an industrial process where he had to stop people skiving all the time. I remember we had big battles about whether we could have an extra lens or whether it was too expensive or not. But you'd find the production car would be taking the producer's wife shopping at Harrods. So there were all these double standards the whole time which made me very unhappy. And I'm sure I made lots of mistakes because it was the first film I'd done and I felt quite overwhelmed by the scale of what was presented.

Were you confident as a director by this point? When you visited locations did you have a clear sense of how a scene would work, where you'd place the camera, the lens you'd use?

Not to that extent. But I was learning. I think if I'd done it on 16 mm, it would have been a much better film, because I would have done it with confidence. I'd done quite a lot of 16 mm films by that stage. But the main point was, why do we want to do the film? We want to do the film because it was these character sketches of this group of people and it was about talent and hope and wit and appetite for life which went into crime, and led to all this dissatisfaction. Why were people like that? Why did that happen? What was redeeming about them? What was sad about them? What was brutal about them? And how did that affect their relationships? This was the substance of the film. But that tended to get steam-rollered out by the conflict of this industrial process. Joe had no sense of that and that was the pity, and in the end that's why I regret having done it the way I did instead of Tony and I doing it together.

What was it like filming in London in the late sixties with a big film crew?

Nowadays film crews have a different attitude. But at the time it was a very unreconstructed attitude that film crews had – barge in and own the place. The worst example of that was when we were filming in the Elephant and Castle in an old Peabody Buildings flat. When we chose the location and started to film, the deal I did with Carol was that there was no trailers. No nonsense about special treatment. We'll do it like we did the others. We'll just turn up, stand around and all do it together. With Carol that was fine. Why shouldn't it be? But I think, as was normal, Terry Stamp's agent insisted on a caravan. There was a kerfuffle outside. I looked out of the window and there was this bloody caravan being inched into the Peabody Buildings. Then Carol got very upset and said, I'm not being treated fairly. She got on to her agent and her agent demanded she had one too, so then another caravan had to be found. The whole thing escalated just because the producer hadn't talked properly to the actors. I'm sure if Terry Stamp had been approached properly there wouldn't have been a problem. I don't blame him. I blame the producer failing to do his job.

What level of preparation did you undertake for the film?

I think I did it on the back of an envelope like I usually do.

Did you have a sense it was an important moment for you, careerwise?

I didn't feel it was any more important than *Cathy Come Home*. Or *Up the Junction* in a way, because I felt more in touch with what I was doing then.

What were your impressions when you arrived on set? Did you feel prepared by what you'd done before? Did you feel confident.

I didn't feel confident at all. But I never feel very confident.

Did you have a sense you were having to work very fast?

It was the most frustrating film because you were always waiting; the unit didn't work well together. There was that constant dislocation where people don't quite know what's expected of them. They start doing the job in the way they're accustomed to and then find it's not what other people wanted. I had a sense it was going to be people from different traditions but didn't know how to overcome that division. There was this constant power battle going between what I, Brian and Chris were wanting to do and what the production office were expecting. They were constantly supplying things we didn't need and not supplying things we did need. And I wasn't experienced enough to be clear enough as to what we wanted. So that's why it didn't function.

In terms of directing actors did you feel at ease?
Sometimes. And sometimes the rest of what was going on got in the way. It wasn't a particularly complex thing, we weren't spending all day evolving stratagems to get my way. It was just like constantly, oh, they haven't done that. Shit, they've done something else instead. We don't want to have a catering wagon there because we want to have a shot of the street and nobody will come within a mile of it. Just obvious things that the normal film crew would not be surprised by but I was surprised because it drove all the life out of the area we were trying to film. It was something that if Tony had been producing, we would have worked it out together. But when you have this big machine producing it they were oblivious of it and they didn't realize they were putting their fist through the cobweb.

What was the schedule like?
We were scheduled to shoot for eight weeks and we actually shot for twelve, which was disastrous. We overran the shooting schedule, just because the thing was badly organized, and because I lost control of it. It was the only film where I didn't feel I was on top of the situation. I really ran out of steam I think.

What made it last so long?
Cock-ups. We went to Wales, which we probably needn't have done in the end. We'd chosen a location which the caravans couldn't get to so we got there and waited for them to come. They then turned back and we had to find a new location. Stupid things. Because people were pulling in opposite directions. Not that anybody was malicious or unprofessional or bad in any way. It was just the structure was wrong. With hindsight you could see that was bound to happen. From then on, I've cast everyone on the film with as much care as the leading actor.

You mean you cast the crew as much as the actors?
Absolutely. The other lesson was if you have a disagreement on set that affects the actors.

Was Joe Janni around?
He'd come at lunchtime and go into Carol's caravan and complain about something. Again, it was a misunderstanding, I think.

What do you think he thought you were doing?
I don't think he knew. I think he had a sense that London was the place to be. That things that had come out of television were the thing to do and if it could somehow be made into a feature film that would be the best of all worlds. But he didn't actually have a sense of what it was. His instinct wasn't operating. And then, I'd done a two-picture deal. The other film was going to be *Flight Into Camden* by David Storey. And he didn't want to do that after we'd agreed to do it. I wanted to do it very much. It was about a couple who come to London from Yorkshire. He'd done *A Kind of Loving* and *Billy Liar* and there'd been all the other northern films, and he said the north is finished now. And I said it's still there, Joe. He said it was a fashionable period that was over. The fashionable thing was now London and miniskirts and all the rest. And that was where we parted company. But he could be very generous, he could be very genial. But he was also somebody who thrived on rows and I don't. He'd come in and be quite happy to shout for five minutes and for me to shout back and then he'd smile. I can't be dealing with that. Some people can. But I'm finished for the day, for the week. I feel demeaned and belittled, I want to go away and die. He couldn't quite understand that.

What was hardest about the film for you as a first-time director?
I think there were too many unassimilated influences in it. I got hooked on this idea that you should try not to cut unless there was a cut in time so that every shot was real time. Sometimes that happened and sometimes I didn't take the covering shots so that when in the cutting room we found that didn't work, I didn't have a shot to cut back to. So that was a silly, obvious lesson.

Any other major mistakes?
I think the structure and the pace of the film aren't very good. I think there would be moments that worked but I just feel I didn't structure them right so they became just moments rather than an overall film. I think there'd be moments you'd be quite pleased with and moments you'd want to hide your head.

What do you like about it?
I think my views of it are coloured by hindsight. I think Nell's book was really nice and I have a great respect for her as a writer. She's very original and very precise and talented. She's very sweet and I liked her and I liked her book. And I think Carol's character comes over quite well. I think it has a taste of the times, which at least was something. The music was quite nice. There were lots of little ideas in it that worked quite well.

What did you feel when you saw the first cut?
You're bemused by then. You don't think anything. I mean, I sit there all the time so nothing ever takes you by surprise.

What was the public reaction to the film?

It was quite good. The person who bought it for America paid a lot of money and also I think wanted to get his hands on Carol so that made everybody over here think it was a huge success because they got all this money.

Nevertheless, you went back to working in television.
Yes. Mightily relieved I think. Lots of good things came out of it. One good thing that came out of it was working with Chris Menges because he did the next film, *Kes*.

When you're directing a film now and you think back to your first film, do you think the two processes are very different?
The thing that doesn't change, which is for me the most daunting thing about doing a film, is that you know that you have to wind yourself up into a state of hyperactivity which is not your natural state, certainly not for me. You just have to psyche yourself up for it, like a footballer before a game.

I imagine you had to do that for Poor Cow *just as much as now?*
More so. Because the weight of the crew and the expectation and the whole machine was much heavier. At the opposite extreme if you go out with a small crew in one car to make a documentary you can almost go out, get in the car and go and start. That's just good fun. But the bigger the circus you take the less fun it becomes. And so that was the least fun of anything I've done, the least enjoyable just because the weight of the whole unit was so daunting. Fifty to a hundred people, as opposed to fifteen or twenty at the BBC.

It feels very much of its time, especially the Donovan music on the soundtrack while Joy and Dave are kissing under the waterfall surrounded by the Welsh countryside.
Maybe I'd be surprised if I saw it again. Maybe it's not as bad as I think it is. Then again, I'm sure some of it is absolutely indescribable.

Mike Leigh: *Bleak Moments*

Did you go to movies when you were growing up in Salford? Were you a movie fan from a young age?

Yes, very much so. I grew up in the forties and fifties when there were still lots of small cinemas everywhere so I went to the pictures all the time. Virtually everything I saw was English or American. There was a cinema on almost every street corner and you could walk to ten or twelve of them from where I lived. They all showed different films – not like today – and there were always two films to a programme, the main feature and the supporting 'B'-picture, with a change of programme midweek, and two different programmes on Sunday. So if they'd let you, or if you could afford it, you could see a lot of films! Virtually everything I saw was English or American. So I was aware of films from an early age. The first film I ever saw – and I can clearly remember the experience – was Disney's *Pinocchio* in about 1946. I think the first moment I was conscious of wanting to make films was at my grandfather's funeral when I was twelve. It was a cold winter's day – thick snow – and while the coffin was being carried awkwardly down the stairs by these old Jewish guys – one had a drip on the end of his nose – I remember thinking, you could film this, this could make a great film. The nearest I've ever got to actually making that film was *The Kiss of Death* in 1976, the one about the undertaker's assistant.

You said you saw American and British films. Can you give me any examples?

You name it. Anything and everything. For example, I remember seeing *The Tales of Hoffman* and *The Red Shoes*. At the time, we weren't going around talking about Powell and Pressburger; they were just films. It was a while before I really became aware of directors, as such. I mean, I saw all the John Ford westerns without particularly thinking that's what they were. Probably the first film I saw where I was aware of the director was Chaplin's *Limelight*, but then I was far too busy falling passionately in love with Claire Bloom – at the tender age of nine! – to be concerned with Chaplin. And if I really wanted to be anybody in the movies at that time, it was Charles Laughton – *Hobson's Choice* and *Abbott and Costello Meet Captain Kidd* particularly spring to mind. The film that was seminally important in terms of connecting my real, everyday life to my ambitions as a fledgling film-maker was *Room at the Top*, but by that time I was fifteen. It was very exciting and remarkable to go to the Rialto cinema in Great Cheetham Street, Salford 7, and watch a film where you saw on the screen the world that was actually going on right outside in the street. It resonated with the sense I had developed of wanting to make real-life films where the characters were like we really are – films about the world we were actually in. Of course this impulse was going on in lots of film-makers worldwide, but I didn't know that at the time. I'd never heard of de Sica in the late fifties, and how could I know that the Nouvelle Vague guys were on the case? I never saw a French film till 1960, apart from the hideous *Red Balloon* and *Rififi*, which only got a commercial release in the provinces because it's got that long sequence where nobody speaks.

What happened when you left school?
By the time I got to the end of Salford Grammar, it was plain that I wasn't academic, and besides, I knew I wanted to make films. I fetched up dropping out of school and getting a scholarship to RADA, where I trained as an actor. I was then an actor for a year or so. I played very small parts in mediocre films by Michael Winner and Roy Ward Baker, and I was a deaf mute on a barge in a *Maigret* episode. I then went to art school – I did a very good foundation course at Camberwell, while simultaneously going to the London International Film School, or the London School of Film Technique, as it was called at the time, on the night course. Then I did theatre design for a year at the Central School of Art.

When you won your scholarship to RADA, were you thinking somewhere in the back of your mind that you wanted to be involved in films?
Absolutely. Unequivocally. I knew that I wanted to make films, full stop. I didn't want to be an actor, I wanted to be a film director. And I wanted to write my own films. I had been writing all sorts of stuff from an early age, including my own ground-breaking production of *Muddled Magic* at North Grecian County Primary School in Coronation year!

So why did you go to RADA, as a matter of interest?
Because I figured, correctly as it turned out, that learning about acting would be a very useful thing to do, and also it was something that was simply available to me at the time. There were no film courses, apart from the London School of Film Technique, and I didn't really know about that. But I was desperate to get out of Manchester, which was a dreary, dead place in the late fifties – not like the vibrant buzzing Mecca it is today! – and the prospect of RADA was positively exotic. So in a sort of a quirky, spontaneous way, I applied to drama school with no real moral support from anybody and got this scholarship. As it turned out, RADA was a mixed thing, a somewhat sterile experience in some ways, but seminal and fantastically useful nonetheless, and the foundations were laid for many things that have happened since. By that, I mean that I spent two years reacting against old-fashioned acting and rehearsal methods and conventions, and in a rudimentary way, started to formulate sort of notions that led to my work over the years. What d'you do as a kid, as a late teenager who wants to go into films? Nowadays, it's not extraordinary but in 1960 it was fairly wanky, really. In the provincial, suburban post-war world that I came from, nobody was a film-

maker! It was pretentious. So the reaction was 'How dare he?', basically.

What happened when you arrived in London? You've talked elsewhere about discovering film-makers like Satyajit Ray, films like Shadows *by Cassavetes.*
Everything was going on, you know. In no time at all, I was discovering international cinema, the NFT, early cinema, Renoir, Fellini, everything in the Italian cinema, the Russians, the Japanese. All the stuff you couldn't see elsewhere. The Nouvelle Vague. It was just a huge revelation and very exciting.

And you saw everything you could?
Yes, absolutely. Relentlessly and passionately. That's what the first half of the sixties was about for me. Drama school, art school, film school and watching movies. Then there was this moment in 1965 when I got offered two jobs simultaneously. One was to go and be assistant director and run acting workshops at the new Midlands Art Centre in Birmingham. The other was to work as a runner for Bob Godfrey, the animator, at his Biograph company. It was a terrible dichotomy. Film versus theatre! A crisis decision, because to be a runner in films, to be in Soho, where film-making was happening, was immensely attractive for ten pounds a week. And, as a cartoonist, I was still potentially interested in animation. And Birmingham wasn't attractive. Not in the least! Yet somehow to experiment and run workshops with actors seemed to be what I should be doing, so I opted for that and it was probably the right decision. In fact I'm sure it was the right decision because fuck knows where it might have led if I'd done the other thing! It was in Birmingham that I began to make improvised plays, and I suspect that if I hadn't had the freedom to do that there, it might have been impossible to do it anywhere else.

What happened when you left RADA?
Almost straight away I got this job on *Two Left Feet*, a film directed by Roy Ward Baker with Nyree Dawn Porter, Michael Crawford, David Hemmings and Julia Foster. I had a very small part – I only spoke in two scenes! – but he cropped up frequently so I used to go to Shepperton every day, whether they called me or not. It was just fantastic. I mean, I didn't much care about the film itself, to be honest. But it was an amazing ten weeks spent on a picture, and it was incredibly educational. I did that and some other film and television work, as I've said. So by the time I went to the film school about eighteen months later, I'd already got some sense of film-making from being on shoots as an actor.

Did you continue to want to be a film-maker throughout the sixties?
Of course. As far as I was concerned, I was a film-maker! I did this evening film course for thirty-six quid and immediately twigged on that you could go there whenever you wanted – not just in the evenings – because they were happy that you were keen. So I actually crammed my time with Camberwell and the film school, where there was this extraordinary Turkish student called Biltin Toker. He

ran something called 'Meanwhile', the London School of Film Technique Film Society. He was a real hustler. The minute he heard that a film-making celebrity was in town, he invited them to the school, showed one or two of their films, presented them with an honorary diploma, and got them to do a Q&A. We had Renoir, Hitchcock, Fritz Lang, John Huston, Alexander Mackendrick, Blake Edwards, Raoul Coutard, Dmitri Tiomkin – loads of people. It was extraordinary!

Did you make any short films at the school?
Yes, sure. The course at the school was very practical. You made a film where everybody directed a bit and then one where one person wrote and directed the whole thing. Mine was a silent movie about a dishevelled guy getting up and struggling round an extremely grotty room and frying an egg. That was the first learning experience; plus Toker's endless screenings. It was all a very rich film experience. There was theatre as well, but for me it was primarily about film-making. I mean, I was very inspired and indeed influenced by Peter Brook: his *Lear* and Marat/Sade, and also his Artaud experiments, all with the Royal Shakespeare Company, where I later worked myself in 1967 to 1968 and 1974. They involved real investigation and improvisation; they were extraordinary.

How did the play from which Bleak Moments *was adapted come about?*
Charles Marowitz ran the Open Space Theatre in Tottenham Court Road. By 1970 he was famous for some pretty arty 'improvisational experimental theatre' – he'd even assisted Brook on the aforementioned *King Lear*. I got him to let me do this late-night piece that was to become the prototype for *Bleak Moments* – which was what it was called. Marowitz hated it. He had an abhorrence for what he saw as naturalism, which it wasn't, but that's how he saw it. To him 'experimental' meant shows that were self-conscious and avant-garde in an obvious, self-regarding way. So he loathed it anyhow. But on top of that, it so happened that he'd got the screening rights to Andy Warhol's controversial film *Flesh* – the only time the Open Space operated as a cinema. It had caused something of a stir, and the Lords had given it a special London licence. Marowitz wanted to screen it all round the clock, and we were performing at eleven p.m. So he wanted to get rid of us. But I said, 'No, you've given us this slot', and we stayed for the agreed three weeks. He was very pissed off. When we finally left, the film played to raincoats queuing all the way to King's Cross: people like the occasional person who went to see *Naked* for all the wrong reasons!

How did you cast the play? Did you know your actors already?
Pretty much, yes. I cast it empirically, really.

What do you mean 'empirically'?
I mean, quite literally, intuitively – on hunches. The way I've cast ever since. Annie Raitt I knew from the Victoria Theatre-in-the-round at Stoke-on-Trent where I'd acted and done some directing; Joolia Cappleman I'd met in an acting

workshop I ran, and in fact went out with for quite a long time. Sarah Stephenson I'd worked with on *Individual Fruit Pies*, an improvised play I'd done at E15 Acting School; and Mike Bradwell had also been my student there. And somebody suggested Eric Allan, who'd just been working with Peter Brook at the RSC, particularly on the anti-Vietnam War play, *US*. Nowadays, of course, it takes me a long time to get through a fraction of the people who want to work on my films. But in those days to persuade five talented professionals to be in something for nothing when you didn't know what it was going to be, and there was no script, was quite something. And the play was put together in three weeks.

Can you tell me a little about how the play evolved?
I evolved it in the same basic way that I still work today. I created the characters, working individually with the actors, and then built the play through a lot of improvisation and, I guess, inspiration. The central events were the same as the film, but it all took place in Sylvia's living room. The main thing, of course, was the relationships.

Did your way of working ever cause problems with actors used to working from a script?
Yes. When I started casting, I wanted an old actor, and Thelma Holt who ran the Open Space with Marowitz said, 'Try "Mad George Coulouris".' So I did. By this time, Coulouris must have been about sixty-eight. He'd been to Hollywood in the thirties and was in all sorts of stuff, most famously *Citizen Kane*, in which he played Thatcher the lawyer. I went to see him in his cottage in the Vale of Health in Hampstead, and he said, 'Oh, this is fantastic, wonderful. I've always wanted to do this kind of thing. Experimental!' So we embarked on it and he lasted four days. Then he lost it. I was about to talk to him, and then he didn't show up and sent me a note saying he couldn't do it, and didn't agree with my approach. My sort of stuff works for some actors and not for others. It involves meticulous material, very subtle, patient, introspective, truthful, and with a necessary sophisticated sense of humour to make it happen. George wasn't on that wavelength, bless him. So he was out. He would have been Sylvia's and Hilda's father.

How did the play lead to the film?
A seminal force kicking around at that time was the team of Tony Garnett and Ken Loach. We're talking about 1970 – they'd done *Family Life* and a number of memorable television films, including *Cathy Come Home*. I got hold of Tony Garnett's phone number, phoned him up and said, 'Please come and see this play.' He hates plays, as I soon discovered – always a healthy sign. But he came to see it and said, 'Fantastic. You're really good. You've got to make films.' I went back to his pad in Notting Hill and was there till three in the morning, just talking about what I'd been doing and wanted to do, et cetera, and getting all this encouragement from him. At that time I had already been turned down twice by the BBC directors course. I remember sitting there with this terrifying board ask-

ing, 'How would you do this?' And I said, 'Well, I'd get actors and I'd rehearse for a couple of months, and then I'd go out and define the film by making it up as I went along, shooting it on location.' And icicles formed in the room . . . I told Tony this, and he said, 'We've got to do something.' And before too long he was on the case, and after the film of *Bleak Moments* he gave me my first break at the BBC, where he and I made *Hard Labour*.

Anyway, Tony was so encouraging that Les Blair and myself were really motivated to get on with trying to set up a film version. I'd grown up and gone to school with Les and when I'd put on the play at the Open Space, he'd brought along a cinematographer called Bahram Manocheri to take production photos, and we all agreed that there was a film in it. Les had said, 'Let's collaborate.' He would produce and edit. So we formed Autumn Productions and set about looking for backing. Bruce Beresford, who was running the BFI production board at the time, saw the play and was very encouraging. But by the time it all happened, he'd moved on and been replaced. But we needed to have the film accepted as a BFI Production Board job because there was an agreement with the film union, the ACTT, that as an experimental film you could pay people a special low rate. So the BFI merely put in the hundred pounds which was the minimum it could put into a production under this experimental scheme. The rest came from Albert Finney. He put up fourteen thousand pounds although it ended up costing eighteen thousand five hundred. Tony came to see it and quietly persuaded Albert to see us through to the end. Albert was immensely supportive throughout and he never interfered with it.

Were you at all anxious about turning a play into a film?
The idea that this material could and should be a film had occurred to me during the rehearsals for the play, when we were working on the bit when Hilda comes back and hears Norman playing his guitar in the garage. My only reservation was that I'd always regarded films and plays as two separate things. I still do. But at this point I thought, 'I've got to do this. It's a golden opportunity.' Apart from anything else, here was a narrative I could actually describe – at least we could say what it was about, because normally my problem was – and has been ever since – that I could never say what the film was going to be. The usual premise was, there's no idea I can talk about yet, and no script – just hand over the dosh! Over the years I've been lucky and people have given me the money and trust, and, except for once, a film has always materialized and it's been a surprise. But at least on this occasion we could be concrete and tangible about it. But it did just feel like a really good idea for a movie.

Was raising the money a struggle? Did it take a lot of effort?
Bruce Beresford suggested that Memorial Enterprises would be a possibility because Albert Finney and Michael Medwin were very much up for this sort of thing. They'd done the Tony Scott film *In Loving Memory* and then Stephen

Frears's *Gumshoe*. By the time that was shooting, we were under consideration for *Bleak Moments*. We went to see Albert and talked about it. Then I remember we had to go and see Michael Medwin at Lee International Studios when they were shooting the Aquarius bookshop scene with Maureen Lipman. They really took a risk. I mean, they could have been backing a complete turkey. There was no real evidence other than one's apparent track record and enthusiasm and apparent CV, not even a track record, particularly, because I'd done very little work that had been reviewed anywhere at that time. So they just went on a hunch. I don't think it took them very long to decide. We were just very lucky.

The orthodox method of raising money is that you have a script, and you give the script to the people with the money. Can you remember how you sold it, how you described it?
I sat in the room and described in a simple, straightforward way what the play was and how, in principle, one would open it up into a film. That is what happened. What is remarkable in the grander history of film backing is that they went for it! They're pretty special guys, let's face it.

To my mind, one of the film's major themes is a crippling inability to communicate, what might be described as a peculiarly English brand of social embarrassment. Is that how you would have described it? Is it how you saw England at that time?
The answer to the first question is yes. It's a film about non-communication, in fact a film which puts somebody who simply cannot communicate, Sylvia's sister, Hilda, amongst others who should be able to, but can't. In some ways Hilda was communicating in the most honest and direct way of any of them. So, yes, it was very much about the pain of sharing and communicating and being able to articulate and be honest. As for the question about how I saw England at the time, that's a difficult one, for a number of reasons. It's difficult because it was very much an emotional and intuitive piece. Even when I'm being more didactic, for example in *Meantime, Four Days in July* or *High Hopes*, I nevertheless make very subjective and emotional films. So it's hard to talk about what I was doing in terms of seeing England like that because it wasn't a conscious statement about England as such. Another thing that I think is terribly important is that the film was made on the cusp of the sixties and seventies. In the late fifties, it was perfectly respectable for anyone who wanted to be an artist to say, 'I'm apolitical, I'm an artist.' By the end of the sixties we'd all been politicized, and very properly so. So here's a film that is both subjective and heightened realism, but at the same time operates through a kind of detachment and very highly distilled sort of alienation. I'm cautious about too easy an analysis of it in terms of a blow by blow critique of English or British society. I think the lack of communication, the kind of pain and loneliness and isolation, that it's about is probably not an exclusively English thing and that's why it's been quite successful elsewhere.

So what you're saying is about those characters as opposed to a statement of some general kind?

Of course it's a statement about us, the way we live. But it makes its point through the characters and relationships and atmospheres, implicitly. And it is a tragi-comedy.

You've talked a little about your method of working. Was there any difference between working with the actors on the play and working with them on the film?

Not at all. The point of the process is to bring the characters into existence. Once you've got them they can go anywhere. So really all we did when we came to the rehearsals about a year after the play was to reactivate the thing, which was fantastically easy. They all put on the costumes and got into character and we picked up where we left off. The interesting thing was introducing various other characters and building the thing in various directions. I spent a lot of time casting. That's when I found Liz Smith who'd not been working for years. She did that extraordinary mother. A wonderful guy, Ronald Eng, was the waiter. He was a Singaporean ex-medical student who'd come to London and worked as a waiter whilst he did his training. I always get people to talk about people they know so we can find a starting point for the character. He talked about this guy who'd been a waiter in this Chinese restaurant where he'd worked. He'd done nothing but whinge about his ailments the whole time because he knew Ronald was a medical student.

The meal in the Chinese restaurant has to rank among the most dismal date scenes in the history of the cinema!

Absolutely. For me it was deliciously autobiographical in some areas. You know, failed relationships and things. In the play they had gone out and come back and in the film you see where they go – to the Chinese restaurant. Or you see Pat's mum or Norman in his garage twanging away on his guitar. And then you have Joolia Cappleman who really is a wonderfully idiosyncratic character actor. I think you can physically feel the tension in the air in the scene when she creeps into the room and happens upon Peter standing there.

You've talked about creating the character with the actor using some circumstance or person the actor knows. How do you see your role at this stage in the process?

My role in the first and last place is that I'm the storyteller. If I say that I ask the actor to come up with somebody that they know and then I create the narrative, that doesn't really explain how it works. What I used to do in those days was give the actor a sort of specification and say it's this sort of a character, maybe a little introspective or whatever, can you think of as many people as possible that this would suggest. And they would then talk about a small number of people, and I'd pick one for us to use as the basis of the character. I don't usually give a specification these days, though obviously I had to on *Topsy-Turvy*. When I worked with David Thewlis on the central character of *Naked*, we talked about over a hundred people that he knew. Now the point about that is that my job is to select the person in question and it's only a jumping-off point anyhow. Both the process of talking about all sorts of things and people, and the process of selecting, are very much creative things on my part. So it's misleading to suggest that a single random person is the source of a character. Obviously my job is to put together characters and to create the context and to move the thing along, both to take from what happens organically and spontaneously in the improvisations and to push them in various directions. But the preparation work is always only the premise because in fact I don't start the final rehearsals until I get out on location. I then define and define and define until in the end what we get is distilled and structured and cinematic.

Both in the context of the play and the film, does the final stage in this process actually yield a script?
A physical script? No, never; unless I transcribe one later, for publication. So you don't need a script, as such. If you rehearse thoroughly, the actors know it. As it so happens, there is a post-production script for *Bleak Moments* knocking around. But it's only thirteen pages long because they say so little and speak so seldom, even though the film lasts 110 minutes.

So once you've distilled what you want from the rehearsals, you've found your characters with the aid of the actors, you don't write anything?
That first, then you distil, then you go on location and you rehearse. You rehearse in a precise way. And rehearsing is writing, constructing the action.

But not actually putting anything on paper?
No. Writing is a creative process where you define that which happens including that which is said. Now you may choose to write it down or you may not. If you don't need to then you don't and on the whole you don't need to. The important thing is to shoot it, not put it on paper!

So when, to take an example at random, Sylvia says to Peter, 'I was imagining you without your trousers. Take your trousers off' – that was not something that was scripted. She simply remembered it from the rehearsals?
No, it was scripted – but scripting doesn't mean writing it down, though it does mean fixing it precisely. If you're asking me whether it's absolutely precise and thoroughly rehearsed and therefore scripted the answer is yes. If you're asking me whether we wrote it down on paper, the answer is no, we didn't need to write it on paper because she knew it. She knew it, we knew it, the cameraman knew it. We rehearsed it and it was absolutely precise. We could have written it down if we'd chosen to, but we didn't because we didn't need to. In other words, writing it down is superfluous to the process because you write by rehearsal. These days I've got a continuity person who works with me and, of course, she'll keep notes and if we all go away and come back to it six weeks later, they'll be there to

remind people of things. But that's a technicality. In terms of what you're saying, the important thing is that it is very tightly scripted but there isn't a script in the sense that there isn't an artefact on paper. The script is what they do. A film is a film, not a novel or a play or a poem.

So you never have anything on paper yourself?
Oh yes. But that's different. We're talking now not about dialogue but about structure. For every film that I make, including *Bleak Moments*, I write a structure. Scene one, Sylvia walks down the street. Scene two, Sylvia meets Peter. Or scene one, Johnny steals a car, whatever it is. That's all it says. It's a premise.

A scenario?
It's a scenario and you go on location and build a scene on that premise and things change, the scene gets cut, the scene becomes something else but that's the thing to work from.

What you seem to be saying is that you know the function of the scene in advance but not the actual content?
The details, that's right. Although there may be things in a particular scene that I know because I've explored them in one form or another in the preparatory rehearsal, there are scenes when I haven't a clue what's going to happen. And, indeed, in almost all my films I never know what's going to happen at the end. At the end of *Naked*, for example, there was a big debate about whether Johnny should stay or go. If you remember the end, he finally comes down the steps and hobbles down the street and we track back with him. It was a Steadicam shot for a huge distance at the end of the film. There was debate about how we should end it. We were having discussions about the character and I was privately having a kind of ideological discussion with myself about what would be the right thing to happen. And every morning I was driving to the location, along that same road towards the house and seeing it there. And finally 'Bong!' it went in. I thought, this is an image, this is a fantastic image. And the minute I thought that, I thought this is the end. He has to leave. Film-making is the fusion of the visual and the dramatic action, and I have to conceive them as one thing.

Is this why you need to rehearse in the location?
Yes. I can never construct a piece of action without being in the location. Once you see the world that you're creating in its environment, you put a frame around it and direct the action by a visual response or by the visual imagination being sparked. The worst misunderstanding of my stuff is that all I do is to make a piece of theatre and ask somebody to point a camera at it. Talk to any cinematographer I've worked with and that is not the case. It's very much about exploring things in a very filmic way and the whole point is the strength of such acting because it's so grounded and organic that the actors can adapt to the needs of the camera. And this was absolutely how Bahram Manocheri and I worked on *Bleak Moments*.

Can you say a little about your preparation for the film?
Under the BFI agreement everybody worked for twenty pounds a week, whatever their job, right across the board. The actors had to do it under the Equity minimum agreement for feature films, which was forty pounds a week, so all the actors invested fifty per cent of their earnings into the picture so everybody was on the same money. The other remarkable thing is this: there was a director, producer, editor, a cinematographer, a sound recordist, a focus puller, who incidentally was Roger Pratt, a boom swinger and a fifth guy who was both clapper-loader and assistant sound man. There were no sparks at all, there was no make-up, there was no costume department, there was no catering. Somebody did continuity and there were a couple of other assistants and a few odd people who were around every so often and so forth. That was it and if you look at the film you could say it's a bit crude, but considering it was shot for peanuts with nobody there it doesn't half look good – 110 mins of Eastmancolor and it's bloody impressive!

Given you didn't have catering, where did you eat?
In the café. We ate egg and chips.

Did the small size of the crew affect the shoot in any way?
Yes. It was terribly tough. It was all very well doing it without any sparks, without any guys to hump the equipment, without catering and all that stuff. But for me it was an even greater struggle because there wasn't a script. You have to make the material, engender it and rehearse it, before you can shoot it. There is always a scheduling tension between shooting and rehearsal because you need rehearsal days and I got into a terrible bind. Eventually we took a week off shooting so we could rehearse. We shot the scene with Liz Smith, we shot all night because we had to get out the next day. People in the other council flats got mad with us. We had very hostile neighbours at the main location. Every time they heard the clapperboard they turned on the Hoover on principle, because they were so anti.

Why were they anti?
We were young people and they didn't like us. They didn't want all this nonsense going on next door, a lot of long-haired, scruffy young people coming in first thing in the morning. Perfectly understandable – they were retired, genteel, humourless folk.

Did you have trucks and camera vans that might have annoyed them?
Well . . . we had a Ford Transit. I had a 2CV, Les had a Fiat 500 and Bahram had one of those little Ford Anglias. Every so often Albert used to show up in his Range Rover with his batman. He once came when there were roadworks going on and there was a kind of trailer sitting in the road and he said, 'Oh, I thought that was the director's car.'

Given this was your first experience of directing, how did you work?
We were novices. I had done those little films that I've talked about and I'd acted

in films but I'd never actually directed a sound film so it was a first for me. In terms of how we worked creatively, we talked about the look of it, about visual references. I know that we talked about Vermeer but the way we talked about the palette was obviously not as sophisticated as more recently, say, with Dick Pope and Alison Chitty when we made *Naked* where we were very sophisticated with the kind of thing we did, including bleach-bypass and all of that. But we talked about colours and tones. I have to say we did *Bleak Moments* in incredibly tough circumstances. It was a very hard shoot, but it was very creative once it got going.

How did you prepare in terms of your coverage? You were a very good artist, draughtsman. Did you draw storyboards?

I have never done storyboards except for one occasion, and that's the bit in *Bleak Moments* when they all come round for tea, and nobody speaks – all those close-ups. They're all looking at each other and twitching and it goes into absolute catatonia. We took off the blimp so the eye-line was clear and you really heard the camera motor. All that sort of acting where you look at somebody's lapel for the eye-line and pretend is crap. That's not what it's about. So I storyboarded for that sequence, yes, but normally I don't do it. My working method is to run the action and then talk with the cinematographer and go through it and make decisions and try bits and plan the shots.

Given that you'd wanted to direct films since you were a kid, did you feel confident about what you were doing? Did you feel that you'd found your vocation?

I'm never completely confident about what I'm doing. You talk to anybody who's worked with me and more often than not at some stage on every film I suffer a terrible crisis of confidence. It doesn't matter how successful you've been, you can't rely on that to make it happen. You've got to work at it. On the other hand, I remember the good times making that film. I was finally doing it and I knew it worked. And there were times when it really, really worked. In the scene where they have tea, there's a two-shot where you've got Pat on the left and Peter on the right. They're framed on either side of the hatch and you can see into the kitchen. When we lined it up, a number of people, including Bahram, said, 'You can't do that because he's looking one way and she's looking the other way out of the frame and they're both on the edge.' And I said, 'No, it will work. That's the whole meaning of it, there's a tension there.' And they said, 'Are you sure?' And I said, 'Yes.' I remember that moment. I knew what I was doing and what I was finding. By that time I'd directed a lot of plays in the theatre and it was just the thing of bringing all those skills that one had discovered and marrying them with the actual film-making process. It was just very positive and rich. I really felt that I'd come home basically or found my feet or however you describe it. But at the same time there were times when you thought, bloody hell! What am I doing? Part of film directing is captaining the ship. You've got to get it to happen and there's never enough time. In this case there was not only no time, but no dinner and no money either!

Did you feel that this captaining role came naturally to you?
Yes, but it wasn't new because I'd done loads of theatre. And I've always run things, since I was a kid. It's just that I hadn't done a full-length film before. So in terms of getting it all done and keeping everybody happy and dealing with the pressures, it was new. But that's no big deal. It happens in all films.

You said earlier that you'd found your modus operandi in terms of working with actors by now. What about your technical know-how? Were you interested in the camera?
Absolutely, I always had been. And I'm fascinated by sound.

So you didn't have to lean too much on Bahram? You could say what you wanted?
It's always a shared thing and it was a learning curve. I mean, it was a huge education making that film because although I'd seen it happen in the studios and on location as an actor, and I'd done the film exercises, I was now actually doing it on what was effectively a real film.

Did you always know where to put the camera? Did you always have a strong sense of how a scene would work?
There are times when you can't find it and you're not sure where to put the camera. But I think for the most part knowing where to put the camera came naturally to me. One of the things that I was very clear and uncompromising about was that the camera should never be anywhere that draws attention to itself as extraordinary or intrusive. And although more recently I have deviated from that in the simplest sense, on the whole on that film we were pretty damn strict about an unobtrusive camera.

So the camera was just there? It wasn't glitzy, it wasn't flashy.
Well, it wasn't 'just there' – I think we shot it aesthetically. But it was unobtrusive. When we shot the famous scene when Sylvia gets pissed and asks Peter to take his trousers off, Manocheri drew a grid on the carpet so Anne could move wherever she liked and Roger could pull focus wherever she went. It just really helped the performance amazingly.

What was the most difficult thing for you?
I think it was the sheer logistics, rather than the content or style. I mean you look at it now and you think it's not epic really. Not much happens. But actually it was hugely epic. The camera is placed in a very considered and heightened way all over the show. Don't forget it's lit in a very extraordinary and heightened manner. You could shoot the same subject by getting in there with 16 mm black and white film and doing it hand held and very rough. That's not what this was about. It was very composed and controlled and that made it a very tough operation.

How fast were you having to work? How long were your days?
The days were very long and it was bloody slow. We went on much longer than we were supposed to, by several weeks. I can't remember now how long but it

traipsed on for a good long time, but we finally got it done.

Did you find the whole machinery, the whole process of film-making dovetailed very neatly into your way of working or did you find it was quite a job to make the two things converge?
It dovetailed very neatly. The only practical difference is that films don't spend months in rehearsal but I don't actually spend months in rehearsal. I spend months preparing raw material and in this case it wasn't as much as months. It wasn't very long. It was about two months before we started shooting. But it was a duck to water, really.

Did you have any pieces of luck when you were shooting the film?
When we shot the film those streets in Tulse Hill were completely empty. I'm bloody sure that those streets aren't empty any longer but in 1971 they were naturally very empty. We didn't have crowd control or anything and I remember shooting all that stuff when we were walking around and it was such magic to be out there in the streets shooting and somehow everything just happened. I mean, a van goes around a corner with 'Lambeth' written on it, the light was just incredible.

It had an extraordinary amount of silence for a feature film. This must have taken some courage?
I wanted those silences and there was no way that we were going to post-sync. But we were near the Crystal Palace transmitter and of course the bloody sound wires started picking up radio stations. So we sat around endlessly wrapping tin foil around sound cables to insulate them against Crystal Palace. We'd also used up our two cans of anti-flare at fifteen shillings a can so we spent the rest of the film using builder's putty instead of anti-flare. There are some scenes in the film where it looks really bad. Sometimes you can see a door covered in putty and sometimes it's shiny. All those things take a long time and can dissipate the momentum. Those were the kind of things that made it difficult. Apart from having to go off and find lunch, or whatever. I mean people came by public transport. Crazy!

You said earlier it was sort of massive learning curve. What do you think were the biggest lessons or the ones you can remember? How would you sum it up?
It was discovering how to make films, how to do it, basically. Everything to do with the procedure of film-making from a director's point of view. I mean, I knew it in a basic way because of the various things I'd done previously but I hadn't actually made a full-length feature. I learnt the way everybody learns on their first film. Having shot it, we then went into the cutting room where Les edited it and I doubled up as assistant editor. We edited it together, as you'd expect.

And was that another big learning curve?
Yes. But editing always is, quite frankly.

Well maybe more the very first time?

Well, of course. Especially when it came to condensing and reducing this quite unwieldy thing. And Les was a very good editor.

Did it all work technically? Did it cut together?

Yes, it cut, because the camera was in the right place for the most part, I think. It's hard to answer without being self-congratulatory in some way. But I think I knew what I was doing: storytelling, really.

Apart from Norman's singing the film has no score. Was this deliberate? Or a further reflection of its limited budget?

It wasn't the budget. I had this notion that not having music would somehow be purer and actually that made some kind of sense. Though now when I think back to it, you think, well, actually the right music would have been rather interesting for it. But it was a kind of philosophy at that time to make a film where the action came without any vinaigrette.

To my mind the 'bleak moments' the film contains are even more powerful without any music.

I think you're right.

It's more painful.

It was and that's where it came from. It felt right at the time and it took me a number of years to dare to make a film with music, which was my fourth film, *The Kiss of Death*. Obviously the scene where Hilda is walking down the street and she hears him sing 'Freight Train' is very evocative and it works as film music, as obviously the convention is that you're hearing him where you wouldn't.

What lessons can you draw from the experience that you think would be useful for film-makers making their first films now?

To have the luxury of making a film that is so personal and idiosyncratic and that you're free to expand and contract as you go along means that there's no tension between you and the material. You're not enslaved by somebody else's idea or an idea that you don't really believe in or something you're merely doing in order to advance your career. It really is organic and it really comes from your bowels and your soul and it appeals to your sense of humour, it's all of those things. It was a great thing to make up one's first film with that kind of freedom. It was also an object lesson in how backers should behave. Albert Finney gave us total carte blanche, which is to his eternal credit. He ought to give lessons to Hollywood.

Bertrand Tavernier: *The Watchmaker of Saint-Paul*

When did you discover movies?

I was very young. Six, seven, eight. But I really fell in love when I was eleven. At the age of twelve or thirteen I'd cut stills from films which I found in children's magazines and put them in a small scrapbook. I'd underline not only the name of the actors but also the name of the directors. The first director I underlined was John Ford, the director of *She Wore a Yellow Ribbon* and *Fort Apache*. I saw them both in the same month and realized there were similarities between them and that the similarities were due to the fact that they were directed by the same man. The second was William Wellman and the third was Henry Hathaway. At the age of fifteen I was already writing screenplays, very imitative of American films, mostly westerns. They were very silly but by this point I knew I wanted to be a film director. I was also seeing a lot of films. Not as much as I wanted because I was at boarding school and could only see films on Sunday. I gradually became involved in the choice of the film in the school. I'd see films because of their stars. I saw all the films of Gary Cooper, even the old films. I saw *Springfield Rifle* which made a big impression, *Distant Drums*, *Mr Deeds* and *The Lives of a Bengal Lancer* which was a big shock. And John Wayne, of course. I think I saw *Wake of the Red Witch* three times in the same week. Sometimes I had to lie to my parents. I'd say that I was going to the museum when I was actually going to see films. I was not like my pals at school who only saw new films. I'd go to small cinemas to see old films like *Thieves Highway* by Jules Dassin.

You've mentioned a lot of American directors and movies. Were French movies as important to you?

They became important when I left boarding school and I discovered *La Grande Illusion* and the films written by Jacques Prévert. When I became a real film buff in my twenties, I tried to see all kind of films at the *cinémathèque*. That's how I met a number of people who are still my friends. We created a film club called Nickelodeon. We met practically every day and saw a lot of different films. When we created the film club we decided to concentrate on American films because a lot of them were more difficult to see than French films, specially in the original subtitled versions. At the time we didn't know that there was a problem with the French films of the thirties and forties. In the art cinemas we were seeing plenty of French films by Feyder, Cocteau, Carné, Grémillon. But the films of Stanley Donen, John Ford, westerns, musicals, were not shown except at the Studio Parnasse which was a very important cinema for a lot of us. So we concentrated on

American films. But we saw all kinds of film. We saw Japanese films – I remember the big shock I had when I discovered Mizoguchi. We saw films from the eastern bloc, Boris Barnet, Donskoi . . .

How did your parents react to your passion for the cinema?
My parents were very upset that I wanted to be in films. They wanted me to go to law school. That was put in my biography and I've had many questions about the influence of law school on my films which proves that the biographical approach is very bad since I only went to a law class once. I went the first day and I got so bored that I only showed up at the end of the year for the exam and handed in a blank piece of paper because I'd never been to the class. We were forced to stay at least an hour and a half even if we were not doing anything and I was very worried because I was missing an Allan Dwan film that was on in the 20th *arrondissement*. So it always amuses me when I read in articles that my law studies were a big influence on films of mine like *Le Juge et L'Assassin* and *L.627*! Anyway, my parents said if I didn't follow their advice and go to law school and if I stayed in their place, I'd have to pay rent. So very early on I had to earn a living. I went to many, many newspapers like *Télérama* and wrote small essays on films like *The Searchers*, or *Distant Drums*. I wrote about ten or fifteen articles. But it was difficult. A lot of the time I was not eating much. I was saving my money to go to see films. There were plenty of cinemas at that time that were cheap, especially when you went before noon. This lasted two or three years when I was eighteen, nineteen, twenty. I then started doing interviews for a monthly magazine. The first of these were with Claude Sautet and Alberto Lattuada. Finally Jean-Pierre Melville and Claude Sautet went to see my parents and told them to let me do film. So they were my two godfathers in the cinema. Then Melville decided to take me on as a kind of fourth or fifth assistant. I was quickly promoted because Melville always hated a few people on the set. So he started to hate the first AD, even before the shoot, and the poor man was forbidden to go to the set. The second AD, Volker Schlöndorff, became the real first AD and as I was the assistant to Schlöndorff, my responsibilities grew bigger. It was a pretty terrible experience for me because Melville was a dictator on the set and loved to humiliate people and I was very shy.

Was he encouraging of your aspirations?
In the sense that he was paying me a little bit of money he was helping. But on the set it was a frightening experience because I saw him humiliate people like his art director several times in front of the whole group. I was always thinking, do we have to suffer so much when we make films? And when I became a director I reacted very strongly against that experience. But sometimes he could be wonderful. When he wanted to charm someone, he was irresistible; he could tell you stories about the French underworld, the Resistance, about his love of American films. So he played a very important part in my life.

When you went to him, did he know you wanted to become a director?
Yes. But at that time he thought that no one could make it. He thought that there were only two directors in France, Clouzot and himself. After *Léon Morin, Prêtre*, which, by the way is a very beautiful film and which is a part of Melville I like the best, better than some of his thrillers, which I find more abstract and mechanical, he said to me you are a very bad assistant. You'll never succeed in that job but you might succeed as a press agent. And he said that to the producer of the film, Georges de Beauregard. And that was a wise thing to say. I would have been a terrible assistant director. I probably wouldn't have got any work and might have given up.

Do you think the two things you did prior to directing – working as an assistant and a critic – helped when it came to directing? Can you learn from watching or only from doing?
I think you can learn by seeing films. The same way you learn by reading books. Not how to write but how to appreciate certain things. The French writer, Paul Leautaud, who also worked as a critic, was once asked if the fact that he had to read and write about a lot of books conflicted with his creative talent. He said he didn't think looking at or admiring beautiful women was in conflict with making love. And this is true! But I never considered myself a critic. It was always a temporary stage for me, a way to learn. Learning by seeing all kinds of films and learning by having to write about films. Truffaut thought that when you write screenplays, summarising the plot was a very good exercise. As a press agent I had to learn to do a small résumé of the action to find out what the backbone of the film was. Nowadays when I'm writing a screenplay and I've done one, two, three drafts, either I or the writers I'm working with will do a small résumé of the action, to see if we have a story that we can tell in five or six sentences and if it makes sense. So I learned many things by being a press agent because when you're a press agent you have all the advantages of being an assistant without the problems. I was able to watch, to study all the different stages of film-making. With the producer Georges de Beauregard I'd start when the film was being written so I was reading the screenplay of *Le Doulos* or *Platoon 317*, or *Pierrot le Fou*. I'd then go on the set and watch the director working. I'd sometimes see the rushes. I'd go to the edit and see the relationship with the distributor and with the exhibitors. I was learning and I met wonderful people. I had the privilege of being there with Jean-Luc Godard, with Claude Chabrol. And a lot of them are still my friends. I even learned my trade. On *Platoon 317*, for example, Pierre Schoendoerffer let me do the trailer. I wrote the text and chose the shots with the editor.

Did you at any time try to make a short?
Yes, I did. When I was working for Georges de Beauregard. And then after leaving him to work with Pierre Rissient. He wanted to make portmanteau films, a series of short films, and give a chance to some new directors, so I used that

opportunity and worked on two films, *Les Baisers* and *La Chance et L'Amour* as writer-director.

How did they turn out?
They got good reviews but I think they're both very bad. They were very imitative of the American cinema. I think they were competently done but were very child-ish and lacked any personality. But I learned because I worked with people like Raoul Coutard and on the second film with the composer, Antoine Duhamel. The most important thing I learned was that I was not ready. It was stupid to do a film if I was going to do empty adaptations of thrillers without any style or indi-viduality. So I decided – and my wife was instrumental in this – to learn more about life and to do a feature when I was ready, not technically but emotionally in my heart and in my head as a human being. I decided to wait, to go on study-ing films, but to live and to be curious about life and politics.

What was the gap between the short and your first feature?
Nine or ten years. I did the shorts in 1964. Then when I thought I was ready I wrote two screenplays. One was an adaptation of a Robert Louis Stevenson story called *The Beach of Falesa* which I wanted to do with James Mason and Jacques Brel, both of whom accepted. But I was tricked by the producer who took the script and hired another director. I then withdrew and could never find the finance.

Let's talk about The Watchmaker of Saint-Paul. *How did you come across the story? What attracted you to it?*
After failing on *The Beach of Falesa* I was trying to find another story and discov-ered two subjects at the same time. The first was about two people called Bony and Laffont who belonged to the French Gestapo. Bony had been a cop and Laf-font was a gangster. They united and created a group which tortured and killed many people during the Occupation. At the same time, I was a great fan of Georges Simenon. I'd read a lot of his books and had worked as the publicist on two adaptations of his work, *Le Chat* and *La Veuve Couderc*, two beautiful films directed by Granier-Deferre. I remember thinking at that time that Simenon had provided the French cinema with a lot of interesting films. When I read *The Watchmaker of Everton*, as it was originally called, I was deeply moved. I remem-ber thinking it would be good if I could transpose it to my birthplace, Lyons. I wrote a thirty-four-page adaptation then thought to myself that although I'd written two screenplays on my own I'd found it very difficult. Sometimes I could stare at a blank page for hours and not write. So I thought that for my first film it would be better to work with somebody on the script. And based on my knowl-edge as a press agent I quickly realized that the screenwriters who were fashion-able and were working with the directors of the seventies were often working on three or four films at the same time and were both too busy and difficult to con-tact because they were so successful. So I thought to myself, well, I'm dealing with

a subject which is based on a relationship between a father and a son. It would be good if I was working with people belonging to an older generation. I was fascinated by the enthusiasm of the blacklist writers I'd met, by the fact that they were so happy to work again, and that they were still very young in their attitude. So I decided to approach some screenwriters who'd been neglected. Firstly, they'd give me more time because they wouldn't be doing three or four films at the same time. Secondly, as they were out of fashion they'd be eager to prove how good they were. I decided to see a lot of the films of the forties and fifties and study how they were written and two names came out. First Aurenche and Bost. And then Maurice Aubergé who had written *La Vérité Sur Bebé Dong* and Becker's *Falbalas*. By watching those films I realized that some of the criticisms that had been levelled at them should have been made of the directors not the writers. Aurenche and Bost, for instance, were writing screenplays which were not only written with a real freedom, but I liked what they had to say politically. In *Douce* there is a scene where a wealthy woman, Marguerite Moréno, goes to see a poor family. At the end of the scene she says 'patience and resignation' and Roger Pigaut who plays the servant says 'impatience and revolt'. To write that in 1942 during the Occupation! I became very respectful towards them because they were taking a very strong position. You have to be brave to put a line like that in a script when the Germans are out there and the words 'impatience' and 'revolt' have a tangible meaning. I was right because the scene was censored by Vichy. Secondly, I thought their dialogue was rich but not overdone. Truffaut had made an attack on them which was preventing them from working but which was totally unfair and totally wrong. In my opinion, his attack should have been on the directors. In *Les Orgueilleux*, for example, he criticized a particular line. I thought if you gave that line to Alfred Hitchcock he could make the scene work. Why didn't the scene work? Because this line is underlined by the direction, by making a special shot for it. If it had been done in a master shot then the line would not have become so self-conscious. And the line itself was quite inventive. It's when Michèle Morgan is sending a telegram and she doesn't have enough money so she says, 'leave out "tenderness" and "love"'. If it had been directed with a greater fluidity it would have been far more effective. So it was the director who was at fault.

How did you make contact with them?

I had a contact from the agent of Aurenche and Bost. They arranged a meeting so I had lunch with Aurenche. He was enthusiastic about working with me, although he and Bost quickly said, don't do the French Gestapo story. We don't want to do a film about horrible people, they said, because even though we're making them horrible, it will be very difficult for the audience not to see them a little bit as heroes and there is a moral issue here. Bost was totally opposed to it. He said, no, we must not touch this subject. But they agreed to work with me on *The Watchmaker of Everton* without being paid. During this time I'd written to Georges Simenon to ask for a free option and he'd said no. I wrote back. He said no. I wrote long letters analysing the novel. After four or five letters, he said, okay, I'll give a free option for a year or eighteen months. So I started working with Aurenche and Bost and at the same time talking to producers. I found somebody who gave me a little bit of money to pay them but for fourteen months I didn't earn anything. I had stopped working and it was fourteen very difficult months. It was tough. We were helped by some friends. Sometimes Claude Sautet helped us but mostly it was Philippe Sarde the musician who was very generous. He invited us to lunch very often.

Can you describe how you worked together? What was the most difficult thing for you?

The most difficult thing was to convince Aurenche to stay on the project. Aurenche was unpredictable, crazy, brilliant, hyper-brilliant. You'd set up somewhere to work for two or three weeks. Then after ten days he'd say I have to go to Ardèche to see somebody there and leave suddenly. I'd go back to Paris and suddenly he'd arrive unexpectedly. One day he phoned and said, come and meet me at St Lazare. I met him and on the page of pocketbook he'd written a brilliant scene, a beautiful scene which was not in the book. It's the scene in the park where they're walking the dogs and Noiret says to Rochefort, you know, one day a little boy I didn't know came up to me and said, you've changed. And Rochefort says, what a mean thing to do. And Noiret says no, it's not mean. It's an act of love to cross the street, meet someone and tell him he has changed. It's a beautiful scene and one which I discovered on St Lazare station! We'd never discussed it but I don't think I changed a single word! Anyway, Aurenche would come up with ideas like this. Some of them were totally crazy, some of them were beautiful. The problem was to keep a kind of discipline. Aurenche had been influenced by the surrealist movement. He was full of poetic ideas. Everything he was saying about life was inspiring, funny. Bost was very much a Protestant. He had the kind of mind that put some order into the beautiful disorder of Aurenche. In fact, very often in that relationship I think it was Bost's role to keep Aurenche inspired and working. Aurenche was always quitting because he said I'm not inspired, I will never be able to please you. In fact, in a beautiful book of interviews, *La Suite a l'Ecran*, Aurenche says a good screenplay is a letter of love from the screenwriter to the director. He adds that he works well only with people whom he wants to impress and names Bost and myself, saying he wrote his best scenes because he wanted to astonish us. That is the condition for a screenwriter, he says. To work well you must want to give the director a gift. I loved both of them, but mostly Aurenche. I've never met anyone as young as him, anyone who was less a prisoner of the rules. He told me he hated working with directors who were too classic in their thinking. He said, 'I'm not a *mécanicien*. I'm not somebody who can do a perfectly constructed plot. I cannot do thrillers. I can write about characters and I can understand characters but I'm not a craftsman.' One thing I learned from Aurenche was not to write a synopsis of two or three pages. Of course we had my forty page treatment. But we didn't work from the treatment. Aurenche said if we work on each scene at length we'll discover a detail we can incorporate into the next scene. We spent a long time discussing how to do it before beginning. Simenon's book is about a lonely man. Aurenche came to me one day and said to have a guy who is lonely, who has no friends, is very banal. Loneliness is more interesting if you're surrounded by people, he said. He told me he had a friend who was always surrounded by people, always at dinner, always making jokes, but who was one of the loneliest people he knew. I can credit Aurenche with these ideas. If you're trying to represent something, don't illustrate it. Go against the idea, give it a different light. In this way you'll make the scene fresher and more alive.

How much did you change the screenplay from the novel?
Eighty per cent of the screenplay is original. Of course transposing it to France changed some situations and some legal situations. I invented the political dimension of the story. We changed it totally to suit the time and because I wanted to make a contemporary film. I think that Simenon is politically more abstract. I learned a lot from working with Aurenche and Bost. I often wanted to say things against society and police. For example, in the scene between the cop and Noiret on the train, I had written a much longer monologue about the brutality of the police. Bost said, no, you have to cut that. I agree with what you say about the police, about police brutality. But look, our character has started to live now and he doesn't want to speak about that. You want to say it not him. We must listen to him now. There are certain things he can say and certain things he cannot say. He made me cut several things like that. And I learned a lot. I discovered that working with people who were older than me was bringing new ideas into the script. For example, Aurenche brought the story of one of his great-uncles, the man with the matches, into the screenplay. It's an autobiographical thing. So he was nourishing the father with his childhood. And I was nourishing the other characters with my ideas.

Do you think three life experiences will create a richer screenplay than one?
That depends. A film written by one person can be very rich. Some films written by five writers can be shallow and impersonal. Then again, some – Italian films, for example – can be superb. The director and the writer can live a lot of experience which will help them. So it's a complex thing. But I think it's more interesting to work with screenwriters who have had an interesting life.

Before we come on to talk about the preparation for the film itself, I just wanted to ask you how you managed to raise the money in the end?
It was a nightmare. I'd met Philippe Noiret and given him the treatment. Three or four days later he said yes. Several weeks later I organized a lunch with him and Aurenche. They met, he liked the screenplay and said yes again. It was then that the nightmare began. I thought having a screenplay, having a producer, having Philippe Noiret and having an interest from the people at Pathé and Gaumont, it

would be easy to raise the money. But it wasn't. Firstly, the producer I'd found had another film he was interested in. It was a first film by a director called Serge Leroy, a gangster film called *Le Mataf*, with Michel Constantin. In the end he decided he'd rather do that than mine. So I had a screenplay but no producer. I went to all the producers I'd been working for as a publicist. I was turned down by every one of them, very brutally, with a lack of respect. They just took the screenplay and said, look at it, it's too heavy, too much dialogue. Most of them hadn't read it. One of them even said, my secretary read it and didn't like it. Several times I went with Philippe Noiret and they received us very badly. I felt insulted, discouraged but I tried to fight back. I was not doing one thing after the other. I was pursuing them all together. I had fifteen rejections. The people working for Warner had to send it to London, then it got lost between London and Paris. Some people didn't respond to us, people for whom I'd done fifteen films as a press agent. They had the screenplay for months and didn't respond.

Were you a problem in the sense that you hadn't yet directed a feature film?
Yes, of course. I was treated very badly. Very rudely. I was unknown so they wouldn't help me at all. Philippe Noiret's agent advised him not to do the film with me. And Philippe stayed despite that. Then one day I went to Claude Sautet's producer, Raymond Danon, for whom I'd done a lot of films as a publicist, *Les Choses de la Vie*, *Le Chat*. I gave him the figures. I had everything: a schedule of forty days, the cost of the film – two million six at that time of which I had one million four from the distribution plus a guarantee from Pathé Gaumont – plus Philippe Noiret who was doing the film for half his usual fee. Danon asked me, is the screenplay good? Yes, I said. Okay, he said. I will call the people at Pathé. If what you say is true, I will do the film. He called me two days later and said he'd spoken to the people at Pathé and they'd confirmed what I'd said. So he made an offer. I accepted immediately and we started preparing with Philippe Noiret and François Perrier who was going to play the cop instead of Jean Rochefort. Then Danon came back to me and said, I've read the script and I don't like it at all. But I gave you my word so if you can do it in thirty-six days instead of forty, let's do that. I will always be grateful for that because he kept his word. But we were really considered as a no-film in his eyes: a very little, unimportant film. At that time they were preparing a film with Annie Girardot and Bernard Fresson. It was called *Ursule et Grelu* and the budget was ten million francs. No one even remembers the film now but at the time their people were constantly reminding us that there was one important film being produced there – and it wasn't mine. I was being paid one hundred thousand francs which was about seven thousand pounds for co-writing, producing and directing. One day Danon came to the office and said you're being paid very little. I'll double your salary if you shoot all the interiors in Paris instead of Lyons and do a week for the location work in Lyons and everything else in Paris. I said no. And I saw in his eyes a look of total astonishment. He just couldn't understand. I wasn't making any money.

I was refusing because I knew that the interiors were important. I also knew that I wanted to move from the interior to the exterior in the same shot and that the interiors in Lyons were not the same as the interiors in Paris. Danon was very puzzled and in his eye I saw clearly the thought, okay, I'm dealing with a madman so it's better if we do the film and forget about it. He went out and it was the end of any kind of discussion. He had just had a problem with a first film with Alain Delon so he put in my contract that if I was two days late by the middle of the second week I'd be fired. Noiret said, don't worry. I'll fight for you. But it was in my contract. Then came a new problem. François Perrier became unavailable. He had to do another film being made by his son. So suddenly I'd lost one of my two leads and had five days to find another actor. In the list given me by the distributors there were only two names. One of them was Jean Rochefort. So I went to see him, thinking if he says no the film is out. I went to his farm outside Paris. We had lunch and I told him the idea of the film and also – because he would have discovered – that he wasn't my first choice. But I knew that he'd acted several times with Philippe Noiret and they liked each other. I left at two-thirty, returned to Paris and at four o'clock there was a phone call at home. I've read the screenplay, he said. When you find such a screenplay it's impossible to refuse. I have to do it. It took him one hour and thirty minutes to say yes.

This must have made up for the producers?
It made up for it, yes. Then everybody made up for the producers. I hired a cameraman, Pierre-William Glenn, who'd only done a few films but they were very good. He was at IDHEC and before becoming a cameraman did research into the psychoanalytical aspects of American B-movies. He chose me as his assessor and I gave him 19 out of 20 because it was very good analysis. I also knew him because he'd shot some of the films I'd worked on as a press agent, including *Day for Night* by Truffaut and *State of Siege* by Costa-Gavras. I had a Viennese executive producer, Ralph Baum, a friend of Max Ophüls, who did all Danon's films and was always trying to get his girlfriends small parts on the films. I think he was getting a percentage from the labs. In fact, he probably got a percentage on everything he touched. He was very showy, wore huge braces, a Tyrolean hat and talked with a Viennese accent. When he spoke it was in pigeon French: 'Who is cameraman of yours? Me not know cameraman.' I used to answer in the same way: 'Cameraman has done films Truffaut and Costa-Gavras. Please you?' It was crazy! And every time a guy came to sign a contract he'd say, too expensive, before the guy had even sat down! But I had a clever strategy. I knew Max Ophüls's films very well. So any time I had a problem I used my Max Ophüls trick, my Max Ophüls credit card! For example, he once wanted to give me only twenty metres of track and I wanted between thirty and forty. So I said if Max Ophüls were shooting this film would he use twenty or thirty metres? He said, oh, more than thirty. I said, you see? Or I'd say, do you remember *La Ronde*? Do you remember how did you do such a shot? And he'd start telling me the story of how

it was done and I'd say I'd love to do a shot like that! He'd say, okay. But we won't tell Raymond. So I got away with it and there was enthusiasm all around me. Once we were in Lyons, what I thought would happen happened. Danon and Baum were not really working on the film. They were not coming to the set. They were not even seeing the rushes. The only person I had imposed on me was the production manager who left after two days and went to visit Lyons. So the fact that we were outside Paris gave us complete freedom. I was completely free, especially because I was never late. I was always on schedule, always on budget, under budget even. They hardly knew that the film was in production because everything was going so well. At one point at the end of the fifth week, Noiret got a little bit irritated and sent a telegram to Danon saying, 'Do you know we are doing a film for you? signed Philippe Noiret'. And Ralph Baum sent a telegram saying, 'I've seen the rushes' – which I'm sure was not true – 'everything looks great. I've recognized everybody'. There was an enormous difference between the tremendous pressure during the preparation, the financing of the film and the joy of the shoot, the incredible joy. I decided to create the kind of spirit on the film which would be the opposite of what I'd experienced with Melville. Everybody was going to be happy. People will love going to the set to work because they'll have fun, the actors will have fun, I will have fun. I tried never to look angry, never to look irritated. Pierre-William Glen was a wonderful help. He helped me overcome some people in the crew.

Let's talk about your working relationship with Pierre-William. How did you prepare in terms of your locations?
Some of the locations were connected to my childhood. I wanted Lyons to be a character in the film. I thought it was a very Simenonian city. It's secretive like the characters in Simenon. It's not a city which gives itself up easily. You have to go inside it and then you discover its beauty, something which is not ephemeral but stable and enduring. For me Lyons was as important as the protagonists of the story, and sometimes I wanted to escape the characters and to have shots of the city, and those shots are not only documentary but have a relationship with what is going on inside the characters.

There are moments I remember where the camera just cranes up and leaves the characters to look at the city.
Yes. That was very important for me. I knew that I wanted a certain style of camera movement. I wanted to use a lot of hand-held shots – that was something directly from the New Wave. There were two things from the New Wave which were very important for me: direct sound and a hand-held camera.

A lot of the time in the interiors – when he's walking through his apartment, for example – you follow hand-held. Is this because it's the simplest way of making a transition between an interior and an exterior?
Yes. I tried to combine my love of the New Wave and certain things I learnt from

American films like the dramatization of places, of topography. You have to learn the nature of Noiret's apartment very quickly. You have to understand the rooms, you have to understand the places he inhabits because that is part of the story. Very often in France, directors don't pay attention to that. I come from a school of film-makers who have learned film-making through a love of directors who knew how to film landscapes. This school embraces John Ford and Joseph Losey – two very different directors, but two directors for whom locations, the design of the set and the way they film a 'decor', all play an important role, and where the characters seem to be rooted in the locations, not only in a naturalistic way, but in a metaphysical way.

Given this was your first film, were you confident about the choices you were making?
No. I was full of doubts. And I still am! Before the first day of shooting I always had angina which was created by anxiety. Nowadays I'm even more frightened because I feel that after each film that I know less. At the time of *The Watchmaker* I was under a lot of pressure and was more crazy. I knew I was dealing with a crew that has made many, many films, I must not hesitate, I have to be sure of myself. So I immediately said something and sometimes I was right, and when I was not, Pierre-William would make suggestions. He would say, it's a good idea, but I would put the camera here rather than there.

Did you always have a sense of how you were going to cover the action?
I didn't have many days in the schedule so I tried to decide everything before the shoot. For instance, I decided to do a complicated shot the first time that we were in the park with Noiret and Rochefort. I said to Pierre-William I would like to start at the statue and turn around it. So we knew we had to build a scaffold in order to do the tracking shot which was a couple of hours' work. Most of the time I had an idea at least of the angle so he could light in the morning. I knew what I was going to use and I tried not to change my mind. Sometimes I didn't know exactly how I would do the scene unless I had seen the actors rehearse. I'd know, for instance, that I wanted to start from the window, pull back, and have the two actors in front of us. But then while rehearsing I discovered I could even go further in the scene before I moved the camera. I'd say to Pierre-William, we pull back from the window, we discover Jean Rochefort, then Noiret goes to his friend, he says a few lines while walking, turns and we stay on the cop who answers, then we cut back to Noiret. And Pierre-William would say, if I do a tracking shot here we can use twenty more lines of dialogue in the same shot. So I accepted the idea. Some I refused, some I accepted. But I'd try to impose myself even when I was not totally sure because I wanted to inspire confidence. Most of the time Pierre-William was very positive. That's a great idea, he'd say. This was incredibly helpful because I had a first AD who was making me doubt myself. For instance, I did a whole scene in one shot and he said, are you going to do some coverage? And I said, no. And he looked at me and said 'this is your film' in a way

that made me think, my God, maybe I should do it like that? And Pierre-William said, it's your film. It's much better without coverage: it's less conventional. One day I was hesitating about doing another take because I was going into overtime and Pierre-William taught me a wonderful lesson. He said, do it and don't care about the overtime. We are on budget. We have not done it most of the time. It's not possible to subtitle the film explaining that the scene is not good enough because you didn't do another take. You cannot subtitle a film to explain your mistakes so let's avoid the mistake instead. This is something which makes the French cinema totally different from the American cinema. In France the notion of crew is very important and a cameraman, especially someone like Pierre-William, chooses not only his assistant, but also the gaffer and the grip. This doesn't happen in America. I talked to many DPs and they all said that with the exception of Michael Ballhaus, who works with the same people, they work with the people who are available, whereas the cameramen in France work with the same people. It's a kind of family. They support you, especially someone like Pierre-William. That was one of the great things that the New Wave brought. Technicians who are working not for themselves but for the film. The only area where I had people that I had not chosen or were not willing to experiment was the set design. The designer was absolutely no good. Nice but no good. I had no knowledge of that area and had to trust my first AD and it wasn't a good choice. But I chose everybody else. I also did something which I still do. I did the casting myself with my second assistant. I never use a casting director because I want to meet all the actors personally and talk to them. Of course I chose Philippe Sarde as the composer because he had been so helpful and generous and at the same time was so talented. The thing that Pierre-William and Philippe had in common was that they were real film buffs. They loved films. They loved to go to movies. I remember during the shoot, once we'd seen the rushes we'd very often go to see a film!

Did you prepare shot lists or storyboards with Pierre-William prior to the shoot?
Never. There was no shot list. There was nothing technical. Not one technical detail. I have to see the actors. I knew deeply in myself that I'd have to rely on the actors. I didn't know if Noiret was going to sit there (*indicating one corner of the room*). Or there (*indicating another corner*). I just knew that after a certain scene, I needed to have fast movement because the scene itself was static. I knew a few things like that. A few principles. I thought, let's adopt the principle that Philippe Noiret dictates the rhythm of the film, the pace of the shots. So the camera has to move like him. Not only like he walks but like he thinks. So when he takes a sudden decision the movement would be brutal. For example, I knew a long time before we did the scene, that, for the trial, I will have only one shot of Noiret saying his line. I knew it would be a very fast forward camera movement. That I knew. But many scenes – especially the scenes between the cops – I wanted to discover. I wanted to discover what the actors would bring to the scene. In one

where I had a preconceived idea and tried to shoot my preconceived idea, when I saw the rushes I said, it's no good. Let's do a retake and do it much more simply because I'm not using the actors well enough. So I did a retake the next day and it was better.

Did you have a major input in terms of the design of the film?
The design of the film for me had nothing to do with the design of the set. The design of the film was firstly that it would be a film with summer colours. It wouldn't be in black and white because Lyons is not a black and white city. It's grey, pink and blueish at the same time. It's very Florentine, close to an Italian city and I wanted to get that look. And at the same time I wanted to do a film which was a kind of introspective study of a man. I wanted a slow pace broken by a few fast movements and abrupt cutting. I wanted to have the emotion, to have the flow of emotion and sometimes I knew I needed to go against it. For me, the design of the film was the design of the camera movement, of the angles. And the fact that I was not going to use a long lens. For me it was a film that was shot on a short lens, mostly between 25 mm and 32 mm. Sometimes 40 mm, but never, let's say, 400 mm. Although I did one or two shots on a zoom.

When they're walking in the park aren't you on a long lens?
It's not so long. It's a 100 mm but it's not a really long lens. Pierre-William loves the long lens because he's a fan of Sam Peckinpah. So he was always trying to sneak in an 800 mm shot! But I always liked a shorter lens. For me that was the design of the film, much more than the sets. I think the story had to be intimate. You had to feel the place around the character. You had to avoid poetry, everything which was softening the image. You had to have the kind of image which was harsh, full of contrast. I think the long lens sometimes softens, diffuses. I had to take out all feeling of diffusion. I wanted harsh rather than beautiful photography.

To give it a documentary-like quality?
Not documentary. Because in documentary the idea would have been to do black and white. The streets were lit. Sometimes we even shot without light. We used some of the first Panavision lenses which opened very wide. And we'd shoot in the night on the Place de Terrome lit only by the fountain. You can say 'documentary' but I sometimes wanted the characters to be silhouetted, to be backlit.

Can you tell me a little about your technical know-how at this point?
I learned it automatically by seeing films. I didn't read books. I didn't learn the grammar.

When you worked with Pierre-William did you say, I want this lens for this shot?
Yes. I wanted to prove to people I knew where the camera should be. I would say, I want a 25 mm and Pierre-William sometimes corrected me, saying I think a 32 mm would be better. And I'd say yes or no, but I was trying to be precise. And most of the time I was right. I had a good notion of the right angle. Sometimes I'd

follow his advice because I think one of the qualities of a director should be to recognize when somebody in the crew has a good idea and not turn him down because it's somebody else's idea. I didn't overdo it because I knew that Pierre-William had an ego and you have to direct the technician the same way you direct the actors. So sometimes I suggested something and sometimes I listened to him. I'd say, don't you think it should be more there and I'd like it a little wider. I wasn't as specific as saying, I would like a 25 mm rather than a 40 mm or a 35 mm. But I knew what the heart of the scene was. When you know the heart of the scene, you know instinctively where to put the camera. Sometimes you make mistakes. When I saw the two first days of rushes I thought it was a total failure. I said to Pierre-William, we missed everything. He was a great comfort. He said, be careful. You must be cautious with your rushes because you can have rushes fever. Either you find everything great or you find everything bad. When it comes to the film you mustn't let yourself be overcome by that. First edit the scenes and then you'll see more clearly what actually doesn't work. The first two days – which I wanted to reshoot entirely – are in the film and they work very well. It's just that I had a problem seeing the scenes without them being mixed. And I learned to think in terms of editing. Sometimes I had no coverage – or very, very little coverage.

How fast were you having to work?
I think there were more than seventy-four scenes in the film and we shot it in thirty-six days. Sometimes we did two or three scenes in a day. We were sometimes shooting five minutes, six minutes a day. And we were shooting quite fast. When I cut the film, the first cut was two hours and ten minutes and I'd shot it in thirty-six days, so you can work it out yourself. We were working so well together that sometimes we did seven, eight, ten pages in one day always with the camera moving.

Did you have any overriding principles in terms of the way you dealt with your actors on the set?
I didn't want technique to overcome the actors. In a way I felt very close to people like Renoir without even really knowing that I did. Later on I talked with people who'd worked with Renoir. In this respect too, I found myself on common ground with Pierre-William. I said, let's try to do the film without marks. Can you do that? It was very easy with someone like Noiret because even while doing different things in each take, he'd always be in a good place when you needed him. Pierre-William said that for an operator he was a dream to work with. He was precise without being mechanical so he could do two takes totally differently but you knew that they'd end up at exactly the same point. And Noiret derives pleasure from this precision. So I tried to have that feeling of spontaneity, of people being happy in the shot. It's something I didn't like in the French films of the fifties. There was a feeling of oppression from the directors and the technicians on the actors. In many films they look frozen.

Did you have much time for rehearsals?
I didn't rehearse a lot. Not even a day. Jean Rochefort came on board the first day of the shoot, or the night before. And with Noiret you don't have to rehearse. What is important is the discussion before. And sometimes it's a discussion where you don't talk about the film. You talk about other subjects. You talk about the props; you talk about the costumes; you talk about the colour of the shirt. And with Rochefort I'll always remember that I'd hardly met him because after he'd said yes he was doing another film. The day after he arrived he was shooting a very important scene so I invited him for dinner. During the dinner we didn't talk about the movie: we talked about a French writer that we both love called Jacques Audiberti. I talked about some plays of Audiberti and there was a moment in the dinner when Rochefort said to me, you know that having talked about Audiberti I now know how to play the character.

How?
He knew what interested me. What drove me. What pleased me. After that we barely spoke. I mean, Rochefort and Noiret are both very educated, they have both read a lot, they both know a lot about painting. They don't need the mass of explanations that many American actors need. Two words and they get it. I think Laurence Olivier must have been like that. You give them an adjective and for them it's a world. They can dream about that and it gives them the key. They don't need to spend a month studying the scene. Part of an actor's job is to dream around the character.

How did you feel the night before you began the shoot?
Full of fear. I don't think I slept at all. I tried to hide it, to mask it, to look very happy, very relaxed. But I wasn't. I remember a letter sent to me by Budd Boetticher who said that on his first film he didn't want to look puzzled so he called one of his friends and said how do you do it? The friend said if you're unsure of yourself ask for a very complicated camera movement. The time they're setting it up will give you time to put together a few ideas. I did that and in fact it was a good idea because the camera movement worked!

Is there any way you can evoke the experience of being on the set of your own film for the first time to someone who hasn't done it?
It's a tremendous pressure and a tremendous joy. Mixed both at the same time, all the time. You have a feeling of anxiety and at the same time a great spirit. Especially if you create a good mood around you which allows you to survive. I mean a set can have a very depressing atmosphere; some directors can only create in an atmosphere of conflict, of guilt, of anger. That would block me. I discovered when I did my first film that I didn't have any problem over power. I wasn't making a film to have power over people. And that helped me a lot. I knew how to get a good mood. I know how to be concentrated. You have to learn that. You have to learn how to cope with a lot of people. And if you can create that

spirit and you are not power-obsessed, then you survive. I was facing many, many problems. I had a very bad production manager imposed by Lira Films who was making a lot of mistakes. For instance, I had one shot of a girl on a mobylette. I begged him to buy one but because he wanted to economize he rented one at the place where we were shooting. Suddenly at midnight the motor goes puff, puff, brumm! Broken. Last shot of the scene. It's a scene which we had shot backwards. Dawn is coming so we started with the end of the scene. That was difficult in terms of direction. I was doing the first shot of the scene at the end of the day. And we were in a desolate airport outside Lyons far away from anywhere with a mobylette that didn't work. It's midnight. Nobody can help you. It took more than one hour. In fact, that false economy cost him two hours with the whole crew at triple time. But you have to survive through that and with the right mood you can overcome these problems; you can even transform that into something that puts more energy into the technicians, into the grip, into the crew, because they'll support you and the next day they will want to prove that they can gain some time. Later on I met a director called André De Toth. On his set he has a sign which says, drama must be in front of the camera not behind. That's something which I would have loved to put on all my films. The most important thing I'd say to young directors is that you have to economize with yourself, with your energy. Don't waste it on scenes that are useless. When I had fights with actors on later films, even if I won most of the time, I lost a little bit of energy. You cannot afford that. You have a specific amount of energy and you mustn't waste it on unimportant details, the money problem, the problem of how you're treated in a restaurant or a hotel.

Did you have a sense that you were learning throughout this process?
Yes. But I still do. I make films because I want to learn. Not only about how to make films but also about life. When I did *The Watchmaker*, I learned details about the life in the factories. I learned things about the police. I learned things about certain aspects of Lyons. I make films where I'm always learning about a historical period or about part of the society, a group of people, schoolteachers, cops. I feel after every film that I've been growing up and I think that it's best to go on being curious, not closing yourself to the rest of the world. Because when a director stops being curious, stops looking at things around him, that's the end.

What was the first cut of the film like?
It was much too long. So I did what I do very often. I brought two or three directors to look at the film, in this case Claude Sautet, who had given me advice on the screenplay, and Jacques Rouffio. They said, you must take out the scenes with Liliane's parents. And they were right. Those scenes were distracting us from the main subject of the movie which was the small step that Noiret takes, the small and enormous step taken by somebody who cannot cross the street if the light is not green. I've always said that the story of *The Watchmaker* is the story of some-

body who goes from A to B instead of A to Z. But that step is enormous at the same time. And to focus on the other characters was taking us away from him.

Was there anything you didn't like about the experience of directing?
Sometimes I didn't like the fear. Sometimes I thought I was too shy. I was never ready to humiliate somebody to get a specific shot. Maybe the shot would have been a little better but is it worth the price? I don't remember anything unpleasant about the shoot. I remember unpleasant things before we started shooting and after we finished. When we showed the film to Raymond Danon and the light went up at the end of the screening, he looked at me and he said, so you did film the screenplay and I said yes. Then he looked puzzled and turned to his driver, a Yugoslavian guy called Boda, and said, Boda, how did you like the film? And Boda said, I loved the film! You did? Yes. I loved the film. So I was saved by this huge Yugoslavian Serb driver who was at the same time his projectionist! When I received the Louis Delluc award, I was interviewed. I was asked what I felt and I said, you don't know the pleasure I feel because it's an answer to all those producers who insulted me during those months when I was trying to raise the money, who treated me me like I was nothing, who humiliated Philippe Noiret and myself during those ten or twelve months. You don't know how pleased I am to kick them back. It was very spontaneous! And then Danon came to me and said, I've been totally stupid. It's a beautiful film and kissed me on the cheek. That was my first producer's kiss! But we won the Louis Delluc award and the public reaction was great. It was a big, big success for a film of its kind. It was even successful abroad. In America, for instance, it got wonderful reviews by John Simon and Vincent Canby. I then received my first two international awards, one in Berlin where I got the Silver Bear award for best director and the Hugo award in Chicago.

Did you feel vindicated?
Yes. But then the problems started again with the next film. I was doing a period film and I was turned down by every distributor, everybody I went to, for the reason that the film was not like *The Watchmaker* and the film was very difficult to do. The same thing happened on practically all my films, including *'Round Midnight* and *Life and Nothing But*. The only one that wasn't difficult to finance was the least successful commercially.

Barry Levinson: *Diner*

Your career as a writer-director has embraced both big budget, Hollywood movies and smaller, more personal movies like Diner, *which have a more European feel about them. Did you see many European movies when you were growing up?*
I saw quite a few, starting in the late fifties. In Baltimore we used to have the Playhouse and the Charles cinemas, and they began to show all these foreign films. I think it all started with *And God Created Woman*. It was like, oh my God, Brigitte Bardot! But then we began to see the work of Bergman, Kurosawa, Truffaut, Godard, the Italian film-makers. So suddenly I saw an enormous amount of foreign films, and they were very influential for me. They were stripped down, in a sense, and they showed human behaviour in a way that wasn't being explored by Hollywood. So I was just fascinated by that kind of work. It shook up your mind.

Did this make you want to go into the film business?
I loved what I saw, but the idea that I could ultimately get to do that didn't occur to me. If you're growing up in Baltimore, who in the world is going to go into the film business? I didn't know anyone who was in the film business. So just to say, 'I want to do that' – well, how?

What happened to make it seem possible?
It evolved very slowly. I happened to get a job working in television in Washington DC, and I was doing on-air promotional spots for various shows. I had access to lots of footage and basically I was cutting images with music, to try and encourage an audience to tune in. I was a little a bit on my own while I was figuring things out; so I started to play around. I got to thinking, this is interesting, or that got someone's attention. Also I got a chance to actually go out and shoot a few television spots. I knew nothing at all about filming so I just shot it all to cut in the camera. A girl goes out, makes a left-hand turn to go down the street. So there'd be a shot of her looking, and then you cut.

That was effectively your technical training?
Yeah. I was exploring the dynamics of certain kinds of music and certain kinds of images. How do they get our attention and what kind of mood do they create?

By the seventies you were working in television as a performer and a sketch writer. Did you see television as a stepping stone to films?
I'd always been fascinated by movies since I was a kid; but film wasn't like something I was working towards. I was a comedy writer, doing sketches, performing,

working with Mel Brooks. It didn't occur to me that 'Yes, I want to direct'. It was an evolution of things that had to happen to get me to the point where I said, 'You know something? I would like to direct what I write. I want to see what it looks like if I do it.'

When did you discover you had a talent as a screenwriter?
That's a good question. I co-wrote *And Justice for All* before *Diner*. So I understood structure and so forth.

Who or what prompted you to embark on the script for Diner?
I think it was Mel Brooks. For a long time I was probably carrying around bits and pieces of it, just in my head. I told Mel some of the stories, about the diner and the guys, and he was amused by them. He said, 'You really should write that as a movie.' And I thought, that's all well and good, but I don't understand what it *is* yet. I didn't just want to write a nostalgic piece – 'gosh, here's what we did then'. And I didn't want to do some kind of slapstick comedy. I wanted something that made sense of the time for me – about why the behaviour was the way it was. So I needed to find what anchored the whole piece, what gave it something that would resonate for me beyond just throwing some things together, getting some laughs and getting the hell out. Once I began to understand its themes, then it just all came together and I was able to write it.

What do you think were its main themes?
What really made it all work for me was this real lack of understanding of women among these guys. We were tribal – the guys got together and did all this guy-talk. And even though there was this whole thing about girls, the great fear was that we didn't quite understand where that was going to go. We didn't understand some basic things. When I understood that, I could write it. Even though it doesn't scream out that this is what it's supposed to be about. But if you look at what they're talking about all the time, it keeps coming back to that.

And once you'd found that, you wrote it very quickly? In three weeks, so legend has it?
Yeah. It just hit me one day. I went 'Oh! Okay', and then I could go. I always write very quickly, all the time.

Do you have any set ways in how you write?
I play music all the time. I'm always driven by music. Even when I was in high school, my mother used to complain, 'How can you study and play music?' It doesn't even have to relate to the movie. You know what I was listening to mostly while I was writing *Diner*? Pete Townshend. An album called *Empty Glasses*. I just played it over and over.

Do you prepare any kind of outline before you begin?
No. I don't know exactly where I'm going. I just have an idea of where that might

be. And even though I write quickly, sometimes I'll stop, and I might not write for a day and a half, I just keeping wandering around, because something is bothering me. But eventually I'll think 'Oh, Okay' and then I go again. I write in longhand, on yellow pads, because I can't type fast enough. And when I get tired of actually writing, then I'll type what I've written. Because I scribble, and if I leave it alone for too long, I may not know what the hell I wrote!

What happened once you had the first draft of Diner?
That was basically it. I always try to test the material. I'm certainly not so protective of the work that I wouldn't change it. Any time I'm doing a scene and something comes up that's better, you know, some little improvisational thing, I'll say, fine, let's go with it. But generally it holds up relatively well, oddly enough.

How did the script end up with the producer, Mark Johnson?
Mark used to work for Mel Brooks as a second assistant director. He had gone to work for Jerry Weintraub who managed a lot of rock groups and had done a few films. We'd become friendly so I showed him the script, and he said, 'How about showing it to Weintraub?' I said, 'What the hell, we'll start there and see where else to go.' You always assume the first person you show it to isn't going to go, 'Oh yeah, let's make this movie!' So Weintraub read it and he really liked it and wanted to make it. He showed it to MGM and they said 'Fine' right away. To be honest with you, I'm not so sure that anybody ever really read it. It was a really inexpensive movie for them, and I think they just thought it was going to be like one of those cheap teen movies – high jinks!

Were you surprised about getting this reaction so quickly?
I was shocked. I had initially assumed there was going to be a little more of a battle, because . . . *and justice for all* struggled to get set up for quite a while before it actually happened. But this was very exciting. By the first of the year we were going to go into pre-production and start shooting some time in March.

You hadn't directed at this point. Was there any resistance from MGM or Weintraub to you directing the movie?
No, nothing. Again, I think they just thought it was a cheap movie.

Still, it was around five million dollars. And for someone who hasn't directed before, that's quite an investment.
I always look on it as one of the flukes. Every so often, it's the right moment in time and someone says 'Yes'. Because, God knows, they say 'No' most of the time. Every year or so, there are a certain number of young guys, and now more women as well, who just sneak through under the wire. It's one of those things – like salmon swimming upstream.

Did you think of it as a very important moment in your career?
To be honest with you, I had no preconceived ideas about what it was going to

mean in terms of my career. It was 'Ooh, I got a chance to make a movie!' That was all that was on my mind.

So you started preparing. How did your collaboration with the cinematographer Peter Sova come about?
I was meeting various cinematographers about the piece and never felt comfortable with anyone. They were certainly all capable, in different ways. But I just didn't feel that their sensibilities hit me right. But when I met Peter, we hit it off. At that point he didn't really speak great English. He spoke like (*strong Czech accent*), 'Barry, I think we put the camera here.' But, as odd as it seems, we had a similar sense of humour. When he heard the actors saying something, he would laugh, and I would say to myself, 'How did he know any of this?'

What had he done up till that point?
Not that much. I think his only feature was a film called *Rockers*, made in Jamaica.

I gather you saw an enormous number of people for the male roles when you were casting the movie. Was this because you had a very precise idea of all the characters?
It wasn't like I was looking for physical types. I just wanted people who had the sensibility that was appropriate to the piece; people who have a certain sense of humour, a certain kind of rhythm in the way they speak. I wanted a fairly naturalistic approach for the movie, and I wanted actors who could somehow do those things without it becoming very theatrical. It's always a crapshoot when you're casting. You say, 'She would be interesting with him, and this would be good with that . . .' And you begin to hear these various rhythms in the way people talk, and see how they apply to the piece. And you want these variations, these different kinds of voices, to be part of your package.

Did it take a long time to find your cast?
We looked almost up till the time we started shooting. I know that at one point, we'd done over five hundred personal interviews for the five guys. Interestingly enough, Ellen Barkin was the only woman I saw for the role of Beth. I might see a hundred and fifty guys for a part but when she came in I said, 'That's her!' There was no question that I had to see any more people.

The majority of the cast – Ellen Barkin, Kevin Bacon, Mickey Rourke – have all gone on to become well-known names. But at the point you cast them, they were mostly unknown. Did this cause any problems in terms of the studio?
You would get names that would crop up periodically. 'How about so and so? This person was big in a television show. Why not him?' But I threw all that out, because it just wasn't appropriate to the movie. At some point you have to say, 'These are young characters, so they're going to have to be played by young – and therefore mostly unknown – actors.'

As far as I know you hadn't worked with actors before. Did you do much rehearsing?

We had a week where we'd meet, talk the lines, play around with it; but only for a couple of hours a day. What I was really interested in was not to work out the beats of the scene or deal with the blocking. All I really wanted was for them to get familiar with one another. Period. To get to a point where they could just talk and not feel like maybe I shouldn't say that; all the inhibitions that come when people first meet. I did all the stuff actually in the diner at the end of the film so there would be as much time as possible for them to feel as if their friendship has gone on for a long time. I've never been a big one to rehearse and rehearse.

So when you got on set, how did it work?
What I would try to do was rehearse only in terms of getting the blocking down well enough so that the cameraman knows what to do, and save the performance for when you shoot. Otherwise you can end up with a performance for the blocking when you're not rolling your cameras, so you just blow it all out.

Did blocking come naturally to you? Moving people around a space isn't the easiest thing in the world if you haven't done it before.
I just took the approach that you let it evolve out of what seems natural, rather than try to force blocking on the actors. You just ask, 'Where would you go, where would you stand, if you're doing these kinds of things?' Then you start to find what makes sense for the piece. I didn't really know any other way.

The film is an incredibly assured directorial début. Were you always confident about basic things like where to place the camera?
Initially the production designer would show me a location that he thought was great. And I'd be baffled because I couldn't figure out where to put the camera. I didn't know how to stage a scene. I didn't have a clue. I was lost with this great location. Finally we went to a location and the second I saw it I immediately saw the scene. And as soon as I saw that, I said, okay, this is what I'm going to do for this movie: when I see a location and I know where to put the camera, that's the one I'm going to use. If I don't, it's not the right location. That was the rule of thumb.

What about your technical knowledge at this point?
You say, let's do this. Then you take a look in the lens and see. In other words, if you didn't know initially one lens from the other, you'd take a look and see and say, no it doesn't feel right. It's a little too in-between. Let's close it up.

So you learned in a pretty hands-on manner?
Yeah. At some point you have to deal with the lens you're using in the shot. It's not like a cinematographer just throws a lens on and says, 'There it is.' It needs to be either this, that or the other. And as a director you have to be on top of that. For *Diner* I knew we weren't going to be using zoom lenses. We used a lot of wide-angle lenses, we felt that was good for the movie. But I didn't know to say that the 29 mm lens would be the one.

How did decide on your coverage of a scene?
A lot of it I had to take from what the actors are giving. I knew that the movie had to be slightly voyeuristic.

What do you mean 'voyeuristic'?
It wasn't the kind of movie where the camera was flashy. I didn't want it to be obtrusive. The camera's just there. It's not flamboyant in any way at all. It picks up the information. I remember I was talking to someone about the movie who hadn't seen it yet. They said, 'Sometimes your first movie doesn't have to do well. If it's got a lot of style, a lot of pizzazz to it, you can get another job because they can see the work of the director.' And I said, '*Diner* doesn't really have a lot of pizzazz. You wouldn't look at it and say the guy's a technical wizard.' And I actually got nervous 'cause I was thinking, what'll happen if it doesn't do well? But I didn't use the camera that way because it didn't apply to the piece. I felt that the scenes had certain rhythms that come out of what the guys are talking about, and the camera style was loose enough that it allowed that to work.

Did the same principle govern the look of the film?
Absolutely. The aim was to be as real as we could to the period, and make a very credible look that you don't pay attention to. You just see the actors and a piece of time rather than 'Oh gosh! Look at that!' Something that occurred to me when I was going to write it was that our view of the fifties is very much through movies like *Grease*. It's like the fabulous colourful fifties. I wanted *Diner* to be a much more straight-ahead look at the time. It had a look of winter, and in the wintertime it was obviously grey. It was a stripped-down thing. And that applied to the cinematography as well. Everything would have this no-nonsense look about it.

What was your input in this regard? Did you use photographs, other films to show what you wanted?
The costumier Gloria Gresham would show me stuff in magazines, and I would show her stuff in yearbooks and whatever else I could provide that I felt was very 'Baltimore'. I found as much as I could to show how we dressed, the kinds of ties and shirts and sports jackets that people were wearing at the time. I wanted to stay fairly accurate to that. It was a very non-cute, non-flashy view of the times.

Did you use locations that you already knew from growing up in Baltimore?
I couldn't use the real diner because it had already been turned into a liquor store. So I needed to find another diner. There was a great looking diner on Route 40, I think, but it didn't work out. Then Peter Sova and I were riding around one Sunday afternoon, just looking at things, and we stopped and saw this piece of land down by the harbour. And I said to him, 'Wouldn't it be great if the diner was just right there?' And he said, 'Yeah, that'd be good.' So I talked to Mark and said, 'Why don't we put our own diner there?' So we tracked down a diner graveyard in New Jersey, and we went up there and there were all these old diners just

stuck around in the mud, just diner after diner. We saw one diner we thought looked right, so we worked out a deal, brought that diner down and put it on that piece of land which the city allowed us to use for a while. In a sense we were much better off than using the functional one on the highway because we would have run into a zillion problems. So we got lucky. And you always need a certain amount of luck when you're making movies.

Can you remember how you felt before the shoot?
I think I went to bed and slept, and that was the end of that. But I must have been somewhat nervous, suddenly to be launching this thing. I remember walking around at the Holiday Inn where we were headquartered. All the trucks were there. God Almighty, all these trucks! They were all over the lot and I went, 'Oh my God!' I think that got me more than anything else. Trucks!

How did your first day go?
The first thing we were going to shoot was the girl, 'Jane Chisholm', riding her horse. When I cast the actress, I said, 'Can you ride a horse?' She said, 'Yes.' I said to the AD, 'Check her out. Make sure she can really ride a horse.' He said, 'She's fine.' So we get to the first day. We're getting ready, we've worked out the first shot. I see her on the horse, then I'm doing something else and suddenly I hear on the walkie-talkies: 'The horse has gone off! Can anyone see the horse?' And the horse has now run away with her. She's off over the horizon somewhere and the wranglers are trying to find this runaway horse. Anyway, she obviously could not ride a horse that well. And basically I lost a half a day on my first day's shoot.

How did you feel?
Oh my God! Terrible. The very first day, it was March and bitterly cold. And I'd lost half a day. The second day was in a pool-hall. We had designed the first shot, with a little move. But our video playback kept rolling: every time we tried to do a shot, a roll-bar would come through it. So by lunchtime, I'd done one set-up. I think I had about nineteen set-ups in my head and by lunch I'd done one. I said to Peter, we're going to have to really move because I can't get another half day behind on this. And what I did was I shot that scene much like I was telling you earlier when I didn't know anything at all. I just shot it in the camera. If that's all I was going to use, that's all I shot. And we ended up getting eighteen set-ups by the end of the day. Just, bang, cut that, cut that, take this, this and this. No room for anything other than just accomplishing the work. The performances were all good but you didn't have the luxury of saying maybe there's something else here. A shot was for only for those two lines, period.

Eighteen set-ups after lunch – that sounds like a long day.
We did it in the allotted time. And after that everything settled down. You begin to find a rhythm for the shoot, things fall into place. And I think I never felt really pushed until we had a fire at the diner. An electrical fire, we lost the better part of

a night. I said to the studio, 'We really need an extra day because of the fire.' They said, 'No, you can't have it. It's too bad.' I said, 'But the movie is *Diner* and now we're doing all the diner scenes.' 'No, you can't have the extra day.' So we had to figure how to do it without the extra day. They didn't care.

During the whole thing, did you think you were given your creative head by the studio?
Periodically they would complain about things. But by and large they left me alone. That didn't mean they liked what they saw.

Did you have any lucky breaks – unforeseen blessings or magic moments?
Once we got to the diner, I felt that the guys really knew one another. That could have been messy. Sometimes in movies you get all these people talking and it all becomes blurred and you can't hear it. There was a naturalism that I really believed. The way they could just slide in and out of these moments in terms of the dialogue was as credible as I could ever have hoped.

Was there a particular pattern to the days?
We had a lot of night shoots. We were getting to the location just before dark and shooting till sunrise. I think we did that thirty-one or thirty-two of the forty days of the shoot.

Did you think you were learning a lot on the set?
I think you always feel you're learning. Always. You always remain a student of the craft. Whatever movie you're doing, because there are new problems that have to be resolved. And the nature of the craft is that it's not like you can figure it all out. I mean, why is it that this particular shot in this particular sequence, a long shot, being way back, may be better than being close? There's no easy answer to that. There are all these decisions you have to make. Is it better in a two-shot? Is it better in a single? I know some people just shoot the scene every which way that they possibly can. But I can't. I need to start to see it: those are the shots that I want and so that's what I'll go after. And sometimes when you're lining it up and you're looking at it, you realize wait a minute, it's better here. It's better when we're not actually seeing the face that clearly. It's better if it's a little darker in this scene.

So you're making decisions right until the camera starts turning over?
Yeah. There's a million decisions that you have to make. When I was doing the sequences in the diner and we'd lost this day, I said, 'How the hell are we going to make this up?' Peter said, 'Break out the second camera. We can shoot the sequence on two cameras, so we can use a two shot and a single.' So that was the start of my using a second camera. Then, after what seemed to me like a good take, the sound-man said to me, 'You're getting these off-camera voices mixed in with your on-camera voices. And you don't want that, because you can do the overlaps in post.' I said, 'But that throws off the actors' rhythms.' Sometimes it's natural to be doing that. So I said, 'Well, mike the off-camera people too, so it won't be a problem in the audio. The only problem we might have would be in

the cutting but I'll work around that.' That was a choice that I made. 'Well, the hell with it, we'll just go with overlaps and it'll ultimately be better for the piece.' And I've always done that since. I've always miked everyone on and off-camera. So that way if you have an overlap, you have an overlap. I need to hear the rhythm of the piece. I can't just manufacture it later on. I want to hear the natural rhythms of the piece because the dialogue I do is so conversational and its humour comes out of its rhythms more than its jokes. If you inhibit the actors, it loses its edge.

Does that mean you fight tooth-and-nail not to use post-sync?
I try not to. I want to get the performance on the floor, not after the fact.

What did you find hardest about directing for the first time?
You need the stamina to stay on top of all the decision-making that has to take place. Somehow you've got to find the stamina to stay clear enough in terms of what you want to accomplish in any sequence. So you can say yes or no, and stay focused on it with all of these people buzzing around you. If you get a little tired and say, go ahead and do it like that, that might be the thing that kills you. If you lose your focus, it's very easy for the scene to completely evaporate. All of a sudden it has no clarity, no point of view, because you're simply going 'All right, the hell with it' because you're too tired to do anything else.

What was the reaction to the first cut of the film?
It was a disaster. The worst experience. I think I did myself a great disservice by showing it to a few friends in an early state. I mean, you would have thought I was showing them this heavy drama. There was not one laugh for the entire screening. Actually, there was one laugh and that particular laugh is not in the movie any more, because I cut the piece out. But it was devastating. And I was thinking, none of this is funny? Even if it doesn't all work, there must be some laughs? Jesus, this movie can't be so out of whack . . . And afterwards people said, 'Well, you know . . .' (*mimics severe embarrassment*) They didn't know what to say. One guy came up to me and said, 'I like the script.' We just shot a whole fucking movie here and he's saying, I liked the script. I guess it was just the fact that it was very crude at that point. But afterwards, I just thought, oh God, this is truly the end. It was a horrible, horrible screening . . .

Did you change the movie in any way because of this response?
We didn't do a lot of work to clean it up. The movie obviously got tighter and a little more focused after that particular screening. But a lot of it stayed the way it was. I said, 'Look, we can't make any sense out of what they're reacting to. If they're not laughing at some of the sequences, there's something that's throwing them out of whack, and I don't know what it is. But we've just got to do the work we got to do.'

How did the studio react when they saw it for the first time?

Not very impressed. I mean, I don't remember the phone going, 'Hey, Barry, great movie!' They said, 'You got a lot to learn about editing.' I said, 'I guess I probably do, but give me an example.' They said, 'Well, for one, the scene where he's asking about the roast beef sandwich? Is he going to eat it or not? Just – boom! – cut past that. Get on with the story.' I said, 'But that is the story. That is really at the heart of the movie, and these relationships.' It was not a great meeting. Then we screened the movie in various cities, where the audience filled out the cards. And the cards were never particularly good: just so-so. They didn't show we had a big hit on our hands, so that the studio might get excited. And then we opened in Phoenix and St Louis and Baltimore, and we didn't open well. And so their plan was basically kill the movie and bury it.

So how did it become the Diner *we know and love today?*
The critic Judith Crist used to have these seminars in Tarrytown. She had scheduled to show a certain MGM movie, but it wasn't ready. A terrific guy called Scott McDougall at MGM-UA liked *Diner*, and he went to Judith Crist and said, 'Look, how about if you show this new movie by Barry Levinson? He's written with Mel Brooks, so you could show Mel Brooks' movies. He did *And Justice for All* so you could show the movie with Al Pacino that Norman Jewison directed. And he had this movie, *Inside Moves*. So you could just show these various films that he wrote and the film that he directed, and make a weekend of that.' She bought that. But the idea of flying me to New York for that alone was like, oh shit, it's a lot of money to fly this guy. They didn't want the critics to see it.

They didn't want the critics to see Diner?
No – because the movie's, like, *history*. It's buried. So what he did was bring it to New York and in order to justify it to the accounting department, he said Levinson's coming to New York to do this and he'll do some other publicity. Now they don't know – it's like one arm doesn't necessarily know about the other – so he showed the film to some critics in New York. Pauline Kael and *Rolling Stone*, perhaps. And it really got a good reaction. So I go to Judith Crist and do that weekend. Then people like Pauline Kael said, when is the movie coming out? I'm going to run a review. Well, the studio doesn't say and doesn't say and eventually she said, I'm going to run the review even if the movie's not playing. And Michael Schragow of *Rolling Stone* says, I'm going to run the review, anyway. So MGM didn't want to be embarrassed. They had a movie playing at the festival at 57th Street. It was supposed to run another week but wasn't playing well. So they pulled that out and put *Diner* in. On the Tuesday I heard that *Diner* was going to open at the festival on 57th Street on Friday. So the first ad turns up on Thursday. You know, '*Diner* tomorrow'. So Friday we open and Pauline Kael came out with her review in the *New Yorker* and *Rolling Stone* too. It got a rave review in *The New York Times*. And we do very nice business on the Friday. Well, come Saturday night there was a big rainstorm. I'll never forget this moment because I was

at the Sherry Netherland Hotel where you can see the corner of 57th and Fifth. I was working with Sidney Pollack, who was getting ready to do *Tootsie*, and I was just sort of there helping out a little bit. And I'm looking out of the window trying to see if there's a line, you know, for the movie. It's early evening and I don't see a line. I don't see anything. And Sidney was trying to be nice. He said, 'They'll stand in the cold. But rain, they hate to stand in the rain.' He's trying to be nice and I'm going, 'It's over.' I had one night. Everyone who wanted to see the movie saw it and now it's Saturday and there's no one there. Well, I had to go to dinner and as I ride by the festival I don't see anyone at all. I don't see any line, just a rainstorm. And I go to dinner with Mark. He said, did you stop by the festival? And I said, I couldn't. He said it sold out. I said, how could that be? I didn't see anybody there. He said, well, there's a downstairs or something like that. They let them in and they go down. He stopped there at like ten o'clock and it was sold out. And then Sunday the noon show was sold out. It was sold out the whole day. And then Monday it did well and then the MGM-UA people said, well, if you can do four thousand or whatever the hell it is, well maybe . . . Then it snowed on Tuesday and it did huge business. Then came the second weekend and we broke the house record. We said, now we can start to open. But instead they went to Boston and then to Toronto. We thought at some point maybe we're going to start to open a little wider but we literally went town by town by town. We never played in more than two hundred theatres in the United States. Broke house records in a number of different places. But ultimately it proved itself and that was the key. So you went from being a movie that was going to go on the shelf, you know, a failed opening in Phoenix and St Louis, to a movie that becomes critically acclaimed and is doing quite well in New York and playing quite a long time.

Did it have a big effect on your directing career?
What happens is you finally make a mark which allows you to do another one. It goes back to what the guy said about technical wizardry. I kept saying, shit, they ain't going to notice that in this movie 'cause it's very understated. But the movie ultimately worked. And that opened the door for me to become a director.

Do you think it would be harder today to make a Diner *for a first-time director? Or will a good script always get through?*
I wouldn't be as optimistic as to say a good script always gets through because there's a lot of really good scripts that don't. But it does still happen. Whether it's a *sex, lies and videotape* here or another one there, they do get through. It's a big, big business, with huge dollars at stake. And this business is far more competitive and the dollars are much larger than when *Diner* was made. But there's still these very small movies that continue to creep through. I think it's part of the lifeblood of the business. Even though it doesn't return the dollars, those little things that bubble up periodically are very important to the business and will continue to happen. The business can never live just on the big films.

Oliver Stone: *Salvador**

Who do you think were the most influential film-makers you were aware of when you were growing up? Who did you like?

Like many people, I saw a lot of pictures as a child: from Michael Curtiz to John Ford and so forth. But I didn't know who the directors were. I became aware of the tradition of film-making later on at film school. That gave me a solid grounding in realizing that many people were involved. That it's elitist to pick out a few people as the critics do and always come back to those people because you ignore so much of the effort, so many people. But ultimately you always have certain influences as a film-maker. In my case they're European rather than American. Certainly Fellini was a king. I love Godard and Truffaut. I love Buñuel. Alain Resnais, I loved. Also Welles was very popular at film school. We also had Bergman. Renoir, *Les Enfants du Paradis*. You know, the usual suspects.

What was NYU film school like in the late sixties?

I joined up after Vietnam when the G.I. Bill came in. I paid all my tuition, pretty much all of it and I went to film class. Scorsese was one of the first teachers. Haig [Manoogian] was a great teacher, as was Marty. They used to make us make these short films. They were crudely done, very low money, 16 mm, black and white. It was a radical time. We would critique each other's films in a collective situation. There would be twenty-five students in the class, you'd show your film and the reviews would range from 'a piece of shit' to 'it should never have been done'. We also used to discuss the films before we shot them. We'd have to sell them to the collective. That's not so easy, so it was an interesting concept. It was very helpful to me later in my life. Movies are a one-man vision but the vision is at the same time a collective one, a strange amalgam. I always find that my NYU experience helps centre me in my editing. For several years now I've used a system of three editors. We bring our work together, we criticize openly and we grow stronger as a result of that critique.

You made three short films there?

I did three short films, yeah and they grew in length. The first one was ten or eleven minutes, the second one was twenty-two and then I went for twenty-five mins.

* Prior to *Salvador*, Oliver Stone made two films, *Seizure* (1974) and *The Hand* (1981). When approached about this book, however, he said he wanted to discuss *Salvador* as it was the film that launched his career as a writer–director and the first film where he felt a true sense of authorship and ownership. After some hurried soul-searching, I agreed.

Out of the work you did prior to Salvador, *what taught you most about directing?*
I learnt a lot from De Palma on *Scarface*. On the set with Al and Brian and Marty
who were actually in the pits, way over budget and three months over the schedule. They had me around the whole six months practically, doing changes to the
script. So I saw the process first-hand and learnt a lot. I learnt a lot from acting
school and from writing, from film-making at NYU. Making short films helped
an enormous amount and influenced my films. I was a PA on several films which
taught me things. You learn from everywhere. But as I remember, it was very
competitive, very tough. People were contrary; people were not giving information out. It wasn't easy to get on a film set. Alan Parker didn't want anybody on
his set. He was not an easy person to get along with. I think if you have done the
screenplay you should be invited to the set by the director. I think that's really
wrong. It's rude.

Do you think writing is a good preparation for directing?
Yes and no. Some people can be very stodgy and academic about it. Pedantic.
They don't understand that this real thing happens between director and actor.
There's something about that which always fascinates me. It's a knowledge of
other people, that you have or you don't have. It's something you are given –
observational power – whatever. For me it's a delight to be with an actor and talk
about behaviour. I enjoy that process. And also I really enjoy the technical part. I
like to feel it is multi-dimensional.

How did your collaboration with Richard Boyle come about?
I was in San Francisco. He picked me up from the airport. On the back seat of his
car was this oily manuscript and he said 'Oh yeah, that's my Salvador story' and
I said 'Oh? Interesting'. I picked it up and read it in the back seat. Immediately I
saw that there was the potential here for a very funny story about a journalist in
Salvador and I loved it. And I brought Boyle down and paid for his life for the
next six months, boarded him in my house, much to my wife's consternation. He
just drank anything he could. He drank the baby formula one night. Completely!
But we wrote a script and hashed it out and got it financed quite quickly with
Gerald Green, John Daly and Mr Arnold Kopelson.

How did you work together?
I did the writing. He did the talking. Richard has lived a very colourful life. He is
a colourful person. He had no money. I knew him from the days when I wrote
Born on the Fourth of July. He had written a book called *Dragons*. It was a very
good book about the Vietnamese war. He had Left inclinations, but the Irish
kind, you know, like 1930s Irish: a bottle of booze and go into battle and don't
give a shit. He was a character, no sense of possessions, no materialism. Beyond
materialism and yet a great materialist at the same time. I mean, he would grab
whatever he could. Anyway, he was a wonderful companion and a great storyteller and a great Irish guy. So, half of it's fiction, half of it's fact.

Which of the two main characters in Salvador, *Boyle and Dr Rock, do you identify with?*
Dr Rock was his other friend. But he would never have gone. The real Dr Rock was so chickenshit he would never leave San Francisco. He tried to get famous off the film, too. And tried to hold us up for some money. He was a character too. They're all crazy.

Prior to Salvador, *you'd been trying to break through as a writer-director for quite a long time. Did you have a sense that this was your last chance?*
Salvador was very much a learning curve film. It's one of the ultimate first-feature films. It was a movie in which I invested my entire being. There was no other choice. It was this – or dying. I said to my wife at that time, 'We're mortgaging the house. We are going to sell everything we have. We are going to raise money, borrow money from the bank and I am going to make this movie for five hundred thousand, six hundred thousand dollars. If necessary, I will go to Salvador and use Salvadoran troops. I will con the Salvadoran army' – which I did. Richard and I went down there and tried to con them into giving us all their tanks and all their troops for nothing. In return for which we would portray them as the heroes and the rebels as hard, as monsters. And the idea would be, then we would go to Mexico, on the back end and would rebalance the film there. But it didn't work when our advisor was killed. Actually he was shot down in cold blood, playing tennis and the FM flag was draped on him in the public square. We saw the pictures in *The New York Times*, on the front page and we knew that the project in Salvador wasn't going to work as well as we thought.

But you kept going?
I had to do it. My back was to the wall. There was no more fucking around. I wasn't playing. I had to put my body and soul into it. John Daly stepped in and saved me from doing the picture financially myself. Otherwise I would be in jail, or bankrupt as a result. It was all financed crookedly, under a fake bond. It was so bizarre. We were using this phoney letter of credit for which later somebody died or went to jail. It originated in Belgium or Holland. The other film was called *Outpost*, a Dutch film. A letter had been given already to them because they were supposed to have Schwarzenegger who was hot. That was being done as *Salvador* by a crazy guy with no stars. And we had to keep the title, *Outpost*.

How did Hemdale get involved?
I met this character called Gerald Green. He is a character. He belongs in *The Mask of Demetrius* or something like that. He's a very, very funny man. British. Anyway, he, in his impeccable sort of style, wanted to work with me and he knew I was a free option at that point. He said *Salvador* was a great idea and he sent the treatment on to John Daly at Hemdale. John responded immediately. Meanwhile, Arnold Kopelson had a free option on *Platoon*. He had also sent it to John. His option ran out and John wanted to do that, too. For some reason, John

believed in me, even if many people had given me a bad rap, saying I was trouble to work with, and *Scarface* was not received well. I was considered a tough kid. A rebel. And here was a British company that didn't give a fuck. John had been around a long time. He was a boxing promoter, a real tough guy. He'd been in prison. He'd been under pressure. He'd been thrown into jail in the Congo for not paying taxes by some crazed Congo dictator and had survived that experience. That's what I liked about him. He could handle pressure. So he came into this thing and said, which one do you want to do first? *Salvador* or *Platoon*? After years of rejection, to be asked that question is like 'which pussy do you want? The golden one or the chestnut brown one?' I said *Salvador*. I didn't want to say *Platoon* because I thought *Platoon* had been cursed by so many defeats. I thought, if I pick that one something will happen. So I did *Salvador*, which John, many years later, regretted because he always said to me, you know, if you had only done *Platoon* first, it would have been such a success and they would not have ignored *Salvador* when it came out. We would have made a lot of money.

How did you find your DP, Robert Richardson?
He had been in Salvador. He had done a documentary. He had interviewed some of these guys. He knew the scoop, walked into my office. By this time I had been turned down by three or four top, not top but you know, young hot DPs. They turned me down. Then Bob came in and he seemed like the right mix. We went with each other for the next few films; eleven films we did together.

How did you work together? Did you do a lot of preparation?
No. Me and Bob were both winging it. We were shooting fast, in documentary-like fashion, which is what I wanted. I didn't get much indulgence which you get as you get bigger and bigger – till you have so many toys you don't know which one to fucking use! But at that point you didn't have a choice. Because really, it was pretty limited.

So how did you prepare yourself as a director?
When you write the script you have this mental image. That's how you are shooting the movie. You are thinking it through. And not everything is evident. There are many things that are decided upon later, with the collaboration of your DP, your production designer, your producer, your actors, many things, editors. I mean, so much comes into play, because that's the collaboration process. But I feel when I come to the set that I am ready to make *that* movie, the one I have in my head. But if I get a better idea about a certain way to do it, I'll listen. I have no problem about listening.

A director should be a good listener?
A very good listener. Sometimes, the best direction is one word or two words, four. I mean, honestly, if you are communicating, you don't need to say too much.

What can you remember about the shoot?

The shooting was a nightmare of discomfort, of interruptions: constant financial problems. Gerald Green was down there, barricaded, taking calls left and right. The crew were constantly striking. There was one strike in the middle of it, I remember. I yawned and went to bed in the car. I went to sleep in the car. I just didn't give a shit any more. You know, you reach a place where you have fought so much to keep this thing together that it's beyond your destiny, it just has to happen. We closed down in Mexico on day forty-two. We were kicked out of Mexico with bills unpaid. And I went back to John and begged him to finish the movie and to do the beginning and the end because I had shot the middle and I hadn't done the American section yet. He thought about it and said, can't you cut the beginning? And I said, that's a ridiculous idea, John. Why don't you just cut the ending too? So we went to Vegas. He gave us some extra money. We finished it in Vegas and San Francisco. I had a lot of problems on the editing of it too because of the violence of the war. So that was also a big issue. We had to cut it way back and I think we lost some things in there. Unfortunately the film has a very chequered history. Hemdale went bankrupt. Three of my films went into bankruptcy too: *The Doors*, *Platoon*, and *Salvador*. Plus, *Talk Radio*. So I've always done films with these people who go bankrupt. But the point is that we never lose hope.

There are some very big set pieces in Salvador. *Did you find it easy to stage the action?*
You have to understand that I always considered myself a director. When I got out of film school, call me arrogant but I said, 'I am a director'. It was just an assumption. All those screenplays were written in the belief that I would be the director. I would always write on the paper: 'director, director'. By the time *Salvador* came I was a very hungry person. I was a fighter, a warrior. It had been too long that I'd wanted to direct. It had been thirteen fucking years since I left film school. I'd done two pictures that weren't getting me anywhere and had written some screenplays and I had to get something done with my life. I was pushing forty. I was about thirty-nine. And here I was getting my chance. It was hit or miss now. I mean, it was all or nothing. Most directors have made hits in their twenties. I started very late as a director.

Prior to Salvador, *did you have a constant sense of time running out?*
I gave up several times. I died artistic deaths. I just never thought I would get my shot. That's why when I got my shot I really ran like the devil for ten years. You got to understand that they all think that was all very militaristic but the fact was it came from a desire and fear. Because I had been through a lot of rejection. I hadn't had the opportunity to do films – many broken hearts – so when I had one, I figured I had to go, take it, use your power and make the film. Basically I did ten films in a row up to *Nixon*, you know? I got a little tired! I wrote a book and I did a smaller film called *U-Turn* which I loved. I did what I wanted to do. I did ten in a row, fast. Nobody caught me. The critics were always after me and in

the end they hurt me. They all trumpeted each other and they all said the same thing. They came up with 'conspiracist'. But it's not so.

Was part of your purpose to make a political statement about America's support for the right wing in Salvador? Or was it simply a good story?
I said it at the time and I say the same thing now. It was a great story, a great challenge and I was excited by it because I liked the background. I don't think I would have liked to have done it if it had been set in Alaska or fishing. There are certain things that interest you. Politics does interest me but it's not my *raison d'être*. If it had been, I think I would have gone into it and it's a rough-and-tumble world. I consider myself a storyteller and a dramatist. I worked at it that way and I thought I'd try to tell the story. If it's a real story and it happened, in a fair way. You try to understand. You can accuse me of partisanship and perhaps immaturity. I was a younger man. That's another issue. At that time I felt really strongly that you had to be shocked by our Salvador adventure. The Americans did the wrong thing in Salvador. You had to be offended by it, especially coming off the Vietnam war. And I was very fiery about that. I said things pretty bluntly back then. Probably I'm a different person now. I find *Salvador* a radical film that way. Some people like that. It's certainly more black and white as a film. It's broader, it's more like *Natural Born Killers*, cartoon-like.

Salvador has been described as Buñuelian. Was that part of your intention?
No. Buñuel I love. But my intention was to tell the story fast. It was a montage to get us down to Salvador. I loved the concept of going down there because he is broke and has no money and I think there is delightful and charming hope to the story to have these two bums who can't make it on the fringes of American society, going down to get blow-jobs in Salvador, and maybe get some extra money. There's something very free and adventurous about it. It's a great road movie thesis. And I also had a great sequel in mind. I had a great idea for going to Beirut. It's too bad John went out of business. Because I like John Daly and he always played his hand and got in some messes. If he had done *Salvador* after *Platoon*, it would have made a big difference and we could have gone to Ireland and Beirut.

How did Salvador fare commercially?
Salvador was not a success theatrically. It was a big disappointment to me. John Daly released it through his own Hemdale Releasing Corporation because he was pissed off by the way Orion had handled it. At least it was reviewed, it was heard of for about two seconds. But the reviews were very mixed. I somehow felt good in my guts because Bob Dylan went to a screening and said it was a great movie. That was enough. I knew that somebody had seen the movie at another level and had said it had worked for them.

What were the main things you learned during the making of the film?
A lot of technical stuff. How to do war stuff, you know. How to make do with lit-

tle money. *Platoon* was the same, by the way. Both films were very cheap. *Platoon* was a five to six million dollar movie made in the Philippines: a very low-budget independent movie with a British actor who nobody really knew made through a bargain basement producing house. And it yielded this enormous international return that was unreal. Broke the house. Got everything: Academy Award picture, all that shit and money too, flowing in. It was just a dream come true. Especially if you have spent years like Daly and I in the Congos of the world, in the Congo prisons of the fucking world. It was a great movie. I always will think of *Salvador* and *Platoon* as twins, brother and sister. They were made in the same spirit of madness, back to back. I was moving literally from Mexico to the Philippines. I was taking off from Mexico City to Manila. It was a bizarre world. Everything was weird.

Looking back at it after some twelve films, what's the main thing you remember about the experience?
The thing I remember about *Salvador* was how bold and confident we were. Adventurous young men willing to go forth to Mexico, to Salvador and have dinner with Arena death squads, talk to Americans and show me the spies and hang out in the countryside and hope the guerrillas would come by, you know, and try to con the Salvadoran air force and military army into helping us for free and having all that madness. Going to villages out in the Mexican countryside too where the people would not pay taxes or cooperate with the government. Total vigilante villages we shot in. With the rebels – just the confidence and the feeling of being on top of the world. You know you have made a film that says something, that has guts and colour and a splash. We were very proud of it, and it's at that moment that it breaks like a wave, you know. The first success and you sort of feel it.

Since then, the majority of your films have all been firmly planted in America. Do you still follow European cinema?
No. Films in Europe have got bleaker and bleaker. There was something ironic about that wave: the 'new wave' of films. Life that was despairing yet had a colour and an energy that was the brightest. I feel it's got grimmer and grimmer. So the films now coming out of Europe, especially the hard-edged ones, are to me a little bit cold. Cold and frightening, actually.

Do you think it's easier to make your first film now than when you made Salvador?
Films have become more whorish. It's become too easy now. Then, the opposite was true. A low-budget film was a big *cause célèbre*. Now it seems like everybody and their uncle can make a low-budget film. It's lost some of its sacredness.

Neil Jordan: *Angel*

When you were growing up did you go to movies all the time?
My father was a teacher and he had very strict views, not about what we should see, but how much we should see, really. So I was only able to see movies once every two weeks.

What kind of thing did you see?
Anything that played in my local cinema, the Fairview, in Clontarf on the north side of Dublin. There were a lot of these crypto-teen movies, Tommy Steele and Cliff Richard things. All the *Carry Ons* were coming out. A lot of rubbish, really. Like every adolescent – certainly every Irish adolescent – I thought the movies were exclusively connected with sex. I mean, Dublin was a very uniform society at the time. So that would have been one's mode of escape.

When did you start to take them seriously?
Really it was when I began to watch Fellini and Bergman and Godard. There was an arthouse cinema in Dublin at the time. And the strangest movies used to end up there. I first came across Japanese movies there, Italian films, Bergman films. That's when I began to look at them as something apart from entertainment.

Was there a moment when you thought that's what I want to do?
I always wanted to do it. But it didn't seem possible. I was writing fiction from the age of about sixteen. Then I went to university and I worked in a theatre group there with Jim Sheridan. We took over the drama society and set up an independent theatre group. And when I came out I tried to get into the National Film School in England, Beaconsfield. I sent in some of the plays I'd written. I actually got a place there but I couldn't afford to go, because it was very expensive and you didn't get grants as an Irish person.

When did writing fiction and plays give way to screenwriting?
When I began to publish, and get known. People began to commission scripts off me. But I experienced this tremendous conflict because it seemed a far less pure pursuit than the austerity and isolation of writing novels. It's to do with the culture I grew up in. Irish culture is always dressed up in literary terms. Dublin is a writers' city. When I began writing fiction the whole ethos of it was regarded as terribly important. It seemed to me to be like a handing on of the keys kind of process. One was regarded as the heir to an older generation of writers like John McGahern, Sean O'Faolain, Brian Friel. I was quite a well-known figure in Ire-

land because I won the Guardian Fiction prize for my first book of stories. And a lot of people were quite outraged that I would actually consider making films – on the one hand, literary people, and on the other, people who'd been trying to make films themselves. They were really pissed off. They thought you should earn your stripes, I suppose.

Do you think you still have the conflict between your literary and screen sides?
Yeah, I do. At the moment I want to write a novel. But we don't live in a culture that allows you to do more than one thing. The last novel I published, half the reviews said, surprisingly enough, he should never have taken up making movies or he should go back to making movies. They think it's an act of supreme arrogance to do two things. I don't see why one shouldn't be able to make a film, write a play if you want to. It's a different muscle that you use. The less you use it the harder it is to use.

What's the main difference between writing novels and writing films?
When you're writing a screenplay the words you're using are your best attempt to describe an event that will happen in the future. A screenplay is not the finished item. Whereas when you're writing a piece of prose, the words you're using are the event: it begins and ends with what you've written. Writing a screenplay is pure joy compared to that. It's like skiing compared to walking through deep snow. It's a far less burdensome experience because you know the main burden will be when you're actually making the movie.

Do you think writing is a good preparation for directing?
I think it's totally different. Writing a screenplay seemed a natural progression from writing prose, like another branch of the same activity. But directing a film was like total cleavage, something totally different. It was a terribly brutal experience. Nothing I'd ever done had prepared me for it. And actually that's logical when you think of it because it's a totally different form from putting pen to paper. Movies themselves have disrupted every other traditional literary or pictorial form.

Can you describe the path that led to Angel?
I'd written two books: a collection of short stories called *A Night in Tunisia* and a novel called *The Past*. They were both very influenced by movies, by the way of looking at things in movies. So much so that *The Past* was actually about a photographer and the whole book existed in pictorial terms, in terms of what was seen and heard. It was almost burdened by its visual obsessions. There were no Irish movies so I'd been writing stuff for Irish television. I wrote a script called *Travellers*, a thriller/road movie kind of thing about an arranged marriage between two young traveller kids. I'd done some TV adaptations of my stories for television but this was the first film script I wrote. I got quite excited about the story and then it was made into a short independent movie, a fifty-minute movie or

something, which I wasn't very happy with. I found the experience of seeing my work changed so upsetting that I said if I ever did it again I'd try and direct my own stuff.

When did you direct for the first time?
I'd written a script for John Boorman called *Broken Dream*, an adaptation of a book he'd bought the rights to. I'd gone through the last draft of *Excalibur* with him, we'd talked through all the underlying ideas in it. And he wanted me on the set of the film as a kind of creative consultant. So I directed a small film on him making *Excalibur*. It was an hour-long documentary, a very interesting film. That was the first time I'd ever taken a camera crew around, the first time I was ever on a film set. And to see a large movie being made, based on these ideas John and I had talked about, was kind of thrilling really. So I decided to try and do it myself. When I'd finished the script for *Angel* I sent it to Walter Donohue at Channel 4. They'd just started up. He read it and liked it a lot, and we met. But then I said to him and David Rose that I wanted to direct it, and they were very nonplussed by this. I said, 'Well, if John Boorman agreed to produce it, would you support me?' They said 'Yeah.' So I showed the script to John and spoke to him about it. He agreed to produce it. And they agreed to let me direct it.

So the existence of Channel 4 was crucial in giving you your first chance?
It was a combination of things. On the one hand, Channel 4 had been set up and they didn't want to create a writers' cinema, but they didn't want to go the old Hollywood route either. They wanted to get more interesting material, material that was alive and direct, that reflected people's experiences. So they were quite open to the idea of a writer coming up with a screenplay, and they were also, reluctantly, open to a writer actually directing his first film. But they needed the security of someone with some experience behind them, which in this case was John Boorman. He really filled that gap. So it was a combination of John and Channel 4 that enabled me to make the film.

How did your collaboration with John Boorman work?
He put the budget together. He put me in touch with the organizational aspects of the whole thing. He went through the script with me, the casting. And then when I started shooting, he came round on the first day, and then that was it. Which, to me, is the best thing a producer can do, really. Because as a director, you've just got to go through that experience. You've got to either find a way to express yourself and do what you see in your heart or your brain – or you fail. And I'm sure you generally fail. But even then, you either fail and survive, or you fail and perish.

What was the inspiration for the story?
I had played saxophone in a band when I was trying to support myself as a writer. So I'd toured up and down the north of Ireland a bit, playing at different venues.

And it was around the height of the sectarian killing campaign. The north was quite a dark and horrible place. I remember very well the experience of driving back at night and getting lost in areas that you shouldn't have been in and coming across blocked-off roads and guys with balaclavas and trying to reverse quickly out of it. But it seemed that musicians were immune from the shooting. Then there was a band that was killed, the Miami Showband. They stopped in the wrong place and were all machine-gunned to death. That was the basic stimulus for the movie. At the time I couldn't say that, because it was such a renowned event and I didn't want to make a film about that event. But it was the idea of guys in silvery suits being shot down arbitrarily. It was a bit like circus people being assassinated, even though they did no harm to anybody. Before that, the showband circuit went north and south.

Did it take long to write?
I wrote it very quickly, in about four or five weeks, I think. Then I rewrote it. The first draft was quite realistic, then I wrote another draft which brought out the coincidental nature of it.

Were you influenced by any other movies?
I was influenced by Nicholas Ray's films. I saw it as a *film noir* set in Ireland. But I was also influenced by musicals. *Angel* had a very dark and violent subject, but I wanted it to look like a musical. That's where the lighting thing came from. I couldn't quite articulate this but I could see these golden and purple and glittery costumes, all the things you'd see in a ballroom, against this very grey, dull, leaden kind of landscape. I could see these contrasts. And that was the image I had of the movie. How to execute that was a different matter. The approach of documentary realism would be the natural route to take: to show British soldiers kicking the shite out of people and so on. But I wanted to tell a story where the logic, the impetus behind people's actions, was never presented. I would never show a reason as to why this and that person would be shot. I wanted to remove the social and political context entirely from the story.

To my mind the story itself had a dream-like quality, largely due to the many coincidences it contained. Was this your intention?
To me, it wasn't so much a thriller, really. What was important was what it was about. And everything I did came from the central idea of what the movie was about, what it was meant to be saying. It was not about people taking up arms because they exist in a post-colonial situation, but about the attraction of a weapon, and the attraction of the idea of killing. That was the most difficult thing: just trying to communicate these rather personal and philosophical ideas to all these people.

There's a scene at the end of the film where the band's singer, Deirdre, doesn't want Danny to touch her. Did you feel Danny had been contaminated by his use of violence?

He'd been taken over by the ease with which you can kill people. I just saw the gun in the saxophone case. One thing being glittery and the other thing actually having far more attractiveness than the saxophone. Of course it was the idea of revenge that led him there but once you get there he'd been led to a place where he exists in another world. It was a story about the attractiveness of evil. The attractiveness of the power of life over death, the seduction of that notion. That's the story I wanted to tell. I didn't want to tell a story about the historical roots of the issue or anything like that.

Would you say it's very Catholic in its depiction of evil?
Probably. Or more like William Blake. The guy they keep talking about, 'Nobadaddy' comes from Blake.

Who or what is nobadaddy?
Negativity. The attraction of the night. Of black things, dark things. The attraction of emptiness. Stephen Rea was constantly asking people their names before he shot them. And in my mind, the intimate level of the violence that you had in Northern Ireland was one where people were killing people they knew. And they would know by their first name whether they were Catholic or Protestant. If they were Fergus they were nationalist, and if they were Ian they were unionist. I wanted it to be about somebody doing away with the lives of people with whom, in other circumstances, he could have had an interesting conversation or a drink.

In the preparation of the film, what were the main problems you encountered?
The main problem was realizing that nothing happens by chance. If you want to see a certain image you've got to build it, you've got to prepare it. It may be a simple little image one has in mind but to realize it actually takes probably four weeks' work and preparation. For example, in the screenplay there was this image of these huge circular pipes outside the dancehall. Not only do you have to transport the pipes there, but then you have to make sure you can see the dancehall through the pipes. The engineering complexity even of that operation appalled me. And then you've got to blow up the dancehall behind it and get your timing right. Stuff like that I found mind-blowing, staggeringly difficult to deal with and comprehend. Also there's the fact that you've got to explain yourself every step of the way, explaining what is normally just an intuitive unquestioned process. You've got to constantly explain everything you mean to maybe two hundred people. It's terribly exhausting, really wearing. And any expression of uncertainty on the director's part is interpreted as weakness. It's hilarious. Sometimes I'd go out and they'd say well, what do you want to do next? I'd say, well, actually I don't know. I haven't got a clue.

Can you give an example from Angel?
The thing that brought it home to me was when I was walking up and down on Bray seafront looking for a place where we could stage a little scene. There's a

beach there and a promenade above it. I was walking with Stephen Rea and Chris Menges with a little eyepiece. I'd walk down here and say, no, we won't do it here. Then I'd walk back to this other place and say, no, not here either. I turned around and I could see everywhere I went there was a procession of trucks, electrical trucks, catering trucks, all these vehicles. Every time I stopped they'd park. Every time I turned they'd turn. I'd been doing this for twenty minutes and I didn't realize they were following me. That illustrated to me the cumbersome nature of the thing that's following you around compared to the delicate, essential little thing you want to photograph.

How did your collaboration with Chris Menges work?
We had quite a few conversations about what it should look like and the feeling we wanted. We looked at all the locations and chose the colours we wanted. I didn't want any of that bright emerald green that you get in any independent Irish movie. We tried to eliminate that kind of green so we put sand over large areas of green, like ferns and stuff. We'd look at different camera set-ups. He'd ask me what I wanted here, what I wanted there. There was a lot I didn't know. I didn't know how to move the camera very elegantly. I didn't know anything about complementary close-ups. I didn't know anything about the idea of cover. So I suppose he just had to bear with me and be the eyes of this rather inarticulate man. He was very patient. It was really a matter of him trying to find out what I was trying to articulate visually.

How would you describe your technical know-how at this point?
Non-existent, basically. I hadn't got a clue about lenses. Zoom, prime lenses meant nothing to me. Often it was very obvious where to put the camera because we'd chosen the places before and we'd discussed the way we'd shoot it. I mean the film is very graphic but the camera's very static so you get very strong compositions. Whatever mobility we had, believe me, Chris Menges provided because the orchestration both of the camera and of moving characters, the plotting of that orchestration was beyond me.

How did you feel when you started seeing your film come to life in front of your eyes?
Learning about composition was wonderful. About how objects placed in the foreground or where the camera is can actually change the meaning of a scene, or are the meaning of the scene. That was quite extraordinary. And I had to learn that. I didn't know that.

Did you spend much time rehearsing?
I'd worked with actors before in theatre. And these actors were my friends. On this movie you had this bunch of electricians and hard-bitten crew people. To my mind, they'd be always saying, he's doing that? They didn't seem to me to understand or be friends of the process whereas the actors were my co-conspirators. We knew what we wanted to arrive at. None of us had ever made a movie before

so we arrived at ways of expressing our intentions and getting what we wanted. I had a sense that I was most unsuited to this huge machine of things. Because I was trying to express things through it that made the more practical members of the crew throw their eyes to heaven. I had the sense that my own sensibility had to really fight to express itself through this thing.

Would you say that's the most important thing about directing? Being able to communicate what you want?
Actually, I'd say the most important thing about being a director is having something to say. The thing you learn is how to say it. And I don't even know if you learn anything in the end anyway, because every film is totally different. In a way you should approach each film as if you know nothing.

Did you improvise at all?
No. The dialogue was too loaded. There was no room for that kind of thing.

Did your earlier experience in the theatre mean you found staging action easy?
It's not easy at all. In some sequences, for example, when there are people dancing around in the dancehall, there's a movement there that starts itself. With others it was more difficult, but the main problem was me being able to articulate the images as I conceived them clearly enough for people to be able to deliver them.

How did you feel when you were about to start?
I felt in a real state of panic. But you learn you just have to get on with it and make the thing. It was complicated by the fact that I had some threats. Some people called at my house. And the manager of the Miami Showband had been sent some anonymous letters. The whole issue of the IRA, it was slightly scary. My sleeping patterns were a bit disturbed by apocalyptic imaginings.

How long was the shoot?
About six weeks. Then we did a few bits and pieces. We had to do an extra day's shooting which was actually delightful, a wonderful experience.

Were there any moments of luck on Angel?
There were great moments of luck. For example, the image of a guy wandering around in a purple suit could have looked ludicrous, but in fact it looked terribly, terribly strange and sad.

How about things that didn't go as planned?
One stunt went wrong. The sequence where Danny's hijacked the guy in the car and the guy's saying, 'Shoot me, shoot me.' We'd arranged this shot whereby the car comes towards us, and we pan around, and it skids, crashes through a hedge and comes to rest in an open field. Then I'd planned a series of shots of Stephen emerging from that car, and then we were going to set charges and blow it up, as you would in a normal movie. But the stuntman got so excited about having survived the stunt that he started driving round in circles. So we couldn't do what

we planned, and in the end I had to take this rather conventional thing out of the movie.

Were there any disasters?
No. It went quite smoothly. But we did ludicrous things. For example, it was meant to end with a British army helicopter coming down behind Danny in this burnt-out dancehall. We couldn't afford an army helicopter, we could only afford one that could be got from a commercial hire place. They couldn't afford to paint it with the correct markings. So we ended up with this bloody helicopter that we cannot see. In the end we used it just to create a down-draught – the wind in the last shot.

Did the fairly low budget affect the film in other ways?
We hadn't even got enough money for Stephen's costume, we couldn't afford to dress him correctly. In the end, he wore my coat. I said, this coat looks good. He tried it on and it seemed to suit him. If you look at the sequence in the car where Stephen Rea has a gun to this guy's head and he's driving faster and faster and daring him to shoot him, you can see I didn't have the budget or the means to shoot properly. I should have done sections of that in the studio. I should have created a sensation of speed. You didn't get the feeling that the car was going faster and faster, that if Stephen shot this guy he was likely to die himself.

Do you think that as an experienced director you look at a location in a different way from how you did as a first-timer?
No. I don't. Because actually I've used the same locations in *Angel* in many movies. Where the circus was in *Angel* is exactly the same place as the circus in *The Crying Game*. And I used the same location in *Michael Collins*. I use a lot of these locations just because they suit the kinds of thing I like, and I instinctively knew what to do with the camera once I was there.

That's what I was getting at in terms of the difference between an experienced director and one who hasn't done it before.
I think experience in film-making is often a hindrance. When I go to a movie I don't want to see a series of codes being manipulated very expertly. I want to see something fresh and new. I think your job as a director is to make absolutely sure that you're bold enough to put something on the screen that hasn't been there before.

Was the editing a steep learning curve?
No. There wasn't a lot to do. The editor had nothing to work with, really. Everything I shot was in the finished film. And when we cut it together it definitely had its own logic.

What I remember are sounds like the bells on the wishing tree outside the dancehall.
It was a mono dub so those sounds stand out more than they normally would. It's

more poetic if you do it in mono. I think in the end movies are about poetry. I don't think they're about anything else. I think the reason people do them, the reason people want to make them, it isn't for the money, because they don't make a lot of money, really. They're a lot of stress. I could be churning out a novel every two years like any other eminent Irish author. But the reason I do them is that they express something that nothing else can express. This strange thing where observed life, real events express their own poetry, something mythic, something beyond themselves. Photography is a very beautiful thing. To photograph something, you get into a very beautiful relationship with what you're photographing. The act of looking is very pleasing. I think that's why people make films.

How did Channel 4 respond?
I showed it to John Boorman and he was slightly puzzled by it. And I showed it to Walter Donohue and David Rose and I remember getting this horrible feeling, I've totally fucked it up. And we had to take it to London to show it to Jeremy Isaacs. He was then the head of Channel 4. And John was there and so were David and Walter. And I'm sitting there watching this movie. I'm literally dying. I'm thinking I'll be regarded as an arrogant idiotic dilettante or whatever. This is an embarrassment to everybody concerned. And afterwards Jeremy starts to clap and says, this is exactly why I wanted to start a TV station. Everybody else was a little unsure whether they liked it or not whereas this wonderfully generous man instinctively responded to this thing and endorsed it. And after that everybody felt a bit better. They were saying yes it's very good isn't it? I remembered that for a long time.

What then? Did it find a distributor very quickly?
No. They showed it at Cannes out of competition. There were quite a few rave reviews written about it. Stephen Woolley from Palace Pictures saw it there and bought the rights to release it cinematically.

When you made it, did you think that it was launching you as a director?
No. I had a book coming out around the same time, *The Past*. I remember thinking there was two of me and I didn't know which one would win. But film is an obsessive activity, it takes you over.

Do you think young directors coming up now have it easier or harder?
I think it's much easier now, certainly for young English and Irish directors. The process has become demystified. There are tremendous support systems for first-time directors. They must have made about twenty first-time movies in Britain last year. Also in Ireland where I served a four-year term as a member of the Board. The problem is everybody wants to be a writer-director but some of the scripts are not that good. But in independent movie-making, their very naivety has become a badge of honour. If you look at American independent films they

don't seem to be accepted as authentic unless there's these rather jagged elements in them.

What do you think about Angel *now?*
I was at a festival in Sorrento a few years ago, and they were screening *Angel* so I went in to watch it. I never watch the films I've made again, because by the time you've finished you've seen them so many times it's impossible to look at them, so it was the first time I'd seen it since I'd made it. And it was a very beautiful film but it was very naive, a film made by somebody who doesn't know the rules, who hasn't learnt anything about the genre. It's a bit like a naive painting. I mean, everything about it – the acting, the pacing, the lack of movement in it. It was made by a guy who hadn't seen every Sam Fuller movie. But then the genre of the action movie doesn't interest me that much. I was interested in other things. And that naivety has certain very fresh qualities to it as well as a certain clumsiness. That's the best way I can express it.

What's the best first movie you've seen?
I Vitelloni by Fellini. Nicholas Ray's *They Live By Night*, perhaps. *Duel* was a good film. And one of the great first movies has to be *Reservoir Dogs*. That was fully realized.

Anthony Minghella: *Truly, Madly, Deeply*

You came to directing through writing. Was there anything in your childhood which sparked an interest in storytelling? Did you tell stories? Were you told stories?

I think the circumstances of my childhood are connected to what I'm doing now in two ways. Firstly, I was raised in a small café on the Isle of Wight. It was a large, extended Italian family and we were living above the kitchen of the café. We spent our time in the kitchen – which was also a thoroughfare for visitors and customers – so there was no defined private life. Secondly, my grandmother was a real figurehead in my life. She was a tiny peasant woman from Valvori near Monte Cassino in the south of Italy. My grandfather left her after fathering three young girls very quickly so she'd led a difficult and complicated life. She'd run a café in the Gorbals in Glasgow so she spoke this coarse Italian/Scottish. She liked paddling on the beach, so most mornings I'd walk with her on the way to school, and listen to her talk in a very superstitious, Catholic way about men and women and how the world worked: men are weak, women are strong; women survive, men are helpless and stupid. So on the one hand there was this extremely livid and colourful oral tradition and on the other hand, I'd come from this background of noise, very warm and typically Italian. The one thing I remember absolutely vividly about the first day of *Truly, Madly, Deeply* was being surrounded by what seemed to be hundreds of people who were involved in the film. I was trying to talk to Juliet Stevenson and Alan Rickman about a rather critical and delicate moment and people just kept walking by, talking and moving things and I thought, I feel quite comfortable with all this noise. Suddenly I was a boy sitting on my parents' kitchen table talking about some pain or triumph or whatever it was.

Was film something you were aware of when you were growing up?

Our café backed on to a cinema called The Commodore. We had two derelict cottages, one of which was a storeroom where we kept our cornets and tubs and various other things but one of which we rented out to the cinema's projectionist, Vernon Cook. There was one room there that I was allowed to have and I decorated it with film posters which Vernon let me have from the cinema. He also let me come into the projection box whenever I wanted. So my introduction to cinema was through a sort of mini-*Cinema Paradiso* experience. But I would be lying to you if I said that the effect of this was to make me obsessed with film. I was obsessed with music, particularly American music.

I suppose music rather than film was what people dreamt of in the sixties?
Yes. It was the great escape. The counter-culture for me was imported West Coast music. I think my interest in stories came from music. When I was about thirteen or fourteen I discovered that you could wail out your *anomie* at a piano. I had a piano in my bedroom and I started to write songs. I began playing in clubs and lived to write music and lyrics. I thought that was what I would do with my life and wasted a great number of days in my school career playing in bands or hanging around studios. The other great liberating arena for me as a schoolboy was the art department which was the place where weirdos, creeps and loners traditionally ended up.

What led you from writing lyrics in the sixties to choosing to do drama at university?
I left school in 1972 and was supposed to go to university. But I was in a band that had a record deal, and I fantasized that I would go to the recording studios and never come home. And then in the middle of trying to make this record the band fell apart. We were at the Olympic Studios in Barnes. It was our first trip to London, we were actually making a record and we just couldn't deal with it. So I applied to five universities and an art college. Hull invited me up for an interview and it was an absolutely formative moment in my life because I went there thinking, Hull is the last place I'm going to go. I don't even know where it is! But they had a new performance centre so I went up for a selection weekend. And the experience of going on this weekend suddenly opened up the possibility of doing something that could be called a degree and might be absolutely extraordinary. I was lucky that my enthusiasm about what went on that weekend was matched by the staff's curiosity. I must have appeared very unlikely to them. I had some music and art skills which I think was what attracted them to me. They called me the day after I'd been up there and said if I accepted the place they would give me an unconditional offer. Which, given how badly I was doing at school because I was so seldom there, seemed extremely appealing. So I had this place at a brand-new performance space with an extremely intensive staff–student ratio and almost everything I know and feel about dramatic art comes from the luck of landing in this place at a particular time in its history when it was in a new building with an amazing energy. How many students will ever again say 'I did a *commedia dell'arte* option at university'? But that was me! I had a tutor teaching me for a year on a one-on-one basis. Only at Oxbridge can you hope to get that kind of tuition. Except I was doing a subject where I was almost creating a course for myself because it was so brand new and it was nourishing. In the space of a year I went from being the least academic, the least industrious type of student to becoming the most diligent, library-bound enthusiast.

You found your vocation?
Yes. And it was the luckiest, luckiest thing. It really was as random as opening a book.

How did your parents feel about what you were doing?
They were very dispirited by the choices I was making. My father would obviously have preferred that I went into his business as an ice-cream man, a manufacturer. All immigrant families are preoccupied with survival and it seemed such a capricious course that I was following that at the beginning they didn't see I could make a living. I was also a typical adolescent who felt that anything conventional was unacceptable. And then later when I turned into this swot and suddenly got a First they were mystified, because having been given a job at university, a secure base for life, I so quickly gave that up and decided to pursue a career as a playwright.

You sound like you were wrong-footing everybody?
I was wrong-footing myself if I had any clear scheme. Very few people actually project a career and find their way towards it. Most of us are colliding with opportunities, some of which we may have made for ourselves, some of which we were blessed to collide with.

When did you begin to take an interest in writing?
I don't think I tried to write a piece of original narrative until I was in my last year of university. As a final year student I was allowed to offer a piece of practical work as a third of one paper. I wanted to offer eight songs because all the way through university I'd been hired to write incidental music for plays like *Troilus and Cressida*, *Pelléas et Mélisande* and *Twelfth Night*. I thought they probably wouldn't accept a score, but perhaps they'd accept a series of songs with a thematic connection. So I found a tiny short story and strung together these songs by writing some dialogue that would support them. It was a play called *Mobius the Stripper* based on a brilliant short story by Gabriel Josipovici, a rather metaphysical postmodern story about stripping which I found one day in the library. It was about a man who took his clothes off to make a point. I was interested in directing so I thought it could be a performance piece: I could do the music and direct and perform. I had an idea of how to do it which was to transform a space into a strip club. It was called *Mobius the Stripper* because the 'mobius strip' is a mathematical phenomenon where if you keep following a plane around you end up on the other side of it. For example, if you take a ribbon and twist it into a figure of eight you end up on the other side of where you began. For this reason, the story was a circle: you began it and at the end you came in at the beginning again. It was an immediate success at the university and sold out and people just kept coming back to see it again and again. It then transferred to the Humberside Theatre, which was a local professional theatre, and they gave me a commission to write a play.

You've talked a lot about plays. Did you see movies at university?
At university there was a film society and I studied film in my last year. Just as I happened to collide with a music environment in the late sixties as a teenager, in

the seventies my formative film-going years happened to be some of the great years of American cinema. I just happened to open my eyes to film when films were extraordinarily adventurous. I was recently looking again at *Midnight Cowboy* and *Annie Hall* and what struck me immediately about both films was that they couldn't have been more different as movies. But both are deconstructed in terms of their narrative; they're so wildly ambitious in the way they tell a story. Nowadays people would be preoccupied with previews and market testing and I'm sure many of the wonderful narrative wrinkles would be ironed out. When I was a student in the early seventies, the mainstream cinema, the commercial cinema, was so much wilder than it is now. But I was also discovering and relishing Italian cinema. Rossellini, Visconti, de Sica, the Taviani brothers. I remember seeing Olmi's *The Tree of Wooden Clogs* and Fellini's *I Vitelloni*, which are still two of my favourite movies. *I Vitelloni* particularly spoke to me because it's about kids growing up in a seaside resort dreaming of Rome. I had been a kid growing up in a seaside resort dreaming of the mainland, of going somewhere fascinating. And I was a part-Italian boy and so it seemed so real and true.

Did your sense of identification with these films have any impact on your writing?
Absolutely. I found that the cinema was a much closer venue for texts that fitted me personally. The kind of thing I wanted to write about was not at all the currency of the British theatre. The British theatre at that period was fascinating and rather brilliant. It was Edward Bond, Howard Barker, David Hare: really substantial writing that was analytical in the sense that these writers were looking at how the world worked with great authority. They were bringing together social and political behaviour and I was trying to write about people through their personal behaviour.

You mean your approach was less cool, less analytical?
Yes, I think even people who were interested in my writing were rather disappointed in how politically unanalytical it was. From very early on my plays were often criticized for having cinematic aspirations. However, if you were in your early twenties in 1975 to 78 and were looking for a professional apprenticeship as a writer, the cinema wasn't available. You couldn't say, I'm going to go and work as a movie-maker. You got a job writing for a studio theatre. That's where you got your opportunities. It wasn't that I thought I was most suited to the theatre. It was just where you went to learn. When I saw *The Godfather* for the first time in 1975 it seemed to me the greatest film that had ever been made. It was accessible, moving, individual, psychological, wild. The music was amazing. It was about Italian people, it was about immigrants. What better kind of event could there be? But I could never dare even imagine that I would be in a place where I could make a film like that. Instead I was getting a job to write a four-hander at the Humberside Arts Centre.

Did you try to make any films while you were at Hull?

At Hull you could play around in a TV studio and with a film camera and I started to get interested in that. In my first year as a postgraduate I decided that I wanted to make a film about my grandmother. She died in 1975, which was a wrenching event for me. So I thought, I'll make a film about her life. In 1977 to 78, along with three other people, I ended up borrowing something like ten thousand pounds, which took me nine years to pay back. And we tried to make a film using short ends with help from friends who were at Yorkshire Television who took some time off and some people we knew in the university.

What kind of film was it?
It was a fictional film. I was using friends and friends' parents and my parents' café. I went back to the Isle of Wight, my brother was nine at the time and he was a boy walking along the beach with an older woman who was talking about this relationship she had with her husband. (This later became a play I wrote called *A Little Like Drowning*, which was put on at the Hampstead Theatre Club in 1984.) So I tried to write and direct this film. But I didn't have the first idea what I was doing. By this stage I was writing quite seriously and I was working with students at the university and I just thought I wanted to do something on film. Films appeal to me partly because music has a much clearer relationship to film than theatre. If you were going to make a step from music into a literary art-form it would be film. I think the musical form and the film form are very clearly related.

Did you get much experience of working as a dramatist while you were teaching at Hull?
I suppose I had nearly ten years of thinking about how plays were made, looking at plays, making plays, directing them, being in them, lighting them. Just playing around. We had so many spaces to work in, so many opportunities to work. The more I think of that period the more extraordinary an opportunity it seems. Because we had no money one thing I learnt there was how to make do – which I think is something all film-makers have to deal with. It engendered in me the belief that if I wanted to do something I had to find some way of doing it and that is the way of making films. It's no different from when Saul Zaentz and I were faced with no money to make *The English Patient*. All I knew was that I wasn't going to give up because I was determined to see that film made. However I was going to do it, it was going to get made. I suppose I'm not proud enough to give up.

You mean that you will always find a way of compromising if you have to?
What I mean is that I'm prepared to humiliate myself by going to everybody I know and saying, 'You must help me because I want to make this film.' And just because somebody's saying you can't make it, you don't say, 'I'm going home.'

Once you left Hull you pursued a dual career writing TV drama and stage plays. How did you begin working in television?
When I first came to London I was trying to make a living as a playwright. I had given up a job as a university teacher and was thinking that I was going to live in

a garret and write plays. The week that I arrived in London I got a call from a man called Kenny McBain who was going to have a huge impact on my life. He'd found me because I'd been working on a television series called *Maybury* and the producer had recommended me. So it was one of those 'I have a friend who knows someone' stories. Kenny asked me if I'd be interested in script editing for *Grange Hill*. I said, 'No, I've just given up my job as an academic because I want to be a writer.' Besides, I'd never seen *Grange Hill*. But I had no money and he said, 'It's just for one series and it's part-time.' So I met him and liked him enormously. He was an extremely sophisticated, erudite and interesting man. And he gave me eighteen cassettes which were the previous series and eighteen screenplays for the coming series. Two days later I was a script editor for *Grange Hill*. I'd no idea what a script editor did. They were just about to go into the studios with scripts that they didn't consider were ready. So I was plunged into this fantastic experience of seeing this material turned round very, very quickly and, by the by, forming a profound friendship with Kenny who was a very intelligent, rigorous, mercurial character. He and I formed a partnership to try and find other things we could do together. He found a book by Colin Dexter called *Dead of Jericho* and said why don't you adapt this for a television film or it could even be a series? The next thing that happened was that Julian Mitchell and I had a Colin Dexter book each and we tried to write pilot episodes for *Morse*. I couldn't find a way of cutting my script into two one-hour parts so I delivered a screenplay that was two hours long. Granada were horrified at first, but they said they would do it as a pilot and then they decided that the *Morse* slot would be a two-hour slot. So there I was, and I had never intended to do this job. I was at a period where I really wanted to concentrate on my plays but this series became the most successful drama series on television at that time. And every year they would come back very nicely and say, 'Would you do one more?', and I would say, 'Umm, I don't think so'. And they'd say, 'Please', and I'd do one more.

Do you regard the period you spent writing television drama as a necessary apprenticeship for your later work in the cinema?
I wrote so much between 1980 and 1990 that I completely lost my inhibition for writing. I was writing constantly and because of the metabolism of that period I was writing then seeing things being done, seeing the turnaround of my writing. This was incredibly useful because you could create a scene and within a few months see it acted in one form or another. If you look at the metabolism of my work in the following ten years, it's been so slow by comparison. For example, I started working on my current film, *The Talented Mr Ripley*, before I made *The English Patient*. If I'd known when I was starting that I wouldn't be looking at any images from it until 1999, it would have been painful. I don't know if you can bear the pain of that, the sluggishness. My brother is an emerging and talented writer and screenwriter who's had lots of opportunities to write screenplays. But the casualty rate in film writing is so much greater than television because so few

are actually produced. Whereas when I got commissioned to write a TV play, it tended to be done quite quickly. So I learned in television because of its very fast turnaround. And that has been very useful to me because when I went on to a film set I always felt that people had some respect for me as a writer so they gave me a little bit of room as a director.

Do you think writing for the stage provided a good platform for writing for the screen?
I think that the theatre is geared more towards writing that you could call 'epigrammatic': writing where people say what they want to say in rather elegant lines. Film writing is anti-epigrammatic. In other words, writing dialogue, the thing I find easiest to do, is the least significant part of writing for film. I don't mean that what comes out of people's mouths isn't important in film. I just don't think it's about meaning in the same way that the epigrammatical line is. What I say to you in a film is ultimately neither here nor there. The fact that I'm making noises at certain points in the scenes is extremely significant. But because what makes you look at an image, what makes you listen to an image, is so specific in film, it doesn't really correlate in any proper way with writing for the theatre. Nevertheless, once you have learned to organize a scene as a playwright the same kinds of components fall into place in a screenplay. I don't think writing a nice speech is particularly good preparation for becoming a good film writer but I think having experience of mise en scène is very important. If you look at most movies people come into rooms and leave rooms; they go on journeys. It's exactly the same structural syntax as the theatre. In theatre when they come into the room, they stay home a lot longer but that's the only real difference – how long they stay in! It's still made up of entrances and exits, arrivals and departures of strangers, of conflicts. It has the same conjunctions and devices. It's just that they tend not to be able to accommodate as many in the play and film wants to eat up as much of those things as it can. One of the things that I like best in film is the stacking of events vertically which you're forced to do in the theatre because you can't move. In *Ripley*, for example, there's an opera scene which is organized so that all of the characters collide in a public setting and the public setting itself comments on this collision. In the original version of the screenplay all these collisions happened over time and I squeezed them all into this theatrical moment in an opera house. So there are a lot of clues in the dramaturgy for the theatre that can be properly and usefully employed in the cinema.

Students of film are often taught that screenplays should have a three-act structure. Do you think that screenplays benefit from a particular act structure?
I think that distributors and studios are so nervous of the cost of the negative that they're constantly looking for ways of making what can never be scientific into a science. So being able to find a lexicon that helps them approach a screenplay has been invaluable in two ways. Firstly they have a vocabulary with which they can talk to writers about a screenplay and secondly they can use that syntax to try and

examine whether a film is going to work or not. It gives them a noise they can make and an index they can use. I remember somebody whose opinion I value a great deal read the screenplay of *The English Patient* and said, 'Where is the third act?' And my reply was, 'Where is the second act?' Because it's a film that has an antipathy towards act structures in general. This doesn't mean I'm not extremely sensitive to the idea of structure in a screenplay. It's just that I think it's absolutely intrinsic. In other words, I don't think a screenplay comes in three sections any more than a house needs two bedrooms or five bedrooms. It depends on who is living there!

Did you have much opportunity to observe your work being directed? Do you think you learnt from this?
I learnt by osmosis rather than by design. I wasn't sitting with directors trying to breathe in their oxygen: what does he or she do? I think I learnt from some of the people who directed my plays. Michael Blakemore directed one of my plays in the mid-eighties and I thought that the way he was in rehearsals, his respect for actors, was extremely edifying. He taught me something about the metabolism of actors that I have never forgotten. You can't afford to bring too much technique to an actor because it presupposes that every actor can be dealt with in the same way. The thing I noticed about Michael most of all was that he seemed to have a technique which altered to suit each actor. Some actors require an enormous amount of invasion of their technique: they want to be directed. Other actors require much more space. If you invade their space they feel it's impossible for them to work. I certainly remember that but I remember very few things where there has been a direct lesson. I think there have been a hundred indirect lessons. I certainly feel that I was lucky enough to work with very good directors and I'm sure that I've stolen from all of them what seems to me to work. I think that you get much more from a director in the theatre only because the playwright is plaited into the rehearsal experience in the way that the writer is not plaited into the filming process.

The last television series you wrote prior to writing and directing Truly, Madly, Deeply *was* The Storyteller. *Can you tell me about this experience?*
I was very, very involved with *The Storyteller* because the producer Duncan Kenworthy and I were the constants in that series. I suppose we became editorial staff as well as writing and producing staff. We stayed on and worked with the directors and worked in the cutting room. It was my first experience of working on post-production as much as I worked in pre-production, because I rewrote in the cutting room. We were finding the series as we went along. I was ready then to start directing. I felt my interest in directing didn't come from impatience with the directors I was working with. It came from a feeling that I was working continuously with this group of actors and it was odd that somebody always interposed themselves between me and them every time we got to a certain point in

the work. And also because I loved the post-production experience. I loved the rhythm of the whole filming process, which begins in isolation and ends in a kind of isolation. So I was jealous to have some of that experience and I was lucky to be having repeated experience not only with actors but also with some production people – Mark Shivas and Robert Cooper, who directed a whole series of my plays on the radio. And they were sympathetic to this ambition to direct.

Robert Cooper ended up being your producer on Truly, Madly, Deeply. *How did this collaboration come about?*
I wrote a piece for a ballet called *Hung Up*, which was a telephone conversation. I wrote it for a great friend, Jonathan Lunn, who was choreographing at the London Contemporary Dance Theatre. They had no money so I asked Juliet Stevenson and David Threlfall if they'd come in and record it for me. So I directed them using a home tape-recorder. It was an enormously low-tech weekend event. This play was then remade on radio and Robert took over the directing reins because he was a staff director and I was a writer. But he admitted my input because he had already known that I had directed an earlier version. It worked particularly well and won one of the Prix Italia. After that there was a lot of appetite for this collaboration to continue, though Robert was also alert to the fact that I wanted to see that whole process through myself. So he set up a paradigm where I could write and direct a play with his supervision. There would be at least a paper supervision to give the BBC some sort of security. So I wrote *Cigarettes and Chocolate*, directed it and had a wonderful time. For many years I hoped that if anybody happened on one thing I'd done it would be that. After that I realized I'd found something I wanted to do.

How did the idea of directing a feature film come about at this point? After all, you were still better known professionally as a writer than a director. You were still writing episodes of Morse, *for example.*
Which was very nice except I felt that it wasn't quite what I should be doing. But I liked the actors enormously, John Thaw, Kevin Whateley and the directors who were involved. Then what happened was that Kenny got very sick, gave up *Morse* and died soon after. And I really felt enough was enough. But they came round for the fifth series and asked if I would like to do one more and I said no. They said, what if you directed? They'd obviously known that I was flirting with becoming a director, that I'd done *Cigarettes and Chocolate*. So Chris Burt, who was one of the producers, said I could direct an episode of *Morse*. About a week later, Mark Shivas and Robert Cooper called me and said the BBC was starting a series called *Screen Two*. Would I like to write a screenplay? And I said I would love to write an original screenplay for a film but I'd been offered an opportunity to direct an episode of *Morse*. And they said, 'Why don't you direct this screenplay?' So I was in a dilemma. I couldn't do both jobs. One would have been an extremely well-paid and prestigious job and the other one was for a new, small,

low-budget *Screen Two*. So I thought, everyone will watch the *Morse* and will think what a terrible amateur job I'd done. And at that time the series was getting about fifteen million viewers or more a week, so that's really standing naked in front of a big audience. Whereas nobody will watch this *Screen Two*, which I can make with my friends very, very quickly and it can be personal. And it can be a continuation of some of the things that intrigued me about *Cigarettes and Chocolate*. So I did the *Screen Two*, imagining that this could be a rehearsal for a future as a film-maker, not realizing the impact it would have on my subsequent life.

Given it was commissioned by the BBC, did you think of Truly, Madly, Deeply *as a cinema film when you were writing it?*
From the beginning I always thought that *Truly, Madly, Deeply* was going to be a cinema film. In fact what happened was that people read the screenplay and offered me the chance to make it into a theatrical film if I changed the location and the cast: a common dilemma for all European film-makers. Some of them brooked no interference or opposition but I wrote it specifically for Juliet Stevenson and that to me was a given. Robert Cooper and Mark Shivas both thought that enough people had read the script and liked it to give us a very good shot at a theatrical release, although the BBC at the time were very resistant. The feature-film industry was in such a poor shape in Britain that they actually felt that it would have a negative impact on the broadcast if the film had appeared as a movie. It's the exact opposite of how they would perceive things now.

How long was it before you had a green light?
I delivered it and I think I was in pre-production a week later.

That sounds like a dream experience!
There was great receptivity to the project. You might say that it took a few weeks and fifteen years to make my first film! And one of the strange things about *Truly, Madly, Deeply* was that I never quite felt I'd begun directing because I was so comfortable with the people I was working with. I'd worked with Juliet eight or nine times. And I'd worked with Alan Rickman and Michael Maloney before. It felt so domestic and so familiar an activity that directing sort of happened by default. I don't want to be too disingenuous; obviously I thought very carefully about it, and felt that I had written something that was very easy for me to do. I didn't feel that I set myself an enormous number of production challenges. We had a tiny, tiny budget; the shoot was only twenty-eight days and I tried to write something that was small enough to do in that time.

Let's talk about your crew. How did you come to choose Remi Adesfarasin as your DP?
I chose Remi because I'd seen a film he shot by Angela Pope called *As Sweet As You Are*. I thought it was wonderful, and he had a terrific reputation. I must say that Remi was a huge element in the making of *Truly, Madly, Deeply* and the fun

of it. He has the soul of a poet. He turned out to be the most gentle nursemaid a first time film-maker could hope for. One of the strange things about BBC cameramen is that their experience is vast because they shoot almost every day. You could be doing *Match of the Day* on a Friday, a documentary on a Saturday and a movie on a Tuesday. Because of this background, filming for him was a natural and organic activity. We were shooting day in day out so it was a critical relationship. I'd stumbled into the perfect partner.

How did you choose the other key personnel on the film?
An old friend who'd been at university with me, Peter Markham, who had been a production manager for a long time and was extremely experienced, worked with me as a first assistant. The thing he did for me – which many people have done for me over the course of my film-making life – was to make me feel very secure and calm. He said you know the film you want to make; these are actors who you've worked with many times before. And he helped me a great deal throughout the film in terms of what I needed to know in advance, what needed to be established in advance. People are very quick to welcome you as a new director with their wisdom. Remi was an enormous enabler; he would ask me what kind of film it was that I was trying to make. In the end I suppose what I had in my head were largely emotional landscapes. 'This is the feel of this scene'; often it might have some musical connotations. It's an allegro scene or it's a largo scene. There would be something that made me feel I had found the emotional register of the scene. Is it because it's a very dark scene? Is it because nobody moves? Or is it because the camera never stops moving? What is it?

In a sense you were using your musical background to search for the heart of each scene; for what made each moment unique?
Yes. Although if you'd been with me two weeks before shooting *Truly, Madly, Deeply*, I don't know whether I would have been able to articulate any of these things because some kind of funk overpowers you; the funk of organization. I think that what mostly happens to a first-time director is not art but logistics. It's not 'tell me about your movie', it's 'how are you going to get your crew from Shepherd's Bush to Waterloo in the afternoon? It's never going to happen, can we shoot nearer to base?' It's all about the army on the move. When you do it for the first time it's like standing in the way of some sort of lava. It's just coming at you. That's the most significant emotion you feel: being overwhelmed by all these organizational requirements. Not just aesthetic decisions but do you want three days on that stage and if so, where are you going to shoot that scene in the analyst's room? And can you shoot both of them in one afternoon? Where will you rehearse them? In a way, that becomes an enormous relief because there's so much working out to do that you don't have enough time to panic about whether your movie is going to be like Tarkovsky or Kieslowski or the Coen brothers. You don't have that luxury. In fact, oddly enough, what happens is that as you make more films

PEDRO ALMODÓVAR

Pepi, Luci, Bom

ABOVE:
Pedro Almodóvar

LEFT:
Luci (Eva Siva) and
Pepi (Carmen
Maura)

ALLISON ANDERS

Gas, Food, Lodging

LEFT: Allison Anders

RIGHT:
Fairuza Balk ('Shade')
and Ione Skye ('Trudi')

Steve Buscemi

Trees Lounge

Tom DiCillo

Johnny Suede

ETHAN COEN AND JOEL COEN

Blood Simple

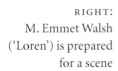

LEFT: Joel Coen (standing) and Ethan Coen prepare to shoot the burial scene

RIGHT:
M. Emmet Walsh
('Loren') is prepared
for a scene

BOTTOM:
Loren (M. Emmet
Walsh) turns the tables
on Marty (Dan
Hedaya)

MIKE FIGGIS

Stormy Monday

ABOVE:
Mike Figgis

RIGHT:
Sting plays nightclub
owner Finney

STEPHEN FREARS

Gumshoe

ABOVE:
Stephen Frears

LEFT:
A spot of light
reading for Eddie
Ginley (Albert
Finney)

P. J. HOGAN

Muriel's Wedding

ABOVE:
P. J. Hogan

LEFT:
Bill Heslop
(Bill Hunter) and
daughter Muriel
(Toni Colette) on
her big day

NEIL JORDAN

Angel

LEFT: Honor Heffernan ('Deirdre'), Neil Jordan
and Stephen Rea ('Danny')

RIGHT:
Danny (Stephen Rea)
stands captivated
outside the Ballroom

Pushing Hands

ABOVE:
Ang Lee

LEFT:
Retired T'ai Chi master Mr Chu (Sihung Lung) takes on all-comers

MIKE LEIGH

Bleak Moments

ABOVE:
Mike Leigh pictured in 1966

RIGHT:
Anne Raitt ('Sylvia')

Diner

LEFT: Barry Levinson with Steve Guttenberg ('Eddie')

RIGHT:
From left, Timothy Daly ('Billy'), Daniel Stern ('Shreevie'), Mickey Rourke ('Boogie') and Kevin Bacon ('Fenwick')

ABOVE:
Daniel Stern ('Shreevie') and Paul Reiser ('Modell')

LEFT:
Mickey Rourke ('Boogie') and Ellen Barkin ('Beth')

KEN LOACH

Poor Cow

ABOVE:
Ken Loach directs
Carol White ('Joy')

RIGHT:
Dave (Terence Stamp)
and Joy (Carol White)

JAMES MANGOLD

Heavy

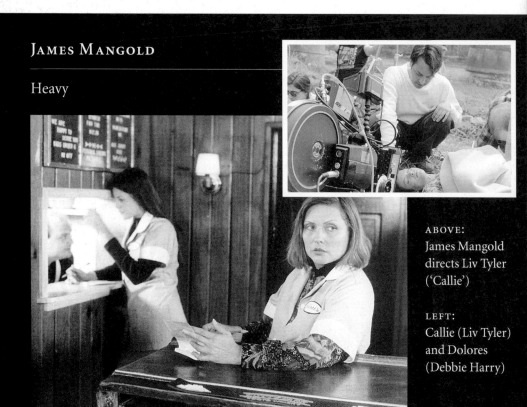

ABOVE:
James Mangold
directs Liv Tyler
('Callie')

LEFT:
Callie (Liv Tyler)
and Dolores
(Debbie Harry)

ANTHONY MINGHELLA

Truly, Madly, Deeply

ABOVE:
Anthony Minghella
(pointing) directs a
scene

LEFT:
Juliet Stevenson
('Nina') and Alan
Rickman ('Jamie')

MIRA NAIR

Salaam Bombay!

LEFT: Mira Nair confers with her actors

RIGHT:
Krishna (Shafiq Syed)
says goodbye to Sweet
Sixteen (Chanda
Sharma)

GARY OLDMAN

Nil by Mouth

ABOVE AND LEFT:
Gary Oldman at work

ABOVE:
Gary Oldman directs
Ray Winstone ('Ray')

RIGHT:
Ray (Ray Winstone)
harangues Janet (Laila
Morse)

KEVIN SMITH

Clerks

LEFT: Kevin Smith

RIGHT:
Brian O'Halloran
('Dante') and Jeff
Anderson ('Randal')

BERTRAND TAVERNIER

The Watchmaker of Saint-Paul

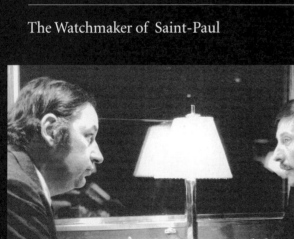

ABOVE:
Bertrand Tavernier

LEFT:
Philippe Noiret
('Michel
Descombes') and
Jean Rochefort
('Inspector Guibert')

OLIVER STONE

Salvador

ABOVE:
Oliver Stone

RIGHT:
Euphoria for Boyle
(James Woods) and
Cassady (John
Savage)

LEFT:
Doctor Rock
(James Belushi),
Boyle (James
Woods) and
Cassady (John
Savage)

more space opens up to worry about what kind of film you're making; probably a dangerous space. You can compress the entire making of *Truly, Madly, Deeply* from writing, directing and finishing it into what I would probably now spend on the first draft of a screenplay or what I would spend in pre-production on a film. That's a blessing and a curse. Many times subsequently, I had the yearning to go back to a metabolism of film-making that is as fast as *Truly, Madly, Deeply* because it didn't give me time to go into that paralysis of aesthetics.

How did you prepare for the shoot? How did you visualize the film you wanted to make?
I think one of the ways to answer that question is to say that I had seen the film before I had finished writing it. I used to tell myself, you've already made this film, just make it again and be surprised. The succour I found when I was frightened and when I was nervous about what was going to happen was to tell myself that I was a dramatist. In other words I dramatized every scene because I tried not to write lines which actors said, but to write action which involved language and movement; moving people in time and space. There was an inner screen where I'd seen them saying a line, on which I'd recorded them, and all I was doing was trying to bring them to life again on the screen. I was trying to find the recorder and press the play button. I've already made the film with my pen and that's what puts me a long way ahead of all my other collaborators. So, for instance, I'm looking for a location with my production designer and I may have to surrender it. What can often happen is that the designer might challenge the inner screen version and say, look, whatever you told me you wanted for this scene, it's wrong. What about this? And then you surrender or you don't and it's a very interesting tug-of-war between this often rather narrow, rather diluted version you've got in your head, and this full colour version. It's like a fretwork of other people's imaginations supporting yours: it's often much more dense and strongly worked than just the thinness of your own mind. And so I'm happy to let go but it also gives me a starting point. So I think when you ask me what was the starting point of preparation, it was writing the screenplay. That's why I think a very clear distinction has to be made between writer-directors and directors. I don't actually think of myself as a director. I think of myself as a film-maker who does a number of jobs on a film. I write films, I direct them, I'm involved in the post-production of them. I don't think that I would make a very good director of other people's work.

What kinds of practical preparation did you undertake?
My wife is Chinese and we have a Chinese wooden man at home to bring good fortune. It's a beautiful old statue that's about four feet high. We had a very long living room so I borrowed a viewfinder and I put the statue at one end and sat at the other end with my viewfinder and drew sketches of it using different lens sizes trying to imagine how it would work. I think it was a very haphazard preparation! I'd done a course at the BBC intended for production managers which gave me

the opportunity to work with a couple of DPs and go out and shoot some film. I'd been on sets many times before and knew many directors. I felt I'd made a version of the film, because I'd been a dramatist all my working life and part of the process of dramatizing material is that you've seen the dynamic of movement: as you've written a line you've seen whether you've been in close up or whether that line was said from a distance. I had a very clear idea of the choreography of language, of the action of language and I felt that my safety net was that I've seen a version of the film that nobody else had seen, and my job was to communicate that. I felt that if I had been a first-time director of somebody else's screenplay I would have been entirely unable to make the film. Obviously the minute you get in front of an actor in an environment, the film that you saw is not quite the same as the one you're seeing in front of you. And you either make some attempt to drag the reality towards your poetic conception, your inner-screen version or you surrender your inner-screen version to what's in front of you. And on the whole it's probably a happy amalgam of both the inner screen and the outer screen.

Did you draw storyboards of any kind?
I draw every day on a film. I still have notebooks for *Truly, Madly, Deeply*. I've got seven or eight notebooks on *The English Patient* which are full of drawings and some of them are quite elaborate, others are just reminders for myself of what I need to achieve in a sequence. But again I'm not sure I knew what a sequence was when I was doing *Truly, Madly, Deeply*. I remember I had ideas I wasn't able to sustain in the film: for instance, when Alan first comes back, I wanted them constantly to be in a two-shot. I wanted to go from seeing Juliet always in singles to suddenly filling the frame with the two of them. And I think that got me into terrible trouble in the cutting room because it was very hard to cut between two-shots. There's a reason why you don't stay in a two-shot all the time, but I didn't really understand that. I just thought it was an interesting theory which in some ways addressed the argument of the film. One of the things that I've always tried to do is to try and shoot towards the film's argument. I try to think of the visual correlative of the film. For example, Ripley is about somebody who finds himself increasingly alone so I've tried to find ways in which the framing isolates the character. I've tried to make sure that there's no landscape frame that doesn't have Ripley breaking the frame so in some way you feel he's always edged in by the landscape and that the film is viewed entirely through his perspective. And I think that's a more worked notion of something I was just feeling my way towards in *Truly, Madly, Deeply*.

Did you find it easy to translate what you saw in your head into actual set-ups? Did you feel confident about where the camera should be when you visited locations?
I've never had any anxiety about where the camera should be or whether the camera should move or not. But I think you could say that *Truly, Madly, Deeply* is more a

recording of a film than a piece of cinema. It's very much a film that wants to record performance. The camera is in service of the acting much more than it is in *The English Patient* or *Ripley*. I think that I now see the camera's agency in the film as being as significant a dynamic as anything the writer or actor has done. But I didn't understand that at the time, and if I had understood it, I'm not sure I could have changed the way I shot the film because there simply wasn't time. To understand a film's sentence, the relationship between one shot and another, is such a significant part of film-making; the degree of coverage you need in order that the film can re-emerge in the cutting room. I didn't understand that and it was a blissful ignorance. Now I go into the cutting room with an enormous amount of material and an enormous amount of coverage – not because I know less or I'm worried more, but because I realize that the phrasing of a film over time is enormously aided by having options: how to compress a scene; how to accelerate it; how to extend it. A lot of what I was doing with John Stothard in the cutting room on *Truly, Madly, Deeply* was just sticking the shots together.

Did you spend much time rehearsing with your actors before the shoot?
I appreciate the fact that many people who work in cinema mistrust rehearsals as a process. In some ways it's enervating: it drains some of the spontaneity. But I'm not a disciple of that school at all. I'm a great rehearser. I come from the theatre. I feel that the more you know before you walk on to the set the better for everybody. Every second you have together before you show up makes you into a team of people doing the job, and actors always come late to projects. Unity of style is the single most important aspect of film-making: to have everybody in the same movie, making the same movie. So I try and steal as much time as I can with actors before the shoot. Not only with actors, but having the cinematographer show up to rehearsals and talk to the actors about the film. In my opinion, there can't be too much shared information.

How difficult did you find the basic mechanics of blocking?
The two things that I don't worry about in film-making are the direct contact with actors and the choreography of actors and the camera. I have many other problems in film-making, but those things have not concerned me. I've always felt entirely comfortable with the process of working with an actor and the performance. In fact, I've always been exhilarated by it. I thought those were my strengths – writing, working with actors. That was an area where I felt, okay, well at least I know about this: I know about these performances. I know what they need. I've written every scene for Juliet Stevenson, we had been collaborating for a long time, talking about this project, what it could be, what we could get from it. There was no apparent alteration, no point where the film got more serious. We were serious the first day we talked about it. We were serious when we were shooting. There are some actors who have this wonderful ability not to alter when you say action. There's no apparent revving up. There's just you calling

action and the scene continues at the same level of adrenalin. When the adrenalin is over-agitated by the word 'action!' something goes wrong with the scene. But if you're comfortable with the actors and they're comfortable with you there isn't that perceptible alteration in energy when you call action.

How did you feel when you first began turning over?
I remember being very anxious about the first five or six shots. The first shot was a very long lens shot of a destination board at Heathrow Airport. I think we were going to come off that and find Juliet amongst the crowds. I can't remember exactly, but I know that I was there for hours before the crew turned up. I had just bought a new car, a Mercedes, which was the subject of a great deal of stick from Juliet and Alan. It was the first new car I'd owned in my life and I'd had it for about a week when we went into production. I parked in the long stay car park at Heathrow and was on my way down to the shoot when somebody said, is that your car in the garage? I said yes. Well, I was obviously in a lot of turmoil because I'd left it with all the doors and boot open. I'm still the same. Even on the ninetieth day of shooting of *Ripley* I still feel sick on my way to the location. I'm sick with nerves, absolutely sick every day with nerves.

Doesn't this anxiety diminish with experience?
I think if anything it gets worse because you become more acutely aware of what is at stake every day. I don't have the skill to coast. If I haven't prepared for every single eventuality, the day won't work. That's what it's all about: seizing the day. *Carpe diem* applies to nothing as much as to film-making.

So you wouldn't describe yourself as particularly relaxed?
I felt the circus element of making films really appealed to me. Particularly given this was at the end of a decade of writing alone. I think having several people holding your pen, as it were, is a much more human activity than writing alone. I really love the crew and also I'm an enormous enthusiast. I was enjoying myself and I wanted everybody else to enjoy themselves too and it turned the film into a real event. I felt that the crew were really behind me. Also, I'm always intrigued by everybody's sense of what's happening. I wanted to know what the gaffer thought about how we were doing. There is an enormous amount of collective wisdom on a film set. There's people who have been doing their job for thirty-five, forty years. Film days are very hard to come by. People should have little badges saying 'I've shot eight hundred days of film' because that changes you. Two days of film, one day of film is different from eight hundred days. One of the problems of being a director is how rarely you do it: you can't practise. So I try and find the 'eight hundred days of film' people and say is there anything that I'm doing that you think is daft?

Did you find it easy to inspire your crew? Including the 'eight hundred dayers'?
On *Truly, Madly, Deeply*, I think we very quickly managed to operate as a group.

There was a lot of larking around which I think is of great value! Film's so weird because there's some people doing these intimate things and everybody else is watching. It's very hard and it's wrong. There was a scene where Juliet and Alan do a version of a Walker Brothers song, so I got the whole crew to sing and dance with them and it freed everyone up; the room became rather stupid. I think that enabled Juliet and Alan to lark about because everyone was larking around. Then there were times where I felt the set needed to be incredibly quiet. I would explain to everybody what we were trying to achieve in this scene to make sure that we were working collectively towards an energy. I still do that all the time. The point is not to imagine that the work is being done in the centre of the room and that the edges are not contributing or detracting from it. I get extremely impatient with people not respecting the set, extremely impatient. I think that most crew feel that they're not required to be part of film-making. That they're workers, and art is going on somewhere else and it seems to me that we're all workers – and art, if there is any, is going to come from our collective activity. I believe that passionately. One of the things I noticed about *Truly, Madly, Deeply* was that because it was a film about somebody who was a translator there were a lot of people of different nationalities on the set. There was a Pole and several Chileans, an Argentinian woman, my wife – who is briefly in the film – is Chinese. Film-making is an international activity. The more films I've made, the more international the collaborators I've worked with. That also means that people are brought together by the common excitement of film. However jaundiced we become, we're all basically film fans. I was a huge fan of Alan Rickman, a huge fan of Juliet Stevenson. I felt the enormous buzz of having them do my work. A lot of the time, I just felt, I'm very lucky today. That's what's happening here: luck is happening.

One of the things the film is remembered for is Juliet's performance when her character visits her analyst. Was this hard to achieve?
I have a very strong image of driving down to Bristol rehearsing the analyst scene in the car. My driving and Juliet sitting next to me wailing! But also it being rather fun. It was very much of a guerrilla film in the sense that we grabbed some time in one of the seminar rooms at Bristol University to do that scene; very much a sort of smash and grab. We got there, went in, did two takes and we were out again. There wasn't much preparation. Juliet went into another room and I talked to the crew and said, look this is an odd scene, it's a tough scene. We've got no time. Let's make everything right for her, so she can come in and do this scene and feel like she's supported by us. It all sounds slightly pious, but it wasn't.

Were these very emotional scenes the hardest ones to realize?
No, they weren't the most difficult scenes to do. Here's a dumb thing to say: hard scenes are scenes with three people in them. Two people is easy, one person is easy. Three people or five people is very, very hard to shoot because you get stuck into the geometry of the eye-lines. In *Ripley* there are endless scenes of triangles

and when one person moves, the camera moves and you're constantly having to go back and pick up new angles to make the equation of the scene cut. It's very hard to describe without diagrams, but the cutting angle requirements of three people are many times more than two. Even now I feel I don't have enough experience in shooting to be comfortable with scenes like that. I find duet scenes great to shoot - very easy and fun and you can be quite ambitious with the camera. Big scenes are wonderful. I mean that's the great discovery that I made – the more the merrier!

Were there scenes in Truly, Madly, Deeply *where you felt you were at the edge of your abilities, of your experience?*
Every single day. The scene with Michael Maloney in the café was a tricky scene to shoot. It was one of the very first public scenes I ever shot. You start to lean very heavily on the continuity person/script supervisor. The script supervisor I have now, Diane Dreyer, is a constant. I'm in a wrestling match with her from the first scene to the last because she's so belligerent with me and argumentative and insistent and brilliant. Jayne Spooner, my script supervisor on *Truly, Madly, Deeply*, was calm, quiet but reassuring: 'You've got the coverage. Don't worry.'

Continuity is an extraordinarily underrated skill.
It's one of the most significant jobs in film. I think about who is going to play that role for me as much as any other job. Both the women I've worked with, Jayne and Diane, are absolutely brilliant. I've been in situations on other shoots where I haven't had that support and it makes me look a lot less good than when I'm with them! But you have to be very careful in those scenes not to simply to shoot by numbers; to become obsessed with coverage. You have to try and think, am I ever going to need this shot? Why am I shooting it? You have to find the moment in the scene. For example, in the scene where we meet Alan for the first time, the moment is hearing the cello. I'm playing the piano, I hear the note of the cello. That's the moment in the scene. How does everything build around that image? Where is the camera going to be for that image? How am I going to find Alan playing?

How did you do it?
As far as I remember, there was a sort of a little crab around Juliet so he comes into the frame. He's still looking at her but we're moving from left to right and he's revealed in the background.

What do you think are the main things you learnt during the shoot?
The thing I would say – which is not really connected to *Truly, Madly, Deeply* but about film-making in general – is that you have to keep speaking about the film. I can think of many examples of films where you can diagnose a lack of coherence; there doesn't seem to be any consonance between costume and lighting, between lighting and screenplay, between acting and screenplay. So the one thing

I instinctively knew was that I had to keep on announcing the film that I had in my head. But I was never frightened that there wasn't a film in my head. I wasn't frightened about what the film should be. I felt very confident about how it should look, how it should sound, the kind of acting that I was interested in, the kind of actor I was interested in, which isn't to say that I wasn't profoundly nervous and fragile during the making of it. But I want to say several things about the experience as far as I recollect: one thing was that on the very first day of shooting I thought, oh, this is good fun. I like doing this. I mean, I felt instantly as if I was doing the right thing in my life. In the pre-production period I didn't feel I was being asked questions I felt threatened by. I thought, I'm not being undermined by this experience. I feel like I'm at the very edge of what I know but I like being here. I like this precipice. It feels like the right precipice to be on. There have been times when I've done work where I thought, I am not good at this. I might be surviving at it, but I'll never be wonderful. I wanted very much to be a composer but I always knew I would never be a really good composer. I never had a technique that could articulate what I had in my head. There was something lacking in me as a composer. Whereas with directing, I felt very clearly that I'd found something I could do because it called upon so many of the things I enjoy and also gave a public element to something which hitherto I had only experienced privately. I'd felt very comfortable in my room as a writer and very comfortable meditating on writing, thinking about writing and reading and living the life of the mind. But I'm also a social person and so I found this wonderful rhythm, where you're at home and then you're out. And when you're at home you're quiet and when you're out it's incredibly noisy and I like that. I like the sense of collaboration and I like working with other people and thinking that my work is being substantiated and improved by other people in a way that nobody could really improve your screenplay. You get all the credit and blame, rightly or wrongly, as the screenwriter or as a playwright. You get too much credit and too much blame as the director because largely you are working with many other people, all of whom are better at what they do then you are. It's a wonderful and exciting feeling where you sing a note and twenty people sing it back to you more beautifully.

Did you feel you were in control of the film at all times?
One of the things you feel you're doing when you're directing is spinning plates. You're running around fifty spokes trying to keep the plates from falling. Someone was once talking about Leonard Bernstein and conducting. Bernstein was giving a lesson about conducting to some schoolchildren. He said I bet you're wondering what conductors do. You probably think they just stand around and wave a baton and actually the orchestra are wonderful musicians and don't actually need this guy at the front with a stick. There was some muted agreement with this particular analysis, so he walked off the stage. And the orchestra kept playing and suddenly somebody lost time and somebody tried to compensate and then

somebody else tried to compensate and then the music unravelled. It's not a perfect analogy to directing a film, though I think the director is the only person on the film set who is not actually doing anything, who doesn't have a mechanical activity. I neither want to exaggerate the importance of the director nor undervalue it. I think there is no film without a director. It seems to me that one of the scary things about film-making is that you are surrounded by people doing their job better than you could ever do, who would do nothing without your guidance – without you nothing happens. They want somebody to say to them: the camera shouldn't be there, it should be here, the set shouldn't be grey, it should be blue. That door is too heavy. It should be a much lighter doorway than that. Possibly because of the historical way that film has been made, there is a certain reliance on a director's point of view to inform every single decision. And that's either exhilarating or terrifying. I find it absolutely exhilarating, apart from anything else because my background has been so much connected to art, music and language, because I was raised in a café, because I'd been an academic. All these things seem to fit perfectly as a training for the film-making experience. It felt like every bit of experience that I'd had was being employed and examined and challenged. I think that one of the reasons there is a narcotic element to film-making is because it's rather like drug dependency. It's not very nice doing it, but the withdrawal symptoms of not doing it are intolerable. There are no directors I know of who don't find filming a loathsome activity in the sense that it's so enervating, it's so exhausting, it's such an absurd way of spending your time, it involves so much sleep deprivation, it's so sapping of every form of spiritual, mental, physical stamina and yet when you're not doing it you feel less than yourself.

So by the time you're in post-production, half your mind is thinking about what to do next?
Or wanting to be shooting because shooting is also an artistic endeavour, particularly coming from the background of writing. My parents used to say that effort was always rewarded, that the harder you work, the better things will go for you in life. And one of the most demoralizing things about writing is there's no relationship between writing and results. There were days when I was writing when I'd be totally marooned, paralysed by the experience. I would be at a table for about twelve hours and tear up the half a page that I'd managed. There was no empirical relationship between effort and result. One great thing about moviemaking is that on the whole you get something each day. There are very few days on a film when you can't say, look we've shot something! There's an absolute relationship between effort and result.

Did anything come as a surprise to you about directing? Anything you hadn't anticipated?
I think even if I was shooting tomorrow I'd imagine that there's this secret that I

haven't learnt yet that seemed to be the one that everybody else who makes films has. And I suppose what I discovered on *Truly, Madly, Deeply* was that there isn't any secret. The camera records action and you stick it together and it tells a film story.

So that was the biggest surprise? That the camera is just a machine for recording images?

I think the really odd thing about film is that if I now turned a camera on you, I can make it into fiction. I can put it into the middle of a movie and it becomes part of the fictional landscape and sits comfortably in that fictional landscape. I remember the very first day of shooting on *Ripley*. There is a shot of the Forum in Rome with Matt Damon looking at the Forum. Matt Damon's character, *Ripley*, wanted to look at Rome with somebody else and that somebody else wouldn't come with him so he goes alone and goes and looks at the Forum. That's the context of this moment. The shot is fairly wide, probably a 20 mm lens, with Matt Damon right of the frame before he turns towards us and walks out of the shot. That's all it is. So all that happens is that we set the shot up, we waited for the right light, then at five o'clock in the morning, the light decides to come up through the Forum and hits the back of the Forum so it's a very back-lit shot, and I call action. Matt's looking at the Forum. He then looks down at his guidebook, closes it, turns and walks away. That's all that happens. I call 'action' and I call 'cut'. But because of the purpose of that moment, the intention of the moment, when you put that shot into the sentence of the film, into the long book of the film, that shot acquires this incredible loneliness and disappointment. That's all it is. It's a strange thing that in a jigsaw puzzle of a beautiful sky there are many pieces that are simply blue. You need them. If you looked at a piece of the puzzle, it's just some blue. Making a film is collecting lots and lots of oddly shaped bits of blue, and sticking them together knowing that they're going to make a sky for you. And I think the extraordinary experience is that this piece of oddly shaped blue will ever have any emotional value, will be a sky. And the good news is that it is. Or it will be.

In other words, the shots that make up a film only take on a meaning when edited together. On their own they're flat, uninflected.

That's perfectly said. They're uninflected. What I think is the most remarkable thing about film-making is that a left to right walk across a landscape can be heart-stopping. There's a moment in *Ripley* where the camera makes a semi-circular move around Matt Damon's face. It's extremely harshly lit so there's light kicking one side of him and no light on the other side of him. And the move from light into dark is as emotional a moment as any I ever shot. I've no idea what he was thinking about when we were shooting that and it's actually of no significance because it's uninflected. When I was shooting *Truly, Madly, Deeply* I thought I had to keep shooting everything, the whole scene. This became a joke that the crew would make with me. We'd be two thirds of the way through shooting a scene and Juliet would say, 'Could I just go back a speech before we turn over?' I'd say sure. Then she'd say, 'Can I actually go back a couple of speeches?' And I'd say, 'Well, yes, go back as far as you like.' So what we'd do all the time was start at the top of the scene because she wanted to get her run-in and so did I. I believed it more if she'd done the whole scene by the time she got to this moment. Now I've seen dailies of extremely experienced film-makers where they say, 'Just the moment when you put your finger in your mouth. Good. Cut. Just turn again, turn to your left. Good. Cut.'

What do you think was the steepest learning curve in the whole process of shooting?
I think the steepest learning curve as a director is that there is no off day. If you write for a living then there are many days when you can't write, and you have to reconcile yourself to that as a writer. Today has been the day when the muse didn't appear: tough. There's no such days when you're making a movie. You can wake up with a raging toothache; you can break your ankle – tear all the ligaments in your ankle as I did on *The English Patient* – and the next day you're on the set and you're shooting. And that day's going to be in the film. The stamina of film-making is the biggest learning curve, and as time goes on the issue of stamina gets even more significant for me because the shoots have gone from twenty-eight days to a hundred and twenty-eight days.

How do you prepare yourself physically?
I try and get fit. I train and I try to eat well. I try and get as much sleep as I can. I think the issue of pacing myself and the stamina of film-making is the thing that preoccupies me now. I also know there's a fall-out after shooting. Little bits and pieces of you go wrong afterwards and you get sick.

Did you feel there was a lot at stake when you shooting Truly, Madly, Deeply?
No. I felt it was a rather parenthetical event in my life. I didn't have any sense of it working or not working in career terms at all. I thought I was a writer who was directing this film and would carry on writing. I didn't know my life would be turned on its head – which was effectively what happened – and I've not worked in England since that film. That's a huge change of my life.

Is there anything you didn't like about directing? Being cruel to get what you want?
I'm extremely cool, cold even, about getting what I want in film. Ralph Fiennes talked about my being an iron fist in a velvet glove as a director. So I'm not a soft touch as a director. On the other hand, I think that you have to work absolutely with what you have. Some film-makers will not shoot under certain circumstances. If the actor's wrong they'll fire the actor and get another actor. If the light is wrong, they won't turn over. I think I've got a compromising instinct, which is 'We're here and we're going to shoot today'. One of the reasons I work with John Seale is that I know he's exactly the same. He can't bear not shooting and I can't

bear not shooting. And I try to make a series of very good decisions before I get to the point of turning over. It's the same with actors. Even Juliet Stevenson, whom I wrote the part of Nina for, was not always what I thought she would be. But obviously you have to surrender to the actor. You have to say, it's not my moment any more, it's their moment. I need to love and cherish this person in this moment. It's a kind of love affair and you have to love the person. I think you constantly have to work within the art of the possible in film and exploit coldly and shrewdly exactly what there is and not long for what you can't have or what you wanted. Ultimately it is the Faustian compact you make with film because you can't wait for ever for the light to hit. It never really hits the side of the face in the way you hoped. None of the constellations ultimately line up perfectly: the actor is human and erring and often it's in those fault lines that the most interesting work occurs. To me the job is not to feel unsatisfied by any of the elements, but to try and locate them all and exploit them all for what they are.

Let's talk about the post-production. Did you find that another steep learning curve?
Editing is so close to writing that I found myself completely at home in the cutting room. It's probably my favourite part of the film process. I can organize my day in a way that fits my rhythms and not the rhythms of film-making. I like that. I like the rigour of cutting. Somebody said that a poem is never finished, it's only abandoned, I think that's true of film and I love the process of finding a place where you can abandon it. I think that the rewriting process in the editing room is absolutely fascinating and one that I'm learning as I go along. I wrote almost an entire draft of *The English Patient* in the cutting room. I went back and rewrote scenes, remade scenes. We did so much filleting of material it was like making a dress from a suit. There was a lot of opportunity to go back and work again with the actors in quite extraordinary ways. On *Ripley* I'm already in the process of writing ADR lines that I think will clarify scenes. So I love the creative opportunities of the cutting room. In *Truly, Madly, Deeply* these were few and far between simply because I didn't have enough material to manipulate and the post-production period was so compressed. We had twelve or fourteen weeks in the cutting room in total, including recording music and mixing and completion. Nowadays I've barely finished the first cut by that time. So it's a very different rhythm and pace.

Can you remember what you thought of the first cut you saw?
Just bewildered. People say that a film is never as good as the dailies and never as bad as the first assembly. The first time you see the assembly you feel like you're looking at a building site. Knowing it will eventually be decorated and that there will be furniture requires the same act of faith. Unless you know that, the process is extremely disabling and disconcerting. I remember being very worried when I saw the film because there was so much mess.

Such as?

I remember when it came to shooting the hopping scene it was chaotic because we couldn't quite control the South Bank. We didn't have adequate permission to clear everybody; we didn't have any extras and we didn't have a dolly because you can't put down track on the South Bank. So we got an old Ford chassis, put the camera on the chassis and pushed it along. It was bouncing horribly. If we'd used continuous takes it would have been absolutely absurd but fortunately we were able to cut. In the meantime the weather was changing constantly so when I saw the first assembly, the scene looked awful because there were so many light and colour temperature changes. That was very frightening to me, but eventually it got smoothed out as much as it was possible to smooth it out. Areas where music is involved are also very hard to imagine in the assembly, particularly in those days when everything was cut on film. You had to wait until you got into the mix before you could smooth out any sound bumps. The analogy of the building site prior to furniture and decoration is a very good one. You just can't anticipate the process. It's a wonderful thing when you get the answer-print back and you go into the mix and everything starts to get cleaned up. The transformation of the film in the last ten days or two weeks is so huge, you just need to keep faith with the material until that point. And obviously the more you've done it, the more you understand where it's going to end up.

Can you remember the first public screening of the film?
I took the film to Los Angeles because there had been a great deal of interest in the screenplay before we started shooting and my agent at William Morris, Michael Peretzian, had said I should screen the film in Los Angeles once I'd finished it. I think Mark Shivas had seen it and Robert Cooper had seen it several times. Sid Gannis was the president of Paramount at that time and he was a friend of mine and he said, 'I hear you've made this movie. You should bring it over. Let's have a screening.' So I took the film to Los Angeles. It was very exciting because so many people had somehow heard about the film. And Sid Gannis introduced it. It was all very charming and the film started and then suddenly I realized that there was a huge problem which was not only was this double-headed projector absolutely antediluvian, but also we shot the film at twenty-five frames per second because it was for the BBC. It wasn't out of sync but it was running slow. It was almost imperceptible but it wasn't Juliet Stevenson's voice that I heard. It starts off 'mainly when I'm walking'. I realized that the film was four and half minutes longer at that screening than any other screening. And it was so painful because already when you sit with an audience your film slows down to half its normal speed. But it was literally slowing down as well and nobody noticed! Nobody knew except for me and I was in agony watching it. And then what ensued was a sudden flurry about buying the film and then I was suddenly a film director. Up until that moment I was a writer and the next day I was a director and the odd thing was that people were not remotely interested that I had written the screenplay whereas to me that was the most significant thing about the film.

How did you feel about this reaction?

It felt good. I was so proud of what Juliet had done and still am proud. I still think it's an amazing performance and an absolutely fully realized piece of work by her. I thought she'd dignified every moment of the film and I wanted everybody else to see it. I felt disconnected in that respect from it. I felt like a cheerleader for her and for what people would make of her work. That tends to happen in movies, you become evangelical about a particular thing. I want people to see Matt Damon in *Ripley* because again I felt that somebody has done something extraordinary for me.

Did you think that things would come together in such a perfect way?

It's always rather odd when people engage in something you've done, because in the end you can't quite imagine it. You can imagine the screening in which you are in the room. You can never imagine it in any other screenings. The life that it takes on when you meet somebody who says I've seen your film sixty-three times – which is sixty-two times more than I've seen it – is bizarre. Or the person who says to you, 'I hate that film so much.' Both those polarities are so bizarre and I've had them both. How odd that such a strangely personal undertaking, and something so far from iconoclasm, should provoke such polarized responses!

Do you think the experience of Truly, Madly, Deeply *helped you in your subsequent career?*

I think the making of *Truly, Madly, Deeply* is an entirely parenthetical experience. For instance, I probably wrote twenty-five drafts of *The English Patient*. There's probably twenty published drafts of *Ripley*; whereas I wrote *Truly, Madly, Deeply* in a matter of a few weeks. I think it went through two or three drafts. I made the film, very few people saw it before it was finished. The thing about film-making is that it's one of the most public forms of artistic endeavour around. Nowadays people swarm all over my films. But *Truly, Madly, Deeply* was one of the most private experiences I had. There were so few people involved, such a tiny crew, a tiny cast, a tiny production staff, Robert, who I'd worked with before, Mark Shivas. That was it. I think Mark saw the film in rough-cut and the finished cut. Robert periodically came into the cutting room but was a very quiet and empowering voice and then the film was finished. It was so simple and every subsequent experience has been so complex and the metabolism so slow, that unfortunately there's been nothing to take from it except a kind of nostalgia.

Mira Nair: *Salaam Bombay!*

Were you interested in movies when you were growing up?

No. I wasn't one of those people who grew up knowing I was a film-maker or making movies in my backyard or anything of the sort. I grew up in a small town, with one cinema, that was remote even in Indian terms. The only thing I remember which has carried into making movies is that I loved getting involved with people's lives. My mother has a story of my running off when I was eleven years old and returning with the milkman because I was fascinated with what he did in the mornings.

How did you discover film?

Through being an actress in a very amateur way in India, where I studied with an Englishman called Barry John, a disciple of Peter Brook. I then started working with Badal Sircar, a progressive Indian playwright and director in the radical protest theatre tradition. I spent a few years being on stage and thinking this was it. But I was also under the illusion that I was an academic, so I applied for scholarships and when I was eighteen I got a scholarship to Harvard where I thought I'd pursue theatre. But the theatre there was really conventional. It was *Oklahoma!*, musicals, hooped skirts, that sort of thing. So I went to New York to look at the off-Broadway theatre and studied there with some of my gurus – Joseph Chaikin, The Talking Band, Andrei Serban. On the basis of some photographs I had made that summer, I was accepted in the documentary film-making course at Harvard. And for me it was just one of those blessed things. At the age of twenty I found what I wanted to do in my life, because it was a way of working visually, working with people, trying to capture life. So I became a visual and environmental studies major. You make a film as a thesis in which you do everything. You shoot it, you do the sound, you do the negative cutting. All my films were made in India, but I was living in New York, and I would go back and forth.

What kind of films did you make at Harvard?

My graduation film was eighteen minutes long and was called *Jami Masjid Street Journal*, which is the name of an old Muslim community in old Delhi near the great Mosque. Instead of having a veil in front of me, I had a camera. The film was about how people reacted to me on the street, as a woman who spoke the language, who was from there and yet not from there; also how they reacted to me having a camera. It was conceived as a black and white hand-cranked Bolex silent film, but unfortunately as I was editing the film my friends got me to tell them what was actually happening in the scene. So I added a narration which I later greatly regretted. This taught me my first lesson in cinema: never surrender your own idea of the film, your own instinct, for the momentary pleasure of pleasing those around you. Anyway, that was my first film – an impressionistic portrait of a very traditional Muslim community, using the camera as a veil.

What happened after you graduated?
With that film I moved to New York. Much to my embarrassment it actually got a theatrical release which at the time was a really big deal for a student film. I soon became unemployed so I worked as a waitress by day, and by night I got a job synching up medical films on backache and amnesia. The weird part was that I shared my editing room with Robert Duvall who was cutting his gypsy movie, *Angelo, My Love*. Robert was a blast. He insisted I was a gypsy and would take me out late at night, after we were both fed up with amnesia and gypsies. And we'd drink and have a really interesting time. You meet these kind of cronies in the nether world of New York when you're trying to struggle and work as an artist or whatever you think you are. Anyway, I finally got a more respectable job in an African art gallery. Nobody wanted African art at the time so I used that time to write proposals for my first documentary film, *So Far From India*, a *cinéma vérité* portrait of a subway news-stand worker. He was fresh off the boardwalk from India and had been married off to a peasant woman in India. I hung out with him in New York, seeing how he dealt with life, selling newspapers on the subway. And then his wife got pregnant and had a child so he went back to India to see the child and I went with him. He was welcomed by his family but he had changed so much – thought himself such a cool American – that he refused to talk to his so-called peasant wife. She was in absolute agony that he wouldn't speak to her so I became the go-between on camera between the husband and the wife. It was very painful for her, but to sound ruthless, always interesting for my camera. I lived with them for about two months and assumed this whole silence and estrange-ment. And although everybody was pressuring him to take his wife with him to America he returned alone with the promise that he would send for her. So it was a portrait of the American dream and the other side of it.

Did you finance this yourself?
No, I got my first grant, twenty thousand dollars, from the New York Council of Humanities. I made my difference my strength. You know: 'I am an Indian woman who has access to worlds that you will never have access to.' I got all these American liberals to feel terribly concerned and give me twenty thousand dollars. I then shot ten minutes and went to another foundation. There was a series of three or four foundations I went to over an absolutely brutal ten-month period and then I had a film. *So Far From India* was my first professional film, a fifty-two-minute documentary. I was invited to various film festivals, did fairly well and then Jane Balfour became the sales agent and sold it internationally. That

gave me a step into getting my next documentary pre-financed by the people who had bought it. So I was in the fairly enviable position of having my next film already financed. That film, *India Cabaret*, was about strippers in Bombay and was financed from a combination of sources outside India. I never touch Indian money because it's feudal money in a way. Everybody who gives you money wants some sort of pound of flesh. Besides, Indian financiers do not understand documentaries. They barely understand a film that isn't in the commercial arena, in the commercial form they know. My films have now made a lot of money, so they've told me that they would look at me now in Bombay as somebody who is viable. But even then they would think it was a huge risk because I am not giving them twenty songs and dances and a multi-star cast and whatever is the norm. Documentaries? Forget it!

What kind of piece was India Cabaret?
It was actually the direct precursor to *Salaam Bombay!* I made it as an investigation of what makes a good woman in India. What is the line that we draw between a woman who is 'good' and a woman who is considered improper or outside goodness? Goodness and badness are always to do with sexuality in our country and I chose to tell it from the point of view of women who are considered improper, strippers. I found two amazing women who were strippers outside Bombay, and I lived with them for four months. In fact, people thought I was a stripper because I was always with them. And it's very interesting and very paradoxical in terms of using your sexuality, because although as strippers the women take off their clothes on stage, as soon as they come off the stage they wrap themselves in petticoats and saris and bindis. The movie is riddled with these paradoxes. And it's a very moving film. One of the strippers told us that she was earning money because her sister was getting married, and she needed to make money for her sister's dowry so that the sister would get a decent match: a match that was beyond her because, as a stripper, she herself was considered polluted. When she went home and we accompanied her across India to Hyderabad, her family accepted the money but did not let her into the house because then the house would be polluted for the wedding. That's India. That's the reality. So, it was a film about their lives, a male customer who comes very often to the club and his wife who stays home: the eternal triangle, Indian style. But it was *cinéma vérité*. The film was in Bombay Hindi which is what they speak in *Salaam Bombay!* Bombay is the place where everybody comes to from all over India, so even the language is a pastiche. It's a bit of this, a bit of that. *India Cabaret* was filmed in that very bawdy, ribald, fantastic language. I was invited to the opening night film of the Indian International Film Festival in Hyderabad in 1985. It was very interesting because the two protagonists of the film, the two strippers, were by complete coincidence, both from Hyderabad. And of course, they were at the screening. I invited them and made sure that they were there. In a highly repressed society like India, a film called *India Cabaret* means that the audience

will literally burst the door down to get in. So it was five thousand people, mostly men, seeing a documentary film on 16 mm in a huge theatre like the Ziegfeld in New York! It was like a riot.

After this, did it seem a natural step from documentaries to features?
I never saw documentaries as a stepping stone to fiction. I was a resolute documentary film-maker. I was so totally absorbed in what I was doing that I was never really looking for the next step. That is a disease you get later. But as a *cinéma vérité* person, you're basically just there. It's as boring as sin sometimes! You know, for four days you're not getting anything, then suddenly, it comes. You get something and it's an epiphany! But I was getting tired of waiting for things to happen and wanted to make them happen. I wanted to control the light, the gesture, the mood, the storytelling. Also this impatience came from the struggle I had to get an audience for my films once they were finished. I mean, the films I made were supposed to be successful but I know how many people saw them. *India Cabaret*, for example, was not shown on television because it was too risqué. It was a reel around my arm. I would go to women's unions; any workers, any union, any colleges, any film societies, anybody who wanted me, I would go and I would present it. Just myself, and then speak afterwards and then leave. I did that to make a living everywhere in the world.

You said India Cabaret *was a direct precursor to* Salaam Bombay! *In what way?*
A friend, Sooni Taraporevala, and I were going to make our first feature film which was supposed to be autobiographical. But when we saw and felt the visceral response to *India Cabaret* in Hyderabad, Sooni thought we should do something closer to the streets, recalling an idea I'd had a while ago of working with street children and their lives. In 1983, I had an experience while I was making the film with the strippers, when I was living in this very bleak area of Bombay called Antop Hill. By every traffic light there were street kids begging. I was in a taxi one day when the light turned red and one of them came up to the window and I gave him some money. He had no legs, just a stump on a board, a makeshift plank with wheels on it. The street was crowded with traffic and the light turned green. I was terrified for him but he propelled himself right up to the middle of the street and then, as the taxi left, performed a pirouette and then bowed to an imaginary audience. He had become a showman, I thought. For me this was the essence of the spirit of the street kids. It was nothing to do with wanting your pity but instead was saying, 'Here is our life. We just get on with it and make the best of what we have.' And many years earlier, I had been deeply affected by Liz Swados's *Runaways* at The Public Theatre – I would hang around her rehearsals; and also Hector Babenco's *Pixote*. I happened to hear Babenco talk about his film just after I saw it, and suddenly I had the courage to make my own film. In India everybody will tell you till you're blue in the face that nothing will work if you don't have a commercial formula. But I'd seen how you

should never underestimate the audience. So putting all this together, we changed direction and came back to Bombay to start the research for what became *Salaam Bombay!*

To go from the image of a street kid at the window of your taxi to a finished feature film script must have been an enormous leap. How did you approach it?
I approached it as a documentarist first. But very clearly appreciating the irony that my camera, the non-documentary camera, the fiction camera, would actually have greater access to these real-life situations than a documentary camera, because I didn't want to enter a world and record it in a hit-and-run manner. I wanted to organize and suss. So I approached it as I would my documentaries. Sooni and I would literally walk the streets of Bombay. She's from there so she knows certain areas. We would start trying to talk to rag-pickers and gangs of street kids and I remember the first time they just took one look at us and ran the other way. We started chasing them and then finally they stopped and they said, 'Look, the chiller room!' 'Chiller room' is the street slang for the way kids describe the government remand homes. But 'chiller' is also the street Hindi way of saying 'children's home'; instead of saying 'children's home', they say 'chiller room' which also has this feeling in English of the 'chill' room, a place to chill out. Finally the kids told us that the chiller rooms were sending people out in plain clothes these days, and they thought we'd been sent to get them for the chiller room so that's why they ran. Finally after days of talking to kids on the street, we met a gang of rag-pickers just below Sooni's house. They embraced us completely and we hung out with them, played cards with them, went to the movies with them. We talked to them over a couple of months and then we went off to a little island off the Bombay coast called Manori and stayed in this ramshackle bungalow owned by a friend. We had to invent a drama, a plot where we would use these stories that we had bought from these children. We riffed about many possible chronologies of plot, then Sooni would write and I would edit and shape and collaborate and then she would write some more.

It's such a rich, elaborate story. Had you had any experience of doing this before?
No, not at all. I had never even been to a movie set before. When you are beginning you are just mad! Everybody asks you, 'Did you think it was going to be such a hit?' And I thought, are you mad? I was just thinking about whether I could make it to the next day. It was that kind of feeling. Not a fear or dread, but just how to carry on. At this stage we were just experimenting. I am a focused dreamer. I was twenty-eight when I started, so I had seven years of making movies where I was on my own creating a narrative in the editing room. So the principles of narrative were vaguely entrenched in me. Sooni was a short-story writer who studied film at Harvard at the same time as me; she was also an English Lit major and we both loved movies. Moreover, she was also a stills photographer who saw the world visually, as I did, and she had an ear for dialogue which

neither of us knew she had before we began. So she had that and I had this other stuff and we put it together.

Did you know where the money was going to come from at this point?
Farrukh Dhondy was one of the three or four pre-financiers of *India Cabaret* when he was a commissioning editor at Channel 4. I had a verbal agreement with him that they would put up half the money for the *Salaam Bombay!* idea. We agreed that whenever we had a new draft we would give it to him. He was the one who believed in the film from the beginning. I think we showed him the fourth draft. He was always a terrific script analyst and he shaped a lot of things. We also had a friend in India, Anil Tejani, the executive producer of the film, who was another extremely valuable person on the script level. I knew I wanted to set up a workshop for street kids at least two months before I shot the film, in order to find my actors and to refine the script for them. And I wanted to shoot the film starting around this huge Bombay festival, Ganpati, a celebration of the birthday of Ganesh in the middle of August. So I was working backwards from that because I couldn't stage the crowd scenes which were the climax of the movie. So everything had to work. Based on the draft, based on me, Channel 4 had committed themselves to fifty per cent of the budget.

Once you had this notional backing from Channel 4 where else did you look?
I went to a very close friend, Michael Nozik who had started to make American independent features. We knew each other from Cambridge days: I chose the documentary route; he chose the feature route. I gave him the script and asked him to tell me what the realistic budget was. I went to meet him on Broadway, I remember, and he gave me a budget of nine hundred and sixty thousand dollars. I remember feeling like somebody had hit me in the stomach. I just thought to myself, I raised a hundred and fifty thousand dollars for my documentaries which was mega at the time. I said, 'I can't raise nine hundred and sixty because that means I'll have to find four hundred and fifty or five hundred.' I felt like a warrior; like somebody had hit me in the gut but I was going to show them. This is my normal reaction when I am rejected. At first my spirits darken and then I get angry, like 'fuck you! I'm going to show you'. I remember walking back from there, fighting the tears, saying, 'I'll show them. I'll do this whatever it takes.' I made three budgets. I made a 'bare bones' budget, a scam budget and a realistic budget based on what Michael had done. The bare bones budget was just about what I needed to shoot the movie 'and then we'll see . . .', which is a terrible way to go, but I decided that was the way to go. And somehow I had the wisdom not to cut corners on the screen, not to make a 16 mm blow-up and all that. I wanted never to apologize for this movie. The second budget was the scam budget. This was actually three different budgets. Let's say I'm going to see Indian backers. They would never give me more than a hundred and fifty thousand. So I show them a three-hundred-thousand-dollar budget and say, 'Look, a hundred and

fifty thousand is here from Channel 4 so if you give me a hundred and fifty we are in business.' There were three scam budgets, depending on whom I was going to see. I told Channel 4 and they were great. In those days they were great. By this time we'd already started the workshop for the street kids. I couldn't wait because of the festival coming up in September. So there we were doing the workshops and there was no sign of any other commitments by that time; the workshop was in full momentum, the kids were proving to be amazing, Ganpati festival was around the corner, and we had to begin shooting in a month at the latest in order to get what we wanted to get. So in come the strange bedfellows. I had put in proposals in America. I had put in proposals in France. There was no money coming in, anywhere. I had to bite the bullet and go to the National Film Development Corporation of India, which is a boring, bureaucratic, government organization which exists to support films like mine but which takes every pound of flesh from you and makes you weep for your Bisleri mineral water receipt. It's horrendous. But I had to do it because I had no money. I remember this chiffon-clad lady-bureaucrat coming out to the workshop to check out what was going on and the kids making fun of her. NFDC's limit was the equivalent of a hundred and fifty thousand. Finally they said they'd give me a hundred and fifty in exchange for twenty-five per cent of the movie. The bonus for me was getting the Indian government stamp, so that even though I was making a fairly risqué movie, indicting Indian society, indicting the remand homes and all that, because they were investors, I could get access to any government property. Shooting on the railway in India, for example, is unheard of. You can never do it! And I shot my whole movie on the railway station because I supposedly had government backing. So it was very useful, although they took their pound of flesh like you cannot imagine. I needed at least four hundred and fifty thousand to shoot the movie and process it. So I said to Channel 4: 'I will tell you that I have three hundred thousand dollars – a hundred and fifty thousand from the Indian government, a hundred and fifty thousand from other sources – so you can match it with another three hundred thousand.' It was really just an open hoax that was understood by both sides. So they gave me the three hundred thousand, and I had the four hundred and fifty thousand in total. I decided at that time to spend almost the entire amount on shooting the film in 35 mm, get all the money on screen and worry about post-production later. By this time we had already begun shooting. And at night after wrap, I would try to raise extra money. Because of the time difference – India is ahead by ten hours from America – I would try to raise extra money. For instance, we wanted to shoot in the monsoon so if the bloody rain wouldn't come down we'd have to pay extra for the rain machine.

Who were you calling when you made these calls at night?
I was calling the Rockefeller Foundation to whom I'd put in a proposal, God knows when. I was calling Canal Plus. I was calling La Sept. I was calling Holland, VPO Television, whoever had bought *So Far From India*. I was calling Jane Bal-

four to ask if she had any other leads. I was calling Gabriel Auer, a friend in France who was trying to get some French money. I was calling everybody.

But you went ahead on the money you had?
I went ahead because of the timetable. What happened was that in the second week of shooting the French came in and said they would put in the remaining three hundred and sixty thousand dollars. I was using Michael's original nine-hundred-and-sixty-thousand-dollar budget and saying I had six hundred thousand. They put in three hundred and sixty thousand in exchange for owning most of the movie. I didn't have six hundred thousand, but that was okay because they were giving me three hundred and sixty thousand! So I was fine. It was great. They came in, everybody took their pound of flesh. Twenty-five per cent owned by the Indians, thirty-five per cent owned by the French, twenty-five per cent owned by whoever. Forget about the creative owners! Then I shot the movie.

On eight hundred thousand dollars or something like that?
I actually only had four hundred thousand at this point. So we shot the movie, we processed it and went to New York, sat in these free bedroom-editing rooms and did the movie at night. Spike Lee and I would share editing rooms. It was wild. Spike and I started at the same time. On *India Cabaret* we split the daily editing room cost by me working ten hours in the morning and him working six hours in the evening. We like to believe that guerrilla film-making was defined in New York! And then because the French had come in, I had to do all the post-production in France, I had to spend all the money in French francs, so I had to go there. We finished shooting in December and I came back to New York and in January we got a call from the Rockefeller Foundation saying they had given me a hundred thousand dollars, which was a grant and which is the only reason that my company, that is to say the creative owners, Sooni and me, actually own any of the movie. Once the government came in, it was all pari passu. It has nothing to do with who is struggling or anything like that. So thanks to the Rockefellers, we own seventeen per cent of the movie, which means we still get cheques every three months!

Let's go back to your preparations for the film. How did you find the kids who actually appear in the film?
I had a lot of help. Firstly, I had a team of friends who I call the international Bhenji brigade. 'Bhenji' is a Hindi word which means women, sisters. But it is a vernacular way of saying 'not-so-hip sisters'. It's just a fun thing; it's actually saying it in a super-hip way, but it means they aren't hip! It means 'my team', 'my gang'. You know, 'girl power' in English. So I have a lot of right and left hands. And this was the team that made the movie. We rented a church space to hold workshops in. We knew from our research on the street how much the kids made: twenty-five rupees a day rag-picking or cleaning windows or selling newspapers or whatever. Almost seventy-five cents a day, ten years ago. Now they

make about a hundred and fifty but in those days it was twenty-five. One of our assistant directors, Nilita Vachani, went to various places in downtown Bombay and handed out cards for about ten days. If they wanted a job they had to take this chit from her and come to this location at such and such a time, and then I'd tell them if they'd got a job, and if they had I think we offered them fifty rupees a day, or something.

Did they know what the job was?
All they knew was that there was a girl on the street who had cards with an address. If you want to come, show up, they said. Nothing else. A hundred and thirty kids showed up on the first day! I had asked my old guru, Barry John, to run this workshop with me. He had run drama workshops and is also really amazing with children. So he was there, with Nilita and my other assistant, Dina Stafford, who was a child psychologist by training. This was her first film and her responsibility was to do two things. Firstly, to mother-hen the children that we finally picked and worked with. Secondly, which was much more important for me at that time, to design a programme for these children once we'd finished the movie. So we had this team and a hundred and thirty kids turned up. Within the first five days we whittled this number down to twenty-four. These twenty-four I was committed to. If they were committed to me, I was committed to them. There was no charity. They were fined if they got there late. Nobody had watches, you see. They would be there early, I tell you. They were never late.

Were they still sleeping on the streets at this time?
Yeah. Most of them were on the streets. They were floaters. They'd sleep anywhere.

By the time you shot the movie, the kids were extraordinarily unselfconscious, grace-ful even. Can you tell me a little about what you did in the workshop?
A lot of it was about physical focus and concentration, physical coordination and mental coordination. They started with a kind of yoga in the morning then did dancing. They would pick their own music, Madonna or whatever. Then we'd have debates on issues that were important to them and they'd divide themselves up and talk back and forth. Sooni was always there working like a classic dra-maturge, recording and constantly aware of what was good in what the kids said. And then we would do improvisations where we would think of situations and the kids would do what they do in the movie; they'd be waiters at these weddings or put on little plays of what happened at a wedding, of being the police com-missioner's son or being harassed by such and such. And we would constantly be enhancing the script with such things. And then we would show them movies. We showed them a lot of Chaplin. We showed them *The 400 Blows*. We showed them things that they had never seen.

How did they react?
They loved movies. They are brought up on Indian movies, on a flamboyant act-

ing style. But in our movie that kind of acting became a bad word. We went for an understated naturalism, the less is more variety. In the workshop amongst the kids, they would critique each other's performance constantly – it became a curse if you were considered to be 'acting'.

So in a way you were training them not to be self-conscious?
Yes. But they would also teach me how to interact with them. We would mother them sometimes. They were children, after all. But they were also looking for discipline. They would want to be told, you know. Then in the fourth week we brought the script in. We would present them with scenes and they would say, 'This line? We would not say this. This is the way.' And they would come up with something better and that would carry on.

Did you feel you were learning a lot during the process?
Constantly. Obviously I was not teaching these children. It was a totally two-way process. They had their lives. I didn't have those lives and they had to make it clear to me what their life was. And they would shame us also by saying 'this is absurd, this is not how it is' or whatever. The script was born out of the research but let's face it, we were never in their place. We were never far wrong but still the nuances, the kind of dreams they had, the things we talked about, were amazing. Things like, are chiller rooms necessary? You'd think they'd say, 'Fuck off. We don't want to have remand homes.' But half of them said, 'We want remand homes because when it's monsoon and the rain comes down, I like that roof over my head and I like that dhal and rice, however shitty it is. I know it's going to come at noon and I like it!' Another guy would say, 'I used to work as a porter before they took me to the chiller room and when I came out I was so skinny I didn't have the strength to do my job. Why don't you take away my livelihood rather than just taking away my strength?' Then another kid would say, 'But where do you want to sleep in the monsoon?' It was surprising. You wouldn't expect these kids to like these places.

What about casting the professional actors? Was it easy to find actors prepared to appear alongside the street kids?
I made it a requirement that the professionals come to the workshop. Manju's mother, Rekha, was played by a brilliant actress, Aneeta Kanwar, a television star. This was her first film. I found Nana Patekar, who played Baba, on stage and cast him. He was amazing. This was his first film but from this film on, not necessarily because of this film but other things he has done, he has become a megastar. He is the highest-paid film actor now in India. The guy who played Chillum was a professional actor from Delhi, which is a very different style from Bombay. He did brilliantly in the movie but it was, I would say, an entirely imitated performance. I had to do line readings for him. This is the thing about my bull-headedness. You do whatever it takes. I've met American actors who will kill you if you give them anything that vaguely resembles a line reading. But there, it didn't

matter! If you need a line reading I'll give you a line reading – 'You do it like this.' Anyway, my work with the professionals was mostly to preserve the freshness that the children brought to their performance.

What were the reactions of the professional actors to the street kids when, like you, they ordinarily might only have seen them from the inside of a car?
Aneeta Kanwar, who played Rekha, was such a consummate actor and such a humble person that there was never any question that these kids were as valuable to her as any other actors. Nana Patekar had never really quite had this experience. He's a lot like Baba in life. He has an attitude, not against the kids, but he was tough with them. You know, tough love sort of thing. He is really a populist but he was not going to mess around, get involved, get emotional. He never told me that he was impressed with them. People thought I was starkers. They thought I was starkers from day one. Why was I doing all this for these ruffians? You know, all this shooting on the street? We'd have these silks to diffuse the light which had never been seen on Indian movies, so they would say, 'Why are you putting all this junk on the street and banning traffic and all this? For what? For these children? At least get a decent movie star.'

Can you remember the first rehearsals you had with professionals and the children?
Chillum was always there from day one. I purposely made Baba and Rekha not come every day because I wanted Baba to have an aloofness from the kids.

Did you rehearse the professionals and the street children together before you shot?
Yes, just for a couple of weeks. Not exactly, but just for them to know each other and be comfortable.

Did you rehearse the action before you arrived on location?
No. I didn't do any rehearsals. After the screen test had been done and I knew who was playing what, I didn't do any rehearsals. For one thing, the kids didn't read so Dinaz would draw cartoons of the script. We had a cartoon script to remind the kids where we were. And lines had to be memorized not read. So it's not like you memorize your whole role. You only memorize the scene you're about to do. Even though you know what scene it is that you're going to do, you only memorize your lines.

Given they couldn't read the script, how did you communicate the role they were playing to the children?
It came from their life. For example, for the scene with Manju eating the biscuits, I said to her, 'These biscuits are from your sister, Jyoti, but she's made you angry so you are eating these biscuits like you are eating her. You just want to eat her up.' And she was getting into it. I guess she was really an amazingly gifted method actress. When she was listening to me, she would get that expression and then I would start rolling. Shafiq was different. He was much more of a pro in the sense that he would turn it on and off. Manju would get into it and you would have to

film. And then, of course, they had a lot of pride. I remember the first day. I never told her to eat the whole packet because I knew I wouldn't keep the camera rolling for the whole packet.

Because you didn't have that much budget?
Because of the stock, not because of the biscuits! So she ate the whole packet and I found myself riveted by how she was eating them because she was eating up her sister. And I remember she had such pride. She was waiting for me to say cut and was getting furious that I wasn't. She came to me and said, 'I am not going to do another take for you on that because I am not going to eat another packet!' But I'd got more than I needed. It was just brilliant. So, yeah, it was done like that. A lot of times, even now with real actors, this happens. I observe what they are doing when they are sitting around, when they are not on a take and I love some things they do. Like Krishna had this thing when he got shy, when he couldn't remember anything, he would bring his palm to his ear, and look up tentatively. I love hands and the map of his life was on his hands. They were like leather. They had thick lines on them like those of an old man. He was actually fourteen at the time, but he played eleven. So he would show his hands when he got shy or vulnerable, not even aware that he was showing them. It was a beautiful gesture. And I would see a gesture like this and say to him, now you do that, what you just did. I would always do that, always, even now. Then, right after they think it is cut and it would have been a cut, I would not say cut because when they think it's over they are actually so truthful. That's always the way. If Shafiq was asking for tea from his boss, I'd say to him, ask twice. And after the second time, I wouldn't cut and he would just plead without saying anything – just with his eyes.

I thought the boy who played Krishna was extraordinary. How did you find him?
After the fourth or fifth week, when we actually started acting the scenes, I wanted to do some screen tests, largely to see how the blend between the professional actors and the non-professionals was working. But also to find Krishna. I was already crazy about the girl who played Manju. She is still my number one. I'm a sucker for her and I always was, so there was no question. But who Krishna should be, I genuinely didn't know. So it was just this screen test that we did largely to test the professionals really and in which he became completely luminous, he just shined. It's like what you see about actors, you know. In life they are okay but you put them on camera and they glow. He had that quality, so that was very apparent. There was no heartache over that choice. He was it.

A lot of the film was shot in public spaces like the railway station. Given India's reputation for bureaucracy, was it a struggle to get permission to film in these locations?
Filming on the railway station was a combination of having the government behind the movie and this gorgeous assistant of mine called Joyce Barneto. It was considered impossible to get these permissions since a Bollywood producer had made a film called *The Burning Train* and apparently had actually burnt a train

during the shooting! But Joyce didn't take no for an answer. She used to go to the railway offices. She'd go with the railway bosses into the elevators and keep saying, 'Please, just please sign this.' She would chase them until they were so charmed that they finally signed. But our agreement, our pedigree was right. You have to have persistence and charm. You have to make sure that they don't feel threatened. That was the good thing about having so many women on my team. I distinctly remember Joyce coming in waving this permission slip. The final approval.

How long did it take to get it?
It took two months. And that's with all this ingredients being right. It takes a lot of time. But once you have that 'yes' there is nothing like it! There is no way to replace the visual madness, the richness, the cacophony and life of an Indian railway station.

How about the other locations? Did you have a location manager?
I had one of the sisters on it but basically it came out of the research. The locations were mostly born out of *India Cabaret*. Basically I'd been hanging out with quasi-prostitutes. I'd therefore already met the madams who were the heads of the brothels. So I knew those faces and I just returned to them. A lot of the locations in the script are in the film and came from the rag-picking gang that we met during the early days of research. Everything was real, but we would heighten some of it; for instance, there were these fab murals of all the gods that would be painted on street walls to prevent passers-by from pissing on those walls. So we got the street painter who would do these murals to paint one just like it against the wall where the kids sleep in the film.

A substantial part of the story was filmed in a real brothel. Was it difficult to persuade the brothel madams to help you? Was it simply another business deal for them?
That was wonderful because I respected them. That is the cornerstone of documentary film-making. You have to have respect and you have to be humble and you have to submit to the reality that you wish to capture. I had met them before, the union heads, the brothel leaders, the madams, all women, for the other film, *India Cabaret*. I just went back to them and I said, 'This is our story now and I want to shoot in your place.' And they said, 'You are a woman, you are one of us, you are welcome.' Because I'd done the right thing. I hadn't sent some little man in to represent me. I'd said, 'This is your work, the film is hopefully going to be my work. What do I need to do? I don't want any charity. Tell me what you need and we'll pay.' There was never any charity but when we asked a great actress, Shaukat Azmi, to play the madam in the film and we were shooting in the brothels, she was dressed by the madams. 'I like that earring, I like that ankle bracelet,' she'd say. They'd say, okay, put it on her, pass a comment and tell her how to swing. That's the thing I love about India, the thing I love about working at home. After the film I met Shaukat for dinner and she cannot get over the experience. She still talks about it.

Let's move on. How did you find your DP, Sandi Sissel?
I wanted somebody from a documentary background, but who had also done fiction, because I hadn't. I am a very visual person and I come from a very strong photographic tradition. I know what I want visually so I have to really respect a person's style. Sandi had done some really interesting documentaries, films she'd produced and shot herself. And she'd also worked in India. She had made a seminal film on Mother Teresa but she had also done a zillion commercials for bread and butter. With all the lighting she had to do for that, I figured that she was my woman. Also she was willing to go for the ride. I am very much a fierce Indian. I don't want to apologize for my country in any way. Anybody who comes along with me for the ride in India has to love it. They have to have a certain sensibility, a curiosity about the world and she certainly met the bill. She came in time for the last week or ten days of the workshop. Incidentally, she adopted the youngest kid in our workshop, the kid who played Insect, Raju Barnard. Keera, we call him, he is one of the street gang. He has got a little role, but he is always there. He is her son now and lives with her in Santa Monica and is a Boogie Board champion of the Santa Monica beaches as well as a camera assistant for Panavision!

How did you work together? Did you show her other films? Did you show her photographs?
No. I do that all the time now. But on that film she only saw the locations. We spent almost ten days breaking down the script before even seeing the locations. You always intend to spend more time on it but it never happens. She was the first person who taught me how to break down a script. We never got beyond the first third of the script but we did break down every scene, first liberally, you know, twelve set-ups or something and then eventually we'd whittle it down to four. We did that together in pre-production. We would draw a rough storyboard, stick figures and such like. So we did a third of the script in pre-production and then we winged it as we went. Because of time, I never had the time to finish designing the whole film. So she was the first one who taught me that. But a lot of the scenes were already based in locations we knew from our research, so a lot of the way to shoot a scene was in my head.

You would go there and you would say how you wanted it?
I'd lived there already so when we went there, or even before we went there, I'd say this is how I want it. Sometimes the designer, Mitch, and I would drive ahead in a taxi to find the location for the next street while the crew were joining us and we would walkie-talkie them, 'We are here now.' We never had every street that we had to have beforehand.

'Fifty-two locations in fifty-two days' as it says in the credits?
It somehow happened, yes. 'What problem? No problem.' as it also says.

Were you ever nervous when you were about to embark on this mammoth shoot?

I am a bull-headed person. I don't even think if I can do it. 'The film is bigger than all of us' was my mantra.

You know you can do it?
I don't even think I know. I just want to do it so I do it. I convince myself. It's a terrible thing because sometimes things aren't ready.

Did you have the same confidence in the kids as you had in yourself?
What happened in the workshop was that the kids learnt how to concentrate. That was the most important thing they learnt. I would say that three-quarters of the film had between five hundred and five thousand people watching every scene from behind ropes. Three-quarters of the film was crowd controlled. It was amazing if I felt like I'd directed for five per cent of my day because most of the time I was crowd controlling!

You mean when you were on the streets or throughout the film?
The streets. But three-quarters of the film is on the streets so nobody could sit on their butts. There was never any question. In fact my sound recordist couldn't come at the last minute because his wife became pregnant. So we hired these professionals from New York, you know, these big guys. I remember this guy I didn't even know telling me, 'Directors are not meant to be like this, yelling, screaming with megaphones. You have to have assistants.' I genuinely did not know what a first AD did.

So you were doing that yourself!
I had a megaphone. I had a megaphone and huge sneakers. I burnt all my clothes after that movie because I was just in shit all the time, literally in the gutter. Anyway, each person has to do everything. The kids who are not in the shot are crowd controlling. The most important factor is concentration. Because we also didn't have stock to burn. We had three takes for every shot.

What was your shooting ratio?
I don't know exactly. But I never ever shot more than five takes. I still don't. But some things, like that last shot where he takes the top and looks up, I think we didn't actually have enough stock to go beyond her take for the last shot of the movie. And it was in that space with at least four hundred people at least watching him cry and do all those things. It was a long take and in the middle of the second take, somebody just dropped a flower pot from a veranda right through the shot. You think it's a great take and bang! It's fucked. I had no cutaways, nothing. The film was entirely, not fully, but largely edited in the camera. There were never master shots or anything like that. It was completely 'only do what you need you do'. So that take was gone. On the third take, I remember this amazing concentration not just because you've got to do a good job but because you ain't got no more stock!

What was your input in terms of the look, the design of the film?
One hundred per cent. I felt it should look very close to reality but a very heightened photographic view of reality. For instance, the brothel we had chosen was
one kind of architectural space. But there was this fuchsia-pink wall that I had seen
in another brothel and I had them reproduce that wall in the brothel where we
were shooting. Or this fantastic mural that you see on many streets in India of four
different gods which is what these kids sleep against. The way of having people not
piss on where you live is to put the gods up so that they won't defecate there or piss
there. Simple story. And when everything is on the streets, that, too, happens
largely on the streets. So this is a way of keeping your little sleeping area clean. So
we created that. We got the same guy who did the graffiti to come and do it there.
Mitch was a photographer by trade and he brought a lot in terms of how to film
something. We understood each other completely and he always took me further.
In India, there is a certain kind of phosphorescence about so much of the street
and I always went for the jugular, design-wise. I just love that. I love the way those
carnations look and play. There are so many to choose from but you just go to the
real place and get it. And then shoot it. So it was this marriage all the time of reality within reality. But those two realities were put together by us.

And taking elements all the time from other places?
All the time. Clothes, for instance. We asked all the children to bring their clothes.
We marked them and then we bought them from the children for the continuity of
the film. I love saffron so I took the shirt Shafiq was wearing and dyed it with saffron and made a mixture of dirt and saffron, things like that.

*What about the professional actors? Did you have to dress them carefully to blend in
with the street quality of the rest of the film?*
We just bought the things which the people there would buy. Amazing stuff.
They had vendors who would deal with prostitutes, who would sell things I had
never seen. The girls never go out so a street vendor comes and knocks on each
brothel and shows them stuff. They bought a roll of pink carpet fabric. I'd never
seen that so I bought that for Solarsol to wear in the photo studio scene. Because
this is what they would wear and lust for. We would just take it from what we
knew, from what was there, from what they would show us.

*Did you have any feedback from your friends about the movie while you were shoot-
ing it?*
I don't mix with anybody when I am shooting a movie. I'm only with my squad
and my team and I don't have any interaction with the rest of the world. Now it's
different. My family comes with me and everything. But when I was doing that,
people hardly knew what I was doing. I never saw anybody. I lived alone in a flat.
Sometimes Mitch was there, or Joyce. And Raghubir Yadav, the actor playing
Chillum, lived in one room and any kid who for some reason didn't want to stay
on the street would come.

Did you ever think, 'I am crazy. I am trying to do something that is impossible in India'?
I am too bull-headed. But I can remember moments of abject pain.

What kind of pain?
Like getting money from the Film Development Corporation. They would expect accounts every week, boring things like that. And everybody had to deal with the boss, with me. This is a terrible Indian disease. You only deal with the boss. Often I would have to leave the set to explain a receipt. That's when I felt I would shoot somebody. There was no respect given at all to anyone who was working like I or my team was. There was the feeling 'I've got the power and I will use it. You are at the end of the stick and you dance.' And I have a lot of pride so there was a lot of tension. I never realized that you had to go through such strain to make movies.

How did you feel the day before you started?
I just felt we were doing it. I am bull-headed. That is the only good way of saying it. I say this word so often because I feel the same thing now that my next movie is starting. I feel that and I have to guard against it because now the stakes are higher. But then I was like Arjun. I could only see the eye of the storm. There is too much to do, physically and otherwise, to even have a doubt. But I remember a lot of frustration and pain and worry and never being able to relax, and looking at the rest of the crew thinking 'I can't have a drink, there is no time'. When we finished shooting, I remember that feeling of 'This is reality, this is the world and I am trying to re-enter it.' Even though I was in that world, I was completely of another world. There was a lot of stress on me and there was a lot of personal stress.

Let's talk about the shoot. Can you remember your first day?
The first day was the most climactic. We were in the multitudes of the festival. We were in a billion, thousands, I don't know, a thousand people or more, a million people in the street. So it was like taking our crew, putting them round our actors and flinging them into this crowd. There's a fantastic photograph of Sandi holding the Aaton on the shoulders of our biggest lighting man. She was on his shoulders, looking down and then we had a hidden camera, a static for a wide shot above on a building and so often in the wide shot you'd see Sandi doing the shot. And I would be there, pushing and creating those waves. Often you see Nilu, our continuity person. Even in the final movie you can see her there in her glasses. It was like a documentary, but the pressure of shooting the climax of the film on the first day was really intense! We were there designing the very end of the movie right till we shot it. We did not know what it was. And then finally we understood that it was Krishna's story and so we should end with him. And then the idea of the top just came. That was what he had come to the city with and that is all that he had left. I talked him through that last shot to give us the beats because it was a three-minute shot; it was about having the accoutrements of being a boy but becoming a man, since he had murdered and since there was no going back. So he would cry and then he would stop crying and then he would look up almost

into the camera with an expression that he would never cry again; a kind of man-hood expression. So those were takes that I would talk through. I would do any-thing. There are no rules ever in directing, I think. Whatever the actor needs, whatever the situation needs, you have to come up with. And you have to realize that that is what it is. So he needed this and we needed it because we didn't have the stock to fuck around with so we'd do it. He would do it, then I'd take it and run with it.

Can you give me some idea about how the shoot unfolded?
Because of the lack of money and time, we tried to be as organized as possible and to shoot as fast as possible. The film was partly set in the monsoon but we couldn't afford rain machines so we always had to have a plan B in case it started raining. For example, we needed a big wide shot of Chaipau delivering tea in the rain, which is when he goes into the barber's and says, 'How can I help it if there's water in the tea if it's fucking raining?' We were shooting a very important scene with Solarsol in the brothel when it began to pour. We had sussed out a place from where you could see the whole cityscape, which was actually another brothel. So when it started to rain, me and Mitch rushed to the brothel from where we had to get the shot. An Arab customer was being serviced by two women so the madam, with whom I had already made a deal that if it started raining I'd be coming, said five hundred rupees and drew a curtain round these three pairs of legs. So we passed the 35 mm camera past three pairs of legs to the window. I had the walkie-talkie and said 'action' and there was Chaipau in the rain and we got the shot. It was a one-shot thing. A lot of things were done like that. The kids in the film were getting more and more sussed out about continu-ity and what they had done before and after and such like. As the shoot pro-gressed, they were helping keep it on line.

How fast were you having to work? How many set-ups a day?
About eighteen – so very fast.

How many hours were you shooting?
Whatever it took really: eighteen hours. We never stopped. We just had to do it. Whatever we had to achieve, we had to achieve. There were never any childmin-ders or anything like that so we just kept working. I don't remember ever having downtime. It was a sort of guerrilla operation. Maybe it's like having a baby. You can get all the pain out. I don't know if it was eighteen hours. It felt like that to me.

What do you think the hardest thing was about the experience? The sheer stamina required? Or were there other things?
The hardest thing about directing is to be a leader all the time, to feel that you are the rock of Gibraltar. And the fact is that you are human, just like anybody else. And it is a feeling of real loneliness, of not being able to lean on people and need-

ing to sometimes. At the same time I'm a communicator. I like to answer a zillion questions because usually I know what I want. What is tiring at the end of it – not bad or hard but tiring – are the personalities. My work is very much about tuning myself to other people and what they need: to try and get from them what I want to see. It's always that. I believe actors are fragile but that is their power. Because they are fragile they can expose themselves on screen. I have to then find the way to get that from them, from every single person in the cast and crew.

Did you find it was a great leap from making documentaries?
Oh God, it was huge. You have to be sure of how you are shaping a scene because you can't suck it out of your thumb in the editing room. You have to have it. Because of lack of money and time, you have to be completely planned about it and hope you are not making any mistakes. I have never understood directors who have the luxury to speak about mood. 'I was not in the mood,' they say. Or be whimsical about a scene, like 'I felt like this'. I was operating it like a military operation. It was luxury for me if I spent ten per cent of my energy in a day on directing. I was mostly a hand holder, a production person, getting permissions, 'pataoing' – an Indian word for greasing the way; I was greasing the bloody way all the time. Getting it done.

Did you find it came to you easily? Did you know instinctively where you were going to place your actors when you were doing a scene?
Sandi and I would do it together. I wouldn't rehearse scenes that were in public places. No way. We would just put the kids there and say, 'Say this'. And it was about where to put the camera. We would find the camera and we would do it. We'd be hitting and running on the streets all the time, which is most of the film. Internally, inside the house, we would do minimal rehearsals in the sense that the mother would lie there and I'd say, 'You're sitting with Manju and then the song comes on and you'll come up here and do this dance.' And then they'd rehearse that. And while they were rehearsing I'd be talking to Sandi, much like any other movie. Then we'd make marks and all that and then we'd finesse it while we were shooting. Because it was always about time. Occasionally there is an absolute fear, an exquisite terror. I remember the scene where the mother and daughter are on the bed and Chaipau comes in. It's raining and she's put on his favourite song and they dance. It was supposed to be lively, upbeat but it took seventeen hours because there was some lighting problem. And we hadn't got it after fourteen hours. Sandi then declared that she had to re-light the whole thing. To sit there and to hope that when she is ready and I say 'let's get up', the kids who were now absolutely fast asleep will give me the life and the liveliness and the energy that I need for the scene – that feeling was like staring into an abyss. How am I going to get something from these poor little kids who are sleeping? Not to mention the camera crew that has flipped out because they have to re-light and it's so hard and we are all on our first movie so nothing is happening like clockwork. But I didn't

have an option. It had to be done because I couldn't come back tomorrow.

Did you frame the shots yourself?
I set up the frame a lot. That's what I love. I use a video tap only for the frame, even now. And then look at the actors straight.

So you were a lot of the time responsible for composition?
Yes. I am very involved. But I trusted Sandi totally on that, too. But I just love it. It is one of the highs one has.

Did you allow there to be moments of improvisation while you were shooting?
All the time. Especially in the streets. I love improvisation, but good improvisation, fun things. And once the crew understood that, they started participating in making the film richer all the time. I think it was the carpenter who brought me those great street singers who are in the film. We just put them in the background of a scene and had them sing a song that goes with the emotional mood of the scene in the foreground. And I would always put my own crews in the movie, everywhere, all the time. When they're in the theatre, I put Dinaz in front and there's a guy pinching her. There are all kinds of little stories going on in every frame. I love density so I pack it in. That is the fun part.

How did the kids react to the camera crew?
The camera crew became part of the family. They were part of the workshop by the end. Sandi certainly was. And the camera was just an extension of her. And as I said before, the kids were very smart. Often these day-actors, professionals from Bollywood, would come in and treat the kids like shit. It was amazing how the kids would deal with them. The tea seller, who was an actor, would say, 'You can take the tea with the right hand.' And Krishna would say, 'No, I have to take it with my left hand.' And the actor would talk to him like he was a street kid and say, 'Fuck off. Take it with your right hand – it suits me.' And Krishna would say, 'I know it's with the left hand because I shot the next scene last week. The tea is in my left hand so please don't mess with me because I know continuity.' This is all Krishna would do. And the other guy would say to him. 'You motherfucker! Take it with your right hand and shut up.'

How did the edit go?
It was great. It's the only time you have the peace to control what you have. I was also working with a great editor, Barry Brown, who'd done all my documentaries so we're very close. He just has the instinct. I'm ruthless in editing. I have no sentiment about this scene or that scene. And it was pretty exciting. We were editing so much while we were shooting that it looked like we had a hundred shots and we'd chosen twenty-five. But it was never that way because what you see is pretty much what we had! And it was Barry's art that made it seem so full and edgy.

Were you going to dailies?

There were no dailies! Indian labs are horrendous – especially then. There was only one good lab in Madras. So we only saw dailies twice in the whole time. I just saw what I had in the editing room when I finished the movie, went to New York and edited.

What did you feel when you saw the first cut? Did it approximate to your vision of the film?
I liked it but I didn't have any idea that it was something special. I suffered a lot and I kept suffering. But I was always involved with the next day. It was always painful, right till the end. When people saw it in New York it was not subtitled so they didn't understand the language. It was only me and my Indian friends – all of whom were making the movie with me – who understood it. So the first time I really knew the impact of the movie was at Cannes, the première, which was three days after we finished the movie.

Was the film now subtitled?
Yes. Nasreen Munni Kabir had done the subtitles and we worked closely together in Paris during the post on the film, just juicing the translation with contemporary French slang and such. It was enjoyable to do. And I think it made a big difference to its success in France.

Did you have a distribution deal by this time?
We had nothing. We went to Cannes with one of our French producers, Gabriel Auer, who is also a political documentary maker. We were invited to take part in the competition but we chose to go into the Directors' Fortnight. I didn't know why those decisions were made, but I went along with it.

How did you feel when you got into Cannes? That must have been a pretty amazing moment.
I was so overworked and so obsessed, and there was no assistance, there was nobody there. It was just like, the buck stops here. So I didn't have any experience of Cannes. Okay, Spike had made his first film and it had reached places, but it was an American film. I had no idea that an Indian film about street kids in India could do anything like that so I didn't even have dreams! When I got to Cannes I was happy of course, but I didn't know what it actually meant, which is the best way to go to Cannes: poor and with a buzz. The film had arrived with a major buzz.

And how did the screening go?
It was a big evening. It was the last night of the old Palais, which is where the Directors' Fortnight used to happen. They were tearing it down to build a Hilton and there was a huge amount of protest. They knew that and felt that *Salaam Bombay!* was probably a big film for them so they'd given it closing night status and had invited all the directors in the world who'd ever had films at Cannes for the night of *Salaam Bombay!* Can you imagine? So it started with thirty bloody

directors coming on stage from Wim Wenders to Fernando Solanas, to this one to that one, to Kurosawa to whoever.

And they were all going to sit down to watch your movie?
That was before the movie. Then the movie happened and there was complete uproar. It was amazing. They just started clapping for about twenty minutes and they took me out. People didn't leave and they shut the outside door and all came out. They know how to put up a great show, the French. And then it is the 'Gherao', an Indian word for 'there is nowhere to go'. It was like that. It was very emotional.

How did this extraordinary reaction affect distribution of the film?
The première was finished at eleven p.m. By six a.m. we had sold the whole world except America which we sold about two weeks later.

This must have been like a dream after the struggle to make the film?
I was very happy and very fat. I'd done the post-production in France and you were paid a *per diem* that you had to spend. They had amazing restaurants so I would just eat and drink the whole time. By the time I got to Cannes, I kind of rolled in! I met all these film-makers who had all their buttons and their posters and I had nothing. I had no money. And I remember there was a film called *Taba Taba*. I think it was Filipino. And they had a big button with the name of the film on it. And over the button we put *Salaam Bombay!* and pasted it on with Sellotape. That was my promotional item!

Were you immediately besieged with offers? Did you have an agent at this time?
No, I got an agent a few months later as a way of getting all the other agents to stop bothering me. And I chose a legendary agent, Sam Cohn. It was a bit of a joke because I knew I would always work independently and I didn't really see myself as needing one. So I said to a young agent who was pursuing me, 'If you get me lunch in the Russian Tea Room with Sam Cohn, I might take you seriously.' He actually swung that! And I met Sam and really loved him, and that was that.

Did the success of Salaam Bombay! *make it much easier to make films? Did it give you the keys to the kingdom?*
If you begin to believe all that or any of that for one minute, you've had it. And I somehow never did. I was always slightly bemused. And now I realize how diffi-cult it was to be in that place. I mean, how rare it is. But even while I was in it I was aware of the ephemeral nature of things somehow. It is enjoyable in retro-spect. But I didn't really enjoy it so much then because I had a lot of work to do, even after it was a hit. I promoted it alone for nine months all over the world – called it the 'Rape and Pillage Tour'. There were no stars to sell the movie. There was never an Indian movie that had been screened in Japan, for instance. Or Italy, or anything. So they needed a hook. And a young Indian woman was the only way to go.

Did the street kids help promote the movie?
Only in India, across India.

What was their reaction to the film?
They loved it. Not only the street kids, our kids in the movie, but other street kids. They said it was their story, which was the best thing I heard.

What was the reaction in India generally?
Our dream was to make a film to show in Liberty Cinema, which is the cinema the kids go to on Grant Road where we shot the movie. That was the only dream we had. And that dream came true: it played for twenty-five weeks there. And that was the best because all those pan-strained distributors from whom I wanted money, they all came to that silver jubilee celebration – twenty-five weeks and we made little statuettes of the god Ganesh and we gave them to every kid, everybody, as a little memento. In India you have big celebrations when you have silver jubilees. That was the biggest.

I imagine it was quite controversial?
It was controversial while we were shooting because the first kiss on the Indian screen was in *Salaam Bombay!* It was less controversial when it actually opened in India because it was such a huge international film success before it came home. It was the first time an Indian film had achieved those things, the Camera d'Or and an Oscar nomination and all that. By the time it arrived at home, it was pretty much a fairytale.

Mike Figgis: *Stormy Monday*

When did movies first begin to make an impression on you?

As a teenager growing up in Newcastle, I suppose. I had a girlfriend who worked at the Tyneside Film Theatre so I used to sneak in. I saw films like *The Knack* and *Morgan, a Suitable Case for Treatment*. I think that was the first time I became aware there was a form of film-making that wasn't mainstream. Then I went to college. I studied music but it was really an excuse to come to London. The Arts Lab in Drury Lane was an incredibly vibrant place for happenings and their cinema in the basement showed really controversial films, Kenneth Anger movies, Godard, Warhol's *Chelsea Girls*. I saw a short there called *Incident at Owl Creek*, which really influenced me. At the same time I was totally into music. I joined an avant garde free jazz group and started working with a theatre company. I think that set up the idea that you don't separate the arts; that painting and music and cinema are very closely related. And performance art, which is what I then got into, was an attempt to marry the technique of cinema and music and painting in live performance.

What did you do when you left college?

I worked for ten years with a group called the People Show. The live performances were very cinematic. I'd make a stereo recording of a landscape with a train in the distance and planes going overhead and the sounds of animals. So you'd be listening to this in a dark space and a light would come up. A hand would come into a spotlight and open a door. Fade to black. Another light would come up and you'd see a woman sitting rocking in her rocking chair, in and out of the light, and the light would go out. The soundtrack continues, some very frightening music starts to come in, some Bartók or music I would have created. Lights would come up on, say, some dead roses in a vase. A hand would come out and take a rose. You'd get these images telling a story, linked together by an ongoing soundtrack.

What happened after the People Show?

I formed my own company. I became intrigued by the possibility of using projected images. So the same actors were on screen and on stage and the action on the screen was an integral part of the set. I had live music and pre-recorded music and live sound and pre-recorded sound so the final show ended up as being an almost seamless marriage of live performance and cinema – to the extent that when people talked about it afterwards they couldn't remember what had been projected and what was live.

Had you had any training in film at this point?

No. I had been rejected by the National Film School and was very pissed off at that and determined to go ahead and make a film, not to stick my finger up at them but because I really wanted to do it. I was in a hurry because by then I'd already been working for ten years in music and theatre. I was very hungry to learn the techniques of film-making, which on close scrutiny I realized are very simple. If you are even slightly technically minded, mastering a cinecamera is not a huge feat. Certainly the rules of lighting and of exposure are fairly simple and are often a matter of trial and error. And you learn very quickly. It's not like classical painting where you have to have a kind of digital talent and if you want to learn about the techniques of oil painting – colour and mixing and that sort of thing – it really is quite complex. Cinema is not that complex.

How did your performance art work lead to your first television film, The House?

I got a very good critical reception, everywhere except England, with a performance art piece called *Redheugh*. I was then commissioned to write a second performance art piece. As I was preparing that, I met Walter Donohue who at that time was a commissioning editor at Channel 4. I went into Channel 4 and said I wanted to be a film-maker. They seemed pretty underwhelmed by the film I'd made for *Redheugh* and asked if I had anything original I could do for them. So I pitched the idea of *The House* which involved moving England into the middle of Europe in 1880 and having it being invaded by the Latvians and the Russians, then creating a kind of doom-laden drama out of that, set on New Year's Eve 1880. They thought that was an interesting idea so I said I would do a performance art piece using Super-8 film, slides, music and so on as a development. Then having done that, end up with a script which I would film. They agreed with this so I went ahead. They then came to see it at the ICA and said they'd thought what I meant was that they should come with a video camera and film a live performance. I said no, you've got that entirely wrong. That's not what we want to do at all. I want to make a proper film on film. I think what happened was that Jeremy Isaacs intervened and said let the lad do what he wants. So we then set up it as a film. Roger Deakins shot it, Nigel Stafford Clark produced it, Stephen Rea and Nigel Hawthorne starred in it along with a cast of stalwart English character actors. It was very faithful to the performance art piece but as a film obviously had a lot more vision.

How did the shoot go?

The producer, Nigel Stafford Clark, had scheduled the most complicated dialogue scene in the film, a group scene, as the first scene to be shot. It was an incredibly complicated scene in a drawing room. It's night. There's people standing by the fire. There's someone looking out of the window and they're talking about whether the Russians are coming. I think Nigel thought, if there's a fuck-up at least we'd know early on. But it's not like I did theatre where people talk to each other with the aid of scripts. All my work was improvised so I'd never seen a script before. So I arrived on the first morning. You get your coffee. You get your bacon sandwich. Everyone's looking after you. It was a jolly atmosphere. The set looked fantastic and Roger had pre-lit much of the scene. So there's all this activity and you feel great and you're standing there feeling like the king of the world when suddenly the first AD comes up and says, 'What do you want?' At that moment a kind of a white TV interference entered my brain. I suddenly couldn't function. I couldn't think of anything. At that point everybody turned and looked at me because they had heard this question 'what do you want?' I just froze. Everybody began staring at me and the more they stared, the more para-noid I became. I thought, I just haven't got a clue what to do. No one has ever told me what to do. There is no preparation for this. I haven't even gone to film school. It had never even crossed my mind that somebody would ask me. I thought we'd metamorphose into some form of activity. So this went on for what seemed like an hour but was probably twenty seconds until eventually Nigel Hawthorne rescued me. He said 'How would it be if I walked across to Alun [Armstrong] by the fireplace, warm my bum there and say my line? Then perhaps the camera will come over to us?' He gave me enough of a break to get on the train and I said, 'Absolutely.' Then Roger said, 'Why don't we do it as a wide shot first? Then we'll go in and do close-ups?' And then I was OK. I was saved. A day later I couldn't even remember the feeling any more because I was having such a good time. I felt I was made to make films. I have never been unhappy on a film set since that time. You have moments when you have problems with actors and so on but I have never experienced the stark terror of not knowing what to do since. Often the best way to work out a scene is just to be with your actors and block it with them and see how they feel. When you've worked out what you think is comfortable, you work out how you are going to film it. Not the other way round – the camera's doing this, what are the actors going to do? – which is the way a lot of directors seem to direct. I decided early on that I didn't care if the focus drifted momentarily. What was important to me was the sort of naturalism and acting that came from my own background.

Was The House *important in terms of what came later?*
It's an exquisitely filmed piece and was really important to me as a showcase. It got the kind of short but strong notices that can help you. It came to the attention of David Puttnam who, ironically, had been on the panel at the National Film School when I didn't get in. He saw it and his development woman, Susan Richardson, got in touch with me through my agent and invited me to come and have a drink with him. They said they loved the film; they thought I was poten-tially an interesting film-maker, did I have anything else in development? I had learned by then that you never say no. I'd submitted a short script called *Mindless Violence* to the BFI: two very very frightening gangsters knock at this guy's door. He walks with them down the hill leading to the River Tyne. At the bottom of the

hill, they execute him. He falls in the river. I still have the rejection slip, saying: 'whilst we think your film is visually interesting, we find it politically vacuous and therefore are rejecting it'. So I improvised on top of my rejected idea. They said, 'That sounds great. Why don't you do a treatment and we'll commission it.' So they commissioned a treatment for four hundred pounds. I did it in about a day, put it into them and then spent nine months waiting for David Puttnam to read it. Susan Richardson kept saying, David is travelling. I have put it in his briefcase, but I think you ought to do more work on it. I kept saying, why don't you just commission a script? A treatment is to give you a flavour. Let me cook the meal. I wasn't even asking for any money. No, no, no. Then eventually, the ultimate insult: I got a call suggesting I spend some time with the director of the National Film School, Colin Young. Colin could give me some hints on screen writing. I thought, what qualifies Colin Young on a screen writing basis? I mean, running a film school is one thing. Screen writing is something else entirely.

How were you living while this was happening?
I'd been on the dole. I was now part-time teaching at Middlesex Polytechnic in their media department. The students I was teaching were very dissatisfied because they thought they were going to learn film and then were presented with video equipment. I was persuading them to take the one portable camera, treat it as a film camera and go out on location – and becoming very unpopular in the process.

Had The House *led to any interest from other producers?*
It led to this treatment and no response, I couldn't even get a rock video going. Then one day I was walking down Newman's Passage in Soho. There was a skip there absolutely full of five-inch reel-to-reel audio tapes that had been thrown out by some commercials company. The film course at Middlesex had no money and were scrambling for materials so I decided to raid the skip. I went and got my Ford Cortina, double parked and got in the skip. I was unloading the tapes when I suddenly became aware that Nigel Stafford Clark, who'd produced *The House*, was walking down the street. At that point he was working for the Moving Picture Company. God knows what he thought when he saw me in the skip. He said, 'Hello, what are you up to?' I said, 'I'm trying to get this feature off the ground and it's all going disastrously wrong.' I told him roughly what was happening and he said, send me the treatment and I'll give you a quick response. I sent him the treatment and within twenty-four hours he rang me. He said, it's far too complicated but I think there's a movie there. If you're prepared to lose two or three elements, I'll commission a script. I said OK. We quickly agreed on a structure and then I sat down and wrote it in two weeks.

Given your background was in performance art, were you confident about dialogue and plot?
I think Nigel said that the ideal plot is like a Swiss clock. If you take out one more cog it ceases to work and if you add one more it won't work either. So your rule

always should be, minimal writing that doesn't abandon logic and at the same time calls on all those things that thrill you when you see other films. I'd grown up with French movies where character and quirk is uppermost. So I like to incorporate as many quirky observations about human beings as possible. To me a good script is a marriage of a series of interesting observations that somehow link to a plot. The best cinema dialogue is not necessarily naturalistic. It's a sort of funny quirky understatement. Really great American genre writing has very obscure dialogue in it. It's not schematic. It's not: 'I say, aren't you the chap I saw with that man in the black hat last week?' It's very oblique. I got into the habit of writing a shooting script for me, not a script for an uneducated producer or an uneducated studio executive. Most of them are not very film literate, funnily enough, so they don't know how to read shooting scripts. They only know how to read cheap novels. So most scripts are written like very bad trash novels with endless descriptions in them. A sex scene is written like a really bad comic. You know 'her heaving breasts, her taut nipples'.

Did the story contain any autobiographical elements?
I suppose the Sean Bean character was based on me growing up in Newcastle in combination with me growing up in London. I was a cleaner at Ronnie Scott's club. So I became aware of Soho gangsters by hanging out in a coffee bar opposite Ronnie Scott's and seeing pimps and prostitutes. I overheard things and found out things when I was cleaning the club that were a bit of a revelation to me as an eighteen-year-old. At night I would go and watch Roland Kirk and Ben Webster. I put those experiences together and then added a romantic vision of a love affair.

What happened once you'd written a first draft?
Very quickly we had a working script which Nigel then submitted to Simon Relph at British Screen and David Rose at Channel 4. Between them they agreed to come up with half the total budget of about one and a half million dollars. Bill Gavin who ran The Sales Company at that time also read the script and got enthusiastic. He had close links with Hemdale who were then very successful with *Platoon*. Hemdale agreed to pick it up and announced at Cannes that they were going to do it. We were all set up because that meant we had seven hundred and fifty thousand dollars from British Screen and Channel 4 and Hemdale agreed to come up with the other seven hundred and fifty thousand. Nigel and I set off for Los Angeles and New York and I had my first casting sessions which was an amazing experience because I started to meet people that I had only dreamed about meeting. Some of those meetings were so bizarre. Christopher Walken terrified me. He flew a long way in for the meeting and was completely stoned when he turned up. I was in awe of him and said, 'I am such a big fan.' He didn't say anything, just sniffed a lot. Then very timidly I said, 'Have you had a chance to look at the script?' He said, 'Look, do you like my face?' I went, 'Yes.'

He said, 'That's good. Because if you don't like my face, fuck you. Get De Niro. I'm out of here.' And he stood up and walked out of the room. It was about a five-minute meeting. The casting director said, 'Don't worry, he's sometimes a little abrasive.' It was the same kind of thing with Harvey Keitel. He said he'd be interested in the part that Tommy Lee Jones did if I wrote a big sex scene for him where he could fuck the secretary over a desk or something. He wanted a sexual power kind of thing going. I mean, these meetings were mind-blowing. Then we went to LA. We stayed in a cheap hotel at the beach, rented a car, had to go everywhere together because there was no money. It was then that it started to get really weird. Nigel's job as the producer was to get a meeting with Hemdale's boss, John Daly. As soon as we got there, he rang them. John Daly wasn't there but his assistant said, 'Oh great! I'll let John know you called.' Nigel called the next day. 'Sorry, John's in a meeting. What's your number? We'll call you right back.' No call. Finally Nigel sent a fax saying, 'Listen, we're only here for another three days. We have to sit down and have this meeting.' Nothing. He then rang Bill Gavin in London and said, 'Can you talk to John Daly? We're here but he's not picking up the phone.' He then rang Hemdale again. 'John said to say hello. He has had to go out to another meeting. Things are just really busy right now. Really sorry.' Eventually it got to the last day and we still had not even spoken on the phone to John Daly. The Moving Picture Company had paid for the trip on the basis that this was a go project. We then found ourselves flying coach class back to London not having had even a phone call with John Daly. We get back and Bill Gavin then confirmed that they had pulled out of the project. At that point, having had all the casting meetings, the project then went back on the shelf. I went back to teaching.

It sounds like a complete nightmare?
It was very depressing. Bill Gavin was saying, don't worry. We'll go to Cinecom. We'll go to the independent companies around at the time. But I thought, that's that. I went on holiday to a cottage in Devon that I had with my family. I used to check in every couple of days with Nigel to see if there was any sort of movement. The commitment from British Screen and Channel 4 was still there and Bill was going out saying, look, this is half financed. All we need is seven hundred and fifty thousand dollars. I phoned in one day and Nigel said, listen, don't get excited but there is a twinkling of interest from a company called Atlantic Releasing. Bill Gavin suggests that you call them personally to say hello. Here's their phone number. I was in a cottage with no water, no electricity, nothing. The only phone box was in a bed and breakfast place in the valley about a mile away. So I trudged down and asked their permission. They said OK. I went to the bed and breakfast at about seven o'clock in the evening. There was a party of deaf people staying there who were all screaming at each other. Outside I could hear goats or sheep or donkeys. I remember trying to make a reverse charges call via the operator with all this noise going on next door, and eventually getting through to a man

called Bobby Rock at Atlantic Releasing. He seemed very surprised to hear from me, didn't know who I was and wasn't sure why I was phoning. Even so, he was very pleasant. It's really nice to hear from you, he said. Are you on vacation? I said, yes, actually I am. He said what's all that noise? (*imitation of loud farmyard noises*) I thought, this is totally insane; this is beyond surreal. A couple of weeks went by and they responded again and said, yes, they would be interested in a collaboration. Of course, the only thing they could see was *The House*. It was the only film I'd ever shot and was pretty weird. I think they had no idea what to make of it. I mean, it's a performance art film. Bill Gavin said to me privately, the only thing that's going to make this movie happen is if you go over to LA. Just turn up there and and make yourself known as a personality. Nigel agreed to sponsor a coach class fare, a minimal hotel bill, a *per diem* of about fifteen dollars a day, I think, and no car. So I got on the plane again. The next day I tried to walk to their offices on Sunset Boulevard and almost got killed by the traffic. I got to the address that Bill Gavin had given me and it turned out to be an empty office block. The doorman told me they'd moved to an address on Olympic Boulevard so I went on a forty-eight dollar taxi ride and arrived at an empty parking lot. I phoned Bobby Rock who said, yes, we have moved. But only one block from where the other office was. By now I'd spent all of my money. I then turned up on time and was told that the man I was supposed to meet, Bill Tennant, who ran the company, had cancelled the meeting. I went back to my hotel. It was my first day.

Did you ever think you were going to go crazy trying to make this film?
I became deeply philosophical about the journey I was on. I thought there must be some kind of zen reason for it. I wasn't a teenager: I was about thirty-seven then and had done a lot of things already. I was very depressed. I was incredibly lonely during that period in LA. I really felt I had no back-up. The next week I turned up every single day in this office. I sat in in a corner of Bobby Rock's office, reading scripts. Every office in LA has got hundreds of scripts and I'd never seen so many film scripts before. I was pretty appalled by the level of writing. Through the wall I could hear them screaming at each other. I could hear Bill Tennant threaten people with violence. Very frighteningly because this was a very rough independent company. Fuck you! You fucking arsehole! They'd say, 'Well, he's busy today; he'll see you tomorrow.' I was waiting for a meeting. Just waiting. I was really being treated with utter contempt. Bobby Rock was extremely nice to me and took me out socially a couple of times but I got nowhere near the big boys. I was really losing heart and then after about a week and a half of this, I heard through a secretary that if they did commit to the film, it would be months later than the timescale I was talking about. At that point I lost my temper and asked to speak to Bill Tennant on the phone, even though he was only in the next office. He came to the phone, very bad tempered, and said, 'What do you want?' I said, 'I have just heard that you've shifted the start date.' He said, 'Yes, so what?' I said, 'Well, the so-what is that I have got a cinematographer, production

designer and some actors standing by on the date I told them and if you are going to move the date, I think as a courtesy it might be a nice thing to tell the writer/director.' I think he told me to fuck off. Basically he said, 'We'll move the fucking dates wherever we want them. If you don't like it go and fuck yourself.' And I said to him, you know what? 'You go and fuck yourself!' And I put the phone down. Bobby Rock said, 'Oh my God! He told Bill Tennant to fuck off!' And I suddenly thought, well, that's it. I'm on the plane now. I'm gone. And you know what? I don't care. I've had enough. I want to go home. I was just absolutely devastated by the situation. Then the phone rang. It was Bill Tennant's secretary who said, 'Would I like to step into Bill Tennant's office?' I thought, this is it. My knees were knocking. I went into the office, He stood up, came over and said, 'Can you forgive me? You are absolutely right. You deserve courtesy and we have treated you appallingly. I can only apologise and tell you that from now on this will not be the case. Would you please accept my apology?' I said, 'Yes.' He then said, 'We are going to make this film and we totally believe in you.' From then on it changed. Just like that. And Bill Tennant became one of my best friends. Even though they were in LA and I was in Newcastle, they were entirely supportive throughout the film-making process, to the point where they asked, do you need more money? Are you sure you have got the shot that you want? It's your job to demand more if you need more and so on. Entirely supportive. And in the way that they released the film. So that day was the major turning point. From then on it it was a go project.

How did the casting go?

I had originally wanted Melanie Griffiths. But Atlantic said no. They thought she was awful. Then *Something Wild* came out and as is often the case, selective amnesia kicks in and they decided Melanie Griffiths was the best actress in the world, sexy and perfect for the film. Meanwhile Melanie felt I'd rejected her and was very reluctant to come back, although she did agree to come back in the end. I had very much wanted Tim Roth to play the lead but Melanie's manager, Phyllis Carlisle, decided that Tim was not pretty enough for Melanie to be working with. So on the basis of photographs they selected Sean Bean as the only person they would agree to Melanie co-starring with. I'd seen Sean in *Caravaggio* and something that Chris Menges had shot where he played a really tough RAF Private who got drunk and drove a tractor through a wall. He had an edge and I liked him. So though they wielded their power, I wouldn't have agreed had I not thought he was capable of the part. Tommy Lee Jones was telephone casting. He was in Texas and I couldn't afford to go and meet him. Sting was an inspired idea because he's from Newcastle and knew the clubs that the clubs in the film were based on and had a jazz background. It was also the zenith of his career and although he wasn't legitimate box office A-list, he was certainly A-list in his own right. With Tommy Lee Jones, you know he's a great actor so you're are not taking a huge risk technically. With Sting, it's one of those things where if it comes off it'll be very smart and it's worth a risk. As he wasn't an experienced actor Bill Tennant came up with the suggestion that I fly to Montserrat where he was recording and spend some time with him.

Did the fact that Atlantic had come in mean there were no further financial hurdles to cross?
As ever it was not quite as much money as we needed. There were scenes in the film I had written which Nigel said I couldn't afford to do. He'd say, if you have a full Chinese market down on the quayside with neon Chinese signs everywhere, you are going to have to throw three scenes out because there's not enough in the budget for both. So what three scenes are they going to be? I always find it ironic that some of the reviews talked about 'the eerie loneliness of the streets'. It wasn't my intention to have eerie, lonely streets at all. I wanted throbbing, vibrant streets, full of people. I'd seen *Blade Runner* and thought that looked rather good. But our budget killed everybody off so I ended up with two extras walking down the street. There was something rather lovely about it but it wasn't my intention.

How did you begin to prepare once you knew the money, even if not quite enough, was in place?
I had photographed every single location in the preceding three years. The only thing of note the location manager helped me find was the Polish Club in North Shields. I photo storyboarded the whole thing and knew exactly which hotel I was going to use. I had got up at four in the morning to take photographs of the Tyne Bridge so I knew what the light was like and where the sun was. I had revitalized all my old contacts and called on them and got favours. When I needed to blow up a Jaguar in the centre of the town, I had a meeting with the head of the fire service and it turned out I was at school with him. He said, you want to blow up a Jaguar? Fine. You blow up a Jaguar.

Apart from its film noir plot, the film had a very American, Hopper-ish look courtesy of your DP, Roger Deakins. How did you convey what you wanted to Roger?
We talked about Hopper a lot, *Nighthawks* in particular. We talked about the point of view of the camera and the idea that the main character has an obsession with jazz and with American culture which entirely coloured his viewpoint and would influence the way we looked at it. The idea of inventing American week gave us the licence to be almost cartoon-like in our American images. But the fact remained that the three cities that I thought of, Liverpool, Glasgow and Newcastle were very American; or to be honest, American cities are very much influenced by Liverpool, Newcastle and Glasgow. The whole cast-iron thing started as a British idea and was adopted and adapted by the Americans. The scale of architecture and of the bridges on the Tyne was very like Chicago. When I toured with the People Show and had gone to Chicago and New York I was very struck by how much they reminded me of Newcastle, just the scale was bigger. Therefore it only took a slight shift of perspective to make those towns look very American.

How did it work with Roger in terms of your locations?
By the time he and the production designer turned up, I had pretty much found the locations. So with great excitement I could say come and look at this. You get these amazing rolling clouds coming off the North Sea so you always have this dramatic skyscape. When I used to show Roger these photographs he'd go, wow! Look at that sky! It was a very exciting period. At that time there was no yuppie colonization of the quayside so we had a huge choice of these beautiful Victorian and pre-Victorian industrial spaces on the river to turn into nightclubs or restaurants. The irony was that when we designed and created a club called the Key Club and put a neon sign up, on Saturday night there was a queue of people outside trying to get in. We had to tell them, no, it's not a real club. It's a film set! When Melanie turned up, I remember taking her round the set. It was like being in a studio because within walking distance of the station there were five key locations all right next to each other and all geographically correct. So when it says in the script they come out of the restaurant and walk down the hill to the club, that's exactly what they did. I'd designed it all so it made complete sense.

It's a very fluid movie. How did you and Roger prepare in terms of your set-ups?
Roger was brilliant at devising camera moves. For example, when the Jaguar is parked in the underground car park, the camera is already treating this car as a potential danger. We know the car's dangerous but we don't know why. The camera almost wants to go underneath the car. You hear the engine block ticking and you know this car is somehow nasty, people shouldn't get in it. I've always been in love with the idea that it's the camera and the music that let you know what the plot is really.

Did your production designer, Andrew McAlpine, have a lot to do? Or was it more a question of finding the right locations?
Again, I knew exactly what I wanted. I knew the Hopper references. For example, the restaurant that Melanie works in was called Weegee. It so happened that there's an art gallery on the quayside, which for some reason held the copyright to all of Weegee's images in Europe. I knew the guy who runs it, so I was able to say I want to blow up these Weegee images and create a restaurant called Weegee's. I had a wonderful production designer and I gave him the photographs, we had conversations and he went ahead. He did exactly what was needed. A lot of it was the use of neon and plate glass and the very clever use of space. I have always had the idea of economy which is you don't need to build an entire set, just the bit that the camera is going to see. So Jim's Gym was not a gym at all. It was just a couple of guys working out and a sign saying Jim's Gym.

Can you remember your feelings now you were making your film at long last?
Immense pride. Here I was in Newcastle, my home town. We had taken a whole derelict area of a very beautiful section of the city and by turning it into a film set had demonstrated what a visually interesting thing it could be. In fact, if you go

down to that section now you would basically see my film set. The whole area was developed with American style restaurants and galleries. I am really pleased but also depressed that we were so on the money. Walking round at the time I was really pleased to see how bright you could make it and how much that cheered people up – because I knew Newcastle was a depressed town; I was just really pleased to be back in Newcastle making a film, pouring some money into the area and bringing Sting back. There was a local-hero kind of pride thing going on for me which I have never experienced since.

How did you feel when your stars arrived in Newcastle?
I was terribly excited. I remember driving to Newcastle airport to pick Melanie up and saying, I'm so excited you're here. And then seeing this truck-load of suit-cases coming off the conveyor belts. I'm talking about fifteen suitcases. I said, I'll take you round the set. The whole set was this very steep hill with cobblestones called The Side. She was wearing this tiny little skirt, this skimpy outfit and colos-sal high heels and smoking these incredibly long filter cigarettes. She's got these very thin ankles and as we tottered down the hill I kept thinking, oh God, if she falls over she'll snap her ankle. We passed a pub and this guy came out who was wearing a donkey jacket. He had coal dust literally ingrained on one side of his face, like a Bill Brandt photograph where you can just see his eyes. I think he came out and belched or spat and Melanie just recoiled in horror. She went 'yuk', and I suddenly realized, having spent some time in LA, that we're talking about cul-ture shock of the highest order here. I mean, when we drove from the airport, her son had never seen a sheep before. She was explaining what sheep were. There are no sheep in LA, so there's no reason why he would have seen them.

What about Tommy Lee Jones and Sting?
Tommy Lee had been round the block and up and down the motorway as an actor. He was far more mature in that respect. He was just sort of intimidating. Sting was a local, of course. But also a huge star. So we had to have extra security for him. When we were shooting on the street, girls would lift up their skirts and scream at him to look.

Did people in Newcastle know the film was being made?
Yes. We did clever things on local radio with a very small budget. For instance, in order to get the crowd scene we had a competition and from our meagre budget managed to get some decent prizes together on the Saturday of the big parade, we invited everybody to come and be an extra for free and to take part in this com-petition. The marching bands were all in competition with each other. Sting was going to be there. It made an event out of it for people to turn up. We got a huge crowd. Our problem was keeping the crowd after that. We weren't paying them so we had to make damn sure that we kept the day interesting. At the same time, we advertised for extras – I think our budget allowed for maybe four hundred extras or something. One morning I looked out of the window of the production

office and saw this queue stretching right up the street. People just coming for a day's work. That was quite sobering.

Did you have any rehearsals prior to the first day?
We had little read-throughs but one discovers as a director that whatever your theories and your desires about how you're going to rehearse and bond with the actors, no one particularly wants to do it. Actors will always say we want as much rehearsal time as we can. But when it comes down to it, its a bit like being at school, or swotting for an exam. It's almost like, we'd all rather do anything but sit down and really do it. And on a film there are so many excuses not to do things like that. There's always twenty people who want an answer about something very mundane and technical. So you usually end up having to stagger through in a hotel room, and that's about it.

Given this was your first feature, you didn't mind not spending a lot of time rehearsing?
Not only did I not mind. I felt like – and this is a hangover from my experimental theatre days – what's to rehearse? You look at a film script, it's not like reading Chekhov or Pinter or something. You are basically looking at a cartoon. The dialogue is usually so simplistic. Especially if you have any kind of intellectual background of writing. In fact, I'm always acutely embarrassed when I rehearse a film script, because there's not really enough substance there. Film isn't really about what's on the page. It's about a very complex and abstract relationship that you build up with the camera. It's not until a camera has film in it and you start turning over that you get any kind of tension. Actors know if a camera's not running, it ain't happening. They are not going to do the stuff, which is to look in a very sexual way at a camera, or to walk in a very loaded way across a room knowing that the camera is right next to them. It's a sexual relationship between a camera and an actor that is the essence of film. I think the rehearsal process is often just a way of checking that the dialogue works. 'Let me hear your voice say these lines.' Then sometimes you think, that's not very good, I should reverse that phrase. If an actor needs to get their confidence with another actor, I would rather just take them to lunch and gossip so they get to know the sound of each other's voices and can watch each other. They have the excuse of lunch to observe each other – which is all a rehearsal is anyway.

How do you prepare yourself as a director?
I'll get on the set and walk around. First I'll walk around like a camera. Then I'll walk round like an actor. I'll just hang around in the space, looking at windows and thinking, oh, that's a nice light. By the time I get to shoot I'll end up with an accumulation of ideas that give me the confidence to go in. I would hope that this confidence can partly reassure the actors. I think what really throws actors is when they feel that a director doesn't know what he is doing. Quite frankly, the technical stuff does really legitimately require your time more than the actors do at that point, because there are certain technical questions that the set designer

and the cameraman will ask you that are very crucial. They are at the point in their work, pre-lighting or whatever, where if I say this, they're going to go left and if I say that, they'll go right.

How fast were you having to work?
I think it would have been made very clear to me at the beginning of the shoot by Nigel that we were going to be under the gun. There wasn't time to hang around. Funnily enough when you are presented with it as a *fait accompli*, there are two options. You either fall down and fail. Or you get through. And if you get through, you assume that's the way life is because you don't know any other way. The only other film I had made was *The House* and that was made incredibly quickly, like in three weeks or something. So six weeks or whatever this was seemed like a luxury. I never questioned it.

Do you think there is a logic to how you cover a scene which can be learned?
I think it has to be learned. It's like being a doctor. You can be a wonderful doctor but unless you learn certain surgical techniques you may kill a lot of people. You need to learn something about camera coverage and lighting in order to be efficient as a director. I have now got to the point after nine films where I am confident enough to do minimal coverage on a scene. By now I know that the extra coverage I could do would be a waste of money. As a producer too, that's a responsibility. If that sequence is going to end up on the floor there's no reason to do it. So now I can go in and say with confidence we are going to shoot a film in four weeks because I know that's the time I need. I do minimal coverage because I think there's a correct way to cover a scene. But I didn't know that on *Stormy Monday*.

What were the main pressures in terms of working with Melanie, Sting and Tommy Lee Jones?
The pressures were that Sting wasn't a proven actor although to be fair I had seen him in *Plenty* where he was quite good. I wanted him to be a Geordie – so that was all cool. Melanie was always going to be tricky because she's a very fragile woman. At one point she became really upset. She started crying and didn't want to shoot a scene. I talked to Nigel and he said no, this is not an option. It was the scene in a bar where she first has a drink with Sean Bean and they sort of fall in love. We were shooting in the North of England where it got dark about eleven and got light about four-thirty. And this was one of the nights. She was just crying, weeping and wanted to go home. I was told by Nigel to go and tell her that she couldn't leave. You could argue that that should be the producer's job. But it's negotiable. There are no real rules in film-making. It's like, who talks to her the most? Who's got a relationship? So go and tell her. I would rather not have had to have said that. It was one of the toughest things I have had to do in my life. She said fuck you! I am not going to do it. And I said, this is not negotiable. It is a low-budget film. I don't have another night to shoot this. Either we get it tonight or I don't get it in the film. We will be shooting in ten minutes. Hair and

make-up checks, please. I just wanted to go home as well. The hair and make-up came in. I said, stand by. Action! She started smiling, then gave the most amazing performance. I was absolutely stunned. I think it's a lesson that you have to learn. You don't have to be a nice guy. In fact, an actor often expects the director to be a bastard. If you try and be a nice guy with a lot of actors or actresses, they just think you are weak. Part of your job is occasionally to go in and be a complete bastard, even though you don't want to be. Once when I was on tour with my theatre group in Italy I wanted to get a certain projector. They said, 'No, it's impossible.' Someone said, you have to pretend to be insanely angry; call their bluff and say, OK I'm not going to do the show. So I did. I went back and said, no projector, no show. You've got ten minutes to work this out. Suddenly they found the best projector in Florence and the show went on. You have to be prepared to follow through too because if somebody calls your bluff you are going to look really stupid if you don't.

How did you fare with Tommy Lee?
We were shooting in North Shields when he turned up which must have been a bit of a shock for him. He walked on the set, looking very handsome and powerful and all the rest of it. Said hello, all perfectly charming. I remember immediately feeling very inadequate. I wished I could have been a big man. A good old guy like John Huston. I felt I was about ten years old, talking to him. I was burbling about how honoured and pleased I was to have him in my film and on the set, in the world and being born basically. We went and had lunch and he said, 'How's it going?' I said, 'It's going fantastically.' He said, 'How are you working?' I said, 'Well, of course there's the script but we are improvising a lot.' He said, 'Oh, improvising?' I said, 'Yeah it's great. Sometimes we just read a scene and then we throw it out.' He was nodding his head wisely and said, 'Any thoughts on my part?' I got terribly excited and said, 'Yeah, actually I've had a great idea.' The scene at the end of the film where Melanie goes back to her apartment and Tommy Lee is waiting there – it's a very frightening scene. I said, 'I've thought of a way of staging it. She goes in. She hears this kind of whooshing noise. The noise gets louder and we realize it's the sound of a shower. There's someone in the shower and it's terrifying. It's a kind of reverse *Psycho* thing.' 'And who would that person be?' asked Tommy Lee. I said, 'Well, that would be you.' He said, 'Naked?' Thinking it would be silly for him to be wearing a suit, I said, 'Yeah.' He said, 'You want me naked in the shower?' Then a loud bell went off and I became very cautious. I said, 'Well, hmmmm.' He said, 'Will I have fresh underwear?' 'I haven't thought that one through,' I said. He said, 'Because my character could not get out of a shower and put on underwear that he had already worn.' 'That's a very good point,' I said. He said, 'OK. You want me naked in a shower, improvising? I learnt every line for this part four weeks ago and you are now telling me you want me to take my clothes off and improvise?' Melanie and I were trying to crawl under the table. I said, 'You know what? You are absolutely right. That's the

worst idea I have ever had in my life. It is gibberish. I don't even know why I am saying this to you.' He said, 'That's OK. It's just when people say "improvise" to me, I see a red rag.' Then Melanie and I said, 'Gosh, we've got to get back on the set now.' Melanie and I stepped outside of the caravan and we just looked at each other. I think we bonded at that point. And from then on in there were good days with Tommy Lee and then there were days when he was just frightening. At one point he came to me and said, 'Look I don't want to cause trouble and at the end of the day it's not that important to me, but I have measured my trailer and I have measured Melanie's and hers is a foot longer than mine. Just letting you know.' Another time, we were doing the American banquet in the hotel with the Polish jazz band playing 'The Star-Spangled Banner'. He and Melanie walked off the set because they'd seen the American flag on the floor of the prop room and in America the American flag is never supposed to touch the ground. They said that this was an insult to America. When Tommy Lee heard the Polish band playing 'The Star-Spangled Banner' he walked off the set. He said he suddenly realized he was in an anti-American film. I think the line was, 'Every donkey fart from those motherfuckers is saying, "fuck you, America!"' I said, 'They're Polish. They are an avant garde jazz band. They don't know the tune and they are doing their best. You are not in an anti-American film. You are in a gangster film.'

Did these larger-than-life personalities affect what ended up in the film in any way?
Yes. At the end of the film there's a scene where the car blows up and Sean Bean pulls a gun on Tommy Lee. Tommy Lee lights a cigar, then says to Melanie, 'You need a ride someplace, Katie?' And she goes, 'Fuck you!' And Sting says, 'Put the gun down, Brendan. You don't wanna do this.' We did a couple of takes and then I asked Tommy Lee if he would look at Sean Bean. I said, 'I need a look to cut with and to show what a ballsy guy you are.' We kept on shooting and he just refused to look at Sean Bean. In the end he got the better of me. We were running out of darkness and I convinced myself that I had got the scene. The next day Sting flew to London on his way back to America and we saw the dailies. I realized I hadn't got the shot. I had lost my nerve and I hadn't got a shot of Tommy Lee looking at Sean Bean. Although I'd almost pleaded with him to do it, he'd refused to do it. It was the only major fuck-up in the film. Sting had to fly back from London. Tommy Lee got a phone call saying there was a technical problem with the scene; we have to shoot again. We all reassembled on the street having shot whatever the night scene we were supposed to shoot quicker than we'd planned in order to re-shoot this. We had to get the Jaguar back, set fire to it again, pay extras to stand on the street. So we reassemble and I said I'm sorry to drag you all back, but really what I need, Tommy Lee, is for you to look at Sean Bean. And he sort of looks at me with a grim face. Now the scene involved him throwing his cigar into the gutter before drives off in his Porsche. He had insisted on Havana cigars which for a low-budget English film, funnily enough, is quite a large expense. By now we are into the second night. We have gone through a box

of Havana cigars. We have a couple or maybe six left and he insists he won't smoke anything that's not a Havana, even though you can't tell it's a Havana. It's Sunday morning so there's nowhere to go and buy Havana cigars. I have a word with the prop boys who tell me of this problem. So we work out a scheme where every time he throws the cigar into the gutter, they pick it up, run back to the prop truck, get their razor blade out, carefully cut the end off, re-package it and wrap it up again. So we are handing Tommy Lee cigars that he has already spat out and thrown into the gutter. We start shooting. We get through five takes or so and I say, 'I don't think I got the look there, Tommy Lee. I think you need to make it a bit bigger.' Which was a way of saying, you didn't do it. Could you please do it this time? We get to the fifth take or whatever and at that point my insecurity or nervousness has vanished with fatigue. I say, 'Cut!' And I scream at him, 'Just fucking look at him, will you!' And he looks at me, sweet as pie, and says, 'Okay.' So we do it again. He gives a big cinematic look at Sean Bean, does the whole thing, gives me what I want. I say, 'Cut', check the gate and we ran.

Do you think this kind of testing is something that affects all first-time directors?
Yes. I've heard stories about other directors coming up against such horrific emotional/psychological crises that they lose their bottle. A crew can very quickly smell when you have lost it and if that is not nipped in the bud immediately that can affect the entire shoot. I have heard stories of directors who really don't come out of their trailer other than to stand in for the actual take because they are so frightened and I can understand exactly how that happens.

What would you say the main role of the director is from the actors' perspective?
You are there to be strong for them. However strong they seem to be and how-ever aggressive they seem to be, that's all a front; they're very vulnerable. When I did *Internal Affairs*, I did a cameo with Andy Garcia. We were just about to go and he said, 'Are you nervous?' I said, 'I am absolutely terrified.' He said, 'Good. Never forget that.' Whoever you're dealing with, however many films they have made, whether it's De Niro or anybody, it's always better to assume that they are nervous when they are about to act and they may be just aggressive as a way of showing that. I think my job is to say there is a reason for this aggression. There is a reason for this hysteria or these tears. What they want is almost like a dad there. They want you just to say, well I'm standing by my guns. Or at a certain point when you realize that it's not going to help to force them to do something, it's better to be soft with them and say, you know what? Go home and have a good night's sleep. We'll talk about this tomorrow. But your job is to make that decision. To make the right decision and be strong about it. You are not one of the boys. You can't necessarily go for a drink with the crew and expect to be accepted as one of them. I don't recall anyone ever really saying to me, other than maybe the make-up department, are you all right? You know, you want a cup of tea? Nobody would ever ask you that. I mean you could be having a nervous

breakdown and nobody would notice. Your job would still be to ask if they were OK.

Did you make any mistakes due to lack of experience?
There are certain things I wish I'd spent more time on in terms of the performances. And once we got into the editing room, there were real logistical problems to deal with through lack of coverage. For example, there's a scene where, having fallen in love and gone to the Polish club together, Melanie and Sean drive back into Newcastle in a thunderstorm. Suddenly a car pulls over and the guy says, you've got a flat. They pull over and then get the shit beaten out of them. A gun is pulled and in the ensuing mêlée, Sean picks up the gun and shoots someone. It was a night scene. To create the rain storm, we had a rain bowser – a water truck with a rig on the back that sprays water in all directions. I had never done anything like that before. It's immensely frustrating because most of the night seems to be spent hanging round waiting for the grips to put the camera rig on properly. The camera gets damp, the lens gets condensation on it and it takes ten times longer than an ordinary scene. What then happened was that the rain bowser ran out of water and broke down. So by the end of the night Nigel said, 'Well, that's the coverage. We can't afford to have it another night. There is no insurance for this and so that's it.' Basically, we got one wide shot with an inadequate rehearsal. You know, bollocks! Also, it was my first experience with stunts. You know: 'Melanie, put your head back when he swings his fist.' Then you look at it and it looks like really bad TV. You know that's not going to work so you try something else: 'Melanie just jump on his back and try and strangle him. Let's go for it.' Then the dawn appeared and the rain bowser broke down. I thought this is definitely going to be a problem. When we assembled it there was no scene there. It was one of the producers, Jonathan Dana, who'd made a few movies before and therefore knew how to cheat, who said, 'You know what you can do? Blow up a section of the neg and get your close-up like that.' So we did that but we still didn't have the shot which was really crucial for the drama. I got a shot of Sean Bean firing the gun and then putting the gun down but I had no shot of him picking the gun up. So Jonathan said, 'Why don't you just run the shot backwards?' So we ran the shot backwards in the Steenbeck and, sure enough, what is him putting the gun down, looking at the gun and thinking, God, what have I done? becomes him looking at the gun thinking, God, what am I going to do? Then picking the gun up. If you look carefully at the scene, the rain is going backwards. There are raindrops going up his nose not down his nose. So one shot basically run backwards and cropped and then the wide shot repeated gave us enough to create a montage of him shooting the thing and with a very powerful bit of score going at that time it worked. You either have to fight and insist on re-shooting or be prepared to be immensely creative in the cutting room.

Can you remember the first public screening?

When the film was cut and dubbed and mixed and locked and we had our first answerprint, Bill Gavin arranged a distributors' screening in Dean Street. It was the first time the film was going to be seen with an audience. I was terribly excited so I went to this screening. I sat there and nobody laughed at anything and when it was finished there was complete silence. I really wanted to kill myself. I just thought the film was a complete and utter failure. Roger was there and I think even he was depressed. He sort of said, 'Oh well, better luck next time.' I came out and just thought, crikey, what a complete failure. I remember I went to a party that night and got drunk and then couldn't get a cab and had to walk back to Barnet in the freezing cold. Someone said to me afterwards, never ever go to a distributors' screening. The whole point is no one is going to say anything. They are all bidding for the film and no one is going to appear enthusiastic because that means the price goes up.

What about the critical reaction to the film?
I was staying in the Hyatt Hotel on Sunset and doing the beginnings of publicity. I had been told that no reviews were going to come up for another couple of weeks because its first outing was going to be Cannes. So I went down to breakfast and picked up *Variety*. I was flicking through it and I got to the review page. Suddenly I see the name, *Stormy Monday*, and I closed it immediately. My heart started pounding. I opened it again and I couldn't help starting to read it. It was about the worst review that you can possibly imagine. It was slick. The performances were dreadful. What plot there was was so thin that it was laughable. It said that I was from rock 'n' roll. You know, 'Ex-rock 'n' roll player Mike Figgis attempts to make a film' and that the only passably decent thing about the film was the music and I should basically go back and stay where I belonged. I remember going back to my room on the 15th floor, going out on the balcony, looking down and thinking, you could jump. Your career as a film-maker is over. I had a day of complete depression. Then that night the phone rang at about four in the morning. I picked it up and it was Jonathan Dana. He said, 'Have you seen the reviews?' I said, 'Yes.' He said, 'Really? They only just came out about an hour ago.' I said, 'No, I saw *Variety*.' He said, 'Forget that. Have you seen *The New York Times*?' I said, 'No.' He said, 'Shall I read it to you?' And it was one of those reviews that people pay money for. By Janet Maslin. So then the film went to Cannes and started to have its own spin.

How did the film fare critically in the UK?
Alexander Walker described it as the crudest calling card to Hollywood he'd ever seen. Like I'd made a film for the sole purpose of being able to get a studio picture in Hollywood. I remember the day the reviews came out, I was actually on a plane to LA. By complete coincidence I was on my way to make a film which ultimately didn't get made but it allowed me then to make *Internal Affairs* and so I actually had the unique experience of reading the reviews on the plane. There was some-

thing very sad about it, very depressing. Some of them were grudgingly OK but no one ever really came out and said, 'This is an interesting film-maker', or 'There's a future here for this guy'. They didn't crucify me: they just made the film sound indifferent and second-class. They missed all the things that I'd really laboured over, the little idiosyncrasies that I put in, the Polish jazz band, the funny characters that pop in and out of the film. I mean, I'd pay money to see Heathcote Williams playing the PR man, or Alison Steadman doing her impersonation of Mrs Thatcher. And then there were the vacuous comparisons to *Get Carter*. Well, excuse me, you wouldn't review a film made in London and compare it to another film made in London. It just showed a real kind of élitism and North/South kind of stupidity.

How did you feel about this, after the struggle you'd been through to make the movie?
I have always felt deeply sorry for anybody doing anything innovative who by the nature of their work, are limited to working in this country. The level of criticism in Britain is appalling. It's so reactionary, so class-ridden and so catastrophically unhip.

Pedro Almodóvar: *Pepi, Luci, Bom*

Let's start with your background. Can you describe the region where you grew up, La Mancha?

La Mancha is a very, very large region. The part where I was born is probably one of the most austere. The earth is very dark, verging on a reddish colour, and there are terraced vineyards, one on top of the other, forming a series of geological layers. This creates the kind of landscape you see in surrealist paintings. If you think of Dali, for example, the base is infinity and then there are figures placed on top. And this is the landscape that I remember, especially in the place where I was born. The horizon is totally flat – it's very unusual to see a tree. And there's a very heavy sky above it. Curiously, however, the artists who come from La Mancha – painters, writers – and there are quite a few – are very exaggerated and very baroque. I think that a landscape like this, with so few decorations, forces you to put your own fantasy there.

As a child would you have thought of yourself as a typical Manchegan?

When you are a child, you just feel like a child. You don't have other references. I didn't know what it was like to be from Madrid or from Cataluña. I was born in La Mancha and I stayed there for eight years. After that, I moved out with my family to Extremadura, although I am really more *manchego* than *extremeño*. I'm conscious of these things now and can analyse them but at that moment I didn't analyse at all. I thought only that it was very oppressive. But now it's a landscape that I like. As far as decoration goes, what I like ranges from a very baroque Mexican altar to Lloyd Wright, which is almost the opposite, and I like both things with the same intensity. I participate in these two extremes without it seeming to be contradictory. Anyway, the countryside and the landscape in La Mancha are very cruel. Its climate is very brutal, very cold in winter and in summer, extremely hot. When I speak about the landscape of La Mancha, it's the land of farmers that I'm talking about, the land they work. The farmers are people who work very hard: very, very hard. But at the same time, they are very conservative – a conservatism that I have fought against all my life. That's why I don't identify with it much. Although I also think it is very important to be born in a place that you don't like, because it establishes very early on the things you are going to confront in your life.

How do you think La Mancha affected your work? For example, you've said that the use of colour in your later work is a reaction to the austerity of the region.

When I said that, I was trying to find an explanation for my use of colour because it's completely instinctive. I work with colour by instinct and by intuition. And that colour didn't exist in La Mancha. Strangely enough, I found those colours much later in many places in the Caribbean – Santo Domingo, Cuba, Mexico, a lot in Mexico. And when I first went to those places – I was already halfway through my career – I identified so much with those colours that I began to wonder if I had some genes linking me to these places.

I gather you had a reputation as a storyteller when you were a child. Do you think this was also connected to La Mancha? Did you feel a need to fill this rather barren landscape with stories and monologues?
While I was living in La Mancha, I don't think that I was very talkative. I began to talk, or to talk more, between the ages of eight and sixteen when we were in Extremadura, in Cáceres. I began to talk, when I could talk, about other people, about external things. I found that expressive exterior in novels or in cinema, and before I was eight I hadn't begun to read novels or see films. From then on I entered a world that was very oral, where I tried to communicate what I read and saw. Because films and books not only provoked in me the necessity to communicate what I was reading and watching, but also inspired in me other parallel stories that I constantly wanted to tell the people who surrounded me, my sisters, my sisters' friends and the friends I went to school with. I also remember ordering books by post when I was nine, which would come through the post from El Corte Inglés (a large Spanish department store). My sisters ordered things for the kitchen and things for themselves, and I would order books, usually bestsellers. From that time on I also saw many films in Madrigalejo and Cáceres.

Can you remember the first movie you saw?
I would like to lie but I don't remember the first one. I have memories of some of the first but not the very first. I remember, for example, Griffith's *The Two Orphans*. I don't know if it was *The Two Orphans* or *Broken Lilies*. Anyway, it was about two orphans and they suffer a lot – a big, big melodrama – and I suffered a lot with them, and at the same time I was completely fascinated. That really was one of the first movies I saw. I mean, perhaps it was not the first one, but it was the third, fourth or fifth. My first memories – because this is what I am talking about – was of *The Two Orphans* and Gloria Mairena. The latter was a movie with a folk singer, very kitsch, from Spain and I was also very impressed by it. It was a complete contrast to the other film; it was a very typical Spanish film with Spanish singers, folkloric, very, very kitsch and very Andalusian, very exaggerated and in bad taste. I'm not sure if the memory of these two films is a complete coincidence. I mean, I can see that they represent two of my extremes. On the one hand, the Griffith film, great, epic, wonderful art, wonderfully done, but at the same time very close to the heart. And the other, bad taste, very kitsch, with singing and a lot of ornamental details that belong to the South. They both have everything

that I was interested in; maybe not everything but a large part.

You've talked about your love of Billy Wilder, Ernst Lubitsch, American comedy. When did you start going to movies on a regular basis?
That was in Madrid. In my village the way I saw films was totally casual and they were almost never current ones.

What sort of films did you see in your village?
They were mostly Mexican horror films, vampire movies, a lot of Westerns and children's musicals, some Spanish and some foreign. We have several divas here from those children's musicals – Marisol, Joselito. But the only child star who interested me was Hayley Mills. Then when I was thirteen or fourteen I went to Cáceres, which is the big town of the province. Cáceres has five theatres which show current movies. What predominated there were American comedies with people like Tony Curtis, Natalie Wood, Sandra Dee, Gene Saks in films like *There's a Girl in My Soup*. That was not the best era of American comedy, but it was funny and I liked it.

Did you have a television at this point?
In Cáceres we had a television but not in La Mancha. I don't know if it existed in Spain at that time. I remember very well the first programme I saw. It must have been around 1960 or something. It was the marriage of a Spanish woman, Fabiola, to the King of Belgium's son. It was a big event in Spain, and I remember that in the little village where I was living at that moment, there was only one TV and all the whole village went to watch it. It must have been 1962, 1963 or something like that when we bought one. What I remember are not the movies, but the pop music programmes. I fed myself on them. I really liked them. This was on a black and white TV.

What about reading? Were you an avid reader?
I started reading when I was eight or nine in this little village of Extremadura. At this point my reading was very casual. Nobody recommended things to me. I was completely alone. I selected the books I was interested in by looking at their covers in a big catalogue – the same catalogue that had bras and household electrical goods. Some of them were very interesting. I remember very well books by Morris West, which didn't interest me. But, for example, they also had *Bonjour Tristesse* by Françoise Sagan, I don't know how. Another one I remember is Lajos Zilahy – a Hungarian writer. There was also one by Hermann Hesse. I think it was *Steppenwolf*. So my collection was very eclectic, very mixed, you know. It was thrown together absolutely by chance. When I started studying in college in Cáceres, I began to choose books more precisely, but it was really only when I came to Madrid that I began to read much more and with much more direction. At that point I started to read Latin American literature because it had just exploded in Spain. Writers who interested me at this point included Guy Debord,

Jean Genet, and other writers of the time. But I'd already begun to read voraciously in Cáceres.

Would you describe yourself as a movie buff at this point?
It was only when I came to Madrid in '68 or '69 that I began to see everything in contemporary cinema, and everything from other times that I hadn't been able to see and which was a discovery for me: all the neo-realist films, all the silent German films, the expressionist films, all the American comedy of the fifties and the thirties. The whole history of the cinema. And curiously, I remember very well the good movies I saw when I was in Cáceres. For example, I remember, I don't know why or how, that in Cáceres I saw two or three Antonionis at the same time – *L'Avventura* and *La Notte* – wonderful!

And L'Eclisse?
L'Eclisse, yes; it was done at the same time. I was very impressed, really was. I remember the couple in *L'Avventura* talking about what to do at night because they're so bored and thinking that Antonioni was talking about me. I remember sitting there in front of the screen saying, 'Oh, my God, how close I am to them.' I don't know how because I was only thirteen or fourteen years old!

Was there a moment when you looked at a film and thought I want to do that?
No, not yet. At that age I was very enthusiastic about the actors. I remember at school in Cáceres I used to talk a lot about the actors and actresses of that period. Because, for me, they were really sacred images, you know, like images we collect in books. So I was a collector of a lot of them. I remember I used to talk about the actors and actresses of the time but I only had photos of them. I had never seen them in films. So I talked about Lana Turner or Brigitte Bardot but I didn't know their films. Of course, I dreamed of being in movies. I think that's quite common. For me it meant something superior to real life. It was the best way to vanish – to run away from my reality. So I dreamed of being part of that world. But it was the actors I was interested in because in my ignorance I thought the actors made the movies themselves. But it wasn't a vocation. Later I discovered that while I like to use actors, I don't want to be treated like one of them. When I came to Madrid I discovered the roles of the film-makers rather than the actors. I then started to pay more attention to the photography, to the set and to the fact that someone wrote the film and someone directed it – and the two of them were behind the camera. And when I discovered that – I think it was in Madrid when I was eighteen or something like that – I was absolutely sure that that was what I wanted to do.

Were you ever under any pressure from your parents to pursue a different career?
Absolutely. I finished school with very good grades and the next step was to do the pre-university exams. I really wanted to go to university but my father, who was from a humble family, thought that the best thing was to look for a job for me in the town's bank. While all this was going on, I spent the only summer in

Cáceres that I have spent entirely there, after finishing school. That summer was enough for me to know that the last place I wanted to live was in a small town and that the job that least interested me was in a bank. The struggle against that brutal destiny lasted about nine months. When I told my father I was leaving home he threatened to send me to the Guardia Civil and I said to him, okay, because I was going to run away anyway. In the end I left home and came to Madrid. I decided that if I wanted to make my life, to be the owner of my life, I would not ask my father for money. So from the very beginning I worked in many, many different jobs in Madrid.

Did you have any kind of plan of what you were going to do? Or was it more like an escape from your apparent destiny?
That was the main thing. Madrid at that point, the very late sixties, '69 or something, was a land of freedom for me, particularly sexual freedom. Also during that time there was the hippy movement which was very strong in Madrid. So, for a young boy it meant freedom in that sense too: the possibility of cultivating yourself in the way that you wanted to. I didn't spoil myself at all. In fact I was even more controlled than if I had been in the local town. To have access to the things I wanted, the things I was interested in, was enough. For example, I went to the cinema every day, to the *cinémathèque*. In spite of the fact that Spain was still living under a very powerful dictatorship, for me it was a moment of total freedom. I could see the policemen and I could feel the dictatorship nearby, but in the way I was living, I had a moment of great liberty and self-discovery and self-development; a moment that lasted for a year from when I finished the *bachillerato*. But I didn't have a plan, no. Or rather, my plans were very general. My goal was just to find a job and try to go to the university; or to start in the film school. There was one cinema school in Madrid at that time, but two or three months before I arrived, Franco and his Minister of Culture closed it down so I couldn't go.

How were you supporting yourself during this period? Were you already working for the Spanish state telephone company?
No, it was a year before I went to work at the telephone company. I did temp jobs, selling books door to door. I also worked as a disc jockey in a club, because there was a girl from my village there. It was a salsa club, an American bar. It was the hippy era so I also learned to make necklaces, which I sold. And because I had long hair (having just arrived in Madrid, I didn't want to have my hair cut) I was an extra in several films where they needed hippies dancing like madmen. I made two or three appearances, always as a hippy, always dancing. But in that first contact with film I didn't register that it was cinema. I didn't realize that I was already working in film.

When did you first start making Super-8 movies? When did you get your Super-8 camera?
A few months after joining the telephone company. I saved some money and then

my first investment was to buy a Super-8 camera. It was 1971 or 1972. So, very soon, I started making movies with the people that I knew, because at the same time as working at the telephone company, I was in an independent theatre group in Madrid.

What were they called?
Los Goliardos. They were very famous at that moment. I mean, they disappeared, but at that moment they were very famous, very leftist, very courageous. They put on very important productions of Bertolt Brecht and things like that. They were very good actors and very good productions. I was definitely the worst actor in the group. But the experience still gave me the feeling of being in touch with the world of interpretation. They were the first actors in my Super-8 films and, in fact, many of them were professional actors. I used to shoot my films at the week-end, so they gradually became my friends. I invited people, they came, and on the whole, it was a kind of party for them. It was just a good excuse to get together, have some drinks. But I was giving them their lines and telling them they had to get dressed and play the roles I wanted them to. At that point I already wrote the dialogue of my films. It looks completely improvised, but it wasn't. I wrote it all.

So whereas other Super-8 film-makers of the time were making experimental, non-narrative films, you were already telling stories?
Yes. Super-8 was really my only school. So I took on almost all the genres. There were melodramas, musicals, biblical films, comedies. The only genre I didn't touch at that time was the thriller. My films were all different lengths – from ten to fifteen minutes up to very long features – an hour and a half. My dream for many years was to be the author of a double programme: a short film followed by a long one. News – invented, of course – trailers, also invented; and then the actual film. All made by me. Of course I wasn't very self-aware at this point – I was only twenty or twenty-one – but these films show very clearly what I wanted to do in film. To me what was happening on the screen was like a big theatre with many people watching. At the time I was doing my Super-8 films, narration was not approved of in the underground movement. To be part of the underground you had to do things like the group that Yoko Ono was part of, Fluxus: put a camera in front of a window for twenty-four hours just to see what might happen. They were underground films in the most radical sense of the underground but also the most comfortable. And it was assumed that fiction was something you were against. They imitated the first Warhol: five hours of a young man having a shower. Or seven hours of somebody sleeping. However, without being aware of it, what I was doing was more like the later Warhol factory, particularly Morrissey: telling marginal stories with marginal people, and telling them in a joyous, playful and happy way. If you see my Super-8 movies, you can see me there, absolutely.

Where were they shown? Did they find a large audience?

No more than a thousand people. Of course there wasn't commercial distribution for a substandard Super-8 movie. But I was extremely active as a distributor of my own films. And I then became very famous locally because I only put sound on the longer films, the features. It was very difficult to record the sound so I put a little of my own in. On the others, I would play all the characters. I sang and I put music on them. So it became something that was complementary to what was happening on the screen.

Do you think that the experience of narrating your films in front of an audience helped you when you came to direct actors?
I learned to be in front of an audience, sometimes justifying things they didn't like and having fun with them. In particular, I learned to do questions and answers. If ever I stop making films, I will dedicate myself to doing tours with questions and answers where I can recite roles, sing, go into the audience. I mean my concept of Q&A is a little bit of Q&A and a little cabaret too.

But what I meant is that being a director is partly about being a showman?
Yes, the actors and the people who saw me in these question-and-answer sessions thought I was a very good actor. But in reality I'm not very good. When I talk about the films, when I explain them, I am. Because then I'm enjoying myself with them, I'm making fun of them, making fun of what they say to me and commenting on aspects of their characters. And nowadays when I'm filming, I play all the parts. But if I gave up directing for acting, I wouldn't be any good. I've been asked by many would-be directors to play a part in their films. But I don't feel passionate about acting the way an actor does and I don't think I'm good enough. So for the moment I refuse.

Let's talk about Pepi, Luci, Bom *How long had you been making Super-8 movies when you made* Pepi, Luci, Bom?
Six years. When I started making *Pepi*, I thought that it would be a Super-8 film. In fact, to be more precise, the idea behind *Pepi* was to make a kind of punk film – because it was the period of punk, at least in Spain. In England it started four years earlier but we're always two or three years behind. So I wanted to make something really very dirty: funny and dirty. *Pepi* started life as a photo novel in an underground newspaper from Cataluña called Star. When I wrote the story I thought it was interesting enough to turn into a Super-8 movie. At the time I started writing the script I was working with Carmen Maura in a commercial theatre company. I was the intern in the company and Carmen was already a star at that time. But she was a big fan of mine, even though I was the most junior person in the company. I think she thought I was very talented because she paid a lot of attention to what I was reading in the dressing room and was one of the actresses who talked to me. I explained what I was writing and she was very interested. 'Oh, I'd love that part,' she said, 'I'd love that part very much.' At this point the distribution of my films had been through private parties, the *cinémathèque*,

photographic academies, Super-8 festivals; I was showing a film every week to groups of twenty, thirty, fifty, a hundred so throughout the year it added up to thousands. But now some of my fans, who already belonged to the world of cinema, decided that I should take the step into 16 mm and asked their friends to put some money into it. In this way we collected half a million pesetas. We started to shoot it in 1979 with a lot of inexperienced people. For example, it was the first thing the cinematographer did; the make-up person was the same; some of the actors were professional like Carmen, some of them came from the music scene, which I was very into at that point. So we started doing this in 1979. Carmen had a lot of confidence in me but the rest thought that it was fun, like the Super-8s that I'd done. It was like going to a party. At that time Madrid was very similar to the New York underground. When I read all about the Warhol factory or even the things that happened after, and what they have generated, it was very very similar to what we were doing. Of course we didn't have the projection that the Americans had. But the way of life and the personalities were very similar. Parties were the place where everything happened. The party was the place where you learned things, where you related to people, where you bought or sold things, where you had fun, where you could read – it was truly the unit of development for every aspect of people's lives. So nobody except Carmen thought that it was a real movie. But with that five hundred thousand pesetas we made a fifty-minute film.

We'll talk about the shoot in a moment. But first I'd like to ask you about the writing. Did you write it all in one go or did you write it in bits?
The first script was shorter than the film turned out to be. I didn't know at that time how to measure what was needed for a feature film. So, seeing that it wouldn't work in the marketplace, I converted it into a feature film. To get to that point was a very tortuous, very long way because the money ran out before I'd even finished the first script. People were giving us small contributions like fifty thousand pesetas. So from June 1979 until December 1979, we continued shooting whenever we had money – never straight through but over a weekend, two or three days consecutively. During those months I was adapting the story to the people with whom I could continue filming. During those months many people stopped turning up. So, like the television soaps, I was adapting the story to the people who were still living in Madrid.

You have described it as your most technically imperfect film. Yet it seems to anticipate your later work in a number of ways. It has melodrama; it has revenge; it draws attention to artifice yet at the same time has a lot of emotional pain – I'm thinking particularly of the abuse Lucy suffers at the hands of her brutal husband, the policeman. You seem almost cruel to her in a way?
I love Lucy. I'll try to explain. I think that my world or part of the world which makes up my interests is already present. I believe that the seed of my films and the stories that interest me is a group of women talking. And that's already there

in the film: they're sitting around a table, which is a very feminine place for talking. This for me is the seed of drama, of the show and of fiction. When I am in the street and I see a group of women talking, I would pay them quite a lot of money to know what they're talking about, because, besides being very entertaining, there's bound to be a good story there. Perhaps this is because when I was a little boy in the yard of my house I saw my mother talking with neighbours, and for me that was fiction, the real thing, because I could determine the relationship between fiction and life. In *Pepi* there are other characters, for example, the girl who comes from the small town to live in Madrid, to be successful, or at least to survive. In fact this was the origin of *What Have I Done to Deserve This?* In my films I often use a person who comes to the big city. Generally they are girls who come from the small town to settle in the city and I show their struggle to live there. There is also another element, very dear to me, which is the housewife. She's the centre of the consumer society and therefore the centre of everything that relates to pop. It's my response to all the characters that Doris Day played in her time. They're similar to the housewives of John Waters but that doesn't prevent you from enjoying Doris Day too. In Cáceres I saw a lot of Doris Day. When I told you about Tony Curtis, Natalie Wood, I also saw films with Doris Day and Rock Hudson. And also, it's like my 'Holly Golightly': the modern girl, Pepi, by which I mean independent, liberal, atypical, promiscuous: very free in many senses and, at the same time, quite naive. This is also an element that appears a lot in all my movies. It's Pepi and at the same time it's also Pepa, Carmen Maura herself in *Women on the Verge of a Nervous Breakdown*. And then also it's the torch song and female solitude, a solitude that arises between women. This is already there at the end of *Pepi*. At the same time, the film is deliberately pop. Its roots are in the comic, which I see as frivolous and apolitical by nature. Comics are also a genre in which prototypes are used – the bad policeman, the policeman's wife, the modern girl, the girl in the group – without going too deeply into them, because that is the style. But it's already clear in *Pepi* that I show an antipathy towards the world of the police, and also serious doubts about the basis of conjugal happiness – or what living together as a married couple means. I remember one of the lines that was used in the publicity was Lucy saying 'my marriage is based on hate and on the mutual lack of respect'. It is a theme that has concerned me in many of my films: a couple living together. I think I have always been critical of authority, but in any political system. So the political dimension which *Pepi* has, is the pleasure and the freedom to make the film; to make it under these conditions; and to make it with these characters at this time in Spain. What I remember is that it was the most unusual film in the whole panorama of Spain of that time. This feeling of independence and freedom is the most important thing about it, politically speaking. What I mean is that it was absolutely risky and personal and this it what was most important for me at that time and it continues to be the most important. This is a seriously political attitude. I think the political attitude that was most important at that moment was a celebration of something completely personal – of your individuality, of your pleasure, of your freedom – completely turning your back not only on the cinema being made, but also on its customs, on the people that you know, on how people live in your country, even if that leads you to solitude.

In films like Women on the Verge *you use colour and set design to emphasize the theatricality of what we're watching. In* Pepi, Luci, Bom *you punctuate the film with billboards or chapter headings to achieve the same result. Do you think your lack of interest in naturalism is also an expression of the freedom you're talking about? A desire not to be shackled by reality?*
It was more the fact that I wanted to narrate something and I narrated it using the means I had at that time and the cheapest means. And also your independence or freedom can lead you to make a film in a studio. And independence for Spielberg means making a film about the war in black and white, which is cheaper and therefore freer. But I understand what you mean. The reviews of my work keep saying that it's more colourful than other movies. But I'm more interested in austerity now, simplicity. I'm trying to make it more simple all the time. Perhaps my work is less outrageous or less surprising than before, but I wasn't trying to surprise anyone or provoke a scandal. I was just trying to do it in the way I thought I could do it and with the means I had at my disposal. And this is exactly what I'm doing now. Now it's more difficult. I learned to do things in a particular way but now I think, no, I don't want to do it like that. So it's difficult. But this feeling of being independent and free and to approach the movie with that feeling and with that decision – this is something I feel in the same way I always did.

Were you very confident when you started making Pepi? *For example, did you always know where to put the camera and the actors? Or were you still learning?*
It was completely by instinct; completely casual. I didn't know how to do it, but I think what is important is just to dare to do it. If I'd thought too much about it, I wouldn't have been able to do it because I didn't really know how to do it. For example, I didn't know anything about crossing the line. I didn't pay attention to eyelines in my Super-8 films. I avoided the problem by always putting the camera in front of the characters so I didn't have a problem. You feel you can make big mistakes but what I discovered twenty years later – and it's very important if you know it at the beginning – is that there are no rules, or at least they are very, very small rules. I mean the point about the eyeline, for example. If you are looking at me and I move the camera from one side of the line to the other, there'll be a jump cut which looks ugly. That's the theory. But if you look at the movies of Orson Welles, say, and watch how he cuts one take with another, you can see what he's doing is not technically correct. I mean, if I tried to do it my editor would refuse! So you need a big and strong idea and a strong feeling beyond that, and you have to push and to impose them on the technician because they're not

really correct. But you can do it. Fortunately now there is much more freedom as regards continuity – curiously as a beneficial effect of a subgenre which to me seems abominable – pop promos and advertising. They have both made rhythm more important and made editing in general more flexible as well as the rules concerning time and space. Before this there was very little freedom. When you see Godard's *A Bout de Souffle*, it's all there already. And this is because of the freedom he allowed himself. So you can choose how you want to do it, even without knowing what you are doing. And if you are strong enough and persuasive enough you can edit it like this. But you need to be very sure of what you are doing. With *Pepi*, I wasn't sure the film was going to be finished. And that experience itself made me passionate about it: I felt I absolutely had to make it. And although I didn't know how to do it I still felt I needed to do it. I don't want to be seen as an example, but it was really like that. I was passionately interested in it and I couldn't avoid it: I just needed to do it. I was conscious that I didn't know how to do it. But I didn't mind. It was so important for me that I just did it.

What was technical knowledge like at this point? Do you think directing came naturally to you?
What has always been easy for me has been to direct the actors; what I have had to learn was the technical parts like the camera movements. It was like a very difficult language for me because I didn't have the rapport, the knowledge: I didn't know the alphabet of that language. Later in my career it became difficult for me, for example, to move the camera because each camera movement was so full of significance that I hesitated too much or I thought about it too much. But at the time of *Pepi*, I didn't have doubts about it because I didn't think about it. I wanted to think about it, but I didn't know how to. But going back to that confidence I was talking about in regard to Welles, I was confident about my desire, and about the strength of my desire. That was the only thing that I knew and that gave me confidence. But I didn't think at that moment about making a career, about success or even about the chances of the film being released in a single theatre.

You just had to do it?
Yes. I was just doing it.

Were you heavily dependent on your cameraman for framing the picture and so forth?
Totally. Because I was still learning. Often the team you have supplements your lack of knowledge, but they supplement it in a very academic way. It isn't exactly what you wanted. For me, a film like *Blood Simple* is a masterpiece because the Coen brothers knew how to shoot a film. This was not the case with me. I come from a different tradition with other motives – not specifically cinema. I wanted to tell stories with characters, which I have had the ability to do since I was a boy. And I managed to tell them through a language that was totally alien to me.

That's not the case for the Coens: they come from the cinema and they knew perfectly well how to make a movie. Spielberg, too, knew the language right from the start. And what he wanted to do was cinema. Me, I wanted to tell stories. Cinema was the means to do this and I did it through cinema. I went to the cinema very often but I was always eyes and ears, listening to the actors, but unconscious of the skills behind the camera. My work came from the need to tell a story, whether orally or through writing. I wasn't aware of the techniques of the cinema but I think my need was so great that I could transcend this language. This is not to be humble: I just didn't know. And even now, it's hard for me. Now that I know how to move the camera, I don't like to move it very much. If I do, it has to be a very sincere movement, one that comes from something inside and that brings with it an idea of narration.

What kinds of things does the movement of the camera signify?
It depends. Sometimes just the frame is very important. I mean the width of the frame is very important in relation to what you are saying. A director who is a master of how to move or not to move a camera is Hitchcock. And he's a director who's very artificial. When I say artificial, I mean in this case the opposite of banal: each shot is a masterpiece of reflection and each shot is something very concrete. My experience over thirteen movies means I'm conscious of this now but I certainly wasn't on my first and second movies. The same is true of lenses. I don't think it was until the third or fourth film that I started to notice the difference between a 40 or 50 mm lens.

You've talked about about the impact of close-ups. Were you aware of that when you made Pepi?
No, no. I think I only really became conscious of that when I saw some of Ingmar Bergman's movies. Bergman sometimes does extremely lengthy shots in close-up, where a character confesses and spends ten minutes confessing. And yet, it has the opposite meaning to what Warhol was doing when he was making underground movies.

Because it was composed rather than random?
Yes. A close-up shot is difficult because it doesn't allow for any mistakes. You have less margin for error because it's showing the guts or the soul of the actor, something very deep. It doesn't allow any slowing up in the rhythm of the film because otherwise it will immediately fall apart. The same thing occurs with the text. There can't even be one word that's not important. Everything that occurs in close-up has to be much more distilled than the rest. So it is much more risky and much more difficult. But when everything comes together and you manage to do it, it is wonderful. It is the most immediate means to communicate what you are saying. People think that to use the tripod in this way is the most comfortable, the least risky option, but I think it is the most risky and the most difficult.

Going back to Pepi, *how did you prepare yourself? Did you do storyboards, shot lists? Or did you just turn up and start working?*
I used to rehearse with the actors when they arrived. Sometimes I did drawings for myself to explain to myself how I wanted to see them. But, no real story-boards, no. I rehearsed with them and then I would place the camera and see how long that camera position worked for me and as soon as it seemed to me that the shot was not working, I would try to change it to make another shot. Curiously, what I did by intuition, was to rehearse a lot, probably because I have always had fun working with actors.

Which you still do?
Yes, but I was already doing it then. I think it was because it was the game I most enjoyed, rather than because I knew it was important.

You're very well known for creating strong female characters. Do you think it's different directing women from directing men?
I think it depends on the culture. For example, I think it's easier for me to direct Spanish women than Spanish men. It's almost a question of numbers: there are many more good Spanish actresses than actors. It's been the same for a long time. Lorca said that he wrote for women because at that time there were more good actresses than actors. There's also another explanation: Spanish women, Latin women in general, are more spontaneous, better at expressing themselves than men. Men are more uniform. But I don't have problem with actors. I mean *Live Flesh* is a movie about men, about male characters, and really the girls are the support characters to them. And when I used to work with Antonio Banderas we worked with exactly the same intensity and the same pleasure as when I was working with Carmen Maura or any good actress.

Do you think you learnt much from the actors you were working with while you were making the film? I'm thinking particularly of Carmen Maura as she was already a professional actress, the star of the show you met on?
Yes. At that time Carmen was very good, and with the time, she became even better – with me, I have to say. I mean she needs a good director and then sometimes you get it or sometimes not. She was completely different from the others. She sounded so natural that it was weird just to hear her on stage. She was also good because she was mixing with people that didn't belong to the profession, people who were just being themselves. She was a professional but she was acting like one of them. She was fantastic like that. So when I saw her, I realized that what I need are more actresses like her.

How did you find Alaska?
We were very good friends because at that point I was more a part of the music scene than the film scene. So we saw each other very often; we went to concerts very often. We were very close friends. She was the only girl that could play a

young punk because she was the only young punk I had.

You've described the shoot elsewhere as 'zany'. Can you explain what you meant?
I was really talking about the people who worked with me rather than myself. I mean, *Pepi, Luci, Bom* demonstrated my absolute vocation to be a director. But they didn't know it was a movie. Really. I mean it was a comedy but it was also a movie – with a chance of being shown in the cinema. They didn't understand this because when I shoot I organize a sort of party for everyone so they're comfortable and then I say, 'Well, now we're going to make this sequence . . .' So we'd rehearse a scene and it would be incredibly funny – because the whole movie is hilarious in Spanish – and they were like 'Ha, ha, ha, let's do it!' And then we did it. But it always felt like a party rather than something serious. In fact, the whole thing was completely crazy. For example, the film took so long to shoot because we didn't have enough money, so that the boys from the group Bomitoni (a play on the words vomit, Bom and Toni) had to go off and do their military service. So I had to constantly rewrite the script and adapt it to reality. And I did all that in my office in the telephone company where I was working. The whole situation was almost surreal and completely extraordinary. The biggest surprise was what happened at the telephone company. I tried to do my work there very well but very fast so I'd have a couple of hours in the morning to work on my scripts on my typewriter. There were always four or five guys with me in the office and they liked to hear what I was writing. So I read them the script of *Pepi, Luci, Bom* and it got a lot of laughs. I'd explain the golden shower scene or the contest to find the biggest penis and these guys were laughing and laughing but they didn't think I was serious about making a film. So a year and a half later when I said you can go to the cinema and see my movie they froze like stones. They said, 'What?!' In fact, it was only shown in two small theatres that showed B-movies but when they went and saw it contained the same things I'd been writing, they were completely shocked! The day after they came into my office and said, 'Oh!' From that moment they were scared of me because they never seriously thought that what I was writing would end up in a film. I mean, I wrote the whole of *Pepi, Luci, Bom* in the company of these people, very common, very ordinary people. But they were so shocked by it in the end!

Given the mixture of people working on it, did you ever find it difficult to keep control of the film?
I put the focus of the film on the three girls because they were the most committed to it. I mean Carmen was professional so when I asked Carmen to come over, she came. Alaska, she was fifteen, she was very young, but at that moment she was very conscious of being professional. So if I called she'd be there. The least professional was Eva Siva. Her real name is Mercedes and sometimes I'd call her and say, 'Mercedes, can you come over because I want to shoot?' and she'd say, 'No, no, I don't want to. It doesn't suit me tonight. No, no, no, not today.' I'd say,

'Mercedes, this is a movie! This is a film!' But she was always pretty casual. For example, a year after we began I wanted to redo a couple of shots at the beginning of the film. Being a true professional Carmen tried to have the same hairdo but Eva Siva's hair was completely different. So I said to her, 'You have to cut it.' She said, 'Why?' I said, 'Because there is something called "continuity".' So she said, 'But I'm not thinking about cutting my hair. I mean, I'm not even dreaming about it!' I said, 'But you have to. I mean, it's impossible to do it with hair like this. Ugh!' 'No, no, no, I don't want to do it,' she said. So we didn't cut it. We just restyled it a bit. And this is a real lesson for the people who get very upset about continuity – you don't notice it! It was a year later, a whole year later and you don't notice it at all! I wanted to redo the scene – and it ended up being very funny – but the price I had to pay was that I couldn't demand that she cut her hair. So in the end we did it how we could do it.

Apart from being occasionally disobedient, did the actresses have problems with any of the scenes, for example, the golden shower scene?
Not at all. It was as if they were playing a game. They didn't have any prejudices and also if you see the movie, you can see it's really like a game, something very simple, very naive. That was the way I did it and that was the way they did it. So it was funny rather than outrageous for us and no one had any problems with it.

You said earlier that the important thing for you was to finish the film. Did you ever think you weren't going to be able to finish it?
Yes. I became obsessed with finishing the film. It didn't matter how I did it. I just wanted to reach the end, but without cutting out any of the story. And there was a moment when it seemed almost impossible. I'd asked all my friends for money. Everybody had helped me out and there was really nobody else I could approach. So in the office one day I thought, okay, I have forty-five to fifty minutes and I need to shoot twenty or twenty-five more. What's the minimum negative I need to go on my own, shoot the exteriors with natural light and just tell the story myself? I mean, I would say, you remember the scene where Luci was doing that? Well, on this morning, here, Pepi was doing this with Luci. I thought if I did this, I could finally put the words 'The End' on the film. That was a moment of real desperation. But at the same time it showed that I wasn't prepared to give up. I mean, I may not have had the money to buy the negative but I had myself, I had ideas and I had the script. Perhaps I only needed ten thousand pesetas to buy a small piece of negative to finish the film? That was my final idea before the arrival of this producer who put up the money to finish the film.

Did you ever worry that you didn't know enough about the technical aspects of film-making?
You have to make your first movie under any conditions – including not knowing anything about making movies! I was so ignorant of the technical side that I wasn't worried. There was only one idea that obsessed me and that was just to

make the film. So although it was full of technical defects, it didn't matter to me. In this respect, I was inspired by the American underground in the late seventies and even earlier. People like Warhol did my generation a lot of good because they got rid of our obsession with technique. So we'd say, we don't know about the technical stuff. We just want to tell a story. And that's what I did. I managed to tell a funny story which had a point of view. Nowadays first-time directors know much more than my generation, technically speaking. I watch someone's first movie and they have all the elements of the film under control. But it's not enough to be fascinated by the language of film-making. If you want to make another thirty movies you have to know the language. You have to use it and to develop it in the way you want. But I really only became aware of it in my third feature, *Dark Habits*. It was then that I discovered the tracking shot partly because for the first time I had the money to do it. But at the beginning I was always focusing on the actors and wanting to be close to them.

Looking back at it, what do you think is the most important thing you learned about directing during the making of Pepi?
I learned about working with actors. Ever since I started, I'd give them the lines. I knew that that was important. But, of course, they didn't learn them by heart and they improvised a lot. So I learnt to be very dictatorial. I'd say, 'You learn this. Now we are going to rehearse it and you are not going to add any words to it because otherwise the sequence may be too long.' At the same time, although I wanted to learn the language, I realized that things like continuity and so on are not so fucking important. I mean, you can get completely obsessed with continuity! I also discovered the rule about not crossing the line although, in fact, I did cross the line quite a lot in *Labyrinth of Passion* but it's funny and it's good and it works – I mean it doesn't give a wrong impression of the geography. So you learn that there are not so many rules that you have to respect.

Did you also learn a lot during the post-production?
Yeah. The editing was a miracle. I learned that you really make the movie in the editing room. I mean, you have to shoot, you have to prepare everything, but really the structuring of the film takes place in the editing room. It was at this point that I learned how useful it is to have reaction shots for all the characters, but of course I hadn't got them because the shoot was so casual. So my editor, Pepe, had to solve a lot of things in the edit. I was fascinated by the editing from the beginning. I learned that I had to get more material if I wanted to play with a sequence. I needed to shoot and give him more shots than we needed. And I learned that you establish the rhythm and the structure of the film during the edit.

You said Pepi *played in a couple of theatres once it was finished. What kind of reaction did it get?*
Well, it was a big surprise because it was the 1980s and Spain had just woken up

from the dictatorship and I think that that it was probably the first film in which the audience could see how much Spain had changed. If somebody was able to make a film like that it was proof that the country had changed. Of course the majority rejected it as something dirty and uncivilized but it was very successful with young people, you know, modern people like club-goers and immediately became a cult movie that played at midnight in those theatres for four years. So for me it was a great success because I didn't want a big audience. It was a miracle that it was just released. So I think it was a perfect birth for me as a director.

Did you anticipate this response?
The reception was similar to the one given to my Super-8 films, which was a lot of laughs, a lot of fun, but within a larger group of people. There were also quite a few protests about it at the time – which I expected although I didn't think of it as outrageous. Perhaps I'm very childish but I would like to keep this way of approaching my own material. The film was trying to be both a photo novel, and also, a parody of punk. It was the punk era when I was writing it so I decided it had to be as unconventional as possible; this was part of its style – for me it was a punk story told in a punk style. I didn't want to scandalize people just for the sake of it, but because of my decision to make a punk film I needed really outlandish material. I didn't have the intention to provoke, to shock people, but they were shocked all right! I was happy because that reaction was an expression of the fact that democracy had returned to Spain.

How do you feel about the film now? Do you think it's very much a product of its era? Or do you think it's very much Almodóvar?
I don't feel like, oh my God, this is so bad! I'm very glad I made it. It represented me very much at that moment. Of course I could make it a lot better now. But it's good that I made it the way I did because it represents the conditions in which it was made. And also there is a link with the American underground insofar as the technical details are not such a big deal. I also think that many of my concerns are present in it. There is female loneliness, which is a subject of many of my movies. There is also female friendship or female solidarity, which is one of the themes of my most recent film, *All About My Mother*. There is also an enjoyment of music: that is also one of the elements in my films.

You've talked from time to time about working under a pseudonym, 'Harry Cane'. Why?
Because although I have the same fantasies and the same passion now as when I began, my consciousness has almost become a burden. By that, I mean my consciousness of myself, of the story I want to tell, of the best way I can tell it, of how far can I go, of the form, of the perfection of everything that I can do, rather than a consciousness of the market or the audience. It's a pressure that I exert on myself when I'm making a film. It's like being in love. When you're young you just screw around. You don't think. You just act. But later on you fall in love. You

know you're in love. You know that it's a passion. You can't live without that passion. You start to be afraid and then you suffer! Anyway, I thought that if I worked under a pseudonym I could recapture the kind of innocence, the kind of freedom I had when I began. After all, when you begin a new relationship, a new love affair, you have great freedom. But now I think it's a lie because I know I'd only be changing my name, not my mind or my memories. Also there's a real danger that people would think I want to make something but I don't want to have the responsibility of having my name attached to it. It's like in the fashion world where a company has a second line. Armani has both Emporio Armani and Armani Exchange. Versace has Versus. I don't want to be like having Versus where everyone knows it's me but a kind of cheaper version of me!

Steve Buscemi: *Trees Lounge*

You're a well-known screen actor. Did you always harbour a desire to direct too? Or was it just Trees Lounge *that you wanted to direct?*

It was a combination of having written a part for myself that I wouldn't be cast in; and also the notion of creating my own work, which I used to do a lot when I was doing theatre with my partner, Mark Boone Junior. We wrote and performed mostly one-act plays and sketches known as 'The Steve & Mark Shows'. We never really considered ourselves 'directors', but we did direct our own material. It was just part of putting the show up. When I was writing *Trees Lounge*, I thought of other directors; but all the directors I really like were directing their own scripts. So naturally the notion came to me that maybe I should direct. Then if I was going to direct, I started to think that maybe I shouldn't act in it. But it seemed harder to find another actor and explain to him a character I'd written for myself. So having decided to direct and act, I then realized I should make a short film so I could see for myself if doing both jobs was something I could handle. So I wrote this short film, based on some dialogue from a 'Steve & Mark Show'. The funny thing is that, having written *Trees Lounge* in 1989, I then got cast as a film-maker in *In the Soup*. After that, I did *Reservoir Dogs*, and after that, I made this short.

So by the time you'd directed your short, you'd already played a director?

And by the second time I played a director, in *Living in Oblivion*, I was able to draw on my own experiences as a director. That's a question I get asked a lot for *Living in Oblivion*: did I base that character on any director that I worked with? Yeah, myself . . .

Can you tell me a bit about the short?

I financed it myself and shot it over a weekend. Mark Boone Junior and Seymour Cassel are in it; but it's really different from *Trees Lounge*. It's just an odd little piece about an incident in a bar: my character is a real psychopath but you don't realize that at first.

You said somewhere that everything went wrong that could have gone wrong on the short.

In the beginning, you are not directing; you're producing. That's the hardest part – to get other people involved. I asked some of the people I had worked with on *Reservoir Dogs* to help me out. Mark was helping me produce it but it was really hard for me to have that leap of faith that it was going to happen. I remember going to look for a bar that we could shoot in and being so nervous that I needed a couple of drinks before I had the nerve to say I might want to shoot a film here and ask the bartender who the owner was. I felt it wasn't going to happen. It was 'who am I to think that I'm going to make a film?' I had people who were willing to work on it for free. It was just hard to get the logistics of it right, to find somebody to make all the phone calls. Finally Seymour Cassel hooked me up with this guy, James Hardy, who ended up being the first AD. I explained how much money I had and where I wanted to do it. I asked him if I could do it in this amount of time and he said to me, absolutely. Don't worry about it. It's easy! He seemed so at ease with it I was convinced it would happen. And it did.

How did the shoot go?
We shot exteriors on a Saturday with no sound, then got into the bar on Sunday morning at six a.m. Most of the crew were working on other projects the next day. So by seven or eight in the evening they started drifting away. By ten o'clock we had just the bare minimum crew, including James. Then he had to leave. But I was thankful that at least he got me there, because once you're shooting you can't stop the train. We shot for twenty-four hours. I remember the next day having to drive some of the equipment we'd borrowed to a place two hours away and just feeling totally exhausted. And when we finally went to see the dailies, they were all out of sync. We had borrowed the camera from Declan Quinn who had just been shooting a music video in Europe and it was set for 25 frames per second. No one checked it, so we shot the whole film at 25 frames per second. But we were recording at 24 frames per second so the film would start out okay, then go out of sync. I would watch it, yelling at the projectionist, 'Why is it going out of sync?!' Once we figured out what the problem was it was easy to fix. But it was an additional nightmare.

What was most difficult about directing for the first time?
The biggest problem I had was figuring out how to work with the script supervisor who'd tell me I couldn't do certain shots: that it didn't make sense. Of course we were shooting out of order. We had to shoot everything that looked this way and then everything that looked the other way and jumping round the script was hard to keep track of. I felt like I had it in my head but it was really hard to have the confidence to say it's OK to the script supervisor. There were a lot of times that I was trying to figure out if I was shooting in the right direction.

But you must have been used to this?
No, because as an actor I never really paid that much attention to what the director was doing. I was always concerned about what I had to do and it just seemed like a big mystery why the set was being lit in a certain way, why the director was using a certain lens, why they would use a dolly, why they wouldn't. And it's not something I really pay attention to when I am watching films either. I pay more attention to it now.

Do you think you learned a lot?
Yeah. I relied on Phil Parmet, my DP a lot. I knew what I didn't want. I didn't want elaborate camera moves because I knew that stuff takes up a lot of time. I wanted very simple camera set ups and different angles because that was the way to keep it interesting although the film uses very long takes. So I learnt a lot in the shooting of it. I was aware of being very tense and hardly being able to speak with anybody.

Did you feel very different to how you feel on set as an actor?
Absolutely. I've worked on a lot of low-budget films as an actor and I'm used to the pressure of having to get a scene done in a short amount of time. As long as nobody's yelling, I'm happy. I kind of like that pressure because it focuses you. But as a director I didn't really like that pressure on set because there was so much to think about. You realize that you're really the only person who cares if this thing gets finished or not. There were some paperback books, pulp novels, that were important in the short and I knew that I had to get some insert shots of them. I remember James Hardy saying we could pick them up later. But I knew that if I didn't get them then we just wouldn't get it together. Get it later! he was saying. But I was thinking, the camera's here, everybody's here! Let's get this now! You look around the room and everybody's relaxed but you're dying inside because nobody's lifting a finger. I suppose it was good that nobody went crazy. You want people to be relaxed. I remember directing Seymour Cassel and just wanting to get some reaction shots from him, talking him through it without really taking the time to do the scene for him to react to. Because he was off-camera I didn't want to go through the whole scene and I remember him stopping me and saying, wait a minute, slow down. And thinking, there's an actor I really love and respect and I'm totally fucking this up and he's getting pissed off with me. But he was great. Very patient. I learnt a lot about dealing with that pressure. It was almost too much. At the end of it I felt I don't want to do this. This is too hard. And then the editing was a whole different process. Luckily my wife, Jo Andres, has made films. So she edited the short and taught me a lot. There were some real problems that I didn't know how to fix and she figured them out. We both did together. Once we'd completed the film and I had a little distance away from the awful feeling of being on set, I started to think, I made it through that. I think I can do it again. And I was proud of the way it came out. It turned out well enough that I wanted to show it to people.

What happened to it?
It was shown in a few festivals. It played on Bravo. I never ended up getting all the rights I was supposed to get, so it's not something I'm comfortable about showing that much. Having done *Trees Lounge* now, it's not something I'm that interested in showing any more.

What about your tastes as a filmgoer? Does Trees Lounge *reflect those tastes?*
Working with people like Jim Jarmusch and Alex Rockwell and seeing how

important the visuals were to them, I absolutely picked up on that stuff. One film that I love and that was part of the inspiration for *Trees Lounge* was the John Huston film, *Fat City*. The other person who was a big influence was John Cassavetes. I had taken a screen writing course one weekend where this guy tried to give you the basic formula for writing a Hollywood script. I didn't want to write a Hollywood script but I thought I should at least know the basic rules if I wanted to write something. He said that you should know your beginning, middle and end. You should have an outline. You should know what the characters are going to go through and the rest is just filling in the dialogue. Well, I was just the opposite. I was good at writing dialogue but terrible at story, at plot structure. So I tried to start writing and I couldn't. I was just totally blocked. I then saw a retrospective of Cassavetes's work at the Museum of Modern Art in New York. I had always known who he was but I thought he was too 'out there' for my tastes. But when I saw all his films together I was inspired because they didn't seem to have a strict structure. Watching them a few times since, I think they do have a structure but it's unlike any other films. The thing people say about his films is that they look improvised. From knowing Seymour Cassel and hearing him talk about it and from reading about Cassavetes, they weren't all improvised. The first one, *Shadows*, came out of a series of improvisations but the rest he wrote. He gave his actors a lot of responsibility and I'm sure there were improvisations that happened within the scene. But basically they were working from a script.

Did seeing Cassavetes's work directly inspire you to write Trees Lounge*?*
I had already had the idea for the screenplay for *Trees Lounge* before I saw the retrospective. But the thing that inspired me was that you couldn't figure out what his characters were going to do. It just seemed like everything flowed so organically. It didn't seem like anybody could possibly have written this and it was so inspiring to see that he'd done it. He broke every convention, every rule and yet he made these films that were so personal. That's the other thing. The films were personal to him and yet they were touching me. I didn't find them esoteric or indulgent. I remember watching *Faces* and for the first half, thinking this one I don't like, I don't get, and by the end of it, thinking this was my favourite one. So, that really inspired me – to start writing and not care about where it was going. If I got into trouble, fine. It was one of the things that this guy at the workshop said: 'You don't want to get into trouble.' And the thing I learnt was, well, why not? I mean, you may have to start over again but everything you write is of value. I would show scenes to Boone and to my wife and hear their comments and write a little bit more. It took me a period of about seven months to finish the screenplay because I'd also get work and go off and act in a film.

That sounds pretty fast if you were working at the same time?
People asked me how I worked on so many films. But I only worked on them for a few weeks!

Was it always your intention to make the film partly autobiographical?
Mark Boone and I had collaborated on a screenplay before with someone who
wanted to direct the piece and had tried to gear it towards this guy's notes and what
he thought would be commercial. That took us about seven months and we ended
up with a screenplay that was okay but basically a jumble. So I wanted to write
something totally on my own, make it personal and not worry about any prospects
of it being commercial. Boone was the one who said, why not do something on
Long Island? That really threw me because I thought, Long Island? There is nothing interesting there! I was in denial about where I was from and what that whole
experience was. So he really gave me that idea and the more I thought about it, the
only way I could think about writing about it was, what if I hadn't left? What would
I be doing? In that way I could use stuff from my own life while I was living there.
Driving an ice-cream truck is something that I did, working in a gas station, and of
course, hanging out in the bars I did a lot. So that was the genesis of the idea.

Did you find it hard to write the screenplay?
It was tricky, frustrating. And it was enjoyable too. Writing dialogue is my
favourite part of writing but you just can't write dialogue for ever. Every scene
has to end some time or it has to lead into something else. That was the tricky
part because I didn't really want to have an imposed story: that these characters
had to do something because the story dictates that. I wanted the story to come
from the characters. So I thought of all these situations that these people were in,
put them together and saw how they'd interact with each other. And that was
basically it. In the beginning, I saw it more as an ensemble piece. Like a Robert
Altman film where you follow a few different characters at the same time. It took
me a while to realize the character I wrote for myself was the lead. That's something I had to face in the edit: we're going to have to follow this guy's story. And
that's what it became, but with all these other characters that he interacts with.

How long did it take to write? Did you write it in one go?
I went through a lot of changes. A lot of stopping and starting. And a lot of stopping and thinking I couldn't start again. I somehow finished it and over the years
would constantly rewrite it. It was more a process of taking stuff out. Taking out
the fat. You're constantly trying to figure out what's the interesting character
stuff that's useful? That happens in the edit too. You're constantly taking out stuff
that you love but which doesn't help the piece as a whole.

Were you bouncing ideas off other people?
People would read it and say to me that they just didn't get it, that it was too dark.
In the beginning, a lot of people didn't seem to get the humour. And that's some-
thing that I always knew would be in the film.

*It's a long way from the Hollywood archetype. It is quite a sad film and Tommy's
life is unresolved at the end.*

Right. You don't know what's going to happen to him. But in my mind, the character I play, Tommy Basilio, is for the first time thinking about his position in life, his actions, his future. He is thinking about what he has done in the past, and what may happen in his future. Granted he's not talking about it. He's just sitting there, thinking about it. But it's the first time you see him in the bar where he is actually thinking. Every other scene of him in the bar, he is oblivious to what's going on. That's his place to forget, not to deal with his life. So it's the first time you can see on his face that hopefully he is dealing with something. Whether he will do anything about it – I didn't know.

When you had written a draft you were happy with, did you go out and try and raise the money immediately?
For long periods of time I wasn't even actively trying to get it made. I was working on films, trying to get the short together. Various people knew about it. Sometimes I'd go through a long thing with a potential producer and it wouldn't work out. For the first couple of years I wasn't really showing it around that much. It was a lot of different people who floated through to make it happen.

Who or what made the difference?
It was Julie Yorn and Claudia Lewis who were both really behind it. They worked at Addis Wechsler, the management company I was with. Claudia ended up leaving Addis Wechsler to go to Fox Searchlight and then we got the money from Live Entertainment. I was always sad she wasn't able to see it through because she was one of the first producers that really cared about the script, one of the first people I talked to about the script and actually made changes based on her notes which were very good. Before Julia and Claudia I didn't really have a producer who was active on my behalf.

When did you actually go into production?
I completed the screenplay in 1989 but didn't shoot the film till 1995. I had to shoot it in fairly good weather; and I had to be in Long Island. That wasn't something I could fake. So I'd start to get my hopes up right before spring. Then I'd go, okay it's not going to happen this spring. Maybe this summer. Or fall. And then a certain point I'd just say, it's not going to happen this year. This went on for two or three years until l felt it wasn't going to happen. The trouble is it's always in your head. You're obsessed with it and you think if this doesn't happen, how will I live with myself? I have to do this. It really becomes something you feel you have to do. Otherwise you feel like a total failure. 'If I don't get this movie made, I am a total failure.' Yet at the same time, you're absolutely scared to death of doing it – 'Oh my God, what if I do get the money?'

Where did you try and get finance for the movie?
I knew that no Hollywood studio would be interested. Or if they were, they'd

want to change certain things and certain people. So we tried independent companies here and in Europe, mostly France. I can't tell you how many meetings I had, and then writing various drafts where I would try to keep the integrity of the script but listen to their notes. Endless meetings. In the end, Brad Wyman, a producer who lives in LA, called Julie Yorn one day and said, 'I heard Steve has a script. I love Steve. Can I read it?' Then he said, 'Look, give it to me for thirty days. If I can't get a deal, it will come right back to you guys.' At that time Brad was partners with Chris Hanley who I'd known from my East Village days. So I thought, why don't I give these guys a shot? Brad took it to the people he knew at Live Entertainment. We had a meeting and by that time we had certain people in the cast, like Sam Jackson and Mimi Rogers, who were strong enough names to make a company like Live interested. In retrospect, they were looking at the video market. Video distribution was their main business. But still there was the issue of the script. Mainly it was a question of clearing things up and reassuring them that I didn't intend to make a deeply dark and depressing film. There is humour in this. If it's not coming across, I'll do my best to try and show you it's there. But the ending was a problem.

What was the problem?
No one could get over the fact that the guy just stays in the bar and it ends. So I ended up writing a tagged-on ending: he goes out, works on his car, is able to fix it then drives away. That was some sort of hopeful note and that seemed to be enough for them to give me final script approval. But I had to let Live think that I was planning on re-shooting the scene. We only had twenty-four days to shoot the film and I said to them, look, this is an easy scene to get. Me and the car, and that's it. And they said, okay. But you will shoot it, won't you? Well, I never shot it. When the day came to shoot that scene, I couldn't. I thought, I don't want this to be in the film. If I shoot it, they could very well force me to use it. What I did do was shoot my character leaving the bar. I left myself that compromise, if the film did end up being too down. In the editing, I tried using the take of me leaving the bar. We even had a test screening and in the focus group at the end some people said, 'Well, it's good that he left the bar. It shows that blah blah blah.' But most people said, 'Yeah, but where did he go?' And I used their comments to say, look, the ending is confusing. The film ends with me just sitting at the bar, which I think is the strongest ending. It took a lot of talking to the executives there. But to their credit they agreed that I'm the film-maker and they let me have my way.

So, once you had ironed out the wrinkle in terms of the fictitious final scene, they agreed the money?
Yeah, but there was a lot of haggling along the way. They still weren't satisfied with the casting.

You had some fairly well-known names. Were they difficult to get?
No, they were friends of mine. Samuel Jackson I had asked before he hit it big in

Pulp Fiction. Mimi Rogers was with Addis Wechsler as well and I'd met her and liked her. Anthony LaPaglia was also with Addis Wechsler. I had wanted Stanley Tucci to do a part but he was doing *Big Night*. But for the main roles I wanted myself, Mark Boone Junior, Elizabeth Bracco, Eszter Balint, and my brother, Michael Buscemi. These were the people you see the most. I think I could have got the film financed earlier if I had let those parts be played by better-known actors. Besides the script being dark, Live was saying, who do we sell this movie on? I had enough supporting players who were names. But they still felt I needed more. It drove me crazy. When I cast Chloe Sevigny, one of my agents at William Morris, Cassian Elwes, had to convince the president of Live she was a name. *Kids* hadn't been released yet. But she was on the front cover of *Interview* magazine and he said, look, she is going to be so big and you're getting her in this film. She's your other name. And they bought it. If Chloe's picture hadn't been on the front cover of *Interview* magazine, I don't know what I would have done.

What was the budget?
About a million dollars. That was the other crisis meeting we had with the bond company: them telling us that we didn't have enough money and going back to Live and saying, they are not going to insure the film unless you give us more money. It amazes me that any film gets made. Especially an independent because the bottom can drop out at any moment. That's the thing I didn't realize as an actor. It is a miracle that we all show up on the first day. It made me really appreciate what Alex Rockwell went through, getting *In the Soup* made. Basically he had to finance the first day himself because the financiers weren't writing the cheques.

Did you do much rehearsing?
I wish I'd had more time with the actors. Some of them were coming from LA. Boone just got there maybe a week before we started filming and once you're in pre-production there's so much other stuff you're thinking about. That was one of the things that surprised me: that even while I was directing, I would forget that the actors needed attention and direction. I had a great cast and they pretty much took care of themselves. When they asked me something, I was able to articulate what I wanted most of the time. Or I would watch a scene and be able to guide them in another direction. But the pre-production was a wild time. I was working with the DP, Lisa Rinzler, and I spent a lot of time with her making shot lists, watching other films and trying to articulate to her what I wanted and how to do it in the least amount of time. And how to make it visually interesting. And then scouting locations. For the short film we just had to find one bar. For the movie there was so much. So many decisions that have to be made. You have to cast your crew as well as your actors. So it was really overwhelming.

Did you find that some of the locations had changed since your days in Long Island?
Well, the bar itself, Trees Lounge, was an old place, and for years I thought at least

I have that. Then six months before we got the money I got a call from my brother saying he'd heard that the bar was sold and that they were taking down the neon sign. And I said, we've got to get the sign at least. I remember going down there and asking if I could buy the sign. They thought I was crazy and that they were really getting one over on me because I paid two hundred dollars for this neon sign that they were just going to toss away. But the guy had changed the bar so much that when we went back to him and said that we wanted to shoot there, it just seemed too expensive undoing what he'd done and having to put it back together the way that he liked it. Also the extra travel time of going to Long Island was a problem. So we ended up finding a bar in Queens that was closer to Manhattan where most people lived. Plus we really didn't have to do anything to it. The way it looks on the film is pretty much the way it looks in real life. So that was a heartbreak, not being able to film in the bar that I had envisioned that we were going to be shooting in all these years. And not being able to use the neon sign because it didn't work on the new bar. But what was also great about the bar in Queens was that it had an apartment on top where the owner lived. In the original script my character had his own place. But when the location manager, the production designer and me looked at those apartments we said, could we use these? I mean, these are great. We looked at each other and I thought, could Tommy live above the bar? Is that too much? And the more I thought about it the more I thought, it's perfect! It makes it that much harder for Tommy to get out of the bar. His life really does revolve around the place. And then I also had the older character, Bill, live above the bar. And it actually added another dimension to the script that I didn't have in my draft. They both share this apartment – and part of Tommy's function is helping this guy get up to bed every night.

Did you shoot most of it in Queens or was some of it shot on Long Island?
I felt it was really important that the scenes with the ice-cream truck were shot in Long Island. We had scouted places in Queens that looked like Long Island but it didn't work. Long Island does have a very specific look to it. So the ice-cream scenes were shot in Long Island, the exact same route where I drove my ice-cream truck fifteen years before. Fireman's Field, where the softball game was and those blocks around there, that was my ice-cream route. And the truck that Steve Rosenzweig, my production designer, found looked exactly like the truck I had driven.

Was it a strange experience? Revisiting your past?
Very strange. The time when I was driving an ice-cream truck was after high school. I had gone to community college for a semester and dropped out. I had started taking some acting classes but that whole world seemed so distant to me. The first year I drove the truck I had a partner, who actually got me into it. The first year, I was eighteen or nineteen and everybody thought it was just a summer job. I had told everybody, I'm going to acting classes. I'm going to become an

actor. I am serious about this. Come another season, there I am again, back on the ice-cream truck. People tended not to believe me any more about being an actor. Most of my friends had gone to college. Actually, most of my friends were still in town, hanging out in the bar. And I was driving that ice-cream truck. I would park my truck outside the bar. Driving around thinking, something has got to happen. I don't have any other skills. If I don't make it as an actor, what's to stop me doing this every summer? How am I going to live? So fifteen years later, to be driving the ice-cream truck but now being followed by a camera, was an amazing experience. Very moving too. We were doing a scene where I was driving the truck down the street and these kids were banging, hitting me with their plastic ball bats and I was yelling at them with the camera outside the truck. We would do about three takes and then I would ride around the block and start up again. But in that ride around the block I was alone: just me in the truck, driving the same streets and feeling like, 'Oh, my God!' One day my brother, Ken, was driving to the set. He saw me drive by without the camera crew and he said it was the weirdest feeling to see me all alone in that truck again.

Tell me a bit about how you collaborated with Lisa Rinzler?
Even before we got to the location, we would think of shots. We would imagine what the basic layout would be and then when we got to the locations we spent a lot of time just shot listing, even while we were filming. Once our AD, David Wechsler, was hired, we did it with him. The three of us would figure out the quickest way we could get in there and cover the scene. And a lot of it was them asking me questions: do you want to do this and this and that? I would say, no, I just need this particular shot with maybe one other angle. But, no, I don't need singles. So really, it was just figuring out how we could use our time the best way. Also for Lisa and I to figure out the look of the film and how we could make it visually interesting without spending a lot of time on it. I didn't want to do a lot of dolly shots and she had to make sure that I wasn't not doing things because I felt we wouldn't have the time. I really had to impress upon her that in certain films I like, the camera is static. She was great. She really wanted to know what was inside my head.

What can you remember about pre-production?
The whole pre-production process was just wild. I was lucky to get Sarah Vogel and Kelley Forsyth, who were hired as line producers and really ended up co-producing the film because they were the ones that really got the crew together, the nuts and bolts of production. They set up the production office and once you have a production office it becomes real. At one point I remember hearing Lisa talking about the colour scheme to the various department heads and really feeling that I was losing control; that they were taking over and really feeling panicked about it. Then I remembered something Phil Parmet, my DP on the short, had told me. It was the simplest thing: just let people do their jobs. At first I

wasn't sure what he meant by it and then it started to sink in that it was their job to be very anal about everything and pay great attention to detail and talk amongst themselves. And it turned out that they would always come to me and say, here's what we think. What do you think?

Did you find it easy to make decisions when you were on set?
No. That was something I had to get used to: all the constant questions you get asked. I remember working with John Carpenter on his *Escape From LA*. I was in his office when he was in pre-production. Somebody came in and said, which thing? This one, this one, or this one? And he went, that one. The guy left and I said, that's pretty good, John. And he goes, always give them an answer. You can change your mind later but you got to give them an answer!

How did you go about conveying the look that you were after?
Just by going around different bars and talking about different places. Colour was something that my production designer, Steve Rosenzweig, discussed with Lisa Rinzler and then came to me. And I really trusted what colours we should stay away from. I remember talking to Stanley Tucci when he was in pre-production on *Big Night*. He also paints, so the palette of the film is something he's very artic-ulate about. I remember listening to him and thinking 'Oh man, I don't know any of that – I'm in trouble!' But the thing is, you don't have to know everything. You have to hire people who know their jobs. It's their job to figure out what you want.

When you visited a location, did you know what the shots would be or did you dis-cover it when the actors were there?
The hardest thing to shoot was the scene in the middle of the film where the soft-ball team comes into the bar. Boone is on the phone with his wife. Anthony LaPaglia's character is there. My character comes in and sees him. There's a lot going on. When we rehearsed it, it wasn't at all like I thought it should be. I had-n't really taken into account that the room is filled with these softball players, and Anthony was at one end of the bar and I was at the other, and we were supposed to be having this dialogue with all this going on in the background. And then Boone was meant to come out and be a part of that dialogue. We were so spread out I knew it wasn't going to work. I started to feel panicky because I knew we had to start shooting, otherwise I was going to lose the day. I looked around the room and was asked a question, where do you want to put the camera? And I looked at everybody in the room and said, I have no idea how to shoot this scene. I don't know what to do. And there was a moment of, okay, I guess we are not going to get any help from him! And Lisa and David Wechsler talked and said, well, we should start shooting this way towards the window because we are losing the light. I said, okay. You set it up and I will try to re-think this scene and I got together with Anthony LaPaglia and Boone and said, something's wrong. Anthony said, yeah, do we have to be that far apart? So I said, no, we can be

closer. Then I said, Boone, right now it is too hard to try and include you. I'm just going to leave you in the phone booth. I'll cover your stuff separately. And we literally changed the dialogue and rewrote the scene while they were setting up; even while we were shooting. On each take I would try something different with Anthony because me being that close to Anthony changed the whole dynamic of the scene. I didn't know what we were getting or if I was going to be able to use it. I just had to go on trust that something would work. It was a hard scene to cut but it works. I ended up getting something that I was able to use. I was afraid that the whole thing was going to be unusable and then I'd have this big gap in the film. So that was the worst day of me not knowing what to do.

The other really difficult day came before that. It was the last day of the first week and I only had Debi Mazar for a small amount of time. It was the scene where Debi comes with her child to get an ice-cream; and the child was played by my son, Lucian, who was only four years old. I was so nervous about using my son that I told my casting person, Sheila Jaffe, to get a back-up kid who was older. So she got another kid who was on the sidelines. I went up to the kid's father and I said, you know the deal, right? I may not need him. And he said that his son was looking forward to it. That morning the crew had concerns about what we were doing that day. It seemed like we were trying to do too much. I thought, the crew's not happy. Nobody really wants to be here. It's no fun now. The last thing I wanted to be was a director on a movie where people weren't enjoying themselves. It's like, oh, man, not another fucking low-budget film! Not enough money, not enough time to shoot. Anyway, my son was great. He was such a professional. We had to rush to get this done then they called lunch. And I looked over at this other kid, and I could see his father telling him; and I saw a look of such deep disappointment that I went over to the kid and said, 'Okay, now it's your turn.' I called for quiet on the set and we just shot it using a video camera that my wife had. The kid cheered up a little bit, but I still felt like I scarred him for life. Later, when we were shooting in the bar, I went into the bathroom stall and locked the door and practically broke down in tears. I thought: what am I doing? I'm fucking everything up. Nobody wants to be here. I felt like the biggest jerk. And then we got through that day and then after that things started to go a bit better.

Every director will probably say they don't have enough time. But twenty-four days does sound fast.
What was funny was that when we were in pre-production, Living in Oblivion was released. My whole cast and crew went to see it and of course saw this madman on screen yelling. I thought, I can't become that! So I ended up internalizing everything and making myself sick. And trying not to show it. On Chloe's first day I didn't want to make her nervous by showing her I felt I was losing control. But after about two weeks of that I finally started to let go and told myself, it's okay. If you don't finish the day, so what? I'm not going to die. The worst they

can do is fire me. Either another director will come on or we will go over budget. These things happen. People do go over budget. Part of it was exhaustion too. I realized I was spending so much time worrying and it wasn't useful because I didn't have that much energy to be spending like that. So I was able to let go more and let my AD worry about stuff like that, understanding that while it was his job to move things along, it was my job to say, no, we can't move along yet, we didn't get this yet. Most days we got most of what we needed. There were some scenes that we didn't get to, that I thought, I guess I am going to have to make this up. But once we got in the editing room it seemed like I had enough to make it work and I eventually started to feel a rhythm. Finally it became – we get there, we look at it, we decide, we rehearse, we shoot and we move on. So towards the end I started to enjoy it a little bit more, reminding myself that if I want to direct films, I should be enjoying this; there has to be joy in it, the same joy that I get from acting. If I'm not getting that, how can I create that? And so sometimes it would be in the afternoon and we'd be hustling to get a shot and I'd be joking around and I heard my AD saying, 'Steve, that's very funny but really we have to get on.' And I was thinking to myself, I know what his concerns are, but it's very important that I joke around right now. It is really important that I do not take this too seriously because I know how much of a pressure of time we are under. In fact, towards the end of shooting . . .

. . . you were totally laid back?
Right! 'Who cares?!' The scene we were shooting at night, with me and Boone in the car, I was drinking real beer. The prop guy literally didn't have time to pour out the beers and pour water in the beer cans. Even though it wasn't a lot, it was enough. I was thinking, God, this is what I need right now. I mean, anything that helps you get in character! Another time, when we were shooting the dinner scene with Danny Baldwin, Mimi Rogers, myself and Chloe, Danny wasn't there. He had been in a car accident and wasn't going to show up that day. So I had to shoot the scene without him. What I ended up doing was shooting a three-person master and singles. Then a week later when Danny was there, I shot a master of me, Danny and Chloe and then his single. In the editing room it works, even though Danny and Mimi were never in the room together. But I think if that had happened at the beginning of the shoot, I would have been saying, 'Oh my God! This is terrible! I'm jinxed. What do I do?' I was lucky that the choreography of the scene was that Danny and Mimi are sitting at opposite ends of the table.

Was it difficult to be the director and the lead character at the same time?
Mostly it was just exhausting. I don't think one job suffered because of the other. Sometimes it was hard being in a scene where I was in the background and I wasn't able to listen to what the other actors were saying. I remember the first week I was asking for a monitor to play back the scenes and when I finally got it, I realized I didn't really have time to look at it. So I would only check it to see

what the framing was. If we did a take and Lisa thought maybe something wasn't up to par with the camera, then I would look at it. I never checked it for performance. I always felt that I could tell the performance from what was going on in the scene with the other actors. If I stayed in character, then I felt that they were also in character. But if something they did took me out of it then I knew that something was up.

Were you constantly involved in the composition of the shots? Or did you leave it largely to Lisa?
I had thought I would be an actor's director, but really the person I worked most closely with was Lisa. But I was very concerned about the visuals. When I see films I often see camera moves that I think are unnecessary or too many close-ups or over coverage. Lisa, of course, was concerned that we weren't getting enough coverage. Or tight shots. I tended to shoot a lot of things wide and not get in very close and Lisa would always be asking me, do you want to go in tighter? And sometimes we'd be out of time and I'd say, 'It's okay. I think we got it.' A couple of times we had to re-shoot, because I did need those tight shots.

Did you make any efforts to mug up on the technical aspects?
No. I guess I'm more concerned with the performances. Though to me the way the camera photographs them is important to the performance. It's just that I can't say, give me a 50 mm! I can't say, give me this lighting! I just don't know about that. Basically what it comes down to for me is looking through the eyepiece and saying whether you like the frame or not. Even if I knew the lenses it wouldn't mean I'd know which one to use.

How did you feel about the experience of walking on to the set of your own film?
I do remember a general feeling of being in the last week of pre-production and wanting to get started: thinking, I'm ready. I don't want to wait another five days. I just want to be shooting. Four days before we were going to start shooting, I was casting the role of my parents in the film and I got a call from my wife saying my father had had a heart attack. He was okay and actually had a little walk-on part in the film. But having something like that happen, so close to filming, just makes you think about what your priorities are. It was an amazing connection between my father and me. Being that there is that element in the film – the disconnection that the character feels with his family. To have a connection like that with my father right before going into the film was very strange.

The night before I'm sure I was nervous. But I was also ready. On the first day I was very aware that this was the day that everybody would be looking at me, at how I was presenting myself. I had to act like I knew a little bit. I knew I had to keep things moving along and had to have some semblance that I knew what I wanted and what I was after. The first day it was just shots of me job hunting. So it wasn't big scenes. And they were all outside. Later that day we did an interior barber shop scene where I get my hair cut, but that was cut out of the film. The day ended just grabbing shots in a car because I needed a scene of me driving. By now I was feeling really pleased that we'd made the day. But in the morning, I was feeling pretty nervous but trying not to show it.

Was the post-production another revelation for you? Had you been involved in the edit of any of your films, apart from your short?
Working on *In the Soup*, Alex Rockwell let me see every cut of the film although I was never in the editing room with him. But just seeing all those different cuts gave me an idea of how drastically films can change and what you can do. What little things you can do to make them better. What things you have to lose for the sake of the film. But this really was a whole new experience for me. You feel like you are sculpting, scouring, looking for moments. Trying things different ways and trying to cut it in a way that gets back to the feeling I had when I wrote it. 'This is what I was feeling. Now I'm watching it, I'm not feeling that thing. How can I get back to that feeling?' I remember going through a deep depression, being so immersed in it and not being able to figure out why it wasn't working. Especially after spending all this time on it. Plus, it was such a personal film that it was bringing up all this stuff. I was pretty much a wreck. But I enjoyed collaborating with my editor, Kate Williams.

Did the finished film change much from the script?
The whole beginning of the film changed. What I had written, we tried to make work and couldn't. It just didn't make sense. You were left in the dark for too long. So the scene that we started with in the bar was the second half of a later bar scene, which on its own was way too long and which I thought I was going to have to give up. Kate and I were banging our heads against the wall, thinking, what are we going to do for the beginning of this film? And it was the assistant editor, Jane Abramovitz, who suggested starting in the bar.

How did it start in the script?
It started with Uncle Al having the heart attack on the ice-cream truck almost running over a kid. The bar scene that we started with was actually a continuation of the Debi Mazar drinking scene, after she's gone and I'm passed out in a booth. We figured, why not start the film this way – this way you immediately know this guy's life.

How long did it take to edit?
In all, it was about four months. It was broken up by the fact that I needed to get some work, so I went off to do an acting job in LA. By that time we had a cut but I knew that it needed work. The music wasn't right, the ending wasn't right. So I was still trying to do some editing while I was working on the film in LA. But Live Entertainment were pretty good about it, and they gave me an extension.

What was your reaction to the first rough cut?
I could tell that we had something but the beginning was still too long. It's not

really a movie in three acts. It's really in two halves. The first half establishes Tommy's life in the bar and introduces all the characters. Then in the second half Tommy gets to work in the ice-cream truck and that goes on until the end of the film. Once we got to the ice-cream truck there was only a certain way the scenes could be cut. Whereas the beginning was really up for grabs. How much time do you spend on introducing this character? How much of Mike's story is important? So besides editing the final scene which was a killer, the first half of the film was the toughest to figure out.

Do you remember first showing it to your friends even before the public?
We just showed it in the editing room. In the beginning we didn't have the money for a work print so we had to watch it on the Lightworks. And we just invited a few close friends. I felt okay because although they said the beginning isn't there, at least they hooked into it emotionally. They were with my character: they cared about what happened to him. Everybody had ideas but you can't try them all.

What was it like the first time you showed it to Live?
We knew it wasn't ready yet but they wanted to see something so we said, 'All right, let's show 'em.' They gave us some notes, which we were expecting, some of which were very good. Part of the problem with editing is that it is really hard to get the distance, to be objective.

Was the question of the ending resolved?
The ending was the hardest thing because they were pretty insistent about my character leaving the bar. There was talk of re-shooting but of course it never happened. And like I said, we had that test screening in LA. We had the focus group. That was really weird. Me, sitting there, trying to hide myself, not wanting them to know I was there. Just listening to the comments, some of which were useful, others of which weren't. I felt that the audience was very young. They weren't going to get it and I didn't care if they got it or not. They seemed to be from eighteen to twenty-five.

What were their comments? Do any stick in your mind?
There is one scene at the beginning of the film where I am driving to the bar and there are four guys in a parking lot across the street dressed in black suits. They weren't extras, they were just guys walking across the street. When we showed it at the test screening, there was a laugh. I was then in the bathroom and I heard these young guys of about eighteen saying that they liked the *Reservoir Dogs* reference. I just shook my head. It even came up on the form about favourite scenes. I almost took it out but I didn't have anything to replace it with. Another thing I remember was listening to them talking about the ending. I heard a couple of them say that it was unsatisfying. 'He left the bar. Why? Where did he go? We are left with these other people in the bar and we want to know what happens to

him.' Well, what happens to him? I don't know. To me the strongest statement that you could make was that he was still there. He is there and if you just end on him that is the simplest, strongest, clearest ending – even if you don't know what's going to happen to him.

So Live finally accepted your ending?
Finally, yeah. I had a long talk with one of the executives there, Yalda Tehranian. At that point *Leaving Las Vegas* was being released. I hadn't seen it yet but I said, I know it's a lot darker than mine. The main character dies at the end. Yalda said, yeah, but when he dies he's in love – he has a smile on his face. I couldn't argue because I hadn't seen the film. But I thought, he still dies. He dies! At least I don't die. Why won't you let me end my film my way? Finally she said, all right, we'll go with your ending – even though she disagreed with it, which I really respect her for.

Did you have a guaranteed theatrical release for the movie?
No. I thought I was supposed to have consultation on who the distributor was. But they decided that they would distribute it themselves with Orion Classics. I was disappointed in the way it was distributed because they spent all their money on big ads for the first weekend. It threw me at first because I thought, they really are behind the film. But after that first weekend it went down to a tiny ad in the Friday *Times*, not any other paper. There were no posters put up. I remember arguing with the head of marketing, saying, why don't you put any other ads in? And him giving me this whole line of well, it's our experience that when people decide what movies they are going to see, they check the Friday listings and that's how they plan their week. I said, that's not how I do it. If I want to see a movie, I look in the paper and see what's playing no matter what day of the week it is. I don't plan what movies I go and see on Friday if I am going to see a movie on Wednesday. And I had friends calling me, saying, we want to see your film but we don't know where it is just because they couldn't find the ads. It was released in the fall, but too close to the Thanksgiving period when the big films come out. And we were just pushed out. We were in a good theatre but I felt maybe we should have been in a smaller theatre. Or that it could have been moved to a smaller theatre.

How many prints did they release?
Not as many as I hoped for. Now I see that what they wanted was to get the reviews for that first weekend. They wanted to release it so it had a theatrical profile and after that it was marketed as a video, because that's what they're good at.

How did you feel about this?
I felt extremely grateful that they put up the money for the film and allowed me to make the film I wanted to make. On the other hand, I felt like they really didn't know what they had, because I feel like the film could have stayed around. Had

they known it was out there, I think more people could have enjoyed seeing it on the screen. Since then I am thankful that a lot of people have rented it. I've had some weird comments. Just the other day someone came up to me and said, I saw your film. I liked it very much. Was it rough on you that it wasn't successful? And I thought, what is it? He's thinking that it didn't make a lot of money. But to me it's a successful film, because I made the film I wanted. I've also had other people say that they saw it on video and liked it – and were surprised because it had gone to video so quickly. And I totally understand that.

Gary Oldman: *Nil by Mouth*

You're well known as a British screen actor. Did you discover theatre or movies first?
When I went to drama school at sixteen, I thought I'd better go and see a play –
because I'd never read one or seen one! So going to the theatre was something
that came really late. But I'd always been a big fan of films. When I started going
to films I was immediately drawn toward social realism. I like that kind of cinema: Pasolini, *The Loneliness of the Long Distance Runner, Saturday Night and
Sunday Morning*, Bergman – the ones that just deal with people, issues and relationships, and love. That's all we want: we want to love and be loved.

Given your international success as an actor, what made you want to direct?
The nature of film acting is that you throw your creative imagination into the
cocktail, but ultimately it's the director's vision. At its lowest basic level, you come
in, you learn lines, you hit marks and you're moved around like a piece on a chess-
board: 'Can you do it a bit more like this? Can you stand there? Turn your face a
bit more to the window because I want to get that angle. Come away from the wall
a bit because I want to put a light in there.' And somehow, in all of this, you've got
to focus, you've got to concentrate on what you're doing under very difficult circumstances. It's also very fragmented. You come in, you do a little piece, then you
break. You do another little piece, then break again which can be very frustrating.
You spend a lot of time waiting. The lighting cameraman spends two hours lighting the scene, but often you're not given the time to do your work. You will wait
all day and then you've got five minutes to do your job! So when I'm on set, I like
to watch what's going on. Often I'm the person who's looking at his watch in a
rather producer-like way. This set up's taking a bit long, I'd say. What's the problem? I'd ask questions and find myself looking at the monitor and thinking, I don't
like that shot very much. I'd bring the angle round a bit. As an actor I'd read
scripts and visualize them in my head. Sometimes I'd be completely and utterly
blown away and surprised by what I saw. And other times I'd go and watch the
movie and it'd be nothing like I saw it – which can be good or bad.

When did the idea of doing a London-based movie first start to take root?
I used to like watching films on TV and at the cinema. But I'd go and see stuff and
think to myself, people don't really talk like that. I wanted to see the London
where I grew up, with real people. So the initial germ of *Nil by Mouth* was sparked
by the frustration of what was not there: a gap that I thought could be filled. You
know, I thought, someone should do a film about London that really shows it

how I remember it, growing up, being in the pub, the colours of London. Then one day – it was March '95 – I said I'm going to write a script. I wanted to do a cheap movie about a bunch of people who are fifty up talking about the age of nonsense we live in. It was going to be five guys in a room. Five guys come back to a flat after the pub. They're telling anecdotes, being funny, like the guys I can remember. I started to write it and then these women started talking and I thought, this is interesting. After that, it just sort of wrote itself.

Did it go through many versions?
Nil by Mouth became a film about a young heroin addict living rough on the street, drawn very much from my experiences and from my family. The opening scene was Billy sneaking around in the kitchen doing drugs while someone was upstairs. Then that changed and found its way into the film in a different way: someone was turning the light on in the kitchen, obviously doing something that they shouldn't be doing. Then there was a scene where Billy went to see his mum, Janet. I started writing her, and I thought, God, she's fantastic. Why can't she be kipping on the sofa round at her mum's? She's got a daughter and my sister's got a daughter she had when she was very young. So I started to draw on that and it just grew from there. I'd write down or draw ideas and things. That shot zooming through the lightbulb when he goes into the garage was the first shot I saw.

At the time the film came out, it was claimed that Ray Winstone's character was based on your father. Was that true?
Ray is a composite of different people but not my father. The press just got the wrong end of the stick. We gave a press conference at Cannes, and perhaps I didn't make myself clear because the next day the tabloids said two things: Oldman makes film and my dad used to beat my mother up! In his big speech towards the end of the film, Ray talks about his dad always being in the pub; just coming home to sleep – but he's always in the pub himself! But he naturally doesn't see it. My father was never violent. He used to just come home and go to bed.

So where did the violence come from?
I'd just seen it. The neighbourhood was very violent. Talk about testosterone! You only had to walk up the street or sit in the pub. The most extraordinary thing about *Nil by Mouth* was that it was really fifteen years of my life. I went to drama school, did plays, lived in the States for a long time. But when I sat down to write it in New York, it all just came out. It's that old thing: no matter where you go, you pack yourself in your suitcase with all your issues, all your baggage.

How long did it take to write?
I wrote it in five weeks. If I'd write scenes that felt like a movie I'd throw them away. If scenes felt too long, I'd say to myself, why should a scene be a certain length before you cut? I was just throwing all of that out. I remember when Isabella Rossellini read it, she said (*falsetto Italian accent*), 'It's like an anthro-

pologia.' She was very encouraging. I then said to Doug Urbanski, I don't want to hear from anyone. I don't want to give it to anyone. I'm not rewriting it. I'm not doing any of that bullshit. We're making the movie in September/October. It may have been arrogant of me, but I was reacting against all the rubbish that goes on. If I'd sent it out to people for coverage, they'd have said, the accents are too thick, the language is too strong, there's too many characters. Who do we follow? Can you give it a bit more hope at the end, make it more optimistic? I'd have had notes and stuff like that and it would never have been the film it was. It wouldn't have had my voice, it wouldn't have had my honesty. So I gave it to Doug in May and said, I'm making it at the end of the year. I want the winter. I want to make it a winter film. Sunless, no leaves on the trees, grey – that's how I remember London. Always raining and grey. Grey sky, grey buildings, people in grey. We had weather cover for the sun. If the sun came out, I'd say I don't want that in my movie. I just didn't want any sun. I wanted it very oppressive.

Once you had a draft you were happy with, where did you go for money?
Where do you think was the one place that didn't want to give us any money?

The UK?
Of course. We didn't get a dime out of them until the film was finished.

Who else did you try?
I've got a relationship with Columbia as I've made several movies for them. But I didn't want to use friendship in that way. And I knew that if I went down that route, they'd do coverage on it and it would hurt the piece. They'd tone it down, they'd tone down the accents. All that stuff. So we tried various places. It was a British film so we went to Channel 4 and British Screen and people were being very sceptical and very cynical. It's that typically British thing: he's getting too clever for his boots. He thinks he can do that now. While we were trying to get money, I was saying to Doug, we're making this. We're doing it. And while he was trying to get finance, I was doing a very early prep. I found the locations, chose the colours of the walls, what pictures they put there. The clothes. I went round taking pictures. I revisited some of the old places. I'd set a scene in the Liberal club in Deptford, and I had to go to Deptford because I thought, is it how I remember it as a kid? I'd just been in New York at a typewriter remembering all these places. They could all have been knocked down. So I went and did an early scout.

What was it like to go back to South London?
Obviously I go back and forth to England but actually to go back to New Cross – which I'd only done five or six times since I'd left – was very strange. Here's someone who's not lived there for twenty-odd years, someone who sits in an apartment in New York and writes something from memory, and you go back and it's hardly changed. What amazed me is that it was still blokes in a pub going, 'Fucking nigger, fucking cunt!' It was still those chaps. I just went, God! There I

was, sitting in an apartment in New York, writing a script and thinking it may have changed a bit. But I walked round the whole area and it hadn't really changed at all. So that was a bit of a shock and also quite sad. But I had fun going around. I mean, I miss the humour. I've always been fascinated by it, although I've never been one of those boys round the back of the pub.

So while you were scouting how was the finance progressing?
I had been very friendly with Luc Besson. When we did *Léon*, he'd say, if you ever want any help, or maybe one day you make your movie, call me and I'll help you. And if there was something that needed doing, I'd always joke, call the Frenchman! So this was just chit-chat on set. Then one day Doug was going through some fan mail. Like the lottery he put his hand in the box and pulled out a card and it was from Luc. It said, 'I haven't heard from you for a long time. Where are you? You are my friend. I miss you. Give me a call. PS: Remember if you ever need any help, call the Frenchman!' He was in town so Doug sat down in a diner just round the corner and Luc said, of course I'll help. He did a quick deal on a napkin and that was it. Basically he was going to work as an intermediary, as a middleman. He had a deal with Sony and Columbia so when he went in with *The Fifth Element*, he twisted their arm. He said, I'll do *The Fifth Element* on condition that you do this one, too. It was a multi-million dollar science fiction film and it was Luc Besson so they said, okay, we'll take the little movie too. But I don't think they really wanted it. It's a dark subject. It's violent and all those things that say we're not going to make any money at the box office.

How much did they invest?
They put a ceiling on it of one point nine million dollars. I could make the movie at a kick, bollocks and a scramble on a budget of one point nine million. I admire people who can do it. If you're Sidney Lumet, you can make *Dog Day Afternoon* in twenty-seven days and they'll love you for it. Or Kevin Smith and *Clerks*? Just knock it together. But I didn't want to work like that. I wanted to do twenty-five takes. I wanted to work at my rhythm. Long before the experts came in I boarded the movie at fifty-five days. I think we shot fifty-seven in the end so I was two days out.

What did the budget end up at?
We ended up making it for three point five million, three point seven five, around there. The actual cost of the film was a little under three million dollars but there was fat in there. There were a lot of backhanders in England. Doug was flying to New York searching for money. I was selling my furniture and my piano. We were getting costings on everything I owned, I was selling everything I owned. In the evening I'd be on the phone: how do we pay the crew because the cheques hadn't come through? I would then wake up, go in, do the movie, go to dailies. I then was up talking to America, working out all the politics, all the stuff of how we were going to pay the crew, what we could do. It was a miracle that the movie was ever made. Another problem was that I couldn't get bonded. I hadn't

directed and because of my reputation they saw me as unstable. I'm the writer-director and producer! I'm not going to be able to take my hands off the film and let the bonding company come in and take over the picture. I mean the confidence in me was completely zero. But in the end, Luc put up the bond.

Did this apparent lack of confidence upset you?
I just said, fuck 'em. I had a vision. I had a passion. I knew what I wanted. I knew what I could see. I didn't know whether it was going to be any good but it was going to be my film. I was going to stand or fall by it. If it was no good then it was no good because of Gary. So I was happy to have the responsibility.

How did you come to work with your DP, Ron Fortunato?
I met several English cameramen who weren't really listening to me. One of them came in and the first thing he said was, 'I think the script's got some problems.' The first thing he said! And I went, okay, and listened to him. But he didn't listen to me. I felt like he was interviewing me for the job. Then he said, 'What do you mean, you want it on the zoom?' Okay, so he went. Then I met another guy and he said, 'You crossed the line there.' And I went, 'I know. I know what the line is. I've made twenty movies. But I want a hard cut.' He just didn't get it. What I sensed from these guys was that I would have days where I'd say, this is how I want to do it, and they'd go, well, I think it'd be better over here and you go, no I want the camera there. Then I remembered Ron who'd done *Basquiat* with Julian Schnabel. I liked *Basquiat* so I called Ron up and sent him the script. He didn't get it. So I called him and spoke to him for a couple of hours on the phone, explaining how I wanted to do the film. He said, oh, okay. He was very hesitant about the zoom, and he hadn't worked in 16 mm for years. But he was the only one who was willing to go on this ride, this journey.

Why was the zoom so important to you?
I felt that the faces were the landscape and I wanted to give it a feeling of voyeurism, looking at them like a fly on the wall. But also a feeling of claustrophobia like you were on the sofa with Raymond when he's telling those stories, like you were his prisoner. The flats they live in are very small so you're like a hostage to a man like that. You can't go into the kitchen, you can't walk through those doorways without touching someone because they're too narrow. So I wanted a very claustrophobic feeling.

Did you have very firm ideas of how you wanted it to look?
I wanted a 16 mm stock that would give it a grainy look. There's a Kodak stock that I think was used on *Taxi Driver* and I wanted it to have the colours and the feel of that film. We chose the stock by blowing it up to 35 mm then looking at it on the longest throw possible at the Empire, Leicester Square. The first one was a bit rough. It looked like it was raining. So I said, that's not quite where I want to go.

How did you communicate what you wanted to Ron?
I showed him a scene from *The Killing of a Chinese Bookie* where the killer is being set up with the gun and the address and all the information so he can go and kill the guy. It's so dark you could barely make out the people. Ron was familiar with the film but hadn't seen it for years. I want the lights to look like night, I said. I want the inside of cars to look like the inside of cars at night. I want the streets like when you see something from your car. I want those yellow sodium lights. Take the celluloid and dip it in dirty water. And he went, okay. He tried a few things and we did a few tests. We did a test at night using some gels. We were on the corner of the street where Ray gets out of the car and punches the guy outside the Wimpy bar. Ron was setting up the camera on the tripod and I said, 'Let's not just do a test. Let's do something. Get in the car, just sit in the back seat, and put the camera on your shoulder.' I had Charlie Creed-Miles there because we were doing some tests on him that day. So I said, 'Get Charlie to come out of the Wimpy bar. I'm going to get out of the passenger seat, cross the street and punch him. Follow me on the zoom. Then keep me on the zoom as I walk back to the car.' 'No, no,' he said. But I said, 'We'll do it.' So somewhere there's this bit of footage, the same as Ray punching the guy, but it's Charlie and me. Ron put down the camera and said, 'That's the movie you want to make? That felt good!' And I said, 'You see what I'm saying? Let's rough it up!' So then it clicked for Ron. And I'm just glad that I bullied him into doing it!

You make it sound almost documentary-like?
People say to me, 'It's documentary-like', and I say, 'But a documentary holds back and lets it all happen.' Ken Loach does that: he lets the scene play out and keeps the camera very passive. But I'm really in there. I wanted it to have a realistic feel. I've seen violence and it's over very quickly. It's one punch if you're lucky, and it fucking hurts getting hit. I've been hit. You don't wipe your arm on the side of your mouth. Your lip splits open, your head bleeds like murder. It looks like you've had your head blown off and in fact you've just got a cut above the eye. When I was acting, the make-up person would be doing a cut on my head and I'd say, 'My head wouldn't stop bleeding: it'd be on my shoes.' And they'd say, 'I don't want to put too much on.' And I thought, when I do a film where someone gets it in the head, it's going to look real. I mean, the look of the movie is very calculated. It's been great when people have said, 'I love that little moment there. It looks like it just happened and it's improvised.' And I go, 'No, it's not improvised. Actually we did twenty takes to get it.' It's made to look like it's improvised and I just happened to catch it. I don't like things that are absolutely perfect. If the frame was too perfect I'd go, it's too pretty. Let's make it a bit rougher!

Coming back to Nil by Mouth, *did you shoot exclusively on location?*
Yes. It was all location. I had a council estate called the Bonamy estate. I called it 'Burbank in Bermondsey', because it was like an empty movie set: it was quiet,

there weren't too many kids and you could move around pretty much anonymously. And because the flats were being knocked down I was able to jimmy windows and make false walls to give myself more room. It isn't there any more; they've knocked it down.

Did you always have Ray Winstone in mind for Ray?
No. I started to write the character, then one day I thought, I'm writing a good part for someone here. Who could play this guy? They've got to fill the frame, and the character. Then I thought, Ray Winstone could do it. I was looking for Londoners. I wanted the real thing.

And the same for Kathy as Val?
I always saw her as Kath, but the other parts I had no real idea of who'd be in them.

How did you find Charlie Creed-Miles who plays Billy?
The Anna Scher School has a night where they do improvisations. I went down, and there was Charlie looking like Al Pacino in *Serpico*. He had long hair and a beard, and he was wearing a vest. He looked really intense. So I said, who's that kid? He's terrific! He came in but, although he was wonderful in the improvisation, he didn't read very well. So I said, 'I think you're probably a much better actor than you just read. If you want to familiarize yourself and learn it, would you come back and meet me?' He said, 'Yeah', and he came back. He was the only person who turned up early. So he's across the table from me and I said, 'In your own time.' He did the launderette speech about the dog. And he did it amazingly well. I then thought, can he take a note? So I said, 'That was great. But he's probably a bit more stoned than you just played him. Can you just do it once more?' He took the note and did it again, even better. I said, 'You're marvellous! You've got the job.'

What about Jamie Foreman who plays Ray's best friend, Mark?
Ray and Jamie did a number on me, really. Ray put me together with Jamie, knowing that I'd like him. In fact, I made the part of Mark bigger for him. Once I had them I could adapt the roles to the people.

Did you have much time for rehearsals?
We had four weeks on the Bonamy estate. I walked round the estate with the designer, Hugo, and said, I want this flat for Ray and this flat for Kath. They weren't supposed to be on the same estate but they were round the corner from one another so I could rehearse on the location, in the kitchen, in the living room, on the sofa that we were going to use. Often you arrive on a set, you meet someone and you have two days with them. Maybe it's me and Demi Moore and the director goes, you're in love. You get on set and they go, you're man and wife. You have to convey a twenty-year relationship in a matter of days. But I was dealing with a family and I wanted to get a real feeling that those people knew one

another and were very comfortable around one another. That was partly why I wanted the rehearsal time. And also so I could say, look, you've got a good idea. Try the scene like that. Are you comfortable there? You don't know? Well, sit somewhere else. Don't anchor yourself there. Move around a bit. Great directing is giving the actors confidence. They think, god, he's great. I just come in and do what I want to do. But you're shaping and moulding what you're after. Working like this also meant I didn't have to rehearse the scenes to death. I could look at angles and make little notes and then say to the actors at the end of the rehearsal, are you all comfortable with where you are? Actors like to nest and they anchor themselves to geography. If I'm in rehearsals and I'm sitting in a chair like this and the arms of my chair are here, then I get to the scene and (*gets up and moves his chair*) now the arms of the chair are over here, I go, I can't do this now. It doesn't feel right. This is all different. I need the arms where they were in rehearsal. So I wasn't coming in at the end of the day saying, you stand there, you sit there, you say the line like this. I didn't want to do that. It was a very organic process and they were very comfortable with it. And it meant that I knew where I was going to put the camera. I knew the blocking. And of course actors love it – they love to come in and act. That's the great thing about the theatre. What do you do in rehearsals? You come in at ten and you act from ten in the morning till six o'clock at night: you're acting all day. That's what we like to do. Actors will just say, rehearsals? Wow! I'd love to do that. It was like a new idea. It was like I was inventing the wheel for these guys. They would go, fuck, rehearsals, that sounds like a really good idea! So they were all into it and it served a double purpose. It got the relationships cooking and it also enabled me to get a shot list. I had to go off looking at costumes and locations so I couldn't always spend as much time with the actors as I wanted but it was great fun because I was with the actors which was where I wanted to be.

What was it like directing actors in the rehearsals? Did you have a clear idea of the action?

To me great directing is knowing when not to say something. Just giving people the room and the space to be doing what they're doing. Often people have to justify the position of being the director by stopping everyone, coming in and saying something. I go, I'm not going to say anything; just keep doing what you're doing: it's fantastic. You then make an adjustment and say, 'That was a ten: now get angry but make it a seven, because that was a bit too much.' If you've got great actors, people will say, you got great performances. But I say, I actually did very little. I just appreciated what was there. I always thought that Ray was fantastic and Kathy and Charlie and all those people. I never directed Charlie. I just made adjustments. I'd say, you're acting telling the story. Now just tell the story.

There are some extraordinarily intense moments – for example, Ray's breakdown in the flat. Was that a particularly difficult scene to direct?

I'd had those conversations. But it was one area of the role that Ray needed my help. So I directed him in those scenes like a silent movie star. I wound him up, put him in front of the camera, gave him a few key things to say and then at certain points gave him a couple of drinks to loosen him up. I'd say things like, 'You love your dad, Ray. Look up, Ray. Now tell me how much you love him. You love her, don't you, Ray? But she's fucking difficult to live with. Look in the mirror, Ray. Tell her how much you love her.' And he got the vibe. He just staggered round, going, 'Fuck, I love her.' And then we pieced it together.

Did you have any disasters?
Yeah. I had to shoot the 'nil by mouth' scene three times. We lost all the sound. A ten minute scene of someone talking from the heart, talking about their dad, and I had to go up to Ray and say, we've got to shoot it again a third time! I would have gone for the second take but we lost it. I just had the picture. No sound, no guide track. I was told that at lunch! Another time, Kathy Burke calls up sick. I had nothing scheduled for the day except stuff with Kathy so I'm walking along the street going, oh shit! The money is ticking away! I'm going, that's half an hour. Then this fog started to roll in. And I went, this fog's good, innit? Get Charlie Creed-Miles on the phone. They got him on the phone. Charlie came round panting. I said, 'You're going to go round to your nan's. You're going to call up at the window. Get him into costume,' I said. 'Get him into make-up as quick as you can.' And we did that scene in the fog with the pigeons. You can't write that: 'fog rolls in'!

What about lucky breaks?
I was really blessed with my actors. The fact that I won the British Academy Award for Best Screenplay really reflects their work as much as it does mine. After all, until they speak it, a script is just a bunch of silent words on a page. You need actors to come along and breathe integrity and honesty and all of those things into the words. Otherwise a script just sits there between two folders on a shelf. It's meaningless unless it's acted and done. So they're bringing their own sensibilities and their own sense of poetry to it. They would come in and Ray would have an idea and I'd go, that's interesting. There was a certain way I wanted to shoot which meant lots of takes – like Ray kicking at the door and screaming. I mean, he did that all day. I'd say, 'Ray?' And he'd go, 'What? You want another one?' And he would just go after it again and again and again. I was really, really blessed. I mean there are actors who go, fuck it! You've got the scene. I'm not doing it again. That's it. What are they going to do? Shoot me? I know a lot of actors who wouldn't go through what they went through. I had a commitment from them that was staggering. And that was really what I most enjoyed about it, getting on the floor; being with my mates. Harvey Keitel said recently that directors would have a better time at work if they understood the tools they're working with. It's like Van Gogh not understanding colour. Actors are your

paintbrush. They're the thing you're working with. And I find that an alarming number of directors don't always have time for it. You're like a necessary evil for them. They've got to have actors but don't dare come with your ideas! Just stand there and do it!

Did you ever worry you wouldn't be able to realize the film?
Oh yeah. I had all of those nightmares. What if I don't know where to put the camera? What if it isn't interesting? It's just going to look like *Eastenders*. It's going to look like television. It's going to look like all these things I can't stand. When Ron got up to speed, he was my eyes. But there were times initially when I was talking to some of the money people and I'd want to plug my head into the finder and say this is what I'm talking about. I was talking about things very much in the abstract. I had no other film they could watch and say, 'You see what I mean? That's the kind of film I want to make.'

What were the main differences between working in America and working in England?
I liked London although I found it frustrating. I was used to being in America where you really get things done. You send a fax to someone and you say please get back to me as soon as you can. And you get the fax or they return the phone call. But England hasn't moved into the twentieth century! You can't film in the West End! You can't park your trucks! You can't go on that side of the street because it's a different jurisdiction! You can't put a dolly track in the street because it's the Queen's Highway, and on and on! And I would say to these people, but we blew up a building on Broadway in *Léon*! You just divert the traffic. We blew a building up! On Broadway! You have movie police and you just divert the traffic around it. And you're telling me I can't put six foot of dolly track in the road because it's the Queen's Highway? Do you want a fucking film industry?! Does England want a film industry? If you want a film industry just have a film council that can get us permission to film. But it was great being back home, being on the streets. It was great going back. I always knew that if I was going to come out of the box as a director, it would have to be in a world I really knew. I still think that one of Scorsese's best films is *Mean Streets*. I think he would actually say that. Maybe you do the first one and there's an innocence to you; there's that sense of flying by the seat of your pants and not really knowing what's going on. Then you learn more about the camera. You get a little bit too knowledgeable, a bit too smart with it, a bit too clever with it.

What did you particularly like about directing a film as opposed to being an actor on someone else's film?
I wanted to be a composite of all the good directors I'd worked with. What some directors don't understand is that if you say to an actor, you're fantastic, the dailies look great and you're doing really good, that'll get you through the whole week. Some directors play mind games with you. I tried to be actor-friendly. The

first thing on my list at the production meetings was food. They said, 'What do you want?' 'Caterers,' I said. 'I know it's a low-budget film, but within our tight purse I would like nice catering and comfortable surroundings. We're going to be out on the streets. It's South London, it's going to be night filming, it's going to be cold. Let's make the actors feel good.' It's like being a general. If you're good to the troops they're going to get out there and fight for you. I remember working with some directors, who were rude or difficult, and thinking, I'd never talk to an actor like that. So it's like anything. You take the good and leave the bad and try and be an ideal amalgam of the best.

How would you a describe a day in the life of the director on the set of his own film?
It's like saving things from a burning house. You're up at six. You're thinking, thinking, thinking all day. There's twenty-seven questions you have to answer per minute. There's this-that? This-that? This-that? Then at lunchtime they're all coming at you. You're having lunch. You've got a quiet moment. They go, now I've got you. Can I ask you this? Can I ask you that? It goes on all day, then at the end of the day you get in the car and drive to the West End to see dailies. Then you get to the hotel at eleven or twelve o'clock at night. Then maybe there's an hour of stuff on the phone and then it's up again at six.

Did you sleep?
Yeah. I was in a coma, I think.

What happened once you'd shot the movie?
I personally took the film back to America. Doug and I picked it up from the warehouse and went to Heathrow. A guy came on the plane and said, 'See that shipment on that truck there? That's your film.' I could hear it being loaded on underneath our seats. So I got it to New York and started to piece it together. Brad was delayed because he was finishing a documentary he was doing. So I didn't have him from day one.

How did the edit go?
I got quite depressed. The doing of it, the writing of it, the shooting of it was the getting-it-out and then when you're editing it's coming back at you as you watch all the images. I thought, God, it's quite bleak. Do I really see the world like this? I found that strangely depressing. Basically the reviews said, 'For his first film, Gary Oldman has chosen a dark subject' – as if I deliberately went out of my way to find it. It wasn't extraordinary to me. It was everyday. A guy punches someone in the street then comes round and tries to kick the door in because he wants to see his kid. He bites his nose, just a regular row. There's nothing overly dramatic or anything about this.

Did you find it hard to cut things out?
When you go straight into editing from shooting, you're in love with certain things you've done. You can't envision the movie without the writing, the scene,

the acting, the shot. You go, I've got to have this in the film because you're just too close to the physical process of shooting which is about pictures and frames and all sorts of other things. So we got it to the viewing room and did a first assembly. It was good but very long. Then something happened that I think was very fortunate. I knew the phone call from Luc would come, saying one good turn deserves another, will you be in *The Fifth Element*? I was just waiting for it. I hadn't read the script but knew he would ask the favour. The phone call came and I said, sure. I didn't want to leave it but I had to. I had to work on *The Fifth Element*. So I went away for six or seven or eight weeks. The editor, Brad, just tidied up a few odds and ends and then just left it. And I picked it up when I got back. I watched it and I said, it's a lot better than I remember it. It's too long. This needs to go. That needs to go. And I had an objectivity, a view of it, a healthy view because I'd just been away. I would recommend that you get away from it then come back and relook. It was like I wasn't looking through that fog any more. I mean, some of the best writing and some of the best scenes are not in the movie. It was telling me. I would do some little trim, do some little tinkering around and then I would run the movie again but keep the scene in. And every time I watched it I would say, it's getting better. It's getting tighter, but the movie doesn't want that scene in it, does it? The movie was starting to say, listen to me. I can't take this scene. I'm going to be this movie now. It was like the film had become a creature that says, you see this scene? Take it back. Don't keep putting that scene in. I'm a personality now. It was becoming its own thing. Completely separate from Gary. I was still trying to push that scene in: I've got to have that image. I've just got to have ten seconds longer on that really nice frame. And then in the end the movie said, you can't have this. So I had to trim it, take the scenes out. Then it becomes what it is.

How long were you working on it for?
I did nine months. But I did two movies while I was editing which helped me carry on. *Airforce One* paid for my mix. And then we did a lot of screenings, in LA and New York. That was interesting. Just watching, feeling it out. Where we lose them. It was a very encouraging experiment because while people didn't understand everything, they were getting the movie! And it got the laughs. I suddenly started to hear the movie. I started to see the movie working. I did about eighteen screenings. And I was just listening to it, hearing it, shaping it. Then we got to Cannes. You know that scene in *Clockwork Orange* where they open his eyes up and they make him watch that footage. That's what it's like watching your movie! Somehow the more people in the room, the slower the film gets. There were two thousand people at the Palais. We opened the festival. And about twenty minutes into the movie an American stood up somewhere and went, 'Gary, go home!' And there was this deathly silence. And I was sitting there in my tuxedo and we're seeing these scenes and I'm going in my head, and cut! And it goes on for two seconds more and I turn to Brad and go, 'We could have taken a

couple of seconds off that scene, man.' But you just have to abandon it. At some point you just give it up and know, it's kind of ready. I would still be editing it now. So that felt like an eternity. The movie was shorter now but felt like it was four hours longer. That's the other interesting thing. You could take four seconds out and it felt a minute longer. It's not a tangible thing. I mean, maybe you could break it down into a science. But I was amazed that it really had a life to it. That was mystical, that was strange.

What was the commercial reaction to it?
We had a screening in the UK and Luc wanted us to go with someone there. We got an offer. He said take it. We weren't too crazy about the deal. So we had an open market behind Luc's back where we invited people and they didn't know other people were coming. They came under assumed names. Like the two guys from Fox, they were Mr Blue. They walked away and this guy turned to his part-ner and said, it's kind of special isn't it? We should do this. We should take this movie. And we did a very good deal with them. And then of course Columbia didn't want it. But that was part of the deal because of Luc. So they gave it to the Sony Classics Division which is really where it belonged. And they took it and to their credit, they released it very well in the States and were really behind it. And it did okay. It did very good in New York on the wave of incredible reviews, which started at Cannes then continued in the States.

Were you surprised?
Absolutely. There's places where it's not everything I wanted it to be. It's not all the things I saw in my head. It is what it is. It's a first film. And hopefully I'll go on and make a second, which will be good or not as good or I don't know. It's just there it is. That's how I felt at the time. I'm sure if I sat down and looked at it in five years' time I would look at the cuts and just say, we're crazy thinking that that was good. I'm sure. And it was a bit of an experiment. It was something I pas-sionately wanted to do. I did it for six mates, a few people out there. It's like any-thing. You do it for yourself. If people come along and like what you do that's all very nice, too.

Looking back on it, what were the main lessons you drew from the experience of Nil by Mouth?
I learned how hard it is to make a movie. How physically hard it is. Before I started working on it I was at a ceremony that was honouring Scorsese and I met Clint Eastwood there. He asked me what I was doing and I said I was about to direct for the first time. He said, oh, you'll love it. You'll have a great time. You want a word of advice? I said, sure. Get more sleep than your actors. He was so right. I also learned a lot about the business. I had to grow up very quickly. It was a real baptism of fire. Just the mechanics of putting money together: the real nuts and bolts of working. I realized that I had a lot of stamina. That I was a lot stronger than I thought I was. That surprised me – my own energy and commit-

ment to it and strange blind faith and belief in it. What I've taken from it, the more obvious things, I won't know maybe until I do a second one. But I've also learned the meaning of that saying, 'too little, too late'. There were people around me I should have let go a little earlier. You've really got to make those decisions. Bold ones, sometimes.

How do you feel about the film now?

Nil by Mouth is a true independent film. What independence means to me is one hundred per cent control and I had that. It's very unusual. The final cut was mine. I enjoyed the responsibility. I liked being constantly engaged in thinking and the thrill of seeing something in your head come to life. It's thrilling and frightening all at the same time. As an actor you have one job to do: you have the words. So you know that if you've learned the lines and done a bit of homework, when you come in you'll be all right. You have a rough idea of what you're going to do but the ultimate responsibility is up to someone else. When you come in and you direct, each day you have a blank canvas. When it comes down to it, all you have is a room, a camera and some people.

Ang Lee: *Pushing Hands*

Where did you grow up?
Until the age of ten I grew up in the east-coast city of Hua Lung in Taiwan. After
that, most of my upbringing was in the southern city of Taiwan. My father was a
principal at one of the best high schools in the country. It was at high school that
my mind started drifting. I was a very shy, introverted, spaced-out kid: silent,
dull, well-behaved. Not very active. Not particularly good academically either.
And at that time, everything you did was academic, so you could get into a good
college.

Can you remember what you were interested in as a child?
Movies, probably. We saw a lot of them. Mainly Hollywood and Chinese movies.
Mainstream comedies, fantasy, martial arts, melodrama. Movies that weren't too
difficult to understand. Of course, as a boy I always liked sword fighting.

When did you begin to get interested in being a film-maker?
I never really got into film until I failed my college examinations. Then I got the
chance to try out the Academy of Art in Taiwan. I got into the department of
theatre and film, but film was very expensive, so we mostly did stage work. I did
two years at the Academy, and two years in the US, in Illinois. So I had almost five
years in theatre before I decided to switch to film. I'd always loved to watch films.
I didn't start seeing art films till I got into the Academy. Not a lot was available
back then. It was only by mistake that they got into Taiwan, but the kids rented
them privately. Then when I went to the States, I went to see a lot of 16 mm
screenings, good quality films they'd screen on a weekend, where you paid a dollar. But I wouldn't say I was ever a film buff.

When did you discover you had a talent for directing?
Actually I did more acting than directing or writing at the Academy. I was a good
actor, everybody asked me to be in their plays and I won some awards. But once
I came to the States, language was such a barrier, especially to stage acting, that I
had to switch to directing. Still to this day, directing – either on stage or in movies
– is the only thing I'm good at, the only place I can function. In some ways I'm a
pretty unsociable person: not good at anything, all fingers and thumbs. But when
it comes to movie-making, I have to make myself clear. People listen, they get
excited: the whole world changes.

Were you encouraged by your parents?

No. They were actually quite discouraging. My mother is the kind of mother who is happy as long as we are. But my father is a very traditional man. And theatre has a very proud tradition, but the business is very looked down on. It's low in the social rank. That's probably why I did my father trilogy. It's like compensation for this long guilt-trip of trying to be a film-maker. Up till a year before I was thirty-four, even after film school, after years of pursuing a career in film, I wouldn't dare say that I wanted to be a film-maker. I'd say, 'I've got some project.' I couldn't admit that I was a film-maker until I'd nearly done it. So it was a long struggle.

Did you already want to be a film-maker when you were studying acting?
When my father asked me before I got into high school what I wanted to do in the future, I said I wanted to be a film director and everybody just laughed. Nobody took me seriously. But nothing interested me in college. So I think from very early on I dreamt about making fantasies on the screen. Probably the whole time in the Academy of Art I liked directing rather than acting. It was just that once I started acting I got offered all the roles and enjoyed doing it because I was a shy person but on stage, I'm sparkling, strong and powerful, people think I'm five inches taller or something. I had a voice. So I enjoyed that but I think deep inside I'm more of a watcher than a performer. More of a voyeur than an exhibitionist.

Were you also interested in writing or did that come later?
I wrote only because I had to. Directing comes first. I needed material so I wrote. I wrote my first two or three movies and all of my student films and some of the plays I directed. But I never considered myself as a writer. Still, I did manage to make two Super-8 films at the Academy, and with those films I got into NYU later on.

Can you describe one of them?
I made a silent movie, eighteen minutes long, about a guy trying to fly a huge crane kite. I was the cameraman, the director, the everything. And I edited. The editing machine was just a splicer. I had no viewer, so I just estimated: this must be this long and was surprised that it came together. Actually it wasn't a bad film. It was quite innovative, it had a very free style. It was a good experience. It took two years because I only used my spare time. Also, I didn't know kites were so soft. Right before we started shooting we had a test flight. The kite flipped in the air, did one circle and hit the ground and broke. So we stopped, and the next year I thought well maybe I should finish that film.

Did you make any more short films when you got to Illinois?
I had to catch up with what was in the school. The experience was overwhelming because the stage was unlike anything I'd seen. It was huge. Our stage back in Taiwan was very primitive. It was a culture shock. I couldn't get into the acting programme, a three-year programme for actors and my language couldn't carry that

either. I didn't express much or perform much because of the small parts I was given. But I did get to do the workshop and the director's programme. So I spent two years there. It was very educational. The first summer I actually took a course in England. The title of the course was 'Theatre in England'. Half of it was an educational tour. During the other half we saw fourteen plays. We spent ten days in London, ten days in Stratford-upon-Avon. We watched plays and talked to the actors and producers. It was a good experience. That was the summer of '79.

You then went to NYU film school?
Yeah. When I was about to finish I was faced with a decision whether to continue with theatre or go to NYU and pursue film-making. At that time I didn't see much hope of a career on stage. As much as I loved the theatre, western theatre that is, the language barrier was just too big. So I decided to make the leap. I got accepted into NYU. Once I got there, I knew I'd made the right choice because things were much easier. I was top student right away. It was a school system which was particularly good for someone like me who doesn't want to study, who just wants to go and make movies or work on somebody else's movie. You get to know bits of everything from other people's movies. So I probably won't design a shot that the cameraman has a hard time to shoot or the sound man has a hard time to place the microphone for. And regardless of how small it is, while you're doing your film you're dealing with your creative self and you're also exercising leadership. So that was very fulfilling. And then you're making movies in New York – which is a blast!

Can you tell me about the films you made?
The first one was silent. I made a slapstick as the second exercise. Then the third one you do without sync sound. That's the first year. By the end of the first year half of the people are eliminated so two classes become one. Some people decide it's not what they want to do. The other half is eliminated by the school judging your work. I think you can tell a lot from your first little film. The second year you do one film and the third year you do your thesis film. *Dim Lake* was my second year film. It's half an hour long. It's about a suffering New York actor, something I knew about because I wrote the script. Usually the actors would help me polish the language. That film won some scholarship. Then I did my third year film. That took a year to finish. It was called *Fine Line*.

What was that about?
'Fine Line' is a name for Canal Street in New York City that divides China Town from Little Italy. So I have an illegal worker Chinese girl running from immigration and an Italian running from the mobsters and they run into each other. It's a fine line between sanity and insanity. It's about forty-three minutes long. Things actually started to happen while I was doing that film. I'd met my wife in Illinois. We got married in the summer of '83. I finished the film in '84. So I was going back and forth a lot between New York and Illinois. And then when I finished the film,

my son was born. So I was taking care of the kid and couldn't decide what to do. I was thinking of going back to Taiwan. I finally made up my mind that there was no way a Chinese speaker could make a movie in the States. I'm not the type of film-maker interested in applying for grants. I'm not a middle-of-the-road type of a film-maker. I'm a dramatist. So I decided to go back to Taiwan. My father was still hoping for me to teach instead of making movies. But before I went I wanted to show my thesis film. After all, it had taken a long time to make: four months to shoot and about a year to edit. I wanted at least to show the film at the school's film festival. I realized later that it was a big deal because a lot of people were from outside film school and a lot of Asians were watching. Anyway, I was waiting for that and I was packing up all my stuff. It was the night I was going to send all my belongings to the sea port. At seven o'clock, I'm supposed to arrive at the port. The previous night the film was showing. I got a phone call and they said, 'This guy from William Morris is looking for you.' I said, 'William who?' Anyway an agent said, 'Why don't you stay here for a week and let me persuade you that you can make movies here?' 'There's no way. I'm gone,' I said. He said, 'You'll be working, blah blah blah.' The Hollywood type. The next day my film won the Best Picture and Best Director of that year. So I got softened up. I was a hot film student that year. And my baby was only a month old.

So what happened?
Once you stay, you fall into a trap of development hell. They don't find jobs for you. But when you have a script then they'll represent you. That's what agencies are about. At first I thought they would go out and find me a directing job. They're skilful enough to hold fifteen fishing poles together at the same time. They hold your interests and hope. Something is always about to happen. Six years flew by.

Can you tell me a bit more about these six years?
I thought it was going to happen overnight. I started to meet people. It was like a dream world. I was able to walk into any studio company. I didn't realize then that people get paid to praise you. They do it so well because it's their job. There's a way they look at you like you are just amazing. They didn't have to do anything. I was saying, what do you want me to make? I made up something, probably the worst picture in the world. I thought things were about to happen, so I persuaded my wife to stay while I worked on something. And as I looked around, I noticed that of the people ahead of me by a few years, it's the writers who are getting to make movies. The good directors at school are not necessarily making movies. Take, for example, Spike Lee, who was just a year ahead of me. One moment he's making his student film, then all of a sudden, boom! All it takes is one out of a hundred people you know to pop up every ten years and that's good enough, you keep going. You feel like a fool but there's no escaping it. I know people, my peers, who are forty or something and are still thinking that some day they'll

make movies. It's just fascinating, I guess. Plus, I couldn't do anything else. I felt I'd lose face if I went back without something. And as the Taiwanese film industry was in a slump at that time, I just had to hang in there. So at the end of '85, I persuaded my wife to stay. We moved to New York and she found a job near New York in the suburbs. We've lived there ever since. She had a degree, a Ph.D. in Microbiology. But for me she had to stay in New York and not go to a university that was good by her criteria. She became a molecular microbiologist working as a researcher with a modest salary, and we lived on that. We were very poor.

What were you doing during this period?
Nothing. I'm sure you know that film scripts are very difficult to come up with. It's not like writing a song. It has to last two hours. It took me maybe two or three years after school to realize that. In school you make short films and you watch classic art films. But we never wrote full-length feature films. It's a totally different ball game. They're not only longer. They're different from drama too. It took me three or four years to realize that movies are not the same as drama.

In what ways do they differ?
The space and time are different. Drama is about a situation but that's not how films work. Movies are more stretched out: at least in regular commercial feature films. Basically they're created to last for two hours. So they have character development, a structure that must function. You set it up to tell the audience what's going to come, twist it, show it and take it back. A short film is a gust of talent, a gust of energy. But a feature film takes two hours. It's a very, very different ball game. And because I had a dramatic background, it was okay to make a short film. But with a longer film, I found that I wrote complete scenes. Everything had a beginning, middle and an end. It was complete. I was photographing actors, which, it occurred to me recently, was something I've been trying to get away from since the first year of film school. I'm still making the effort to get away from the theatre. With each movie I make, I'm getting further away from theatre and closer to film-making. The exception was with *Sense and Sensibility*. The script was written by an actress so there are little complete scenes and everybody is saying what they think. I had to help her break it up. But I couldn't change the nature of that script too much.

In the six years you spent in development hell, did you try and do anything to make money out of your directing talents? Television or commercials, for example?
Nobody gave me any commercials to do. I did PA work. But nobody wanted me. It was terrible. And the horrible thing was you were always on call: any day people might try and call me up. It could always happen the next day. At the same time, there's so many people thinking up movie ideas. Whenever I thought I had an idea I would call my agent and there would be four or five similar movies being made.

Did you ever think of doing something else entirely?
I was afraid that if I did something else, if I wasn't fully ready, I would miss my chance. That's another thing about development hell. I'd keep working on a project in order to give it everything. It would last more than a year. Then probably half a year down the road I'd have another idea. There was always something going on. Meanwhile there would be people who would hand a project to me and I would supervise the rewrite. There was one project that almost got off the ground. It would have cost two million dollars but the distribution company and the production company didn't get along. I almost smelt the pre-production and then it fell apart. It was a slasher-psychological thriller with Julia Roberts as one of the victims. Then she went off to do *Pretty Woman*. Things like that would happen. There'd be actors who wanted me to write a script for them and direct. Like the Italian actor Giancarlo Giannini. He saw my thesis film and loved it. I wrote a script for him and he liked it. But then we couldn't raise the money for an American star. That lasted for two years and eight drafts.

Did you write a lot of screenplays during this period?
Yes. They're weren't in English. They were all Chinese if I initiated the idea. And then there would be other movies, more on the 'B' level, in terms of quality. Thinking about it in retrospect, I should probably thank God that nothing got off the ground.

So when did Pushing Hands *start to take root?*
I think when I was preparing that Giancarlo thing the central motion picture studio in Taiwan called me because my student picture had won a prize in Taiwan, the Golden Harvest Award. I was tied up with all those promising projects which might never happen. So I thought, well, I want to make a Chinese film in New York about the Chinese there. They said all right. So I wrote a script, *The Wedding Banquet*. A friend of mine suggested I do it because a mutual friend of ours was living in Washington DC with his American lover and when his parents came over they had to switch their furniture. At one time they thought about helping a girl get a green card. I thought that was enough for half a movie. But then an idea hit me. What if the parents insist on having a wedding? Then, boom! I have the second half. It's a great movie idea. I jumped up and said that I have an idea. I wrote it in two months. But there was no way to do it. I showed it to my agent who said it was Chinese so they couldn't make it in America and it's gay so it couldn't be made in Taiwan. So it just sat there. It was six years before it got made. Anyway that's the first Chinese script that I had written by myself. By now it was six years since I left NYU. My wife was pregnant. It was six years in and I'd lost my freshness, my confidence. Everything had been turned down. Things started to quieten down. It was just awful. I pretty much sank to the bottom. I couldn't sleep at night. I felt this big void under me. Anyway, a friend of mine saw an ad in Paris put up by the Taiwanese government. It said that that year its script

competition would extend to overseas. They xeroxed it for me. The prize was sixteen thousand dollars so it was very good money. I thought of putting in this idea which was *Pushing Hands*. I'd had the idea for two years.

What was the idea you had in your head?
It was set in a suburban house. In this house was an old man practising T'ai Chi. So there's a lot of Chinese culture stuck in this house. The other half is an American wife who's a writer, very neurotic. So there's a split and in between they had a son who was between the old and new Chinese culture in America. But it was also a romance between an old man and an old lady. So I never wrote it as a family drama. It's not an artistic piece so there was probably no hope of a festival success. But there was no commercial value either. I never really wanted to write it except for the Taiwanese government. I never meant to make it.

But you did it anyway. How long did it take to write?
Less than two months. I only wrote one draft for the competition. But I did go and see some T'ai Chi master to ask him about T'ai Chi and started practising myself. In any case, my second son was born and as I was about to take him out of the hospital, I got my bank to check some money for diapers. And the record shows twenty-three dollars credit. We were in a lot of debt! My in-laws were there and I was writing film articles, reading for American magazines and writing for Chinese newspapers: odd jobs I really hated. But because my folks were there I didn't want to say anything. I cooked and locked myself in my room with those articles, half translating and half writing. It was awful. I thought I couldn't do that any more. And just then the news came that I'd won the first prize for *Pushing Hands*. And The *Wedding Banquet* as a whole script won the second prize. They were very nice. They realized the round ticket would cost some money so they sent me a free round ticket to receive the award. I was delighted. I hadn't been back to Taiwan for ten years. So I flew back and things had all changed. It felt like visiting and homecoming at the same time. It was a very odd feeling. I felt really detached. Anyway, I received the award and Central Motion Pictures, the new head of which was Mr Hsu, produced my first movie. He was the head of the film library for ten years. From ten years old he wanted to make movies. Back then the studios had already declined and didn't really make anything except propaganda. Mr Hsu said he wanted to make at least three movies a year to give screenwriters and directors a chance and he was going to give one movie to a new director. He said I should make *Pushing Hands* because it had won first prize. But I said I didn't want to make it. I just sent it in for the competition to win the prize money. I thought nobody would want to see it. I didn't want the first film to be a flop, commercially or artistically. I didn't want to waste ten years. He said, okay, think about it. So I thought, what the hell? I haven't done a movie for seven years.

What was the budget?
The budget was four hundred thousand dollars. I didn't know if I could make a

movie on that. I had no experience of producing films in New York. I didn't know any producers so I didn't dare take the job. I was all flustered and then I said I'll do it. What the hell, it was my last chance. It all happened in that short trip. He suggested Mr Lung Sihung as the father. I grew up watching him but hadn't seen him for fourteen years. When I met him he was just right and I asked him if he does T'ai Chi. He said, no, but he could pick it up very quickly because he did meditation for thirteen years and used to be very athletic. He was a soccer player when he was young. So it was a deal. And we both thought the old lady, Wang Lai, was perfect for the role. We called her up and it was a deal. Mr Hsu told me we'd get a government grant and a video deal so only a third of the money was at risk. So even if we lost all our money, it wouldn't matter: somehow we'd get a little back. So I took the money, went back to the States and asked around for producers. I then met Ted Hope and James Schamus through a mutual friend. It was, 'Oh I knew this guy Ted Hope when I was a PA and I heard he's become an assistant director and wants to become a producer. Here's his phone number. Call him up.' Then Ted said, 'I've just formed this company with my partner, James. Come over.' So there they were: sharing two tables with another company in the Tribeca area. It's funny. They'd seen my student film and tried to pursue me but my agent had turned them down. Incidentally, my agent turned out to be a film-maker; the third day into the shoot, he called me up. I thought he wanted to congratulate me. But he said 'I'm calling you because you're an important person to me. I wanted you to know that I'm quitting my job. I hate it. I'm going to make movies like you.' It's kind of funny! Ted and James thought that my agent had sent me over. That he'd changed his mind. But it wasn't him.

Were you able to take a fee for the movie?
I was also the producer. They gave me a sum of money. I wasn't going to go over budget so I didn't take anything. Everything went into the movie.

So apart from the prize for the screenplay, you worked completely for free?
Myself and my son. My son was the little boy, Jeremy. We dyed his hair a little bit, he was helping me. He's a very shy boy. First I couldn't find anybody close to what I wanted. The first day he was grouchy and I was very worried. The second day it was natural. You know what's funny? After the movie he played a butterfly in a school performance and he was shaking all the time! But he was helping me because I was saying, 'If daddy doesn't pull this off, we'll be out on the streets.' So he helped us. My own son. We'd be there until four o'clock in the morning. It didn't matter.

Going back to the story of Pushing Hands, *what do you see as its main themes?*
It's about change in society. When I stayed home a lot, I thought about the old Chinese teaching regarding the essence of life: the only thing you can count on is that everything will change. That gave me a feeling of what I wanted to say about life. It's about people's adjustment to change. And for a Chinese person the biggest

change is the value of change itself. It's about becoming a Westerner – which the whole world will become sooner or later. We all become Yankees. It's the way things are going especially for the East. We try to catch up and the old values are left behind.

Would you agree that another important theme was that of balance, literally and metaphorically?
Balance and change, that's the metaphor of T'ai Chi. It's also the balance inside me between East and West. I grew up in the East where the life philosophy is about reducing conflict and reaching for harmony. Our pattern is that everybody tries to diminish differences. There's tolerance, acceptance until finally things explode. It's a big shock, chaos, then people find new lives, a new balance. Everything comes from this hub, whether it's cultural revolution or whatever. Everything is some explosion. When you see the Taiwanese legislature fighting congressmen, it's all because of this lack of democracy and communication, and acceptance of conflict. That's how I grew up.

So it's about finding harmony in a society which is having periodic convulsions?
Yeah, I grew up under this harmonious teaching and then I came to the West, totally fascinated by western drama. Western drama deals with conflict by raising the stakes, by making it look bigger than it really is, the opposite extreme to the East. So the idea I was always brooding about was to put a T'ai Chi master in a dramatic situation and see him get beaten up. That's where the idea came from. And then, in terms of changing, I wanted to look at people's belief in change and disappointment at it. I think that's kind of Eastern. It's very un-American. America is about wanting to make a difference, twisting situations. But I think most Eastern directors see that at the end, life is disappointing. So that haunted me a lot. Back then, I didn't have to make a happy ending. The movie was about disappointment.

At one point the T'ai Chi master says that persecution is nothing compared to loneliness. Is his loneliness really an expression of the cultural gap between him and the rest of the family? Or is it simply that he is looking for a partner?
The essence of morality in the East is 'filial piety': loyalty to your parents, to your family. It's where you come from. It's where your heritage comes from. Filial piety has been holding back Chinese society for many years. But now it's facing destruction because East is meeting West. Everyone has to level with everyone. So the parents are the equals of the children. And this change is something that will take another thousand years to absorb. So that's the common theme of my first three movies: society, family, the changing world, people not knowing what to do. I also think the father is an extension of my idea of Chinese culture – which is patriotic society. To me, Mr Lung Sihung just has that kind of face. When he's not speaking, you feel the pain in his face. It's almost like a poker face. Inside he's getting weaker but he has to hold up that face so that order will keep going in

society. At the same time, he lets people do things for him. He's very smart about that. He plays up to his role but he's losing his grip with the young people. Everybody is pretending they respect him but they all circle round him and finally there's this big surprise. The pattern that I was talking about in China: every once in a while there's a surprise and people try to find a new balance. So all the three films are pretty much in that direction. I think it started actually on *The Wedding Banquet* and then *Pushing Hands*, which didn't go anywhere after I did it except in Taiwan where it was a hit picture but I think it did capture the essence of the Chinese struggle, the whole Asian struggle. Even now it still has a big audience. In Asia it's still their favourite film. They couldn't get over it. It has some emotional core not only of Chinese but also of Eastern society. It's the filial piety inside you. It's been taught for thousands of years. It's the basic moral code and you cannot follow it. You feel total guilt because you cannot fulfil it. You become a Westerner and you betray your parents. Something you feel unable to deal with: total guilt.

The first fifteen or twenty minutes of the film are completely silent. Starting your film without any dialogue is a very brave thing to do.
Back then I didn't think about it. But now I would see it as brave. Then again, it's fun. One room and two lives: the American wife and the Chinese father. They cannot speak to each other. The harder it gets, the more tension there is.

Pushing Hands establishes a pattern in your work: a preoccupation with the family and with the rituals of family life, especially cooking meals. Do you think this came out of the many years you spent at home waiting for your break?
Yes, because I spent all of my time in the kitchen. The kitchen is my favourite spot within the family drama because it contains different levels cinematically. It's both a battlefield and it's personal. People don't get together in the living room or in the bedroom. They get together in the dining room or the kitchen. You've got all types of business going on in there: different levels of interaction. It's a space I love to film in. My favourite shooting place is the kitchen, then it's the dining room because everybody sits ritually, everyone has to face each other. But it's very hard to photograph. The dining table is one of the most difficult things to film, not to mention if you want a hot meal. The other place I like to film is the master bathroom. For me that is the heart of secrecy. Things are really messed up there!

Let's talk about the shoot. You'd been waiting a long time for this chance to show what you could do as a director. How did it go?
It was the worst experience I've ever had. My wife was ill. She developed a thyroid problem after she gave birth to my second son. She lost ten pounds in a week and had a terrible temper. It was hell for me. I brought in a producer who didn't work out. We'd be gone for sixteen hours a day and come back to make phone calls. It drove her nuts. And our baby was colicky. It was a terrible time. Back then there was no production manager so I had to do everything myself, even the locations,

even getting a Kung Fu master or some stunt man. We'd go to the Chinese community and I promised I'd show respect to anybody who could help me complete the film. We had two weeks rehearsals. The two veteran actors I rehearsed in my apartment, the rest in New York. I cast the Chinese myself and hired a casting director for the American wife. Meanwhile I'd still be rewriting the script. I thought I'd make my first film and quit. I was very lonely. Not until Ted took over and acted as assistant director did I feel like I was a director. I always say that whoever invests in me should be happy that I'm a director trained by Ted Hope.

How did you choose your DP? How did you begin to visualize the look of the film? How did you communicate what you wanted with your DP?
My DP was a graduate from NYU. He's from Taiwan, Jong Lin. His father was the godfather of a Taiwanese cinematographer and they had the biggest equipment house in Taiwan. It was the first time I'd used the 1:1.85 ratio. It was great. There was so much more space. But the composition was a little different. Jong Lin had more professional experience than I did but not much. Usually I'd describe the scenes: what kind of light source I wanted, what the dramatic need was. He'd work from that and then I'd come back. That movie has more natural light than any of my others.

Did you do storyboards?
I would dutifully do storyboards up to my second year of film school. But to me film-making is the process of searching for the life of a film. I like that organic, uncertain approach right up to the last day of mixing: still trying to find the movie. I also found that it's quite hard to make a moving image fit a static picture. Now I only do storyboards when I'm asked to – like when the technicians need the storyboard to sum up or plan the scene for you.

It was six or seven years since you'd directed anything. Did you feel confident you could carry it off?
Making that movie was a lot like making my student films except I had an assistant director who told people to get out of the way. I didn't feel like a new director. Two hours into the production I felt like I was doing something I'd always done. It was seven years since my last project but it was like there was no time gap. I felt quite at home. I always knew what I was doing, what I wanted. It was like swimming or something.

Does the camera position define the staging of the action or vice versa?
It works both ways. But back then it was more the action that defined the shots. I'd rehearse the actors in the morning – we'd rehearse everything even if it was just one line – then I'd do a shot list with the cameraman and the assistant director. We'd spend an extra hour making up the shot list. So the shots were based on the rehearsals. To me, that's natural because the main task is to portray people. If you want to put the camera where the heart of the film is you have to know where

the action is, what you want to emphasize, which line is important. How you choreograph the scenes depends on what the scene needs. What makes it work. To me that's more organic than setting up a shot then having the actors fit into it. However, for more cinematic moments, like when the old man does T'ai Chi, when he walks from one space to another with the wife in the foreground, that's purely visual, it's just something you put there. Sometimes the actors can give you inspiration in rehearsals. But it's not really related to them. But if it's a dramatic scene, I like to rehearse them beforehand.

During the rehearsals do you feel you're taking as much from your actors as they are from you?
It's more that they tell me what they would like to do, their interpretation of the scene. That happened in *Sense & Sensibility*, particularly with the younger English actors. It's difficult for me because they don't see the whole picture, they only see themselves. Things can get pretty chaotic especially if you have to rehearse a scene in the morning when you're about to shoot. It takes longer and is sometimes more confusing than helpful. But rehearsals are the time the actors get to know you and you get to know your actors. I think that part is probably still very valuable. You've somehow got to spend time with your actors even if the rehearsals make no sense whatsoever. Even when you've cast them, it takes time to observe them to see what kind of signal their face sends to the audience.

Do you think English actors are different from their American counterparts?
When they perform, there's a mask. It's a skill they put in front of them. Some directors don't like that kind of performance. They want to strip it away but that can be nasty. Of course, there are actors like Emma Thompson who are willing to do it. But it's hard. Complicated scenes are no effort for her but a simple moment – for example, the stable scene in *Sense and Sensibility* where she blushes because Hugh Grant calls her 'Miss Elinor' instead of 'Miss Dashwood' – that's almost impossible for an experienced actor. But Emma's willing to try something.

How did you feel when you were about to begin shooting the film? Did you have a sense this was an important moment in your life?
Yeah, the thought did come into my mind. The night before the shoot I was cooking. I like to take one day off. I've done that on every film. The day before shooting I ask everybody to take a day off because we'll be working so hard. So I was cooking at home and I picked a hot sauce, some spicy paste. I took it out and the top wasn't screwed on tight so the whole plastic bottle hit the ground and all the sauce flew up and hit the ceiling. It was red like blood. It just exploded and I thought, oh my god! What kind of sign is that? Is it a sign about my career or something? It was terrifying. I spent the rest of the night cleaning up the house, cleaning this red hot sauce out of every nook and cranny. It was all over everything. But I slept very well. I was uncommonly calm. Maybe it was exhaustion. The next day I got up on time. It was raining. In China, all movies have a good

luck ceremony led by the director. You have this sacrifice on the table, then you pray before you put the incense in a bowl and hit a gong. I had an assistant from Taiwan saying I should do that because it brings you luck. But I couldn't decide whether to do it as I had an American crew. Then I found a compromise. There were some Chinese there so I decided we'd do it among ourselves. So my assistant prepared the table, setting things up for the next morning. When it came to it, all the Americans on the crew wanted to take part. I said, you guys will laugh. But for some reason everybody was into this solemn holy moment. For one quiet moment everybody prayed: you could feel the energy. The rain stopped and the sun came out after that. I hit the gong and everybody cheered. It felt great. Then the assistant director, Ted, said to me, 'Congratulations, Mr Director.' That's what they called me. I felt my feet were three feet off the ground. I'm a director now! The crew got so excited they talked about it for the next two weeks. Now the whole crew and I do this ceremony for every movie.

It sounds like the pre-production had been pretty much a one-man operation. Did you find it easy to delegate once you'd started shooting?
Yeah. I think people want to please you. I think it's important that you have good ideas and that you make yourself clear. With my English sometimes they had to ask again but it was pretty clear. You don't have to say a lot especially with actors. You'll probably confuse them. That's how I like production to be: very quiet and everybody in a good mood.

How did you feel about directing two veterans of the Taiwanese movie industry?
I was afraid to direct these veteran actors, because they were such veterans. So I was mainly too polite. I didn't dare say too much. And on the second day of shooting, the older lady, our biggest star, Mrs Wang Lai, came and asked me questions on how she should do it. The way she asked me made me realize that the way I'd showed respect had a negative impact. She felt like she wasn't being directed, wasn't being taken care of. So then I forced myself to lunge in. I got better and everybody felt better. It's not a matter of authority. I think actors are like babies. They need to be cuddled.

How did your collaboration with your DP work?
I was very hands-on. I'd decide where the source light came from and I correct them, do the touch up. I'd decide the framing and work out the camera moves and the timing. With each shot, I'd call to the DP, okay, the shot on the monitor is exactly how I want it. I'd also choose the lens. That's a director's job.

How long were your days on Pushing Hands?
Anywhere from twelve to sixteen hours. I didn't sleep much. But actually I didn't need to. I was so hyped up; and I was younger, too. So a little doze was enough.

Apart from lack of sleep, what was the hardest thing about the shoot?
It was my first professional film and I felt responsible because people live on the

project; they live on the hope and for a low-budget film like that in New York it's the only incentive because you can't pay people much. They have to totally believe their director is a genius and that what they do is significant – which of course I enjoyed! But on the other hand, you're responsible. Of course, what you say, your ideas, have to hold it together. And you can tell that if it's a good idea people show respect. I'm not a bluffer. I'm not a shouter so I have to do my homework. And just by standing there you have the power of consolidating their morale, galvanizing their energy. That's what a professional director does. Everybody's busier than you are. But you're just standing there. It's your presence they need. It's a kind of abstract power. Another thing I've found, which is true for all directors, is that from your first day, your biggest enemy is time. You're always fighting time. That's the first lesson. You plan to do eighteen shots but end up doing nine a day. And then you cannot cover as many places as you want. You have to shrink your shots because the bigger the shot the longer it takes to set up, to rehearse. It all comes down to time. So you've got to do it smaller especially when you do independent films. It was reducing the shots and reducing the area we shot in that determined the shooting style of *The Wedding Banquet*. I almost went back to a schoolbook kind of technique. That was a conscious decision based on the experience of *Pushing Hands*. Shrink the shots, so you can do it well. Because when you spend so much time setting up your shots, you're not refining the acting, the chemistry. Another thing I discovered is also related to time. I'm sure that when they do their first film a lot of directors think their task is just to finish the movie, to make the date. The burden is so great, it's easy to forget why you're making the movie. It's easy to forget that your task is to make a good movie, not just to finish it. You have to keep reminding yourself: no, that's mediocre. And you learn from experience that you cannot make every shot pretty and perfect. In fact, that's probably not good for a movie. You have to choose the right moments. But the rest is storytelling so you have to give yourself the time to accomplish what you really have to accomplish.

What was it like to see your screenplay being turned into a film?
Once I started shooting I wasn't thinking about the script any more. Through the course of pre-production the movie has become something else. It's the reality of the movie you're dealing with and not the reality of the script. But I knew that the script had something to say. Halfway into pre-production the script is important but after that I think the film-making naturally took over.

Once you started shooting did you feel that your struggle had been vindicated?
Yes, totally. There's only one thing I can do. I can make movies. And in making movies I can only direct. The other stuff I'm not up to the professional level. And I can do home cooking. But those are the only two things I can do. I know a little bit about how to do interviews because I have to sell the movie. I manage to do that not well but okay. But that's about it.

Was there anything you discovered you didn't like about directing?
I don't like quick decisions. I don't like not hiring the person you worked with the last time. You decide to work with somebody else and you say how much you appreciate them and the next time you don't hire them. That part I probably hate the most. Fast decisions are part of the job. Once I get used to it I can't really say I hate them. Like all directors, I hate it when things don't go smoothly. Sometimes you have to decide whether to be a nice guy or a good director. Sometimes you have to give people a hard time to accomplish something on screen. For certain things you know the actors are too secure in their performance and are not giving you the real thing. So you freak them out. That's a moment I hate. It's nasty. If I freak them out, I feel terrible. If I don't get the performance, I feel terrible too. I just hate to be in that spot either way. It's something I hate about directing.

What did the post-production period teach you?
The thing I learnt most from editing is how a film works structurally. Shooting is like buying grocery. The real cooking is on the editing table. Of course the better the ingredients, the more chance you have of making a good film. But the cooking is the post-production. Usually that's my most happiest time, I'm in New York so I can go home. That's my ideal of a film-maker's life: I can make movies and I can cook. I don't have to deal with actors. I can think about the film on my way to the editing room. I can think about what I want to do and see how it works. It's really pleasurable. The first part of editing is relearning your footage. Just like when you make your movie you have to drop the script at some point, when you edit you have to drop the experience of shooting. When I sit next to the editor, I participate in every cut, in everything, up to mixing, every sound. I think that's a part of film-making.

How did you feel when you saw the first cut?
I felt very moved. But I was alone. They were speaking in Chinese and there weren't any subtitles so nobody apart from me knew exactly what they were talking about – including the editor. Post-production took about two months. Then I fine-cut for three months or so. The next thing you know it's in theatres.

What reaction did the film get when you showed it in Taiwan?
It was great. There was a première in Taiwan. It was packed and people totally fell for it. They were totally moved. It was a hit right away. We won the Golden Horse which is our Oscar in Taiwan. It was great. It was a very moving experience. But it didn't go outside of Taiwan; it showed in Hong Kong for a week and then it was gone. It didn't go anywhere. But it got me the chance to do *The Wedding Banquet* and that was an international hit. Its success was like a base hit not a home run. That sent me out to do the home run that was *The Wedding Banquet*. In some ways I think a director's real task is their second film. You're not established until you have a successful second film. Everybody has a story to tell. If you're talented,

if you manage to finish the film, there's something to watch. But whether you can have a career or not depends on your second film not your first film. The first film is lovely. It's a honeymoon, something fresh. Even if it's full of flaws, there's still something to watch. The second film shows you have the real thing that can last, that you're a real film-maker. You can be fresh but you have to keep growing.

Do you think your style has developed as you've become more a experienced director?
I think it's become more refined. I have more ways of expressing myself. Since *Eat Drink Man Woman* and particularly *The Ice Storm*, I've used the movie more as a provocation than a medium, a way of provoking thoughts and emotions rather than the movie expressing me. *Pushing Hands*, and my earlier films, was a lot of me, me, me. I don't think I gave the audience any credit. I just wanted to tell them about me, about what I know. The more movies I make, the more I found the essence of movie-making is about the viewer. You just provide a stimuli and let them decide. So I'm taking a step back. It's a skill to do that. I don't think it's quite possible for somebody on their first film. I think the first film is a lot about the film-maker, especially if you're making it low budget, as I did. You want to express yourself. There's so many stories you want to tell. And even if you struggle to finish the film, it still exists; even though you do things clumsily, you have bad luck, you make two hundred decisions every day, you struggle with everything, if it's not you then what is it?

P. J. Hogan: *Muriel's Wedding*

What were you doing when you first started going to movies and thinking 'This is wonderful'?
I think I was being shunned by my peers. So movies were really an escape. I grew up in a small town on the north coast of New South Wales, called Tweed Heads, which I later mocked mercilessly in *Muriel's Wedding*. In the first draft of the script, I called it Porpoise Heads and then thought it was perhaps too close to the actual inspiration. So I changed it to Porpoise Spit. But I didn't enjoy growing up in that town. Like Porpoise Spit, it was very small, and small-minded. I always felt like the odd man out; so did my brothers and sisters, in fact. We were the odd family out!

So Muriel *was in many ways autobiographical?*
I've always said that Muriel was me; but in fact the story was inspired by my sister. She always says, 'You told me you were going to tell my story, but you really told yours.' I think it became a combination of the two.

When did you actually discover movies yourself?
To be honest, movies always seemed to be there. My mother always had the television on and if there was a movie, she would always watch it, no matter what. So I saw everything: the bad and the good. I kept a diary briefly when I was ten years old and I remember writing one day that I had seen two great films that day, *Citizen Kane* and *The Ghost of Mr Chicken*. And you know what? I loved them both equally. I didn't see that one was great and one was crap. I was really touched reading that entry, because at that time movies were a form of entertainment and escape for me.

So you saw movies mostly on TV. Did you go to the cinema?
A lot; and I preferred it, because the films were bigger and more involving and they weren't smashed up by commercials. There was only one cinema in Tweed Heads and they would often keep a movie on for weeks and weeks. I remember in the mid-seventies there was almost an entire year when the only film you could see was *The Towering Inferno*. It was so profitable that the theatre just didn't pull it. So I actually saw this awful movie twenty times!

When did you start to make an attempt to discover other kinds of films?
When I was a teenager. At school what I was best at was writing, telling stories. But it took me a long time to realize that films were written. It was like the quote

in *Sunset Boulevard*. I believed actors made it up as they went along. I didn't know that somebody sat down and wrote it. And when I realized that, I suppose I saw that there was an opening for me. I was very naive about how a film was made. I didn't know what editing was. What I did know about the director indicated to me that that was *the* job to have.

And did you try to make any films at this stage?
I remember coveting this great camera and trying to save up to buy it, but never quite getting there and always spending the money on something else. I did have a stills camera so I took photographs. But no, I was mainly writing. At this point I was getting a lot of pressure from my father and mother to be a journalist because my father was a part-time sports journalist, covering sporting events in Tweed Heads. He was a real jock. So was my brother. That made it really difficult for me because I was a total wimp. So I thought, well, I can't play sport. I should do the family proud and write about it. But I never got that far.

What kinds of things were you writing as a teenager?
My first attempts at screenplays were comedies. I felt that the films I could emulate most successfully were the films that Mel Brooks made: parodies. Everything I wrote at this point was a parody of a movie. They were never any good, they were just fun.

What took you from writing screenplays as a hobby to treating it more seriously?
I had an interview with the careers advisor at my school, the Tweed River High. I'd already heard that my prospects weren't good. I turned up for the meeting and he wasn't there. So I went to his filing cabinet and looked up 'Film'. There was a file there with only one thing in it: a handbook for the Australian Film and Television School. So I stole it. It was an impulsive act. I had no idea that there was a film school you could go to. But I found this handbook and felt like a scientist who'd found the cure for the disease that was afflicting him. I read it from cover to cover and it was like a dream come true. I thought, this is what I want. I want to get into this school. And I had a month until the deadline.

What did you have to provide?
Photographs, evidence that suggested you were creative. I had photographs. And I wrote a screenplay just for them. It was about thirty pages long and it was pretty terrible. But I just sent all this stuff off and didn't tell anybody. I was then shocked because I got a phone call from an officious voice saying I had made it to the interview stage and they were going to fly me to Sydney. They told me over the phone that it was unlikely I would get in because I was seventeen and they usually didn't accept students that age; they liked you to have a little bit of life experience. But they thought that I showed enough promise to warrant an interview and perhaps it would be beneficial. Just the trip to Sydney was an exciting prospect for me! The interview process was actually a whole day's work and the interview was

part of it. There were four tests you had to sit and do. In one you had to edit some film. They showed me how to use a Steenbeck, which I'd never done before. They sat me down and this old Australian editor said, 'This is backwards. This is forwards. This is the splicer.' And I found the splicer really difficult. But I was a sponge: I soaked everything up. I managed to cut this footage together. There were these shots that had no connection with each other and you had to put them together and write a little script for them to suggest a story. I spent a couple of hours doing that and loved it. That was the test I really shone in. So they accepted me and I was placed in the editing workshop.

So, aged seventeen and having applied on an impulse, you got in?
Yeah. As it turned out they accepted another seventeen-year-old who was one month younger than me, so I couldn't claim I was the youngest there – which disappointed me! It was a three-year course. Most of the students were in their midtwenties to early thirties, and a lot of them found it difficult to commit to three years. But it was just marvellous for me because I needed three years to discover myself, as a person as well as a film-maker. I can't underestimate the importance of film school. It was revelatory to me. It got me out of Tweed Heads. And I loved working with the other students and living in Sydney. I discovered foreign films. I had never seen French films, Japanese films. Bertolucci was my new god. I never knew that you could move a camera like that. His shots were operatic and just brilliant. I also discovered Australian films. I had been totally unaware of the resurgence of the Australian film industry during the seventies, the work of Peter Weir and Fred Schepisi. I hadn't seen *The Devil's Playground* or *The Last Wave*. In Tweed Heads you didn't go to see Australian films. You were lucky if they got into the cinema. But if they did play, you didn't go see them because they were Australian.

Why?
Well, the Australians traditionally hate their own art. I remember how shocked my parents were when Patrick White won the Nobel Prize for Literature because he was Australian and my mother hadn't liked the book very much. He wasn't very complimentary to Australia. My mother always described Australian writers or entertainers that she admired as an 'asset to Australia'. So there was a lot of having to show the world that we were somehow well-bred, that we had class. And I don't really know how you show that except by not causing any trouble and not being rude.

What about the technical side? Were you learning?
The fact that you could change lenses, vary the size of your shots – that was a major discovery. And of course I was learning about editing. I still love editing. I think it's a language that film has developed and is exclusive to film. It's in the editing room, for me, where you direct the film for a second time; and that's where you really have to get it right. But at school I proved to be a terrible editor,

because I didn't like having to cut it the way the director wanted. I thought my ideas were so much better than these student directors.

Did you get to try out those ideas and make your own films?
They had lots of equipment and it was all free. In my first two years I shot a lot of video stuff and cut it together. It was all pretty crappy but fun. And there were exercises that the school required of us which involved using a film camera. So we had a certain amount of film to play with. You had a limited budget allotted to make a film, but I kept my budget for my final third-year film because I wanted to spend everything I had on one film; which in retrospect was the wisest thing I ever did. The big thing for me was being with other film students. I was lucky because I was in a very good year, very talented people. I met Jocelyn Moorhouse, whom I later married. Alex Proyas. Jane Campion.

Inspiring company?
Very. All of them knew a lot more about film-making than I did. And they also really had a sense of themselves. They knew who they were. That took me a long time to discover. At film school I wanted to be other film-makers; whoever I happened to be impressed by at the moment; whereas Jane Campion always wanted to make her own movies. But I felt very embarrassed about my life. The whole three years at film school I refused to talk about my family, or where I was from. I just thought it wasn't good enough. So there was no way I was going to make personal movies because I was refusing to acknowledge that self. It wasn't until I left film school that I began to look back. I would tell stories about my family to Jocelyn and she'd laugh and say some of them were so funny! And I realized she was right. If I had anything to say as a film-maker I had to start with me.

Can you tell me about your graduation film?
I wrote a couple of screenplays and showed them to a few people I was close to, like Jocelyn and Jane. And they were very critical. Basically, they said, 'These aren't you. Why should you want to make something that doesn't mean anything?' I thought about that and decided, well, they're right. So I wrote a screenplay about something that had happened to me, and that was the one that everybody responded to, the one that the school wanted me to make. It was called *Getting Wet*. It was the usual film-maker's coming-of-age film, the-summer-I-became-a-man kind of tale. But it did have my sense of humour. It was really my first step toward embracing the odd and the eccentric. And it was actually very successful for a short film and won quite a few awards.

Can you say in a nutshell what the film was about?
It was about two brothers. The older brother is something of a stud and the younger brother is a geek. And the family goes off on holiday. The mother is a hypochondriac so she takes along a young woman as a housekeeper. The younger brother lusts after her but the older brother scores with her and the younger

brother is furious and betrays them both. The young woman is sent away and the older brother beats up the younger brother. It was really, really simple. But it had something – something that I found I couldn't actually repeat. It was confusing for me because I didn't quite know why it worked.

Did you get it into the cinema?
No, because it was twenty-six minutes long, too long to support a feature. So it wasn't really seen outside the festival circuit. But it got me a lot of attention. I had meetings with producers who'd say, well, do you have something you'd like to develop? And I had nothing. I hadn't taken the next step. There were a couple of movies that I met a producer for; but they were probably right not to hire me, because I was very young. Also these were movies that meant nothing to me. I mean, what do I know about middle-aged couples' marriages breaking up? So I did meetings and waited for the phone to ring – waited for them to think of me for something. And they didn't. So I ended up doing television.

Was there a viable film industry at this point in Australia, in Sydney? Was it humming?
It was, but it was bad timing because when I graduated in 1984 the government was supporting the film industry with tax incentives and there was one incentive in particular which meant that if you invested in a feature film you could write it off. That meant there was a flood of terrible movies financed by people with lots of money and no taste. And in a way it killed the Australian film industry. Historically, if you look at Australia's film output from the mid-seventies to now, the eighties were a fallow period. Peter Weir, Bruce Beresford, Fred Schepisi had all left, and yet there were more movies being made than ever. Truly awful movies. And you know what? I couldn't even get one of the awful ones!

So you took refuge in television. What did you do?
Somebody who took a class at the film school asked me to develop television shows for a network. They had this drama unit in the middle of nowhere, it wasn't even attached to the station. They put me in an office where I was supposed to think up TV shows. But I took their money and did nothing much. In fact I worked on a feature script. I thought I had got it right and spent years trying to get it made. I actually got really close. We were in pre-production and then all the money fell through. It was devastating. But that disaster led to *Muriel*.

How?
I was rapidly approaching thirty, and the best film I had made was when I was twenty-one. In between I'd done a lot of TV writing and got some TV shows made. I felt like what little talent I had, I'd trashed by working in television. If you write for television, you are rewritten as a matter of course. And they won't even tell you. When you see it there's very little of you left. And even though I was making enough money to survive, it was dispiriting work. I wanted to direct television but they wouldn't give me a chance.

Had you directed any TV yet?
I had one isolated outbreak of directing in the mid-eighties, 1985. I managed to do a television film called *The Humpty Dumpty Man* and it was a really horrible experience. It was the story of a very minor political scandal in Australia, a typical Australian scandal, in fact: a scandal that wasn't one at all. A man called David Coombe was accused by ASIO – the Australian Central Intelligence Organisation – Central spelt with an S! – of being a spy because he was friendly with a Russian diplomat who was a KGB agent and Coombe didn't know this. He was a lobbyist and he knew a lot of politicians but he had nothing to sell. He was hounded by the press, and then when they couldn't find anything on him, they forgot about it. A producer, Miranda Bank, wanted to do the story and it was literally one of those stories that was so boring you couldn't find anybody to direct it. She was a big fan of my first short film and I had met her at the Australian Film Institute Awards when I won an award for Best Short Film of the Year. As it happened she remembered me and sought me out, and said, 'Are you interested in this?' I said, 'Of course.' I wasn't, not at all, but I was desperate to direct. So I said that I had a great deal of interest in David Coombe and the injustice that had befallen him! Then a friend and I tried to rewrite the screenplay as a spy thriller, which was just ridiculous. I reverted to my old impulse, which is to make somebody else's movie. In this case I think I wanted to be Brian De Palma. It was made for eight hundred thousand dollars and we shot it on 16 mm. The shoot was a lot of fun but the film wasn't very good. It was never very coherent. It took two years to get on television and that was in a recut and remixed form. After the first cut, I was fired from the film. But I still take a lot of responsibility for it. Maybe if I was the producer I would have fired me too. Although it made even less sense after the producer recut it. I looked around at the end of it and I realized I was the Humpty Dumpty Man!

So back to your feature script.
So I'd been working on feature screenplays because I thought, well, the only way to direct is to write a screenplay everybody thinks is great and then when they want to make it, I'm the one they have to ask to direct. And it was a script called *It's Now or Never*. It turned out to be quite a prophetic title. I was particularly fascinated by Australian swimmers of the fifties, because Australians have always taken a great deal of pride in their sporting heroes and in the fifties we ruled the pool. The script was about a small town with one claim to fame, a swimming star of Olympic standards. But this kid is also very unstable and the town is trying to keep him from cracking up, but he does. He fails and the town turns on him. It was very dark but structurally really sound. And it was about something that meant a lot to me, which is failing. And people really responded to the screenplay. There were several producers who wanted to make it but it was expensive because it was period.

And you were attached to direct it?
Yes. In fact it landed in the hands of Fred Schepisi who had a production house at the time. He loved it and supported it. So I got a producer and Fred was an executive producer but in the end he just gave me some script notes, said good luck and was gone. The producer worked for years to try and raise the money and when he did raise the money it actually wasn't really enough money. It was enough to get us started but three weeks into pre-production, after I had fully cast, we lost the money. I'd been involved with this for two or three years and then it was just – one day it was gone. And I remember the saddest thing: we had a party to say farewell to each other and everybody on the crew, right down to the runner, had another job lined up. But I had nothing because this film had been everything to me. And I had no money because I had been working for free. So I was devastated. And that was my lowest point. That was in the late eighties. So I decided that I would write something I knew a lot about and that was feeling like a flop. As it happened, my sister was going through a hard time. We were having lots of conversations on the phone and she was telling me stories of her life in Tweed Heads. I thought there was a story there.

She was still in Tweed Heads?
Yes. She and my father had a very stormy relationship. They had got her a job selling cosmetics but she embezzled money from him, forging his signature on cheques. And when the shit hit the fan, she disappeared. She was missing for almost a year. She didn't contact any of us. And everyone was calling me thinking she could be with me, but she wasn't. Then finally she called me. She'd been living in Sydney for a year with a friend but was too scared to contact anyone because she'd stolen close to fifteen thousand Australian dollars and there was no way she could pay it back.

This sounds very close to the plot of Muriel!
Well, yeah. Right after *It's Now or Never*, I thought, I understand why she stole the money. It was her escape. She'd done a terrible thing. She had stolen money from our parents and left them in dire financial straits. But I understood why she did it. And so I felt that was a good beginning for a story. I had also been toying with this idea for a story of a young girl who longs to get married. And then I put the two together.

You said that you used to sit and drink coffee in the bar opposite a bridal store?
Yeah and try and think of ideas for movies that would save me. The coffee shop was right opposite a bridal wear store. And it was wonderful to watch because you would see these young girls go in and then appear in the window as brides. They were just so happy they were glowing from within. And the mothers were usually weeping.

Was it a gradual process of putting these two storylines together? Or was it more 'Eureka!'?

No, it was more like watching two elephants coming together to mate. I gradually realized that to tell my sister's story I needed something that would embody her dream. My sister's dream was to get married. So then I locked into marriage as escape and also marriage as a way of fulfilling one's idea of oneself. When Muriel marries, she marries not for love but to prove to everybody that she is a worthwhile person; worthy of marriage, worthy of being loved. What Muriel wants more than anything is to conform. And that's what I wanted when I was a kid, a teenager. I wanted not to stand out. I wanted to be just like everybody else. I couldn't bear it if anybody said that I was eccentric or odd, even if they meant it as a compliment.

What were you living on while you were writing Muriel? *Were you having a hard time financially?*
Oh yeah. Jocelyn and I were both broke. Her career was not much healthier than mine at that time. I became unemployable in television because I was too difficult. I would fight for my scripts and I would refuse to change them and if they changed them I'd take my name off them. So, my television credits are in fact quite extensive but don't look that way because I took my name off so many projects. Jocelyn was writing for television too, but she never took her name off things because she just expected it to happen. But eventually the work dried up and we couldn't afford to pay our rent so we had to let our flat go. Thankfully Jocelyn's sister and her husband took us in, because there was no alternative. There was no way I was going back to my parents in Tweed Heads. It was a dark period. The only work Jocelyn could get was writing a romantic novel for the *Women's Weekly*, which she wrote under a pseudonym and denies she ever did.

It sounds like you paid your dues.
It was a very dreary time in our lives. But we were both working on screenplays. I wrote a very detailed thirty-page treatment for *Muriel's Wedding* first, because I had to plot it out. Then I sent it into the Australian Film Commission, asking for five thousand Australian dollars to write the screenplay. But they rejected it, rather brutally in fact. Two film-makers were brought in to do an assessment along with an AFC assessor and all three of them told me that this should never be made; that it was terrible. They didn't mince their words. So I thought, I can't win. They are telling me my actual life is terrible. I remember their argument was that Muriel was a thief, a compulsive liar, that she had no redeeming qualities whatsoever and no talent! They said, why should they care about somebody like this? I remember one of them saying, 'If you were to write this screenplay, you would have to give Muriel a talent. You would have to find her "well of creativity".' And I remember saying to them, 'But the point is that this is a girl who can't sing, can't dance, can't write, and yet she wants to be the star of her own life. How does she do this? Just because you're creative people doesn't mean that everybody out there has a talent. Some of us don't and Muriel doesn't. It was very important to me that Muriel be untalented.

So they turned you down?

Yes. And I went into a depression. But what saved me from despair was that during this time Jocelyn had written a screenplay called *Proof*. It was very important to her, very personal. And it got financed. It was a very low budget film but it took off. And Russell Crowe went from not doing *It's Now or Never* to doing *Proof*. Also we had our first child. So while Jocelyn made *Proof*, I was looking after our son, Spike. Jocelyn was also earning some money so we could rent a place of our own. The success of Proof then gave me enough confidence to begin the screenplay of *Muriel's Wedding*. I eventually got some money from Film Victoria, which was a smaller funding body than the AFC. It was even less than the five thousand Australian dollars I had requested from the AFC. I wrote the screenplay in three months. And then took another two years to get it made!

How did it evolve?

I always saw the story as dark because that's how I was feeling. But when I talked about it to people, it would come out as funny. I couldn't talk about my father without making people laugh. What was funny about my father was that he was a big beefy man yet he had such paltry expectations of us. He wanted us to finish High School and maybe go to college. He wanted me to play football and he wanted me to be popular and I couldn't even achieve those simple things! It was like I was failing my father on the most elemental level. I was just glad he didn't add breathing to that because I probably would have found a way to have failed at that, too. And my father would get apoplectic: what do you mean, you can't kick up a football? What do you mean you can't run? Everybody can run! I remember the first time he put me on a football field. I caught the football between my legs and he was humiliated. I jumped for it and I caught it between my thighs and he was so embarrassed. He looked at me, like, you just should have missed it!

Did the story go through many drafts?

No, the first draft was long and I cut it down. After that, I was just polishing. So I would say there were two drafts.

How do you work? Do you start at the beginning and work to the end?

I always know that there are four or five scenes that are the reason I want to write the script. I write those first and if I'm lucky they trigger other scenes, and at the end of it I sometimes have a structure for the film. I try to write lots and lots of scenes for the characters, some that I know are just teaching me things about the characters. The difficult thing for *Muriel* was when and where to start the story. It seems elementary now but I think in the first draft I started it well before that point. There was a lot more with Muriel's family than there was in the final screenplay.

What did you do once you had a script?

Jocelyn was the producer and we used the production house that had produced *Proof* for her. They loved the script and they sent it all round the world. *Proof* went to a lot of film festivals, all around the world. So we would go along with it and I would have my screenplay under my arm, to give to everybody. I don't think there was a company that did not get a screenplay of *Muriel's Wedding*. Jocelyn's name got them to read it but that's as far as it got. Nobody wanted to make it. It was always the same thing: 'We've never heard of P. J. Hogan, so the script has to be really great. And we don't think it is. It doesn't seem to know if it's a drama or a comedy.' And they all had a problem with Muriel. Nobody wanted to make a movie where the main character was unsympathetic. When you meet her she is already a shoplifter and a liar. So it was very hard for people to see what there was to like about her. The other thing they said was, 'Does she have to be fat?'

So you were hawking around your screenplay. Who were you trying? Distributors?
Yes. We sent it to Miramax, Fineline. But they didn't know me, which was a problem. Another problem was that we sent supporting material to show I could direct and unfortunately, in addition to sending my short film I also sent the tele-movie because I thought at least it showed that I'd done some directing apart from the short film. I was very aware that the short film had 1983 on its credits. What had I been doing for ten years?! So I put *The Humpty Dumpty Man* in. And it didn't help at all. In fact, it made things worse. I'd have been better off just sending the short film and cutting off the credits. A lot of people who might have shown interest in the screenplay were put off by *The Humpty Dumpty Man* and I don't blame them for that. We then got close to an American company who supposedly had money and they wanted to make the film with me if I could interest somebody like Juliette Lewis. But she was totally not the right person to play Muriel. I wanted an Australian actress and an actress who was the character I had written. A girl who thought she was unattractive, who always had a weight problem. That was really important to the screenplay.

How were you feeling by this point?
What really got me through was that Jocelyn and Lynda [House] really believed in it. Even though we received a lot of negative comments about the screenplay, there were always some very positive comments too. The only problem was that the good comments came from people without money to invest in the script. And bad comments from anybody who could finance the movie. But we never stopped believing in it. I just knew in my gut that the screenplay was good, and that I knew what to do with it. I don't write screenplays that are full of hyperbole. I dislike that as a director. I like the screenplay direction to be very spare.

Hyperbole in the sense of direction?
A lot of American screenplays are full of purple prose. They write the feeling of the scene. You know: 'Jim walks into the room. You can tell immediately that he

is a man of heart and he is a good looking guy and he looks at Jane and – it's love.' At least ninety per cent of that you can't show with a camera. In Hollywood the screenplays that they rave about and often make are written that way. A studio executive will finish the screenplay and say, 'Wow, I can really see this is a film.' And of course they can. The film's been explained to them. They don't have to use their imagination at all. I'm as susceptible as anybody to hype in a screenplay, because it livens things up. You go, wow, of course, that's exactly what I want to feel at this moment; what I want the audience to feel. The trouble is, it's not there in the scene.

So going back – how did you find a chink in the wall of indifference you'd been encountering?

I was getting very close to giving up but there was one company we hadn't tried: Ciby 2000. Lynda had enquired about whether or not we should send them the screenplay and they told her they never worked with first-time directors, only with film-makers who had something of a track record. And their output of films at that time was small but reflected that philosophy. They'd just made *The Piano* which was a huge success. They'd supported Mike Leigh and David Lynch. So we didn't bother. But finally as we were reaching the end of our resources, we thought, what the hell? We may as well be turned down by everybody. So we sent the screenplay to this wonderful woman called Wendy Palmer in the sales department. She read it and rang us to say that she loved it. For the first time we actually had somebody within a company that had money who loved it. She also told me, two years too late, that I should stop sending *The Humpty Dumpty Man* out with the script! Because she saw that and it made her think twice. But she really believed in the screenplay.

So was it plain sailing from then on?

Not at all. Wendy hastened to add that she was in sales, so she didn't green-light movies. Her support was important but not necessary. There were films that she hadn't liked that they'd made. They just asked her whether or not she thought she could sell them. But she said she thought she could sell *Muriel's Wedding* and was going to recommend it. What then happened was that Wendy rang Lynda and said she'd heard rumours that Ciby 2000 was going to turn us down. There were eight people on the board who had to pass each film unanimously. Muriel had evenly divided them, but there was one member of the board with a lot of sway who hated the script. So it was going to be a 'No'. But I had one card to play, and only one. Jane Campion was a friend of mine. I called her and I said, 'The Ciby 2000 board is about to decide my fate, and we've heard it's going to be a "No". And this is something that really means a lot to me. Would you do me a favour? Would you write them a letter and fax it to them?' Jane said, 'What do you want me to say?' I said, 'I want you to gush about me as a film-maker. You haven't read the screenplay, and you don't have to claim you have. I just want you to say any nice thing you can bear saying. They don't know who I am but they know who you are. I don't know if it will help, but it can't hurt.' And Jane said she would do it. Now, I had no way of knowing if she would or not, and we really had a clock ticking because they were going to meet that day. But Jane sat down and typed up this letter raving about me as a film-maker, then faxed it to the president of the company, Jean-François Fonlupt. The timing couldn't have been better. As the fax was being handed to Fonlupt, the board was rejecting the script. But Fonlupt then ran down and said, 'Tell me about this screenplay, *Muriel's Wedding*.' When he was told that the board had just rejected it, he said, 'The board have not rejected it until I have read it because I am the president.' So the board was put on hold and the screenplay was sent up to Fonlupt's office. He locked the door and read it, said yes and we had our money. It was extraordinary. I was going to dedicate the film to Jane but eventually I just thanked her in the end credits because I thought she would find it mortally embarrassing if I dedicated the whole film to her. But without Jane it really would never have been made.

Did you get all the money you wanted?
We went to the Film Finance Corporation in Australia and they financed half of it and Ciby 2000 financed the other half. But the FFC would never finance an Australian Film completely. You had to have fifty per cent of your budget from another source. So we came to them with the Ciby 2000 money. The FFC wanted our budget lowered so we had to lop half a million Australian dollars off it. We had to do it for two million Australian dollars and we wanted two and a half.

Were there any other parts of the jigsaw that you had to put together before you could actually get the film underway? For example, the music?
That came later. I didn't pursue Abba for their permission until we had the money. Then they said no. And we found out that Abba had never licensed their music to a film, though they'd been asked several times. They had never licensed it to television shows, never licensed it at all for any exploitation other than their own. Of course the music was absolutely essential to Muriel's character and nobody thought that Abba would say no. But they did. We sent them a screenplay with a letter begging them to read it. We got a message from their assistant saying, 'They won't read it, and even if they did, it would still be "No".' So Lynda House asked the assistant to read it, and she did, and she loved it. So she said, 'Look, I don't know if I can promise you anything because they have never said yes, but I'll tell you what to do. Keep up the flattering letters.' So I did, and she got them to read the screenplay. They liked it. But they still said no. I thought, what can I do? We just kept at them. I would send them a letter once a week. And I was shameless. I compared them to the Beatles. I think I called them good looking. I just did everything! Finally I said to Lynda, I can't replace them. I'm going to fly to Sweden and hang out on their doorstep till they say yes to me. Lynda said,

before we do that, let's warn them that you are coming so that they're there. So she said to them, 'P. J. Hogan is flying to Sweden.'

Purely to hassle you?
Yeah. She sent them a photocopy of my air ticket and they said yes. In fact, on the day I was meant to fly, I came down with the measles and was laid up in bed. We were two weeks away from shooting and I had horrible spots all over me. And the only good thing that happened to me while I was sick was that Abba said yes, so I didn't have to go to drag my spotted carcass on to a plane and fly over there and infect everyone! They wouldn't have let me out of the country anyway. But I had to have Abba. What would the film have been without Abba? It's Muriel's music!

Why?
When I was a kid I spent a lot of time alone in my room listening to music and Abba was the music I listened to most of the time. I suppose I wanted to have the life that their songs suggested. Their sad songs really spoke to me. And I wanted Muriel to like music that was out of date, music that you couldn't justify, music that wasn't cool. But it also had to be emotionally right for her. And Abba just seemed to be it. The song that convinced me that it had to be Abba was 'Dancing Queen' because it's an uplifting song, but there is a melancholy in it, as there is in many of Abba's best songs. I wanted the film to be uplifting but I knew it was going to be melancholic as well. That's why I was not going to let Abba go. I was not going to give them permission to say no.

By now it was long time since you'd directed anything. Did you feel confident?
I never felt rusty as a director and I don't know why. I just felt that it was what I was meant to do. I also had a lot of time to think about *Muriel's Wedding*. A lot of time. I was scared, wondering if I could do it but I always thought I could. Another thing that worried me was that I knew that this was my last shot at it. If I didn't get this right, if this was another *Humpty Dumpty Man*, that was it for me. I would be an ex-film-maker and deservedly so. You can screw up so easily as a film-maker. But if you worry about that too much, you won't take risks. And all film-making is a risk. Listening to your instincts on the set is a risk and you have to do that to make something of value.

After the struggle to raise the money, how did you begin to prepare for the movie?
I remember we cast for a very long time. We started looking very early, before pre-production. We all knew it was going to be hard to cast Muriel and Rhonda because we couldn't think of anybody. Even the part of Muriel's mother, a really key part, wasn't cast until three days before we started shooting. For Muriel, I think I saw every young actress in Australia who was willing to play the part, whether they had had any experience or not. Nobody sprung to mind. Why would they? Overweight actresses don't get work. Toni Collette was somebody the casting director talked about a lot. She was an actress who had a lot of diffi-

culty getting work because she didn't look like everybody else. When she came in I thought she's really good but I'm not sure she's right. And I went on looking for Muriel for another month. But I kept thinking about Toni. I think I needed to see all these other people to prove that it was her. Often I find that's what casting is: a process of elimination. Toni desperately wanted the role and I was asking a great deal. I wanted an actress who was ready to gain weight because I knew there was going to be a scene where she was dressed in a white satin pant suit and you couldn't fake her thighs. And Toni was willing to do it. She said, 'I'll be paid to gain weight for this. That will make it a pleasure.' But I don't think she found it a pleasure in the end.

What about Rhonda?
I thought I'd find Rhonda in Sydney because I thought Rhonda was a real Sydney part. The good time gal! But I couldn't find anybody who was right. So I decided to go down to Melbourne as well. Rachel Griffiths came in and didn't look like anything I'd imagined. Whereas Muriel was plump and plain, Rachel was tall, thin and quite beautiful. But when she sat down and read it, I knew it was her. I almost gave her the role in the room but I wanted to show Jocelyn and Lynda the tape. By that time I was pretty certain it was going to be Toni so I knew that they were really going to click. So I put them together and then I cast them both. And when I was working with them I knew I was lucky to have them because they were terrific.

Given the story was partly inspired by events in your own family, were the locations important to you?
Definitely. We couldn't afford to build the sets so I knew it was going to have to be found. What I wanted to achieve was how I remembered my home town and how I saw Sydney. It was very important to me how Porpoise Spit looked so I combed the Gold Coast for locations. And I knew I had to find stand-in locations in Sydney. In the end we shot about three or four days on the Gold Coast and the rest around the beachside suburbs in Sydney. Porpoise Spit itself was shot in my home town, Tweed Heads.

So you actually did go back?
I didn't want to. I was a little embarrassed that my dad would recognize himself as a character in the film. And if I showed his town then that would be a dead give-away. But it was the only town that looked right in the frame. It had those three tall apartment buildings and the beautiful ocean and the beach. And it was all very compact: two hills on either side. And it was the only thing that I could actually film in a wide shot and it said, 'town'. The rest of the Gold Coast is very sprawling. It's actually a series of buildings. And although not many people live there, and it's only alive during the summer, it looks like a bustling metropolis because of those tall buildings. And Porpoise Spit couldn't look like a bustling metropolis. It had to be a small town. You had to want to escape from it and feel

that Muriel's boundaries were what you were seeing. I also thought, it has to be Tweed Heads because Tweed Heads was the inspiration for the story.

You talked earlier about the dark and light in the script. Did you try to reflect this in the look of the film? For example, the bright, cartoon colours of the beach and clubs contrasted to the gloomy interiors of Muriel's parents' home?

We did talk a lot about colour. The thing about the Gold Coast is that they like their entertainment gaudy: everything is brash and 'in your face'. So I knew that there would be no such thing as bad taste when it came to the decor. I was having a lot of trouble finding the right night club for the scene where Muriel is dumped by her friends, and then we went to this cavernous place in Sydney. It was an Italian restaurant and the first thing I remember about it was there were no windows. There was virtually no natural light whatsoever and then as your eyes adjusted you noticed that the walls were covered in shells – this ocean theme. It was dark and claustrophobic, so unlike an ocean it didn't feel free. You just felt closed in, in this cave without water. And it felt right. This is where Muriel's friends would dump her. This is where the worst thing that happens to her in Tweed Heads would happen. In this horrible dark place. What I like to do is photograph all my locations, make a big book so I can see the location for scene seven right before the location for scene eight and then I became aware that some scenes were open and some scenes were very closed. Some scenes in the location were light and some scenes were very dark and generally what I knew was that when Muriel came to Sydney I wanted a sense of freedom for her.

When you are looking at locations, do you have a sense immediately of how you are going to cover a scene?

I always have a little game I play with myself if I'm sitting waiting for somebody or I'm stuck somewhere I don't want to be, which is 'how would I shoot a scene in this location?' I believe there are some film-makers who just have a great eye visually. They can shoot a location, any location, and bring out what's interesting or eccentric in it. I've never considered myself one of those film-makers because when I get to a location, I either know how to shoot a scene or I don't. I really react to a location emotionally. If I can't see my scene working here, I'll feel like I just want to leave it. On *Muriel's Wedding*, I was driving everybody crazy with the churches. We looked at so many churches before I decided on Muriel's church. Nobody could understand why I was rejecting so many churches because all churches look pretty much alike.

Why do you think it was?

It's hard for me to say. The church I chose didn't have much natural light. I never saw Muriel's wedding as a good thing. It was when Muriel was selling out. I felt that the high point in the wedding scene was when Muriel appeared in her dress. What I loved about the church was that it had a beautiful vestal. That's a really important shot, Muriel coming in through the door, back-lit. I'm always very aware where the sun is and where the light will be coming from and I try to go see the location in the morning and afternoon, particularly if I'm shooting there the whole day. I knew that in the afternoon Muriel would be back-lit as she came in through the vestal. I knew I was going to shoot that at the end of the day and that I wanted it to be almost Dickensian as she walked down the aisle.

What do you mean, Dickensian?
Blackish, dark. With light from the building itself, not from sunlight coming in through the windows. I think that was the only time the DP, Martin McGrath, used smoke to diffuse the light. It just didn't feel right for it to be open and sunny.

As you were going around looking at these locations, did you find that you had very clear ideas of what you wanted and how you thought a scene would work?
Sometimes not. With the Heslop house, where the family lived, I knew that I wanted an open kitchen and the lounge room off the kitchen. That's because that's the kind of kitchen I grew up in.

Sitting watching TV!
Yeah. And I wanted the mother to be part of the family yet separate. The kitchen was her little island and you needed to see her, standing in it, even while you were aware of the family. The house we found was a very old run-down house but it had windows all around the lounge room right up the side of the house. So it was always sunny. What I noticed about it was that you were always aware of the outside but you felt closed in. I knew that the Heslop kids never went out. They would stay indoors and watch television and the mother hardly ever went out. The only one who would go out was the father. So I knew that I wanted a suggestion of the outside world but at the same time wanted to feel enclosed so it was like a fish tank with these strange stunted fish swimming in it.

At what point do you start thinking about where you are going to put the camera?
I suppose at the writing stage, I am thinking about how it will look in pictures. And then when I look out for a location, there is usually something that strikes me as 'yes, that would be a really nice moment'. When I came into the Heslop family house, it worked in every area. It worked in the lounge room, it worked in the father's bedroom, the hall really worked. I knew from people's reactions to the script that I had to be very careful with the character of Muriel. I wanted you to experience the story as if you were Muriel. I wanted your identification to be with her constantly. I wanted the audience to identify with this big, plain girl who lies and loves Abba. I never wanted to do any shots that got laughs out of her predicament, or how she looked, and there were times where I had to say, no, I don't want to do that. That would be a really funny shot because it shows up Muriel but that's not the right thing to do. I found that I was spending a lot of time close into Muriel, or seeing things from her perspective, over her shoulder. That influenced some locations as well.

Did you use any form of storyboard?
I always like to storyboard a scene the night before I shoot it. Usually when I've rehearsed the scene I roughly know the blocking. But I've found there's no point in storyboarding a dialogue scene because the actors will change it to fit the location and you've got to give them the room to do that. They've got to be able to move where they want. Sometimes if I've got a really great shot, I try to influence the movement. Usually I'm pretty successful in doing that, but you know if it's wrong – because it will feel wrong. If I'm trying to stand the actor in some area for a great composition that I've thought about but it doesn't help the scene, there's no point in doing it. So I'll storyboard the night before, just so I don't go in without a plan – just in case everything goes wrong in my day – then at least I can say 'aha' and bring out my shots. Basically I like to have a rough sketch of the shots so I can throw them away.

Did you rehearse, separate from location? Or in the location?
I had two weeks where we rehearsed it scene by scene but only up to a point. I never wanted it to be completely set. And then when I found the location, I hoped that I had really chosen well because the actor will see it for the first time when they come to do the scene. And on *Muriel's Wedding*, the actors were always very happy when they got to the location because it felt right to them and then they would make it their own. We'd then rehearse in the set and when I'd got it the way I wanted it, when I could see who is moving where, I tried to think of the most fluid way to cover it.

It sounds like quite a lot of the blocking is coming from the actors rather than you saying 'You do this. You do that'?
I always have an idea of how I want the scene to be. I find that actors sometimes will want to sit in the nearest chair and do the whole scene from the chair and I always think, that's not exactly how I imagined it. Why don't we try it up on its feet? So I'm always pushing to get something close to how I imagined and my pushing makes them do something.

Can you give me an example of the process?
Let's take the scene where Muriel has stolen a dress and she's been brought home by the police. She is standing with Bill Hunter, and she has two police officers beside her, and the kids are all hanging around because this is really big drama. I know this is a dialogue scene and Muriel has to go to her room. So the night before, I know the following things: visually I know that I want Muriel between the two cops. They are probably going to be standing, but there's no point in me picking where in the room because Bill Hunter will come in and go, well, I'll be here obviously! But if Bill or any other actor chooses an area of the room that is really ugly looking, I will do my damnedest to get him away from there. I also knew I wanted to shoot from between Bill and Muriel's mother. I wanted to enclose Muriel, and the reverse I'd shoot over Muriel's shoulder. So that's what I

go in knowing. Then it's the surprises that you've got to go with. When Bill tells Muriel to go and get the receipt, she turns in my shot, and I thought I was going to let her walk out and keep rolling on the scene because Bill has all the dialogue. But I realized on the day that the scene's not about Bill: this is Muriel's humiliation, her fear of being caught. How is my dad going to get me out of this because he gets me out of everything? So when she turned I took the camera back with her and I found I could take her right up the hallway, while Bill is there in the background talking to the cops, and take her into her room. So that's what I did. But I didn't know that was going to happen. I found out on the day. And that turned out to be better than anything I'd thought of the night before.

How did you feel as you were gearing up for the shoot? Were you nervous?
I had a stroke of good luck or bad luck depending on your point of view. I got measles just before we started shooting so we delayed the shoot by a week because I was laid up in bed. I was still recovering from it in the first week of the shoot. I remember I slept very soundly the night before shooting because I was ill and I needed sleep. Also I really wanted to have my wits about me the next day. The first day's shoot was a scene in the video store, when Muriel is in Sydney with Toni Collette and Danny. I chose a scene I knew I could complete on the first day.

How did it go?
It was a good uneventful first day and that's great. I'd had a good night's sleep and I think I was over my illness. I had two good actors and I was actually feeling pretty good. I had been through so much in pre-production that getting on the set was actually a relief because I knew it was too late for them to take it away from me. We were shooting the film now and it was too late for anyone to change their mind. It had started!

Do you know how many shots you are going to have to do in a day?
Pretty much. Because even if I throw them all out and come up with something else, it's the same number of shots. I find that it really helps your first AD if you give them a list of shots. On *MW* we moved very fast so I would often come in with twenty shots. Now I don't do that because I can't achieve it. On *MW* our maximum was fifteen set-ups per day. On *My Best Friend's Wedding* it was less because we were working with major stars and a big A-list cinematographer so I quickly learnt, don't come in with any more than eight set-ups per day! I always see my shots for a scene like water, cascading down. Each shot flows into the next. And if you've done that right, one scene will flow into the next scene. By the end of it all, you hope to God that you got the script right because all your lovely Japanese flowing will mean nothing if the script doesn't make any sense!

MW looked like it was shot mostly on wide lenses. Why did you do that? How does it affect the meaning of what you are doing?
I wanted a lot of information in the frame. I wanted busy frames and I like it with

the wider lenses when people are in the frame. It makes the frame somehow more dynamic. I get uncomfortable when things get so wide that the faces get distorted. With *Muriel*, I didn't want to distort what were very interesting faces to begin with. I thought the film could just totter over into being mean-spirited. But at the same time it felt right that people be very close to each other, so that the frames were dynamic.

Would you agree that the film makes use of a kind of comical exaggeration both in terms of design and acting?

I suppose I was aware I was heightening things because comedy hypes things up. You do exaggerate for the purpose of making a point, so that people recognize exactly what's happening at certain moments. And it's funny. So there was exaggeration in some of the performances; but not in all of them. I don't consider Muriel exaggerated in any way. The father, I think, is exaggerated.

Really? He is so gruff all the way through.

That's a lot of Australian men! Muriel's dad isn't just my father because the character grew as I was writing the screenplay. He became Bill the Battler, a compendium of men I knew in Tweed Heads, these big, chunky, powerful guys who knew exactly what the world should be and their place in it but who were, at the end of the day, very silly men! Bill Hunter was the only Australian actor I know who can play somebody like Bill and give him his due. Bill is somebody who can give a very exaggerated performance like he did in *Strictly Ballroom* where he was hilarious. But he can also play a man like Bill the Battler where he can tip into caricature but give him some truth.

To my mind, Bill had something larger-than-life about him. For example, the way he interacts with his mistress, Deirdre, is completely heightened; not a realistic take on life. You must accept that?

I do. The situations that I put them in are definitely heightened. I wanted to make the point that they had this great sense of propriety. They are quite clearly having an affair. Everybody knows, even Betty, the wife, and yet they insist on following these rules of propriety. Finally they are so shocked when Muriel breaks the rules and says, are you and Deirdre together? And there's this shock. Somebody actually spoke and pointed out the giant pink elephant in the room. And then Deirdre says, yes, we're in love. Which to me makes that moment so funny because of Bill Hunter's reaction. It's like, Jesus! Please don't embarrass me!

Going back to the idea of light and dark, there are some moments with Bill's wife, Betty, that are pretty depressing. Were you consciously searching for a counterpoint to this slightly caricatured 'up' side of the film?

Yes. It was very important that Betty be desperately real. I was having a lot of trouble casting her, and my agent said, 'What about Jeanie Drynan?' She was in quite a few significant Australian films of the sixties and seventies, like *Don's*

Party. But she left Australia in the mid-eighties – her husband is a director who went to Hollywood, so she'd retired from acting and was raising her children. I remembered her as this stunningly beautiful woman and I said, I think Jeanie is more of a candidate for Deirdre, the mistress. So my agent brought her in for Deirdre, and she was now a large lady, still very beautiful but no longer the twenty-five-year-old Jeanie Drynan I remembered. She loved the script but she was embarrassed to play the mistress, because you could read in the script that Deirdre is all tits and teeth. She sat down and did a very dutiful and smart read of Deirdre's part and I was thinking, 'God, I want to ask her to read for Betty, but I don't know how to bring it up. Because she's here for the sexpot role!' Finally, after the second read Jeanie put the script down and said, 'Look, let's face it. I'm right for the mother, don't you think?' And there was this total relief. I went, 'Yes, yes, let's do a test for the mother!' But Jeanie is an actress who needs a lot of preparation and it wasn't a good reading. I was really disappointed because I thought she looked so right for the part. So I moved on and I cast another actress who read really wonderfully. But then something happened in rehearsal. She was an actress who did a lot of commercials, but she'd never had a role in a feature film or even a television show. She was really excited, for her it was a bit of a break. Every day she came to rehearsals dressing a little bit more glamorously and the part started gradually to change and it wasn't Betty any more. I gave her a good talking to and I said, this is not the part. She finally looked at me and said, 'You know, I understood the character when I first read it. But now that we are getting into it I just find that I'm so removed from this woman that we are going to have to change the role because I'm really losing sympathy for her.' I knew then that I had to get rid of her. So I fired her in the three or four days before shooting and then we went into a panic: oh my God! Who is going to play Betty? And we went back through all the tapes and there was Jeanie Drynan doing her read. And I thought, damn it! I said, I'm going to have Jeanie. She's a good actress; she looks absolutely right; she loved the part. She said the right things. It's just that she wasn't prepared to do it on tape. And Jeanie flew in from the States to do it. She had one day's rehearsal and was just magic.

I thought Betty's sadness gave the film a lot of its power.
Yeah. I felt that without her, there wasn't a point to the film. There wasn't a truth there. And there were a lot of women I knew in Tweed Heads who were like Betty, so she did have a model. Muriel's predicament was funny but it had a seriousness about it. She could become her mother very easily and, I think, was on the way to becoming her mother. I found growing up in a small town to be so full of the pettiness and the commonplace cruelties of small town life. I've never forgotten the horrible things people can do to each other in the name of love. And it's not just true of small towns. I find that in life, goodness is often not rewarded. It's often mocked and derided. We play great lip service to it but in our own lives it's very hard to practise it and acknowledge it. And I always thought of the mother as a

good, selfless character. She is the only character in the story not out for herself. She has devoted her life to her family and is abused for that. That was very important for me and that's why I killed her in the screenplay. I was feeling rather hopeless at the time. I felt I had played by the rules, but no matter where I turned I was knocked down. So maybe the character of Betty was my idealized vision of myself. But at the end of the day, I know I'm Muriel.

Did things go to plan during the shoot?
No. There were lots of disasters. We had three or four days in Queensland and we were going to shoot the exteriors of Porpoise Spit and more importantly, the scene on the Pacific Island that was shot at a resort on the Gold Coast. We had one day of sunshine when we were shooting the exteriors of Porpoise Spit. The three days when I needed sunshine, we were hit with terrible storms. It was so bad I had to avoid the skies. The only reason it looks bright and sunny is because of the costumes. The skies were black and we were shooting between rainstorms. At some point we were shooting during the rain and we covered the actors and everybody with tarpaulins. That it worked at all is a tribute to the actors. They were freezing. But they made it look hot!

What was the best moment?
What I remember most was how absolutely wonderful it was to have Abba's music blasting out when we were shooting the music-only sequences. Everybody loved it; because it's usually such a serious enterprise when you're shooting a film. It's such an unwieldy way to capture a moment of life, this gigantic contraption that we invent to shoot something that is ephemeral. So when you can play music as frivolous as Abba, it somehow breaks the bubble in a good way. The three happiest days I've had shooting anything were when Muriel was getting married because we got to play 'I Do, I Do, I Do' for three days straight – great!

Did you discover any weaknesses in yourself that you hadn't anticipated?
Yeah. When I'm directing I find I am faced with nothing but my weaknesses. Everything conspires to make a scene bad. So it's a constant struggle to prevent that, to keep the scene as you see it. Somehow in the first block-through, the scene hardly ever plays. And you feel a hole beneath your feet. In the rehearsal it seemed fine but now the actor has changed it or forgotten something or you're missing the single moment you should be getting. The DP wants to put the camera over here in a wide shot because he has decided overnight that there aren't enough wide shots in the movie and it's claustrophobic and like television. But you know you need to be over here and if you give in you would have a bad scene.

Do you think you learned a lot from the experience of Muriel?
What I really felt was that I could finally show what I could do. I was like a prizefighter that was finally allowed into the ring. What I had to hold back was my desire to do too much. I really wanted to throw the camera around to show that

I could do that and get lots of shots. The budget and the time restrictions we had went against that, positively, I think, because I had to be very certain what was important in the film. And even then I screwed up. I remember in the last scene in the film when Muriel comes into Rhonda's mother's house and says to Rhonda, I want you to come back with me, and Rhonda refuses but then acquiesces. I encouraged Toni to play that scene as Muriel's big moment: Muriel coming in and rescuing Rhonda. When I saw the dailies, the proverbial hole opened up beneath my feet. I realized I had screwed up a whole day's shoot. It wasn't Muriel's big rescue scene. It was supposed to be a scene when Muriel is forgiven. I had written the script and I'd just missed that. I had allowed Toni Collette to play it as if it was her moment of triumph. Her moment of triumph is the scene after that. But here she needs to be forgiven because she has just betrayed her best friend. And I missed it. And everybody else missed it as well. But in dailies – there it all was – wrong. What I couldn't see on the set, right there in front of me, I could see with a frame around it.

How did you feel about the first cut of the movie?
It was terrible. It didn't work, it had no rhythm, the performances weren't shaped. It just looked shocking. That's when my inexperience counted against me. I hadn't made enough movies to know that everybody's first cut is like this. And as depressing as it is there is no need for you to run off and commit suicide. The film just took a long time to cut because it had a lot of characters and the rhythms of comedy and drama had to be just right. One couldn't dominate over the other. So that was hard.

What was the reaction of your producers?
They seemed to like it, even then I was still embarrassed about it. But then both Jocelyn and Lynda had had more experience that I had. Poor Wendy Palmer flew out and was jet-lagged when she saw it. Afterwards she seemed not to like it, and I was upset. But she was just jet-lagged, so it was hard for her to do the jig of excitement I wanted her to do.

How long did you have for post-production?
We were rushing because we wanted to make Cannes. If you want to be noticed, particularly in Australia, you'd better be in the Cannes Film Festival. Australians don't like Australian movies unless somebody else says they're OK.

Apart from Ciby 2000, did you have a distributor in place by the time it was completed?
We had Ciby 2000 for Europe. In Australia we had interest from Village Roadshow, but they would have to see the movie before they bought it. And in Cannes we sold the US rights to Miramax.

Were you surprised at its success in Australia, given that it was a critique of the quest for uniformity?
Yes. But eventually I thought, well, actually, it makes sense because Australians

really get it. What really surprised me was its success everywhere else. I mean, I didn't expect it to do as well as it did in England and in the United States, because at the end of the day it really is an Australian film, full of Australian characters, like Bill the Battler. I thought you had to be an Australian to appreciate that guy. So that was a big lesson to me: if you have the right story then there is no such thing as 'too parochial'.

Was it a simple step to getting more films to direct?
I always say that with *Muriel* I became a director whose next film was anticipated rather than feared. It changed everything. And the moment it changed was the night it screened at Cannes in the Directors' Fortnight. It was a film that nobody knew anything about, but they gave it one of the prime slots, so it was a crowded theatre. And it just went through the roof. The audience were screaming and clapping, it got a fifteen-minute standing ovation. Toni Collette was with me; and by now she had lost all the weight she'd put on for the film. Her dream, she told me, was that she would appear at the Cannes film festival, thin. I went on stage first and then Toni came on. And for a moment you could tell the audience didn't know who she was. And then when they recognized her, the applause just went on and on.

James Mangold: *Heavy*

When did you first start making films?

I started with my father's Super-8 camera when I was about eleven. It was shaped like binoculars, so you had two handles on either side and you loaded the cartridges in the back. My dad had bought it to chronicle me and my brother as we grew up. But I loved using it, documenting the family doing whatever. I would just start shooting things. Then I decided to make a 'dramatic' film called *The Ugh*. It was edited in the camera and was the story of how everyone in the world is depressed and says 'Ugh' all the time and the words all travel to the North Pole where they form this monstrous creature. I made this miniature 'Ugh' creature myself. I literally wrote 'ugh' a thousand times in marker pen, cut it out and then glued the words together. It looked like Cousin It from *The Addams Family* because it's this woolly thing made up of the word 'ugh'. The creature comes down from the North Pole and starts killing people. I wrote each scenario like 'Cut to an apartment' and then 'Apartment starts swirling around'. My dad shot it for me and he would move the camera like an earthquake as the 'Ugh' shook the building and me and my friends would fall around the room. I shot the scenes that I wasn't in.

What other films did you make as a kid?

Many. Several animations. Claymation. One about a killer tractor. Sci-fi. Time-lapse things to music. They kept getting more ambitious: sound, special effects, music, etc. I made one film called *Growing Up* which essentially takes place during a single day in the life of a fat guy in high school. You watch as he's harassed by a group of thugs, star athletes who like pushing his face into the water fountain or knocking the books out of his hands – all of which are the kind of things I experienced in junior high. And yet at the same time, the film's hero, while enduring these indignities, has these Walter Mitty-like flights of fantasy. He's in a science class; he hasn't done his homework and then suddenly he becomes Einstein explaining a theorem to the class. Athletics play such a big role in the American schools, so in one scene he fantasizes about being the star football player. I got the entire cheerleading squad of the high school to fawn on him, stroking him as he brags how many beers he drank at the party over the weekend. And then the day wraps up with the last of these fantasies in which he's imagining he's a star of the New York Knicks. The heavy-set guy I cast was actually a fairly good basketball player, so I did all these slow-motion shots of him jumping up and stuffing hoops. And this fantasy is interrupted by the now familiar thugs, who are out for one last laugh and find him playing by himself in the gym at the end of the day. They start pushing him around and this struggle culminates with him smacking the lead bully in the face. They're all stunned that he could generate even the slightest act of rebellion or courage against them. They want to fight, but he just walks away. And that's the movie: it's just him finding the courage to shove someone back, for once. It's half an hour in black and white.

Was this in any way autobiographical?
Well, I rarely had the courage to shove anyone back. I can't say I ever felt like one of the coolest, most desired guys in high school. Although I wasn't large, I felt an incredible level of identification with this character, a dreamer who is completely misunderstood. Not only that. The guys playing the thugs who torment him were people I genuinely feared in early high school. Also the girl who played the heroine in the movie was a girl I had a terrible crush on. In this way, making movies was very empowering. I could get the girl I liked to play the romantic interest of my movie – although I couldn't get a date with her myself.

Do you think that at this point film-making was a way of creating an identity for yourself that won you respect?
It was my social activity; my way of making friends and meeting girls. In my junior year of high school I made a film called *Barn* on Super-8, which won some awards. I was also quite proud that I got a free subscription to *Super-8 Filmmaker* magazine because they published a letter I sent them about, 'How to make *Star Wars* laser beams'. Someone made this beautiful machine called the Super-8 back-winder. This device had a little pin that would disengage the plastic ratchet that kept the film from going backward, so you could wind the film backward and double expose your cartridge of Super-8. I devised this way of cutting slits in black cardboard and back lighting coloured tissue paper to make these *Star Wars*-style back-lit coloured beams come out from the tip of a gun. And I got that published in the magazine. That was a very big thing for me!

What was Barn *about?*
My parents had a farm and we had a large barn in the back. The boards had shrunken and rotted to the point where a really marvellous wave of light came through the slats when you were inside. There was also a window at the peak of the roof; some of the panes had broken and it almost looked like a face or an eye. My film was about a little boy who gets trapped in a barn that is alive. The barn knows that the kid's father is going to tear it down so it traps him inside and terrorizes him. But in the end the kid terrifies the barn by pulling out a book of matches and holding up lit matches, screaming in terror, 'Let me out!'; and in absolute panic the barn throws its doors open. It was a very simple movie in terms of what it was about, but it allowed me to do some cool visual things.

Did you edit it in the camera?

No I had a splicer. I had been doing this for three or four years, so by the end of high school I was shooting double system Super-8, recording and syncing it up. I was crazy for this stuff. So that movie got a certain amount of play. I mean it actually went out into the world and I had the proud moment of having my family at a screening at the Beacon Theatre, and seeing my movie up on this big screen. For me, being in an upstate high school and getting asked to come to New York City and receive an award at the Beacon Theatre was just the most exalted experience. I mean, Michael Jackson played there!

Do you think your short films taught you things about directing that you still retain?
Oh, everything. They also taught me about writing but more about directing. The goals are different, you have very little time on short movies and they're more like limericks in that they pay off quickly. When you find yourself writing a feature for the first time you realize how much more elbow-room you have to explore things. But certain things don't change. I always have this idea that within your movie there should be several good short films. You can't ask someone to sit through a very bad short film in the middle of your movie just because you have a good short film at the end. Very often you read the first twenty minutes of a screenplay and it's a really good film, but then the thing kind of devolves; the same sense of design and intention doesn't exist throughout the piece. But you learn all that. And you also get comfortable with the equipment. I mean, I was shooting some of these movies myself as well as lighting them myself. One of the biggest problems I have shooting a Hollywood movie is that I want to pick up the camera and move it myself. I like to operate. When you're directing a movie, it feels sometimes like you can't touch anything; you just speak and sit there in this jar. It's frustrating at times, because film-making is a physical experience, and I want to touch things. I don't just want to be the brain in the jar.

What kinds of movies did you see when you were growing up?
When I first started making movies I lived about two and half hours outside New York City in a town called Callicoon Center. Then around sixth or seventh grade we moved to a town called Washingtonville about an hour and a half out of New York in the Hudson Valley. The town was very conservative so, for example, no Woody Allen films played in the area. The only way you'd see a great old film was on a TV show called *The Million Dollar Movie* where you'd watch a Jerry Lewis film, or *Mighty Joe Young* which was a favourite of mine. At this point I became avidly interested in movies and saw nearly everything even though I'd have to go into New York City to see them. Somewhere around the same time was what is probably considered a great moment in late twentieth-century movies, particularly American movies. Scorsese, Spielberg, Coppola, De Palma, George Lucas, all these people arrived, and to a large degree my wanting to be a movie director was just being wowed by these people's films. Seeing *Star Wars* was one of the most intense experiences of my life. I remember I was on a trip with my aunt and uncle

to Yellowstone Park. When I got to Chicago my uncle insisted that he wanted to see the movie again. We went to a big theatre and saw it there and it was so monumental for me. We travelled to Wyoming and stopped at Old Faithful and all these great scenic sights and I would get on the payphone every day and call my parents and they'd say, 'Well, what's Old Faithful like?' and I'd say, 'I can't wait to get back. We've got to go and see *Star Wars*.'

When did you start to think of film-making as a career rather than a hobby?
My parents are both painters/artists. In the town where I grew up none of my friends could appreciate what they did. The only thing they could possibly understand was that my parents were scam artists, making stuff that didn't seem hard to make and selling it for lots of money. So when I was young I carried around a certain amount of shame about how strange my parents were. After all, fine art plays to about as wide an audience as poetry. I would go to their art openings and it was mainly students, rich people, curators, all incredibly well educated and I thought to myself, I never want to play to such a select audience. By the time I was in high school the political climate was Reagan's America, I was frustrated by the inability of the Left to communicate. It made me think a lot about how one might reach regular people, who seemed to me to be decent and intelligent on the whole. I didn't see reaching average folk as selling out, but as an effort to try to bend them to your way of thinking. I saw it less as compromising than just cooking something your guest would like to eat and slipping one dish that was extremely challenging into the meal. Having said all that, I was also inspired by mainstream movie-making. I guess I wanted to be Steven Spielberg.

What did you do about your ambition?
I had two passes at film school, one very early and one very much later. The cultural change in this country between those two visits to film school was gigantic. Twenty years ago if you asked a twelve-year-old kid what they wanted to be they might say an astronaut, a baseball player, or the President of the United States. Today they'd say a movie director or a rock star. The current level of behind-the-scenes publicity, how movies are made and the culture of movie-making, it's so enormous now compared to twenty years ago. Now, in any pedestrian magazine or newspaper, you can find box office numbers!

Do you think your interest in the film business was to some extent an act of rebellion against your parents?
I wasn't rebelling that much. They may have been playing to a rarefied crowd, but I still found their world and lifestyle inspiring. Most people I met when I went to Cal Arts were people like me; people who'd been driven to make movies by discovering Super-8 equipment. When I later went to Columbia University, a lot of people I met had received degrees in literature and so on, but then they had decided they wanted to explore film – because of a sense of the massive irrelevance of most of the arts, compared to the powerful relevance of movies at this

late point of the century. So film was attracting a lot of people who didn't necessarily have this organic experience of making movies, people who were coming to it more as an intellectual decision: recognizing the way of the world and seeing that this massive industry was now becoming the centre of our cultural world.

Did you always regard yourself as a writer as well as a director?
I never ever thought of myself as a writer. For instance, other than *Oliver and Company*, the animated movie that I wrote for Disney some twelve years ago, I never wrote anything for anyone else, other than an Easter special. To survive, I wrote some strange little things. But in terms of feature films, I've still never written one for somebody else. The act of writing for me is just the first stage of making a movie. When I write I always think that I'm mapping out a movie I might like to make. It's a painful but necessary step. The act of doing it for someone else seems a torture.

How old were you when you went to Cal Arts?
Seventeen. At this point I was anxious to get out of this small town I'd grown up in. At that time both my parents taught at the School of Visual Arts in New York, which had a film school. They sent me to meet the guy who ran the film school, to talk to him about my career aspirations. I sat down with him and he said, 'Look, if you really want to make movies then you should get the fuck out of New York and go to Los Angeles.' This was the Dean of the film school in New York! So I applied to UCLA, I applied to USC, and I applied to Cal Arts almost as a lark. Cal Arts had an incredibly lush catalogue. It was so slick – kind of the J. Crew of college catalogues. Everyone just looked incredibly attractive in it. No one was in a classroom; everyone was out making movies, dancing, acting, playing instruments. The catalogue wasn't designed to please parents, but it was definitely going to seduce young people like me.

What happened next?
My dad and I went on a California trip. We pulled in at UCLA and USC in a rental car and I didn't even get out, I was like, 'I don't want to go in'. It was too big. But I liked the smallness of Cal Arts. I could wrap my mind around the act of being somebody there. And I mean that in the egotistical way, too: not just being one among a thousand film students but someone who stood out. But on any rational level, I had no good idea why, for instance, faculty-wise, I wanted to go there. I had never heard of Sandy Mackendrick who later became the centre of my experience at that school. I had never seen his movies and I had no idea he was there. I just liked the space and the catalogue. It was a very well-endowed campus in Valencia with about eight hundred students.

So you signed up?
Yes. I remember filling out the application and not knowing whether I wanted to apply to the animation school or the live action school. They were that specific

about what you were going to study right out of high school. And I was very torn because all through high school I had also been doing animated Claymation as well as paper drawings that I had animated to music. But essentially the power of making movies with people, with actors, was the deciding thing and I checked off live action.

Tell me a little about your time at Cal Arts. What was it like?
I was definitely the most conservative film-maker there. Very few people were interested in making classically narrative movies. The school really had a lot of activity going on: animation, performance art, video art, abstract animation. I mean, there were incredibly cool people working there; a lot of different ways of thinking about film. But I wanted to make movies, so the second I got there I started meeting members of the faculty. Sandy Mackendrick was a cantankerous, six-foot two-inch, seventy-year-old Scot. Actually he was American because he was born in Boston and moved to Scotland when he was young and then lived the last twenty-five years in Los Angeles. He only had one lung because he had emphysema and when I spoke to him he said (*out of breath, Scottish/British accent*), 'You're far too young, you're only seventeen years old. You're a child.' But I already knew I absolutely *had* to work with him. They had a mentor system and I wanted him to be mine, but he said, 'I'm not interested.' We then had a day when we all showed a movie we made before we came to the school, and I screened *Barn*. As the credits came up, Sandy trundled down behind where I was sitting and leaned in my ear and said, 'I didn't remember which movie you'd made. But I like this film very much and if you want to work with me, I will help you.' And so he became my mentor for the next two years and by the second year I was his teaching assistant. Sandy had reams of handouts and writings; analyses of movies and dramatic structure, Aristotelian theory. He would break down classical films into storyboards, from *City Lights* to his own movies, and he'd analyse what shots these movies were made from, and I would help him prepare all these handouts. He was a brilliant, brilliant guy. He also had this wonderful thing in his office. Along the circumference of the ceiling, he had cards, about thirty of them, that said things like 'Movies come in three sizes: too long, very much too long and very, very much too long'. Or 'A foil is a character who asks the questions that the audience wants to have answered'. When you came in with a story idea, Sandy would sit back and go, 'Well, I think you need to look at number seven, number four and number twenty-two.' And if he was talking about, say, exposition, he'd go, 'You can't open a movie talking about how you lost your wife. Let us see that the man is lonely; let us understand that he has a problem and then explain he's lost his wife. Your exposition is in the wrong place: card number twenty-two.' Then he'd add, 'Of course it also qualifies for "Movies are much too long" because you've taken twenty pages to write what you can write in five.' So essentially a story session could be something like that, totally fantastic. I would hand in a four-page screenplay and he'd write seven pages about it; and

not only that: he'd also draw pictures. And what Sandy taught you, more than anything, was that the lark that had been movie-making for me since I was a child was now becoming a very severe craft. Unlike the other teachers at Cal Arts, who were very indulgent and loved the idea of exploring your creative side, putting your dreams on film, Sandy was very severe about putting craft into film, into stories. But in retrospect, his ruthless sense of what was right and what was wrong and what would work and what would not was great preparation for me, for what I had to deal with in the years ahead. I never came across his kind of clarity and severity again.

Do you think he had this clarity because he had made films?
You could sometimes get very severe opinions from your professors or advisors, but there is just something so powerful when it comes from someone who has been in the trenches and made a film. When I'm working with younger film-makers now, I can point to a moment in their film that bothers me, and say, 'The thing you're ignoring is right there on the screen in my film and I regret it.' Or, 'I had to deal with that problem or they wouldn't have made the movie.' Or, 'This actor solved that problem.' And it's so much more palpable than having someone who has just watched a lot of movies and has read a lot of books.

How did you progress through the school?
After two years together, Sandy felt that there was nothing more I could get from him. So he suggested – quite forcefully – that I apply to the acting school and become an acting student. He said, 'I will not speak to you for the next year.' Of course we spoke all the time, but I happily joined the acting school. I like to perform. When I was a kid I did magic shows, puppet shows; and I was in plays in high school. I was even the star in my own films when I couldn't find actors, and I loved the experience of acting. So for my third year at Cal Arts I was a full-time acting student working on voice, movement, dance, mask theory, and studios and was in play after play after play. I can credit Sandy with this because I would probably never have done it unless I had a teacher telling me, 'Get lost, bury yourself in that other school.'

Did you make many films at Cal Arts?
I made a film a year. In my first year I actually made a promotional film called *Future View* for General Motors and Disney. In the first week of Cal Arts I was actually sent to the Disney studios. This was at the height of the recession and General Motors wanted someone to make a documentary about the building of the World of Motion Pavilion at the EPCOT Centre in Disney World. The producer didn't want to spend the three or four hundred thousand dollars that a professional promotional film-maker would charge, so they had the idea of hiring a student. They called Cal Arts, who recommended two people. One was a master's student who had made a fairly amazing movie, and the other was me – because everyone at Cal Arts loved *Barn*. I was seventeen and I didn't have a car

so I had to borrow one to go to the studios to do this interview. I brought my Super-8 projector and I showed this producer *Barn* and *Growing Up*, the high school movie, and got this job. In the second year I made a film called *Pete and Joe Die*, which was a kind of *My Dinner with André* meets *Earthquake*. It was essentially the story of two guys coming back from college to their hometown. They're both presenting the other with the idea that they had all these romantic conquests at college. They live right at the edge of a nuclear missile base, and suddenly the missiles are fired off and they don't know what's going on; a nuclear holocaust is taking place! And as they're dying together, almost in each other's arms in the parking lot of this bar they've met at, they confess to one another that they still haven't had any girlfriends – and then they're dead!

What did Sandy make of this film?
Sandy hated it! In my third year I was in the acting school but also sensing the end of my college years rapidly approaching. So, I started preparing to make a movie that might get me a job.

And what was that?
It was a remake of *Barn*. I made the Super-8 film again in 16 mm! This time I brought a crew back to my family's farm in upstate New York over the summer before my last year, and shot a much more elaborate version of a similar story. I knew the location and I knew the mistakes I made in my first crude version so I just wanted to go back and do it full on. I hoped I could make something slick enough to impress the Hollywood powers. I so desperately did not want to go back home to work in the photo-shop I'd worked in over the previous summer and become the guy just back from college not knowing what he was doing with his life. I'd acquired a taste for Hollywood and wanted to stay. So in my last year, I was cutting that movie with Sandy and another wonderful teacher, Gill Dennis. It was very polished. And Sandy helped me, although he was very clear that he thought the first one was better.

It was too slick for him?
Probably. Or just not as much heart in it. Sandy was very demanding in a great way. You were never going to get congratulations from him. And, to be honest, although he understood my desire to enter the Hollywood workforce – there was only one way he could perceive the film, and that was on its own merits. And clearly, he saw it more as an effort to get work, than an effort to tell a story.

Did your Barn *remake have the effect you wanted?*
It certainly did launch me into a new world. The president of Cal Arts saw the film and saw an opportunity to put me together with some trustees of the school at a graduation luncheon. Among them were Jeff Berg, the chairman of ICM, Michael Eisner, who at that point had just taken over Disney, and Barry Diller, who was running Fox. So on graduation day, a Friday, I sat at a table opposite

Michael, Barry and Jeff. They were all very nice, and I asked them lots of questions like, 'Why don't you guys make movies with Terrence Malick any more?' At the end of this lunch I handed each of them a 16 mm print of my movie, although Barry Diller wanted video. I remember rejoining my parents after this luncheon and telling them how intense this was. My dad was like 'Yeah, yeah, yeah' and I said, 'No, it was a big thing!' Then, the next Monday morning, I'm packing my boxes in the dorm and the phone rings, it's about nine-thirty. And it's Jeff Berg. He asks me, 'You don't have an agent, right?' and I say, 'No'. He says, 'Michael Eisner is probably going to call you as well as Barry Diller. And I want to let you know that if I was you, I would get down here to see me as quickly as possible.' And then I hang up and Michael Eisner calls. He's in his car on his way to the Disney studio and he says, 'I don't know if you know I left Paramount and we've just taken over this place. We're looking for deals with young film-makers like yourself, because we want to create something like an old Hollywood system. I've given your movie to Jeff Katzenberg to watch. I've watched it, my family's watched it and we all like it very much. We'd like to talk to you about coming over and joining us.' And I'm like, 'Cool!' I hang up, then Barry Diller calls. I say, 'This line sounds awful! Where are you?' And he's like, 'I'm on a plane.' And he goes, 'I gave your tape to Larry Gordon and he's going to watch it. He helps me run the studio. We can't make deals like Disney; but we're interested and I want to tell you, "Good job", and it was nice meeting you.' So then I go down to meet Jeff Berg and he says, 'Okay, I'm going to be able to make a deal for you. Go home like you were planning on. Leave your stuff here. Go home and hang out for a couple of weeks, and maybe in a month you'll have a deal. When you come back, you'll get a pay-cheque and we'll have an office set up for you.' And that's essentially what happened. I went home and hung out for a month and came back to Los Angeles with a writer-director deal at Disney. I was twenty-one! At this point I had no feature scripts so they saw me only as a director. But I did write this TV movie for them that I thought would be a kind of nearly silent fable like *The Red Balloon* and they gave me the green light to direct it. It was about a fawn lost in New York City, and these inner-city kids who find it. I loved the idea of a fawn clopping around through the alleys of the Lower East Side of New York, and these sequences of a little boy trapping this creature. In truth, it was a fairly standard Disney plotline, but the way I envisioned it was nearly wordless. What I never understood was that on television, the last thing they want to make is a silent film. Secondly, I wanted to make it about inner-city kids – kids who had never seen nature before – and, in the minds of the studio at least, the last thing suburban America wants to watch is ethnic kids in the inner city.

It sounds quite a leap from Cal Arts to Disney. Did you feel at home there?
When I arrived at the studio, there were other young directors and writers there, so that part of it was just like school. For example, my neighbour was Chris Carter, the creator of *The X-Files*. He was writing for the same Sunday movie show that I

was working on. Phil Joanou was down the hall. We were the young guns who'd been hired for beans. There were others, but those two were the ones that I was friendlier with. However, among all these 'young film-maker' deals, I was the only one who had an assistant, and this caused a great deal of frustration for Jeffrey Katzenberg. He called me one day when I had only been there a month, and asked me to fire my assistant. I said, 'I can't do that.' And he said, 'Why not? You're a member of the Disney family. There's other talent here of equal level who have not been allowed assistants in their deals and it's screwing things up.' And I said, 'Well, there's another Jeffrey that I have to talk to: my agent.' I called Jeff Berg who at that moment was on the slopes of Aspen. He told me, 'Don't worry about it. It's in your deal.' So we insisted that I keep my assistant. It all sounds a bit ridiculous from the outside. All I knew was that the person I had hired to assist me had just quit another job to take this one, and it would be pretty cruel to throw them out on the street just because Disney didn't want to fulfil the deal that they had made. I had never demanded an assistant – it was Jeff Berg's request – and they had agreed. I was twenty-one – I didn't know what was going on, except my simple opinion that people should honour the deals they make. Anyway – what proceeded to happen was that everyone else in the entire building got an assistant, which must have cost Disney a fortune. One of the senior vice-presidents said to me flat out, 'If Jeffrey told me to fire my assistant, I'd do it! You made a big mistake.' It was subsequently made clear to me that I was now known as the guy who told Jeffrey to 'fuck off'. This stupid thing ended up tainting my whole experience there. I got fired from directing the TV movie and flushed out of the studio at the end of the first year. In retrospect, I have no ill will – I wouldn't be surprised if I ended up making a movie at Dreamworks for Jeffrey in the future. But back then, at Disney, I was Michael Eisner's hire and there was a certain amount of rivalry there between them, even way back then. My only compass in that highly charged environment was my own simple sense of right and wrong.

And what was Jeff Berg telling you?
Not much. In retrospect I wouldn't do anything differently but I would have understood that in that one moment I refused to fire my assistant, I had destroyed my relationship with Jeffrey – because while Michael was running this giant multinational corporation, Jeffrey was really the one making movies. At that point Jeffrey would have personal meetings with you. I remember having a one-on-one meeting with him about my script for the TV movie, and he was giving me notes and I was saying 'no'. Again, I wasn't understanding the system.

So what happened to your TV movie?
I was supposed to shoot the whole goddamn thing in twelve days. I fell behind right away, and the thing was looking very dark – and I don't think they were happy that it was so ethnically cast. The producers of the movie refused to fire me because they felt that I was doing a fine job, given the production issues I'd been

thrown into. So the studio had to physically come down to shut the movie down. On the third day a limousine arrived on the set and they fired me, literally in the middle of production. I'll always remember this image. I was directing a scene where there's this gang of kids hanging out round an ice-cream truck. I had invented a special popsicle called the 'neutron pop', a sort of multicoloured rocket-shaped popsicle that these kids all ate. The prop man had all these popsicles made, and kept them on dry ice so they were very cold. These limousines suddenly drove up and the executives climbed out and said, 'We have to talk to you in the trailer.' And these wonderful children who were just about to do a take were all staring at me and this limo. Two of the kids got their popsicles stuck to their tongues because they were so confused about what was going on that they kept these popsicles in their mouths. Anyway, I never saw those kids again. I was taken away into a trailer and fired. One of the executives was Jane Rosenthal, a friend who now runs Bob De Niro's company. I remember crying like a baby on her shoulder, feeling like this was all so unfair. They then confronted me with the fact that the film was impossible to shoot on the schedule; that they wanted me to rewrite it, split the kids up into two groups so they'd have better hours with the children, and could shoot scenes with each group separately. And in a very weird sense I felt I'd been set up. Where was all this production advice when I started? Where was all this wisdom about how impossible this movie was to shoot when I was entering production? I didn't want to do any rewrites for them but they came to me and said, 'If you do the rewrites we'll give you another movie to shoot.' And I believed them. So I rewrote this thing over two or three days, and it got shot by Jackie Cooper, who was very kind in complimenting the script. He had to step in very quickly and get it done and he did.

And what happened to you?
This was the start of the darkest period of my life. I was very shaken and now didn't believe in myself that much any more. I even remember going to Jane Rosenthal and asking whether I could shoot second unit for Jackie Cooper. I just wanted to be a film-maker. After all, it was this thing I'd written and I just wanted to be a part of it. And what Jane did was suggest I go and work on this movie they were making in the animation department. They wanted to make *Oliver Twist* with dogs and cats in the streets of New York. So, I went off for the next eight months, hung out in Glendale with all these animators, and wrote a screenplay. They had someone come on after me to make it funnier. And to a large degree I had a good time. It was a thrill; I was all of twenty-one at this point and I met men who'd worked on *The Lady and the Tramp*; who drew pictures from what I described. But at the same time I was incredibly ashamed of myself because I felt I had blown my big opportunity. To use a sports metaphor, I was thrown into the major leagues and had lost a game really badly and now didn't know where I was going. It took six months to complete my duties on *Oliver and Company* but essentially my deal was not renewed after the first year.

A year since you'd been fêted by three separate Hollywood power brokers! What did you learn from this experience?

Well, there were a couple of things. One was that I was no Spielberg and certainly wasn't at the age of twenty-one. I mean he's one of the most brilliant of film-makers; the geometry and structure of his films are incredibly brilliant. But I don't think even Spielberg could have come up in the system that I was expected to come up in, where you have to look like Steven Spielberg in the first couple months. In his day, you could direct a bunch of *Columbos* or a *Night Gallery*; there was a lot of time and patience invested.

What happened to you once the Disney deal fell apart?

I was adrift. I was now advised by ICM not to talk about what had happened on the deer movie, which created this incredible weirdness when I went out interviewing. It was clear that something had clearly gone wrong in my deal with Disney but I wasn't allowed to talk about it so it just sounded like I had a bad coke habit or something that had to be hidden. I became very disillusioned, wondering whether I wanted to be a film-maker any more. I started writing narration for trailers for Golan and Globus: movies shot in South Africa starring *Playboy* Playmates. I wrote the script for the *Claymation Easter Special* for the big king of Claymation, Bill Vinton. But I wasn't making a living. I was turning to my parents for help. I was just getting by living in the Valley. And I was getting fat because I was just listening to music all day, cooking, trying to write and feeling pretty uninspired. I probably put on forty pounds. I probably weighed two hundred and ten pounds compared to about a hundred and eighty now.

How long did all this go on for?

It was two years of hell where I banged around and did some odd jobs. I was miserable. I flirted with the idea of becoming a novelist – in fact, the first ideas for *Heavy* actually started unwinding themselves in what I thought was a book about this fat man who was invisible.

Which was how you felt?

True. I also wrote a children's book called *The Colouring House* about a little girl who discovers a woman who controls the world's colour system. I was just trying to develop the quality of my writing. It was all I could do; I didn't want to make short films any more. I didn't want to throw the money away doing it. I guess I didn't know what to do.

At this point you thought you'd put film-making to one side?

The corporate side of the business, certainly. I had suddenly been confronted with the ugly side of what I had only seen on the screen from my suburban movie theatre; the kind of Pepsi-Cola cinema that had developed as a result of the tremendous Spielberg-Lucas success. I didn't think had a chance in hell in that system.

So you thought you might have an easier time as a novelist?
Well, I saw it as a world in which I might have a chance to express myself and maybe succeed at a more modest level in a more modest business. So I called the Dean of the Writing School at the UC Irvine, Oakley Hall, and he said to me, 'Why the hell do you want to be an author? It's just as bad as Hollywood. Your friends will stab you in the back just as quickly. The system is just as corrupt. Success goes to the worst writers; the editors are looking for schlock; good writers can barely make a living going from conference to conference, from teaching gig to teaching gig. It sounds like you've got fairly far fairly quickly in the film business. You shouldn't throw that away.' So after that conversation, I decided to move back to New York and go to film school again.

What made you choose Columbia?
If I was going to work aggressively in film again, it seemed to me that the only thing to do was to put myself in a position where I could feel talented – to regain some confidence and purpose. I had to go to a place where I knew I'd feel special: a small school. Columbia wasn't the most favoured or prestigious of film schools although it was well known. The faculty list was phenomenally star-studded but also misleading. You know, it was David Mamet, Martin Scorsese, Brian De Palma, Milos Forman. I was like 'Wow!' when I got accepted there. I was elated and thought I only needed people like that around me to remind me of why I wanted to be in movies. I then discovered that Marty wasn't there, David Mamet had quit the previous year and Brian De Palma wasn't about to come in. But Milos was really there, and I was fortunate enough to get selected by him. He wouldn't teach large classes. He watched a lot of tapes of people's movies and would then have a five-person class in 'advanced directing'. And essentially what I did when I was at Columbia was write *Heavy* in his directing class. We were supposed to be directing a movie. But I sent him twenty pages at a time and he would come in every week and give me notes and I would keep writing. I was so inspired to be working with someone like him. He was a hero of mine. I produced reams of material. I mean, I never worked so quickly.

How did your short, Victor, *come about?*
I wanted to make a film again but this time I decided that, unlike *Barn*, I wanted to make the least commercial film I could: a movie where basically the strongest voice would be me. I therefore decided to make a silent film because I thought, in that way, the storytelling would be everything. And not in a nostalgic way, with cute little cards and old-time music, but a modernist silent film: a simple love story told with no dialogue, just powerful well-composed images telling a story. And that was a very powerful experience. I did that with another wonderful teacher there by the name of Stefan Scharf who had studied with Eisenstein. He was an eighty-year-old Polish man – a brilliant guy with whom I had a great friendship. And I finished that film at the time I was starting with Milos. *Wings of*

Desire had just come out and had completely reinvigorated me with what movies could be; Jim Jarmusch was in full flower; *sex, lies and videotape* had come out that year. I was just blown away by what was happening in the beginnings of what was the Sundance revolution. So I felt positive; I felt that I had an angle. When I finished writing *Heavy*, what I began to understand is the evangelical side of film-making in terms of raising money. At that moment *Reservoir Dogs* had come out and this whole new kind of very high-octane, violent independent cinema was happening. I saw rock and roll, guns, a kind of violent, edgy revisitation of Scorsese's early years by a lot of film-makers. And my evangelical take on how to sell myself and *Heavy* was basically this: just as, after the punk era, there was a resurgence in roots music, in country music, I believed that after this hysterical high-octane, fast-cutting, violent moment in American movies – which was also beginning to happen in mainstream movies too – there would be a kind of slowing down; people would be craving something like *The Last Picture Show* again. That kind of movie would be 'in' and 'hot' again.

So you thought you were writing something that you could sell?
I have this theory that a screenplay is a weird document that has two purposes. One is to sell, and one is to be a recipe for the movie – and these two goals are not necessarily in alignment. Writing *Heavy* was the first real writing experience that I had which was non-corporate. Writing *Oliver and Company* was a giant collaboration with all the different people at Disney and everything previous to that was for TV movies or something. I'm a great proponent of film schools because I had such great experiences. Milos was the ultimate anti-Sandy. He believed in craft but he was not a 'rules' person. He was a 'process' person. Very gentle. But brilliant.

He didn't have cards on the wall!
No. Sandy was the greatest directing teacher I've ever had. Milos was the greatest writing teacher I've ever had. One day I handed him some pages. There's a moment in *Heavy* where Liv Tyler and Debbie Harry are at the cash register. It almost looks improvised, with Debbie Harry saying, 'No, don't press that button, press reset', and Liv Tyler saying, 'Oh what happens if I press . . .?' Deborah Harry then goes, 'You can't do that or you'll have to ring the whole thing through again', and that's the end of the scene. It's about a half page of dialogue of them at the register on Liv's character's first night. And I will always remember Milos in front of the class saying, 'Let's all go to page thirty-six', and he points at this page and says, 'This page is really good.' And everyone's like, 'What?' And Milos says, 'That is life, right there at the cash register; that moment is life.' And it was just banter on the page! But I was really proud and I realized that Milos had another way of looking at the screenplay. Instead of the Syd Field method of constructing a three-act structure – which is the way screen writing is often taught, there is another way of writing; finding people, spaces, souls and lives and then pulling the shape of the script out of those discoveries. The other thing Milos said

was that nothing needed to happen in *Heavy* other than he loves this girl, his mother dies, and he doesn't tell anyone.

Do you write in a linear way or do you find little moments like this?
I write from the beginning to the end. Sometimes I write a scene ahead of time. Sometimes I get an idea for a piece of dialogue. Sometimes I will write something that I think should be in the next scene. Let me use an acting term. Very often an actor can be playing the end of the movie too early. They know where their character's going and they start to tip their hand too much, too early. They're playing their arc too heavily. You can do that in writing. You can in a sense start writing a scene that belongs later in the film too early because you can't wait to get there. But for me that's the way it generally works. I realize it's too early and then I realize that it goes later. I push these bits away and they become useful for me later. What I find myself doing is making things up and then taking advantage of them and then going backwards and redistributing them so they have more of a sense of destiny or structure in the entire screenplay. But I love the act of just wandering and finding things and editing and cutting and shaping and going back. I'm not the fastest screenwriter in the world but most of the decent stuff I've written, the stuff I'm proud of, has come by this process where I inhabit an outline without too much discipline.

With Heavy *did you have anything guiding you apart from Milos?*
I had the films of Yasujiro Ozu to inspire me. I admire his films immensely. Many of Ozu's films seem to be about a moment passing or a season passing: the world turning and moving by a mere inch but that being enough to somehow resolve his character's tale. That was where my commitment to the stationary camera in *Heavy* came from. Shoot low – a medium wide lens – up at the actor. And let them be. Music also inspired me. There was a song by the Feelies that I'd listen to all the time on the album *The Good Earth*. From listening to this one instrumental track I'd envisioned this spiral of shots near the end of *Heavy* where you visit all the characters and subtly see how they've changed. Sometimes you just get these ideas about the end of the film and you just work toward them. For instance, when I sat down to write *CopLand*, I had this idea for a silent gun-fight. I had dreamed up the idea that the hero is deaf in one ear and then I thought what could possibly happen to him in the end? Well, of course they're going to blow out his other ear. But that's all I knew. I was always working toward that silent showdown and then a lot of the other stuff cropped up.

How would you define the step that Victor takes in Heavy?
The guy we meet at the beginning of the movie is not even in the position to open his mouth in the presence of someone like Liv Tyler. The guy we meet at the end of the movie is saying goodbye to her in the fashion of a hero and then making friends with a young woman in a convenience store. I mean, it's just that he's starting from so far back that the step we're talking about is a child's step. I don't

imagine that that tavern will be the same place any more. I imagine that he will come out and talk to people. In my mind he is somehow a liberated creature, or more liberated than he was in the kind of cage he was living in when the film began; with the secrecy about his weight and his eating, his fear of communicating his needs. I mean, even the anger that he expresses to Debbie Harry's character in the late part of the movie is so far from what he was capable of at the front end of the film. And I see all that as tremendous growth. Pruitt does such an amazing job. Do I think Victor's going to accomplish anything in a grand worldly sense? No, he may continue running this tavern. But sometimes that's enough.

But he's more at ease with himself?
He's alive; he's had things happen to him that he will never forget. For example, the scene with Liv and him at the airport: I can't speak for everyone, but for me the power of that scene is that nothing much is going on, other than the hopes and dreams of a guy who loves this savagely beautiful and incredibly kind girl; and that they come close to something happening. What I think is a miracle, and I credit it to the actors, is that you actually believe it. I mean, a glorious young woman at the beginning of her life and a thirty-six-year-old fat guy are almost coming together. It's hardly believable on paper – yet it's performed at such a realistic level – from the power of our hopes and our feelings about these characters you do believe that something could happen between them. That's tremendous progression for this character.

Did you ever think of making something more happen between them?
I felt that she might kiss him. But then I felt that essentially it wouldn't be good for him or her. I felt that essentially all that had to happen was that he had to wake up and understand that he was attractive in some way. The gift she gives him is that she lets him know that he is special to be with. I mean, he's so ashamed of himself that for someone just to be able to invest in him when they could be in a car with anybody is a tremendous gift. So that's the inch I see him moving: towards expressing himself; asserting himself; and an inch maybe even in going to cooking school. All those forays are things that happen in the absence of this maternal presence.

You're obviously extremely articulate and, by your own admission, talkative. Yet the central character in Heavy *is inarticulate also most to the point of silence. The same is true of Sylvester Stallone's character in* Copland. *Is this reticence something you identify with?*
It's more than identifying. I admire it. I'm moved by people of few words, people who can say things succinctly and shut up. I can't completely explain my attraction to quiet characters other than pointing out that they force a film to be less dialogue-driven. While I often write quiet protagonists, I also like to write very noisy and opinionated supporting characters and I identify with them too. *Copland* is a good example of this. I identify with Bob De Niro's character and Har-

vey Keitel's character just as much as I do with Stallone's. They're all parts of me. But I guess if I was trying to put a simple button on it, I would say I love to make movies about quiet people because I, the film-maker, get a chance to speak more. The more my lead character's expression is built on looks, glances and gestures, the more I can speak through the camera and the more I feel like I'm in front and centre with my actor instead of just making a handsome photographic record of them saying dialogue. I try to make the movie work on a visual level first.

Do you think screenwriters often concentrate too much on dialogue at the expense of other things going on in the screenplay?
Gill Dennis taught me a very simple theorem about screen writing. You should write a movie as if you were describing a finished film to a blind person. The screenplay is a list of everything said and heard but it's also a list of what you see in the most efficient way you can describe it. So very often the visual design of scenes is embedded in the writing. I can only offer you a page of *Heavy* or one of my other screenplays as an example. For instance, I will write 'Victor looks upward' and then I will do two carriage returns and then I will write 'vrroooom, a plane roars overhead' and then two more carriage returns – 'Cally laughs', blah, blah, blah. I try to create a kind of haiku. Every time there is a space between the lines, for me, it's another cut. One of the pieces of wisdom that's been handed out on writing screenplays is that you shouldn't put in many camera directions because it will offend the director. I'm not so sure about that.

But they're probably thinking in terms of the commercial industry where they're trying to get a script sold. Whereas you're directing your own movie.
Perhaps. But there is a way around the problem. You don't have to say, 'extreme close up on Cally as she cries'. All you have to write is, 'a tear runs down Cally's cheek', and from that line alone, you feel that the writer is describing a close-up. It's a close-up because you can't see a tear on a cheek from far away. What you're subtly describing is a shot, a specific camera set-up. If you're describing someone's eyes, then it isn't a wide shot. If you're describing the clouds, it ain't a close-up. This way you may subtly persuade the director to shoot the scene in your style. You can do this instead of filling the script with tech-talk and no one will accuse you of directing on paper.

Let's go back to Heavy. *What was the reaction to the screenplay once you'd finished it? How many drafts did it go through?*
Several. I finished one with Milos. I then got together with Richard Miller who produced it with me and we kind of attacked it and tried to shape it more. I generally have a community of friends who just give reactions and a lot of the time they say very subtle things about the draft which helps me understand what I can do and can't do with it. So I'll be improvising and playing with it all the time. I think everyone thought it was a decent script. But financiers and industry people were very uncomfortable because it was different from what was hot in the inde-

pendent world at that time. And it had two strikes against it. One, it was about an unattractive, unsexy lead character. Two, it didn't particularly cater or depict a world that was going to be interesting to the indie counter culture. When people rail on about the evils of Hollywood and how it's catering to 'mall' audiences, you have to remember that the independent cinema has its own beret-wearing, clove-cigarette smoking, sexually enlightened, rock 'n' roll crowd. They can both be clichéd. And each marketplace can be equally belligerent to something foreign. Given what was successful at that point in the independent world, I think *Heavy* looked a little soft.

How did you go about raising the money?
The best advice I ever heard about making an independent movie came from two wonderful people, both of whom I met at Columbia University, Ted Hope and James Schamus of *Good Machine*. They said that the way to do it is to decide on the day you begin shooting the movie and stick to it. You may not have a dime but you say, on May 3rd we begin production on *Poster Boy*. And if you meet any-one and they go, 'What's going on?' you say, 'I'm making *Poster Boy*. We start May 3rd.' The key is the commitment you make to yourself that you will not wait until the financing is all there. You will make it for whatever you've got on that day even if you have to shoot it on VHS. So even if you only have five hundred dollars, Poster Boy has to begin May 3rd. With *Heavy*, we said we were going to shoot the movie in the fall of '93. At that point we hardly had any money so I gave our casting director Todd Thaler a small drawing of my father's in lieu of cash. And Todd did a great thing for us: as soon as he started working on the movie he said that we needed to meet this young woman he'd seen a couple of weeks before. Todd had just finished casting *Léon* for Luc Besson, and Liv Tyler had come in to read for the character that Natalie Portman ended up playing. She seemed way too old but he thought she was amazing. So he called Liv's mom and had Liv come up to my apartment in New York to read with another actor. I taped it, and I still have this tape: it was just the most amazing thing I had ever seen on my little camera. It was like watching a movie star who'd never been in a movie. She left the house and I called Richard Miller and said we've got to make a deal with her right away. He was like, 'Don't you want to see anyone else?' He was keenly aware that to make a movie like this – a fat guy in a low-octane story – we needed stars, to attract people. But I told him, 'This girl is going to be a movie star. And she's meeting Bruce Beresford later in the week, and I don't know what kind of movie he's making, but he's going to cast her, I'm sure of it.' So we offered her the role the next day. She then met up with Bruce Beresford, and he offered her the role in his movie. And their movie was paying a lot and we had nothing, not even scale.

What happened?
Liv told us that she would do our movie after she'd finished the big one. But as far

as Richard was concerned, this was all the better because now she'd have been in a major Hollywood movie and be a rising young star and we could get her for a very low price. But he was also afraid that when they finished this movie, she'd be so hot she wouldn't do ours. I wanted to take the risk so I postponed making *Heavy* for four months, pushed it to the spring. In this time we got Shelley Winters, Deborah Harry and Pruitt. It was my friend Scott Ferguson, who was making *Nobody's Fool* in upstate New York, who said, 'There's this guy and he isn't as fat as you're looking for, but he is an amazingly powerful actor.' So Pruitt came down to the city and I met him and I was blown away just by his presence.

So you're casting away but you still had to raise the money?
We went to the IFP markets etc. We got some money from Richard's family and my family, my grandmother, his best friend from college, everyone. Even small chunks made a big difference and slowly we were getting to the point where we had about two hundred thousand dollars – it adds up quickly and it's easier for people to invest when you can can say you've got Shelley Winters and Liv Tyler, who's in this new Bruce Beresford movie, and this guy who was in all these Oliver Stone movies, and Debbie Harry who was in Blondie. So now the movie has a profile. The only thing that kills you is the tension of having all these actors signed on and no money to pay them. You're playing all these things off against each other. And that's essentially how we did it. We ended up with about three hundred thousand dollars and we managed to stumble our way through production and finished with about forty thousand dollars of debts on our credit cards and no money to edit the movie with and then had to borrow, beg or steal just to keep the editing room open. Of course the cost once you're cutting is low. You just have to make sure that your editor has this equipment and some kind of paycheque to pay their rent and buy splicing tape. We didn't cut on Avid; we cut on film. When we got into Sundance we still didn't have the money to finish.

Let's talk about preparation. How do you work with your DP?
I arrive with a fairly specific idea about scene design. What height I want something shot from; trying to use the same lenses as much as possible. These are things that I applied crudely even when I started making Super-8 films. I don't want to light it but I'm very, very exacting about the shots. My films don't look as aggressively stylized as other directors'; however, I think that the resistance to a showy style takes as much energy and commitment as the application of showy style. Subtlety is very important to me. As well as DPs, I have had intense relationships with storyboard artists planning out the movie. For instance, on *Heavy*, a close childhood friend of mine, Pete Ortel, storyboarded the film. He lived with me for a month while we charted out what this thing would look like. This was after I found the locations. You can't really storyboard or shot list a movie without knowing the locations. In a low-budget film the way to make found sets look like 'designed' sets is to design your scenes or even rewrite your scenes to make

those spaces and their eccentricities integral to the scene rather than just occupied. I try to design a movie from the moment I begin writing it. The next step is putting it into shot structures with someone who can sketch better than I can. I chatter about what I want, do a lot of thumbnails, and the storyboard lays it out from what I'm describing. The people I've worked with provide a real voice in the matter too. I mean, they're arguing with me about how we should shoot the scene. For me, the discussions with the DP and my other collaborators are easier to handle at this early low-pressure moment in making the movie than they are at the moment when the actors and everything are there and the clock is ticking.

What about lenses? Do you have a lens in mind for every set up? Or do you choose a lens for an overall scene?
I try to use the same lens throughout the entire film. Usually a slightly wider than 'normal' lens like a 40, 35 or 28 mm. I think the material cuts better when you stick with one lens – the image has a consistent quality. Also, it promotes a sense of discipline about framing the scene when you have a fixed lens. You have to physically move the camera in order to change the composition of the shot. There's a physical commitment to changing your mind. Whereas zoom lenses have this weird effect of allowing you to get indecisive. If all you have to do is twist this goddamn ring, it kind of produces this kind of 'all right, let's try it a little closer, let's try it a little further away' back and forth blather. Sometimes it's useful. But the reality about a fixed lens on a camera is that if you want to be a little closer, you get closer. If I physically get in the actor's face with the camera, I can feel that when I'm watching the movie – that I'm not zoomed in with a longer lens, that I'm inside the actor's private space.

When do you make the decisions about the lens?
On the set. But you have to set the general lens strategy in place in pre-production. On *Heavy* we shot almost the whole movie on a 35 mm and a 40 mm. We would only go to the 35 mm when we needed more space, because I didn't have 'wild walls'. But essentially it was these medium-wide lenses we worked with through most of the movie. The decision gets finalized when you start shooting and you're actually looking through the viewfinder and the real actors are inhabiting a real space and you commit to a lens. I might have thought I was going to use a 50 mm for this whole movie but then I realize that I can't get far enough away so then I'm cutting down the length. And then you kind of settle in.

How does it work once you arrive at a location? Can you give me a concrete example?
Okay. For *Heavy*, I needed a tavern with a food slot. I felt that the place Victor hands out his pies had to be present in the space, and from this slot he had to have a vantage point on to all the action in the tavern. We found a great tavern but the food slot wasn't big enough so we had to enlarge it. But the way it seemed to be placed at the locus point of the entrance into the kitchen and was a way to see into the bar was a powerful architectural force that helped me lay out scenes. I mean,

as a writer I need to paint a picture in my head of a place in order to write the scenes. It may not be completely articulated, but it's enough that when I walk into a place that has some of those attributes I imagined, it's a thrilling experience. I'm really moved when this happens. It's as if I've found the thing I've been dreaming of. In the case of *Heavy*, I was also looking for a tavern that had a sense of having been around a while. I could not afford to build a run-down tavern or change one from a modern seventies-looking place into a place of the past. It had to be close. Always most important are sight-lines – that you can see this door from this chair, that someone emerging from this space might sense the presence of someone over there. And frankly, we were also looking for a tavern with heat because we were shooting in winter and one which was not being used. This was very difficult. Try going out shopping for a tavern that meets all these requirements!

Do you have an automatic reaction to a location in terms of how you'll film it? Do you have a sense of where the camera's going to go? How you'll cover the scene?
That's the very first thing I think about. You're not picking a cool-looking place per se; you're picking a cool sequence of shots. So in *Heavy*, the reason the food slot was great was that when I stood behind it and saw the place I thought wow! And when I stood at the bar and saw the food slot I thought wow! It's always the shot that you're looking for. On the scale I'm now working on you can afford to change the look somewhat. If you want wood panelling you get wood panelling. But the fact is I'm still thinking of specific scenes – do we move from the street to window? Do I want to see this character sitting there and then see her mother in the car outside the window? Or am I going to cheat the window and shoot this on the sound stage? I try to decide what relationship is most important.

Where did you shoot Heavy?
In a town called Eldred, New York. It's where Pennsylvania and New Jersey and New York all meet at the Delaware River.

When did you start shooting?
I think we started in March but our pre-production was in savage winter.

How did your pre-production go?
We had to solve issues connected to every location in the movie as well as a myriad of other production issues. For example, we got lucky because we were in the middle of nowhere and we needed some place for the cast to be able to sit that was warm. We couldn't afford movie trailers but there was a Winnebago company only five miles away. So instead of having to pay teamsters and have show-business trailers on the movie, we got this guy who owned this Winnebago place to park five family campers along the street where we were shooting and then move them to the next place we were shooting. So each member of the cast was living in comfortable little trailers through the entire production of the movie – which was critical because it was cold.

How did rehearsals actually work in Heavy?

I never did them. Not once. I could never get all the actors together on a stage on the same day. Shelley was difficult to schedule. Pruitt was shooting another movie, Liv was shooting another movie.

What about the mise en scène, placing the actors in the shot? How did that work?

I'd just place them or find it with them. I never arrive on a set with no idea of where I want the actors to be. Certainly you can manipulate that a lot with where you put objects. If you put the bed over here or you put something else over there, then the logical places for them to move are going to be defined by where all these different objects are. Some scenes require nothing more than finger-pointing rehearsal. You get the actors, the DP and the rest of the crew together and you go, 'Okay, so here's where Victor enters. He'll start here, he's going to cross here and he's going to come around here and we're going to need someone to cross here, and then he heads into the kitchen.' There's no reason to burn away spontaneity rehearsing things that are simple.

You make it sound quite functional in a way. Just walk into a room. Don't invest too much in it?

Take the scene after his mother dies when Pruitt walks into the tavern and goes into the kitchen. That's what the script says – he goes into the kitchen. I wanted him to walk past everyone and feel invisible. There is only one clear way to do that but there's no point in wasting time having him walk by everyone over and over feeling strange. Getting it all set up, the dolly track, the lighting, that's what eats up the time. Then blow some film. If he's not getting it, we'll find it. I always want the first time they get it right to be on film. I always think that first time is irreplaceable. If I see them do something right and I don't have a camera rolling it's terrifying to me because it's never the same. And if you're trying to explain to the actor what it was that was so special about a moment in a rehearsal, you will surely ruin that moment for ever by talking it to death. So I have to be rolling when an actor is really reaching inside and doing the work. I want them to figure out what they're comfortable with, whether they can move here to there. Whether they can feel they can play the scene this way. Most experienced actors will be able to tell you that in even a casual walk-through. You tell them what you're thinking. You start here and you look here, etc. Then this whole negotiation begins. Sometimes to be quite honest I've got an agenda which is that I want them to do something quite specific but I don't want to be that specific with them yet so I'm trying to lead them with dotted lines to the place I'm hoping they'll find. Sometimes they come in with an agenda and they're trying to lead me to a place that I don't expect. Both sides can win and when I see something more exciting than my idea I'll be the first to leap on it. Half of being a film-maker is taking what's good and not being too invested in where it came from. The fact that it originated in your brain is far less important than whether it works.

Can you remember your feelings as the shoot unfolded?
I was sick. All I wanted to do was throw up in the mornings. I was smoking a ridiculous amount, God knows how many cigarettes. Some nights I didn't sleep at all. The level of exhaustion was so great that I couldn't even sleep because I was so tired. I thought it was do or die on this film. I'd had my Hollywood experience and I knew I could never manage to put this amount of money together again. This was it. But however awful the pressure was on me, I was also wired with this innate excitement. One of the things about directing that's interesting is that you have to set goals you can achieve. You have to get the day's work done. So you've got to be careful about those crazy shots that are so laborious and impossible to pull off that they actually render the entire crew feeling like failures. There's that all-in-one, giant, *Raging Bull* steadicam shot that you might design but if you're trying to squeeze that miracle shot into a tough day, you're crazy. Sometimes you succeed but sometimes you will fail to get a miracle shot and everyone goes home feeling like they let you down. So it's very important when you're starting a shoot to structure it so that the first days of production produce a sense of accomplishment for the cast and crew – as well as yourself.

What did you do on your first day?
Over the first two days, we shot all of the scenes in the convenience store, all the way through to the end of the movie. So if you look carefully at the scenes inside the convenience store that take place towards the end of the movie, when it's supposed to be springtime, you can clearly see it's winter outside. Also you're structuring the order in which cast members are coming onboard the film – you don't want anyone on location before you need them. You want to keep the amount of time required on the movie to a minimum, particularly when you're paying everyone so little. So if I remember right, we had Pruitt for the convenience store scenes but we needed no other principal actors. Then we had Shelley start and we were ready to do the hospital scenes and there were more in the script than what actually ended up in the film but we did about two days shooting at the hospital. And then we were moving to the tavern and from there another load of people were coming on the movie: Debbie and Liv and then Evan Dando. Slowly they would all arrive. Evan was working the shortest amount of time. Debbie worked a lot of the schedule, Shelley worked second shortest because we had collapsed her amount of time, so the first scenes we were doing in the tavern were the scenes where she was alive, and then we just put off shooting the second half of the movie until she was gone.

What was the biggest difference between Heavy *and your experience on a TV movie?*
It was my first chance to work without being fired. And to work with actors who brought so much to the table. They were all at different skill levels. Liv had done almost no acting. She had done this one movie for Bruce Beresford and had clearly learned some technique there. Shelley had been in seventy-five movies

and was an amazing presence. Pruitt was a veteran of many films but he'd never had the chance to be the lead in a movie so he was really cherishing that. Also, one of the biggest jobs you become aware of on a low-budget film like this is that you set the cast and crew's mood. You're responsible for all these people getting along and feeling good about each other and working together because their pay-cheques are pretty slim.

Can you give me an example of this?
Well, on her first day on the set, Shelley arrived holding her arms up in the air and saying, 'The star is here!' And for Pruitt this was offensive. Pruitt is a tremendous talent with a lot of pride and *Heavy* was his opportunity to finally be the star. He had been a supporting player in many big actor's movies, from Woody Harrelson to Bruce Willis to Paul Newman; and he had paid his dues; so he felt rightly that this was his chance to dig deep and indulge in his own process because this was, frankly, his film. He's in nearly every scene. But you must understand Shelley is an incredibly powerful force: she is intensely charming and theatrical – I love her and cherish the time we worked together – but she can suck the air out of a room. Anyway, Pruitt and Shelley met for the first time on the set that day. I had no idea what went on in their meeting in her dressing room. But when I started shooting the first scene of them together – with Pruitt seated by Shelley's bedside and Shelley telling him a story about when Pruitt's character was young – something went terribly wrong. First of all, Shelley was in a very emotional state. She was looking at pictures of her ex-husband to get ready for the scene and she was very nervous. Anyway, we were doing a two-shot of them. And they completed the first take and Shelley suddenly turned to Pruitt, with fire in her eyes, and said, 'Stop fuck-ing up my scene, amateur.' A silence fell on the set. And I was stunned. I ripped off my headphones and shouted, 'Shelley, that's uncalled for!' But Pruitt stood up and very succinctly said that he didn't deserve this kind of bullshit from Shelley and proceeded to launch some well-deserved invective back at Shelley. Then he walked off the set. Now, I was pissed off at Shelley. I mean, she'd just attacked a brilliant actor, my star, in front of the entire crew. So I ran up to her and I said, 'What were you fucking thinking?!' And she said, 'Pruitt kept staring at the tele-vision while I was doing my monologue.' And I said, 'But I *told* him to stare at the television because it's in the script – there's a Weight Loss commercial on the tel-evision. He's *supposed* to be getting bored with what you're saying', and she says, 'Well, I don't care, because he told me in my dressing room that he thinks he's as good as Marlon Brando, and, honey, I know Marlon Brando. Marlon Brando's a friend of mine, and he ain't no Marlon Brando.' In her mind, she was playing Lloyd Bentsen to his Dan Quayle!

What did you do?
Well, I had to finish the day's work. There's no room on a low-budget movie to fail to get the work done. So, I played Pruitt and shot out Shelley's angles. Then I

sent her home and went downstairs to find Pruitt. And he's in an absolute state; he's very upset, justifiably so, and he says, 'I can't work with her. I won't take that crap. It's not fair; it's not right.' And this is where my job gets really complex because while I sympathize with him – Shelley was way out of line – I'm the guy who has to get the work done or cut the scene, so I'm not allowed to indulge my feelings or, frankly, anyone else's. I have to get him back on the set. So I say, 'Pruitt, she's seventy-three years old. She's made a hundred movies. Can't we laugh it off? It's only two weeks you have to work with her.' And he's like, 'Laugh it off? Did you hear what she said to me?' And I say, 'Well, she's under the impression that you told her that you were as good as Marlon Brando. And Marlon Brando's a friend of hers. So it bent her out of shape.' And now Pruitt gets pissed off *at me*. He was probably justified, because I was not thinking about his feelings, I was only thinking about keeping my movie afloat. Did Pruitt say that to her? I wasn't there. All I know is, out of the goodness in his heart, Pruitt came and shot out the other half of the scene with me playing Shelley. Then, I call Shelley on my cellphone as we're wrapping up the night's work. And I say, 'You've got to figure a way to make this better', and she says, 'Why?' And I say, 'Whatever Pruitt did or didn't say in the privacy of your dressing room, you could have dealt with it in the privacy of the dressing room. But instead you chose to skewer him in front of the entire crew of a motion picture in which he is the star, and did it on Day Three of production ensuring that he will be walking around with this hurt for the rest of the schedule.' And she's like, 'All right, I'll think of something.' So for a few days we shot some other work, and then it was time for Shelley to come back. We were in the tavern. Liv Tyler's there, Debbie Harry's there, everyone's there, and Pruitt is full of anxiety. He's got to do a lot of intense scenes with this woman playing his mother and they're not speaking to each other! So, I go stomping off to her trailer and say, 'Have you thought about what you're going to do make this better, Shelley?' And she says, 'Yeah, tell everyone to gather in the tavern in five minutes.' And I'm like, 'What are you going to do?' She smiles and says, 'I'm going to give a little speech.' So we gather the entire crew in the tavern and Shelley steps on to the pool table in the centre of the tavern and says, 'Pruitt, I want you right here', pointing to a spot right in front of her. And Pruitt steps forward. He's very suspicious and I'm like, oh Jesus! I hope she says the right thing or this whole fucking movie will collapse. And then Shelley starts to talk. And she says, 'I once told George Stevens that he didn't know how to talk to actors. And I told Stanley Kubrick that he was an anal retentive prick. I told James Dean that he was gonna kill himself. And I told Montgomery Clift that he'd better stop fucking with his face or his career would be over. I told Roman Polanski that he was a pervert. I told Gene Hackman that he was a belligerent asshole who treated women like shit. And I told Robert De Niro . . . And I told Al Pacino . . . And I told John Ford . . . And I told Marilyn . . . And I told Burt Lancaster . . . And I told Charles Laughton . . .' She goes on and on until suddenly she looks down at Pruitt and says, 'And so, Pruitt, you have joined a pantheon of the greatest men in the history of American cinema whom I've insulted!' You could hear a pin drop. And suddenly everyone applauded. Pruitt laughed and we went on with the film. This was one of the most intense experiences I ever had making a movie. I saw the whole film crumbling under the tension of this misunderstanding and I was terrified. I'd never want this story to reflect badly on either of the actors. I love both of them and admire both of them profoundly and, frankly, if I had done my job better, there probably never would have been a problem to begin with. I've told you this story only because for all the theoretical parts of making movies that we discuss all the time, there's a very personal part that rarely gets talked about. There is a whole dynamic behind the scenes of people's expectations, their hopes, and their feelings. Managing this, or at least trying to, is a very important part of directing a motion picture.

Did you have any other problems? Did your budget affect things?
I went over a week and the crew wanted to leave. I had to talk to the appointed shop steward of the crew and beg him to stay. Essentially what I said is we've carried this wagon almost all the way to market and we have a little bit of extra distance to go and I'm begging you if you have any goodwill towards me and this movie and believe in it to just haul that extra week. Hold on to that extra week. But it was a problem until I made a personal appeal. The producer tried to pin this down. The production manager's trying to deal with this but it was a personal appeal from me to help me finish this labour of love which meant everything to me and in fact which my life was relying on, that did it.

What kind of schedule were you working on? How long were the days?
It was a forty-day schedule. We had turnover rules for the actors and the crew. They needed twelve hours' rest so if we went late on one day we didn't pay overtime but we still had to start later the next day. We never did longer than a twelve- or thirteen-hour day because the crew would have revolted. The only way we'd go longer is if everyone was high from the work and it just seemed that we were doing something so great that everyone was committed to finishing. I was inspired by the enthusiasm of my cast and crew: particularly the wondrous youthful enthusiasm of Liv; also the patient dedication that Debbie Harry brought to the set. Pruitt's work was brilliant every day. I mean I barely shot more than one take of him. The scene when he's eating the doughnuts in the film is one of the most powerful in the movie. It was one take. I remember the DP asking me, 'Do you want to go closer?' and I was like, 'Why? That was beautiful.' And I remember Pruitt coming up to me in tears after doing that take and asking, 'Do I have to do that again?' and I smiled and said 'No'. And I remember walking out from that little stock room and seeing the entire crew huddled around the little monitor and they all had tears in their eyes. I think the biggest reason the crew hung in there were the moments they saw getting laid down on film, moments

that seemed magical. When a moment like that happens on camera, all you want to do is get the film developed and watch it on a screen.

Do you think you were learning about directing? As the film wore on, you were gaining knowledge about your craft?
Sure. Sometimes what not to worry about. The learning curve continues. It never ends. I've finished three features now and I'm still learning. Some of what you learn on one film has no application to the next movie. It's very much like leaving a relationship and starting a new one. The scars of the previous relationship, the ways you learned to compensate have no use in this new one. In fact they could be destructive. Every collaboration is different. There are some actors you learn to level with and there are others with whom you need to be very gentle. Some you nudge, some you shove, some you try to relax, some you just have to love them and be their friend. Every time you think you've figured it all out, you think, wow! I really broke through with that person. The reality is that you learned how to break through to that person on that day, nothing more.

Were there any moments where you thought you had messed things up?
Absolutely. At the end of *Heavy*, in the script, Victor rescues his mother's dog from drowning. And we didn't have the money to shoot it properly and we kind of did this half-assed version of him saving this dog from this river and it was so bad. I mean, days when you're shooting something and it looks bad are the worst. Sometimes you pretend it's great and just shoot it out and move on. Very often the process of shooting is a grieving process, feeling like you didn't quite pull off what you had hoped and imagined. The editing process is the way of coming to terms with what you've done and how you can shape it. The material starts to speak for itself in the cutting room.

But it must have also been very exciting to see your first full-length screenplay turning into a movie.
To me, one of the great romances of shooting a movie is the contradiction between the delicacy of the human moment you're trying to create in front of the lens and the enormity of the equipment and manpower that's surrounding this fragile moment. Movie crews follow militaristic rules. You know: 'I'm the general. I have a first lieutenant who tells me what's possible and what's not possible in today's battle.' Yet with all these trucks and cable and manpower, there's Liv Tyler and Pruitt Taylor Vince sitting in a car and tears are running down his cheeks; there's something so tender going on at the centre of all this activity. That contradiction is beautiful to me. Managing it can do awful things to your personality, to your personal life. But trying to straddle all these worlds and energies is extremely exciting.

Let's talk about the editing process. How long did you edit for? Was this also a part of your learning process?

I feel very comfortable in the cutting room and the discipline there is being able to throw things away. It's like writing: you're killing your babies, taking out cute things that don't work for the greater good. Things that you might have believed in at one point and thought were critical disappear. And it takes a while to come to terms with losing a sequence or an idea which you may have spent weeks planning and/or shooting, which may even have been part of the reason you wanted to make this movie in the first place. But you have to see past that. On a simple level, cutting is very natural for me and is a very rewarding process.

How did you feel when you saw the first cut?
The first cut is always painful. It's way too long. The first cut of *Heavy* was three hours long. The first cut of *Copland* was three and a half hours long. Same with *Girl, Interrupted*.

So what did you do?
Become profoundly depressed.

Did the film change a lot in terms of your final cut? In terms of what you saw in your head when you were writing it or did you think you were faithful?
I think shooting a screenplay is like adapting a novel. You're faithful to the ideas, the words and what you can make to work. But it's also about knowing what you're going to throw away. Not just like throwing it away on the cutting-room floor but also knowing what dialogue is going to happen off camera; what is going to be featured. You can't feature everything. The writer would love you to handle every word and every idea in the foreground. But some things need to be invested in, and some can't, and as a budget diminishes, it's clear that you've got to merge two scenes or have this scene take place in this room and not that one. All sorts of compromises are part and parcel of making a movie and certainly that continues in the cutting process. Sometimes it makes the film better.

What was the reaction to the film at your first public screening?
We got into Sundance. The movie was fifteen minutes longer than the final released version. We won a prize at Sundance for Best Direction and the audience was clearly moved but it was still not what was hip in independent movies at that moment. So we came back without a distributor. We were really depressed. But then we were invited to the Quinzaine, the Directors' Fortnight, in Cannes, because their people saw it at Sundance. I was flown to France and we started selling it in foreign territories but we could not get anyone to buy the movie in the United States.

How did you resolve that?
By the time we went to the Toronto Film Festival it resolved itself. Liv was becoming more and more of a star – Bertolucci had cast her in *Stealing Beauty* – and a company called CFP, which is now Lion's Gate, bought the movie for twenty-five thousand dollars.

You mean they paid twenty-five thousand dollars for the US rights?
We only got twelve thousand five hundred up front. But what then happened was beautiful. When the movie opened I remember being at the little dinky première party we had and someone came up to me with an Internet print out of Janet Maslin's review in *The New York Times*. I had to read the first sentence twice to understand it was a good review. In fact it was a very good review. I was like, 'Holy shit! We got just a sterling review from the paper of record.' And when I was at Cannes the next year with *CopLand*, I got the chance to thank Janet. I said to her, 'You must know that you made a big difference for my little movie. I want to thank you from the bottom of my heart. I know that you just follow your instincts about the films you review but it was a great gift in my life.' And she was like, 'No one ever says anything like that.' It was true though. That single review drew people in droves, packed the Film Forum in New York City for a couple of months. Also, in some sense Janet set them up to expect a special tempo, she made the film's rhythm an asset not a liability.

Do you think the fact that you had to go out and make a film independently, outside the Hollywood system, has changed you as a film-maker?
Well, yes. If everything had worked out at Disney maybe I would have been a very groomed and conventional Hollywood film-maker. Whatever I am now, good, bad, or mediocre, is certainly more idiosyncratic than what I would have been had things come together sooner. There is such a thing as being successful too young. I always try to remind young film-makers who are trying to get into the system quickly that there is only one example of the system bringing up a great film-maker, and that is Steven Spielberg. There is almost no one else you can think of who came up through the current system and became a powerful film-maker. Without a chance to make a first statement that is unique, you have very little chance to ever find a voice. You become a member of the factory. The kind of satisfaction you feel when you sit down and watch a film that sprang from your head and is fully realized – that is an incredible feeling. None of that would have happened to me if everything had worked out the first time in Hollywood. Unfortunately there is no funding system to bail you out in that interim time where you may be struggling after school. I was at a writers' seminar and essentially every question was, 'How did you make it?' 'How did you get the connections and money to make your movie?' And what I tried to refocus things on was the craft because I think that's the answer to the question. I mean, knowing people may help. But ultimately there's a lot of people who know people: sons and daughters of VIPs who are sitting on a lot of cash but can't somehow turn the corner as storytellers, because they have nothing to say or have developed no craft in saying it. I always say, 'Let's pretend that we're all in the chair business. How would you feel if a carpenter was to make one chair and then went to the chair capital of the world and started saying, "Here's my one chair, why won't anyone give me any money for my next one?"' It's a very sad state of affairs that although

we all profess to love movies so much, we all feel entitled to be discovered the first time we make one. One of the things that Sandy Mackendrick always said was, 'You've finished your screenplay. Good. Guess what it's time to do? Write another one.' His feeling was always just 'Get better'. And that's true whether you're an actor, a writer or a director.

What lessons do you draw from the experience of Heavy *now?*
I think the greatest lesson I got from that movie was 'Don't despair'. I mean the darkest days can turn completely around. The days you thought were the worst days of shooting often become the best scenes in your movie. The things that you are proud as a peacock of during production may become the things you cast aside in the cutting room. The only thing you have to guide you is your vision of the film and your heart. A film that no one understands can two years later be something everyone understands and tells you how much they love. The thing about *Heavy* that was interesting to me is that we struggled to get it into the marketplace, we finally had a very decent theatrical run and it still lives on video. There's no actor that I've worked with who didn't see it. Sly Stallone watched it twice. Winona said she saw it seven times. Actors are the lifeblood of the industry, and they can look at a movie and they see a room for them to do things they haven't done; and for me that has been very important. Whether or not the film was as much of a success as it could have been, I'm very proud that it's my first statement as a creative force in the industry. Even if someone in the precariousness of this business disappears in another couple of years, I'm proud that at least I said that and I said that with my first foot in the door because now I'm finally getting to what I really want to say. If you're going to make one movie as your first movie, make it something you deeply, profoundly care about. Don't get callous, don't try and just get your foot in the door of the business because your first novel, your first poem, your first published anything will forever be your kind of statement to the world about what you are and what it is you want to say. My pride in regard to *Heavy* is that it's deeply earnest, it's deeply thoughtful, it's deeply felt and it's deeply honest. To have done that regardless of whether it's a hit or not to me was the most important thing and made the journey worthwhile.

Director Biographies

Pedro Almodóvar

Pedro Almodóvar was born in La Mancha, Spain in 1951. In 1967 he moved to Madrid where he worked for the National Telephone Company from 1970 to 1980. In the same period he acted with the underground theatre group Los Goliardos, wrote comic strips, articles and stories for underground papers and shot eleven Super-8 films, including *Folle, Folleme, Folleme Tim!* and *Dos putas o historia de amor que termina en boda*. In 1980 he made his first film on 16 mm, *Pepi, Luci, Bom*, which was his first film to gain a cinema release. He has subsequently made twelve feature films: *All About My Mother*, *Live Flesh*, *The Flower of My Secret*, *Kika*, *High Heels*, *Tie Me Up! Tie Me Down!*, *Women on the Verge of a Nervous Breakdown*, *Law of Desire*, *Matador*, *What Have I Done to Deserve This?*, *Dark Habits* and *Labyrinth of Passion*.

Allison Anders

Allison Anders was born in Ashland, Kentucky in 1955. Despite a difficult childhood in which she was gang-raped at the age of twelve and threatened with physical abuse by her alcoholic stepfather, she enrolled in college and won a place at UCLA film school in her middle twenties. There, she became so enamoured of the films of Wim Wenders that she deluged the director with mail and eventually secured a job as a production assistant on *Paris, Texas*. After graduating from UCLA with a clutch of award-winning screenplays, Anders co-wrote and directed *Border Radio* with Kurt Voss before establishing herself as a solo writer-director on *Gas Food Lodging*. Her subsequent films include *Grace of My Heart*, *Mi Vida Loca* (*My Crazy Life*), and one segment of *Four Rooms*. She has just completed her fifth feature film, *Sugar Town*, starring Rosanna Arquette, Beverly D'Angelo and Ally Sheedy.

Steve Buscemi

Steve Buscemi was born in Brooklyn in 1957. He began to get interested in acting in his last year of high school on Long Island and subsequently studied at the actors' studio in New York under John Strasberg before trying his hand at stand-up comedy. Realizing it wasn't for him, he took a job as a fireman in Little Italy and began to work in experimental theatre with Mark Boone Junior. He first came to public attention with Bill Sherwood's *Parting Glances* in 1986, since when he has appeared in more than fifty feature films ranging from Hollywood main-stream pictures such as *Con Air*, *Escape From LA*, *Armageddon* and *Billy Bathgate* to independent features like *Pulp Fiction*, *Reservoir Dogs*, *The Big Lebowski*, *Fargo*, *Miller's Crossing*, *Living in Oblivion* and *In the Soup*. Prior to making *Trees Lounge*, he wrote and directed a short, *What Happened to Pete?*, on which he says that everything that could go wrong in forty-eight hours did go wrong. He is cur-rently completing his second feature film, *The Animal Factory*, based on the book by Edward Bunker. He is married to the choreographer and film-maker, Jo Andres, and lives in Brooklyn.

Joel and Ethan Coen

Joel Coen was born in 1954 in Minneapolis, Minnesota; Ethan three years later in 1957. Movie buffs from an early age, Joel graduated from NYU film school in 1979 and worked as an assistant film editor on a number of horror movies including Frank LaLoggia's *Fear No Evil* and Sam Raimi's *The Evil Dead*. At the same time he began writing scripts with Ethan, a philosophy graduate from Princeton who was then working as a statistical clerk for Macy's. In 1984 the two brothers shot to international prominence with *Blood Simple*, a convoluted and brilliant film noir about a bar owner who hires a private eye to kill his ex-girlfriend and her new lover and ends up getting killed himself. After the extraordinary reception of their début feature, films followed thick and fast. They include *Raising Arizona*, *Miller's Crossing*, *Barton Fink*, *The Hudsucker Proxy*, *Fargo* and *The Big Lebowski*. The Coens are currently completing their latest film, *O Brother Where Art Thou?*

Tom DiCillo

Tom DiCillo was born in 1957 and gained a masters in film-making at NYU film school in 1976. He then worked as a cinematographer, most notably on the early films of the American independent director Jim Jarmusch, *Permanent Vacation* and *Stranger Than Paradise*. With his sights firmly set on directing rather than photographing films, DiCillo next enrolled in an acting class in New York where he began to experiment with a series of monologues about a character called Johnny Suede. Encouraged by the reaction to the monologues, he turned them into a one-man off-Broadway play in 1985 which he used as the basis for his first feature film, *Johnny Suede*, which was released in 1991. Since then he has made three more feature films: *Living in Oblivion*, *Box of Moonlight* and *The Real Blonde*.

Mike Figgis

Mike Figgis was born in Carlisle, Cumbria in 1948 and grew up in Newcastle. After studying music in London, he worked with the experimental theatre group, The People Show, for almost a decade – during which time he made an unsuc-cessful application to the National Film School – before beginning to write his own stage works, including *Redheugh* and *Slow Fade*, which combined live performance, music and filmed segments. These shows led to a television film for Channel 4, *The House*, in 1984 on the basis of which David Puttnam asked Figgis to write a treatment for a feature film. The result was an early incarnation of *Stormy Monday*, which Figgis went on to make with a different producer in 1987. Figgis has since made eight feature films: *Internal Affairs, Liebestraum, Mr Jones, The Browning Version, Leaving Las Vegas, One Night Stand, Miss Julie* and *The Loss of Sexual Innocence*. His latest film is *Timecode 2000*.

Stephen Frears

Stephen Frears was born in 1941 and grew up in Leicester before studying law at Cambridge. He then worked as the assistant to Anthony Page at the Royal Court theatre where he met Karel Reisz and Lindsay Anderson. After working as Reisz's assistant on *Morgan: a Suitable Case for Treatment* and as Albert Finney's assistant on *Charlie Bubbles*, Frears directed his own first short film, *The Burning*. After a spell directing children's programmes for Yorkshire Television, Frears co-wrote the screenplay for *Gumshoe* with the actor, Neville Smith. Produced by Albert Finney's company, Memorial Enterprises, and starring Albert Finney, Billie Whitelaw and Frank Findlay, the film was released in 1971. Frears then spent the next fifteen or so years working in television drama before returning to the cinema with *My Beautiful Laundrette*. He has since directed a string of feature films including *Sammy and Rosie Get Laid, Prick Up Your Ears, Dangerous Liaisons, The Grifters, Mary Reilly* and *The Hi-Lo Country*. His most recent film is *High Fidelity*.

P. J. Hogan

After growing up in Tweed Heads on the north coast of New South Wales, P. J. Hogan gained a place at the Australian Film Television and Radio School in Sydney at the age of seventeen. While studying there he met a number of other Australian film-makers, including Jane Campion, and Jocelyn Moorhouse whom he later married. He graduated with the prize-winning short film, *Getting Wet*. In 1986 he directed and co-wrote *The Humpty Dumpty Man* for Australian television and subsequently worked as second unit director and co-writer on *Proof*, the début feature film by Jocelyn Moorhouse in 1991. Three years later Hogan gained spectacular international success with his début feature film, *Muriel's Wedding*, which he wrote and directed. He followed this with *My Best Friend's Wedding* in 1996 starring Julia Roberts and Rupert Everett. He is currently in production with *Unconditional Love*, also starring Rupert Everett.

Neil Jordan

Neil Jordan was born in County Sligo, Ireland in 1950 and attended University

College, Dublin where he studied literature and history. While still in his twenties he established his reputation as a writer with two prize-winning novels, *Nights in Tunisia* and *The Past*. After a period writing television drama, he worked as a script consultant on John Boorman's *Excalibur* in 1980 before débuting as writer-director on *Angel* in 1981. Since his first feature, he has made eleven films: *The Company of Wolves*, *Mona Lisa*, *High Spirits*, *We're No Angels*, *The Miracle*, *The Crying Game*, *Interview With the Vampire*, *Michael Collins*, *The Butcher Boy* and *In Dreams*. His latest film is *The End of the Affair* starring Ralph Fiennes and Julianne Moore.

Ang Lee

Ang Lee was born in Taiwan in 1954 and grew up in the east coast city of Hua Lung. He studied theatre at the Academy of Art in Taiwan and then at the University of Illinois before attending NYU film school in 1980. In 1984 he graduated with an award-winning short film, *Fine Line*. Although this film confirmed Lee's reputation as a talented film-maker and helped him get an agent it was another six years before he was to make another film. In this time he wrote numerous unproduced screenplays, worked as a PA and cooked for his microbiologist wife. In 1990 Lee accidentally found out about a script competition being held by the Taiwanese government. His script about a Chinese-American marriage, *Pushing Hands*, won first prize in the competition and an earlier script, *The Wedding Banquet*, won second prize. In 1991 Lee was invited by Taiwan's Central Motion Picture Studios to direct the first of the two scripts. On the basis of the success of *Pushing Hands* in Taiwan, Lee went on to make *The Wedding Banquet* which turned out to be an enormous international hit in 1993. He has since made four films: *Eat Drink Man Woman*, *Sense and Sensibility*, *The Ice Storm* and *Ride With the Devil*.

Mike Leigh

Mike Leigh was born in Salford, Manchester in 1943. After attending Salford Grammar School, he won a place at RADA in 1960 where he studied acting at the same time as taking courses in art at Camberwell School of Art and studying film at the London School of Film Technique. After RADA, Leigh worked as an actor on a number of British films, taught drama in Birmingham and Manchester and was an assistant director at the RSC. He went on to direct plays for the Webber Douglas Academy and for the theatre group, E15, where he met his future wife, Alison Steadman. *Bleak Moments* was first produced as a play at the Open Space Theatre in 1970 before becoming Leigh's début feature film in 1971. Preferring to work in television and the theatre, Leigh did not make another cinema film for seventeen years. He then made *High Hopes* in 1988 followed by *Life is Sweet* two years later. Since then he has made *Naked*, *Secrets and Lies* and *Career Girls*. His latest film is *Topsy-Turvy*.

Barry Levinson

Barry Levinson was born in Baltimore, Maryland in 1942. After graduating with a degree in broadcast journalism from the American University in Washington DC he worked as a trainee for a local television network before moving to Los Angeles in 1967. Once there he performed sketches and improvisation at the Comedy Store before starting to write comedy for television. After working on the Marty Feldman Comedy Hour and The Carol Burnett Show he was hired by Mel Brooks to work on *Silent Movie* and *Blazing Saddles* before scripting the award-winning *And justice for all* with his then wife, Valerie Curtin. Encouraged by Mel Brooks's interest in his stories about growing up in Baltimore in the fifties, Levinson sat down in 1981 and wrote *Diner* in three weeks. Backed by MGM, the resulting film was an instant critical success and firmly established Levinson's credentials as a formidable writer-director. He has since carved out an enviable niche both as a director-for-hire on bigger budget studio pictures and the author of a series of more idiosyncratic and personal films rooted in Baltimore. In all, he has made some fifteen feature films including *The Natural, Tin Men, Rain Man, Avalon, Toys, Disclosure, Sleepers, Wag the Dog* and *Sphere.* Typically, his latest films include the fourth in the Baltimore series, *Liberty Heights* and a studio picture about hairpiece salesmen in Ireland, *An Everlasting Piece.*

Ken Loach

Ken Loach was born in Nuneaton in 1936. After studying law at Oxford he was awarded a director's traineeship at the Northampton Repertory Theatre in 1961 and in 1963 joined the BBC as a trainee director. After finding his feet with *Diary of a Young Man,* Loach quickly forged a reputation for pushing at the stylistic boundaries of television and tackling social and political issues head on – most notably as a director of *The Wednesday Play. Up the Junction* and *Cathy Come Home* were the most celebrated of these plays – causing national debates about abortion and homelessness respectively. In 1967 Loach directed his first feature film, *Poor Cow,* for the producer Joseph Janni after which he set up Kestrel Films with Tony Garnett in 1969 to make *Kes.* Since then he has alternated between film, television drama and documentary. His cinema films include *Looks and Smiles, Fatherland, Riff-Raff, Hidden Agenda, Raining Stones, Ladybird Ladybird, Land and Freedom, Carla's Song* and *My Name is Joe.*

James Mangold

James Mangold began making Super-8 films at the age of eleven and was awarded a place to study film at the California Institute of Arts at the age of seventeen. Four years later, his graduation film, *Barn Revisited,* came to the attention of Michael Eisner at Disney and he was hired to direct a television movie about a deer found by children in New York, provisionally titled *Deer Story.* Sacked from the picture after only two days, Mangold then worked out his contract as a writer on an animated feature musical, *Oliver and Company*. After spending several years trying to find his feet again in Los Angeles, Mangold enrolled in Columbia University Film School where he took a class in advanced directing with Milos Forman. There he wrote a thirty-minute silent film, *Victor*, which he also directed. He subsequently used the central character of the short film, an over-weight pizza chef called Victor, in his first feature film, *Heavy*, which he shot in 1994. The film was an immediate critical success and allowed Mangold to launch the career he had long coveted: as the writer-director of his own films. He has since made two movies: *Cop Land*, starring Robert De Niro, Sylvester Stallone, Harvey Keitel and Ray Liotta, and *Girl, Interrupted*, starring Winona Ryder and produced by Mangold's wife, Cathy Konrad.

Anthony Minghella

Anthony Minghella was born in Ryde on the Isle of Wight in 1954 and grew up living above his parents' ice-cream parlour. After abandoning his teenage plans to become a rock star, Minghella attended Hull University where he gained a first-class degree in English in 1972. He then spent nearly ten years teaching English at Hull before becoming a script editor on the children's television serial *Grange Hill* in 1981. For the next decade he alternated between television serials and plays for television, radio and the theatre. His television work in this period includes *Inspector Morse* and *The Storyteller*; his radio plays include *Hung Up* and *Cigarettes and Chocolate*; and his theatrical plays include *Whale Music, Two Planks and a Passion* and *Made in Bangkok*. In 1990 he was commissioned to write and direct a film for BBC2's *Screen Two* strand. The resulting film, *Truly, Madly, Deeply*, was an instant success with audiences and critics alike when it was released in 1991 and allowed Minghella to enter the world of big budget main-stream film-making. He has since gone on to make three feature films: *Mr Wonderful, The English Patient* and *The Talented Mr Ripley*. His next project is *Cold Mountain* based on the acclaimed novel by Charles Frazier.

Mira Nair

Mira Nair was born in Bhubaneswar in the province of Orissa, India in 1957. After studying sociology at Delhi University she won a place at Harvard to study theatre. Once there, however, film took over from acting as her primary passion and she majored in visual and environmental studies. After graduating with an eighteen-minute film about a Muslim community in the oldest district of New Delhi, *Jami Masjid Street Journal*, she moved to New York where she divided her time between waitressing and synching up medical films before making her second documentary, *So Far From India*, about an Indian news-stand worker in New York. Her next film, *India Cabaret*, a controversial portrait of strippers in a Bombay nightclub brought her to the attention of Channel 4 who agreed to put up half the money for her first feature film, *Salaam Bombay!* After struggling to raise the rest of the finance, Nair was rewarded when *Salaam Bombay!* became an instant hit at the 1988 Cannes Film Festival, winning both the Camera D'Or and Prix Publique. Since then she has made several more films including *Mississippi Masala, The Perez Family* and *Kama Sutra: A Tale of Love.* She continues to work in both documentary and features.

Gary Oldman

Gary Oldman is one of the most prolific and successful British screen actors in the world. After débuting in Mike Leigh's *Meantime* in 1981, he has starred in nearly thirty films for cinema or television, including *Sid and Nancy: Love Kills* directed by Alex Cox, *Prick Up Your Ears* directed by Stephen Frears, *Track 29* directed by Nic Roeg, *JFK* directed by Oliver Stone, *Dracula* directed by Francis Ford Coppola, and *Léon* and *The Fifth Element* directed by Luc Besson. Largely self-financed by Oldman and his producer, Doug Urbanski, Oldman's first film as writer-director, *Nil by Mouth,* was released to widespread critical acclaim in 1995. Oldman is currently preparing to make his second feature film.

Kevin Smith

Kevin Smith was born in Red Bank, New Jersey in 1970, and studied creative writing at the New School For Social Research in New York, and film at Vancouver Film School, where he teamed up with his producer Scott Mosier. His début feature, *Clerks,* made on $27,575, became an instant classic of the American independent film scene when it was released in 1994. Not only did audiences warm to its scabrous and scatological humour; the fact that Smith had been working as a convenience store clerk in New Jersey when he made it and that he financed it using a wallet full of credit cards could only add to its popularity. Buoyed up by the extraordinary success of *Clerks,* Smith has gone on to write and direct three further feature films: *Mallrats, Chasing Amy* and *Dogma.* He continues to live in Red Bank, New Jersey.

Oliver Stone

Oliver Stone is one of the most celebrated and controversial film-makers working in America today. Born in 1946 of a French mother and a Jewish-American father, he taught at a Catholic school in Saigon and served in Vietnam in 1967 before attending NYU Film School in the late sixties where one of his professors was Martin Scorsese. When he graduated in 1971 he took a job as a cab driver and began to write screenplays. Although he soon earned a reputation as a prolific and first-rate writer, many of his early scripts went unproduced. In 1976 he moved to Los Angeles to try to secure studio backing for *Platoon,* a script he had written based on his experiences in Vietnam. Although no one wanted to back it, he was offered writing duties on another film, *Midnight Express*. On the basis of the success of *Midnight Express*, Stone was launched as a major league Hollywood screenwriter and went on to write some of the most celebrated Hollywood films of the early eighties including *Scarface* directed by Brian De Palma, *Year of the Dragon* directed by Michael Cimino and *Conan the Barbarian* directed by John Milius. In spite of his success as a writer, however, the directing career he craved remained tantalizingly elusive. Although he'd already been involved in a couple of low-budget feature films, *Seizure* and *The Hand* in 1974 and 1981 respectively, it was not until 1986 that he secured backing from David Hemmings's Hemdale Corporation and the financier Arnold Kopelson for *Salvador*, a film based on the experiences of Richard Boyle and the first film for which he says he feels a genuine sense of ownership. *Salvador* established Stone as a writer-director capable of fashioning commercially successful movies from contentious political subjects and broke the log-jam of his film-making career. Since 1986 he has worked at breakneck speed, writing and directing eleven films including *Platoon*, *Wall Street*, *Talk Radio*, *Born on the Fourth of July*, *The Doors*, *JFK*, *Heaven and Earth*, *Natural Born Killers*, *Nixon* and *U-Turn*. His most recent project is *Any Given Sunday*, a film about the world of American football starring Denis Quaid, Al Pacino and Cameron Diaz.

Bertrand Tavernier

Bertrand Tavernier was born in Lyons, France in 1941. After abandoning his studies at law school he supported himself by writing film criticism before working as an assistant director for Jean-Pierre Melville. Advised by Melville that he would never make a director, Tavernier became a film publicist working on the films of some of the most celebrated French directors of the sixties, including Melville himself, Jean-Luc Godard, Claude Chabrol and Claude Sautet. In 1973, Tavernier persuaded Georges Simenon to grant him the rights to *The Watchmaker of Everton,* and wrote an adaptation of the book with the two veteran French screenwriters, Jean Aurenche and Pierre Bost, which he set in his home town and renamed *The Watchmaker of Saint-Paul*. After a lengthy struggle to raise the finance, the film went ahead with two of France's most celebrated screen actors, Philippe Noiret and Jean Rochefort, in the leading roles. The film was an instant critical and popular success, winning the Special Jury Prize at the Berlin Film Festival in 1974 as well as the Prix Louis Delluc in France, and launched Tavernier's career as a talented and eclectic film-maker. Since the middle seventies he has made more than thirty films for cinema and television as well as editing numerous books on cinema. His films include *Que la Fête Commence, Le Juge et L'Assassin, Des Enfants Gâtés, Death Watch, Une Semaine de Vacances, Coup de Torchon, Mississippi Blues, Un Dimanche à la Campagne, 'Round Midnight, La Passion Béatrice, La Vie et rien d'autre, Daddy Nostalgie, La Guerre sans nom, L.627, La Fille de D'Artagnan, L'Appât,* and *Ça Commence Aujourd'hui*.